# Georgiana, Like So Many

The true story of a Connecticut woman,
**Ella Georgiana Smith Cook (1849–1930),**
who, like so many women of her era,
contributed her full share to happiness in the home
as America and women transformed

By Claire Smith

Also see companion book,
*The Civil War Letters of Abner C. Smith,*
for letters written by Georgiana's father to Georgiana
and her family in East Haddam, Connecticut

Copyright ©2022 by Claire Smith

This book may not be reproduced, either in part or in its entirety, in any form, by and means, without written permission from the publisher, with the exception of brief excerpts for purposes of radio, television, or published review. All rights, including the right of translation, are reserved.

Georgiana, Like So Many
ISBN: 978-0-9816061-1-8

FIRST EDITION
Published September 2022

Quicksilver Communication, Inc.
qsilver.com

*Cover photo: Ella Georgiana Smith Cook, 1868*
*Cover design by Hayley Smith Hildebrandt*

*This book is dedicated to all women —
the trailblazers and for whom the trail was blazed.*

PUBLISHED WHEN GEORGIANA WAS SEVEN

We do not believe in mental inequality of the sexes; we believe that the man and the woman have each a work to do, for which they are specially qualified, and in which they are called to excel. Though the work is not the same, it is equally noble, and demands an equal exercise of capacity.

GODEY'S LADY'S BOOK, VOL. LIII, JULY TO DECEMBER, 1856

PUBLISHED ABOUT GEORGIANA
WHEN SHE WAS SEVENTY-FOUR

She has been an ideal companion and homemaker, contributing her full share to the mutual happiness that has made married life worth living.

CONNECTICUT VALLEY ADVERTISER, APRIL, 1924

# Contents

    Family Trees ................................................... 1
    Acknowledgements ............................................. 7
    **Prologue** .................................................... 11
1. **Connecticut to the Core** Georgiana's Ancestry ............... 17
2. **Little Girl** Georgiana from Birth to Eleven. 1849–1861 ....... 45
3. **Little Woman** Georgiana, age Eleven to Fifteen. 1861–1865 .... 73
4. **Marching On** Georgiana, age Fifteen to Eighteen. 1865–1868 ...111
5. **Start the Music** Georgiana, age Eighteen to Twenty-one. 1868–1870 .................................................. 127
6. **High Notes and Low Notes** Georgiana in Her Twenties. 1870–1880 .................................................. 141
7. **Riding the Wave** Georgiana in Her Thirties. 1880–1890 ...... 167
8. **The Splashy Nineties** Georgiana in Her Forties. 1890–1900 ..209
9. **Oh Brother** Frank in the 1880s and 1890s ...................249
10. **Turns** Georgiana in Her Fifties. 1900–1909 .................293
11. **Before the Parade Passes By** Georgiana in Her Sixties. 1910–1919 ...................................................355
12. **Coda** Georgiana in Her Final Years. 1920–1930 ............. 391
    **Epilogue** ................................................... 411
    Chapter Notes ............................................... 415
    Selected Bibliography ........................................439
    Index ........................................................445

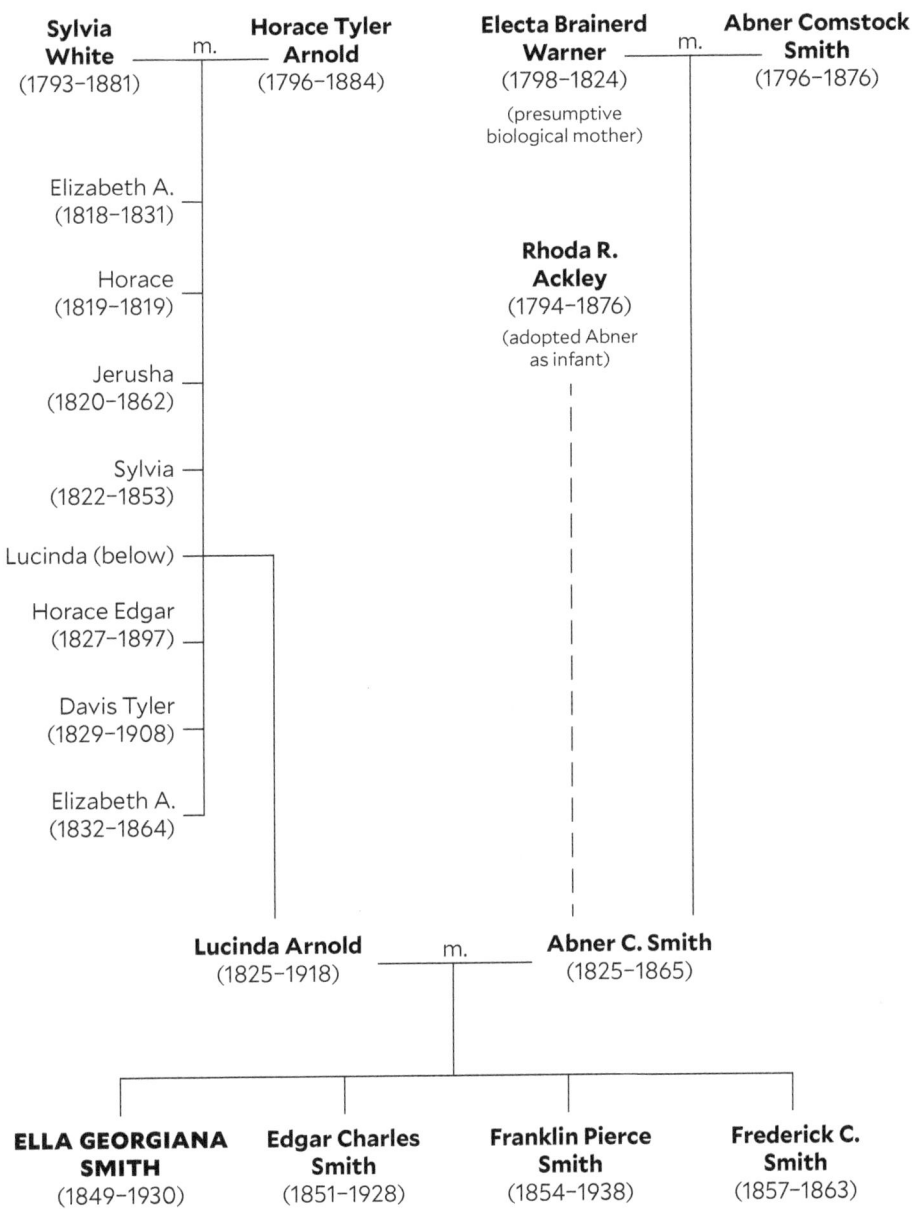

FAMILY TREES

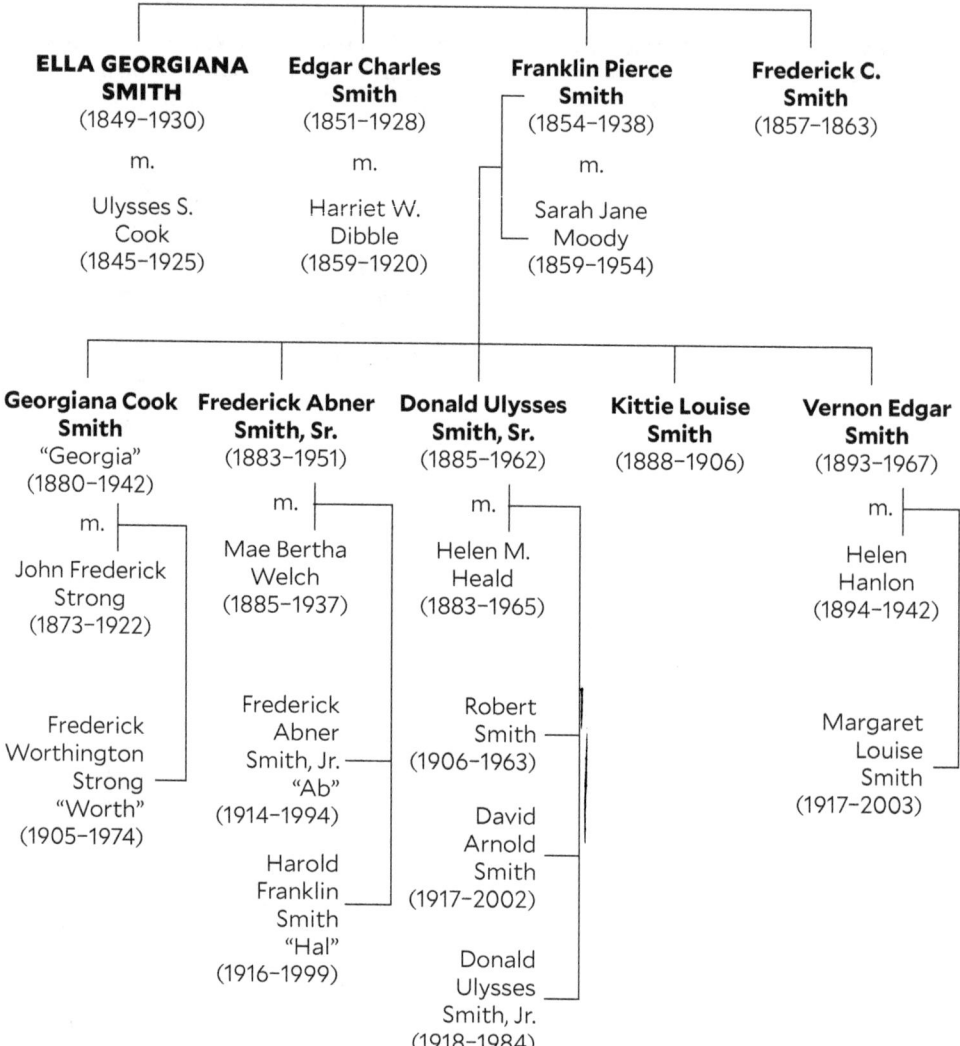

# How Georgiana Is Related to Lillie White

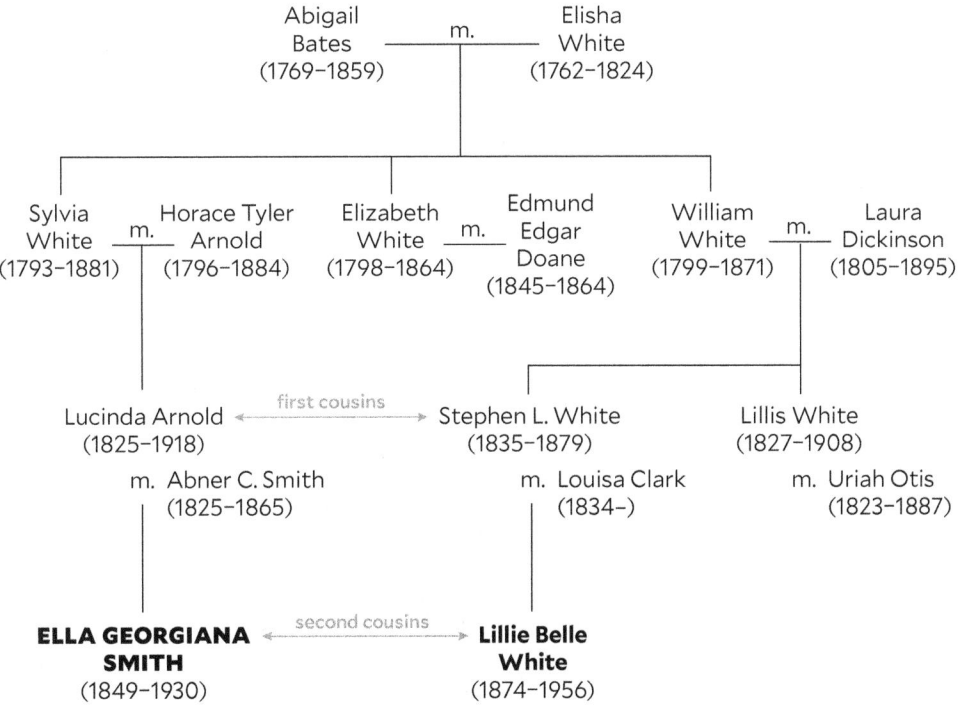

FAMILY TREES

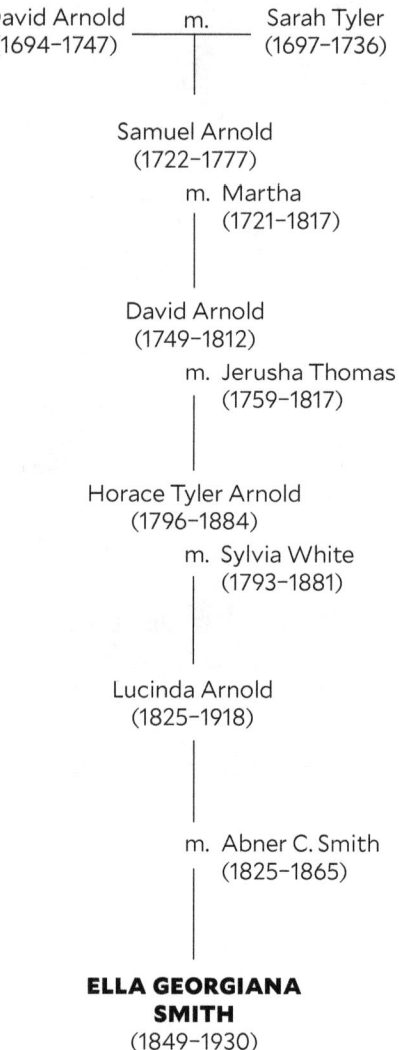

**Georgiana's Arnold Line**

David Arnold (1694–1747) m. Sarah Tyler (1697–1736)

Samuel Arnold (1722–1777)
m. Martha (1721–1817)

David Arnold (1749–1812)
m. Jerusha Thomas (1759–1817)

Horace Tyler Arnold (1796–1884)
m. Sylvia White (1793–1881)

Lucinda Arnold (1825–1918)
m. Abner C. Smith (1825–1865)

**ELLA GEORGIANA SMITH** (1849–1930)

# The Family Tree of Georgiana's Grandfather, Abner Comstock Smith

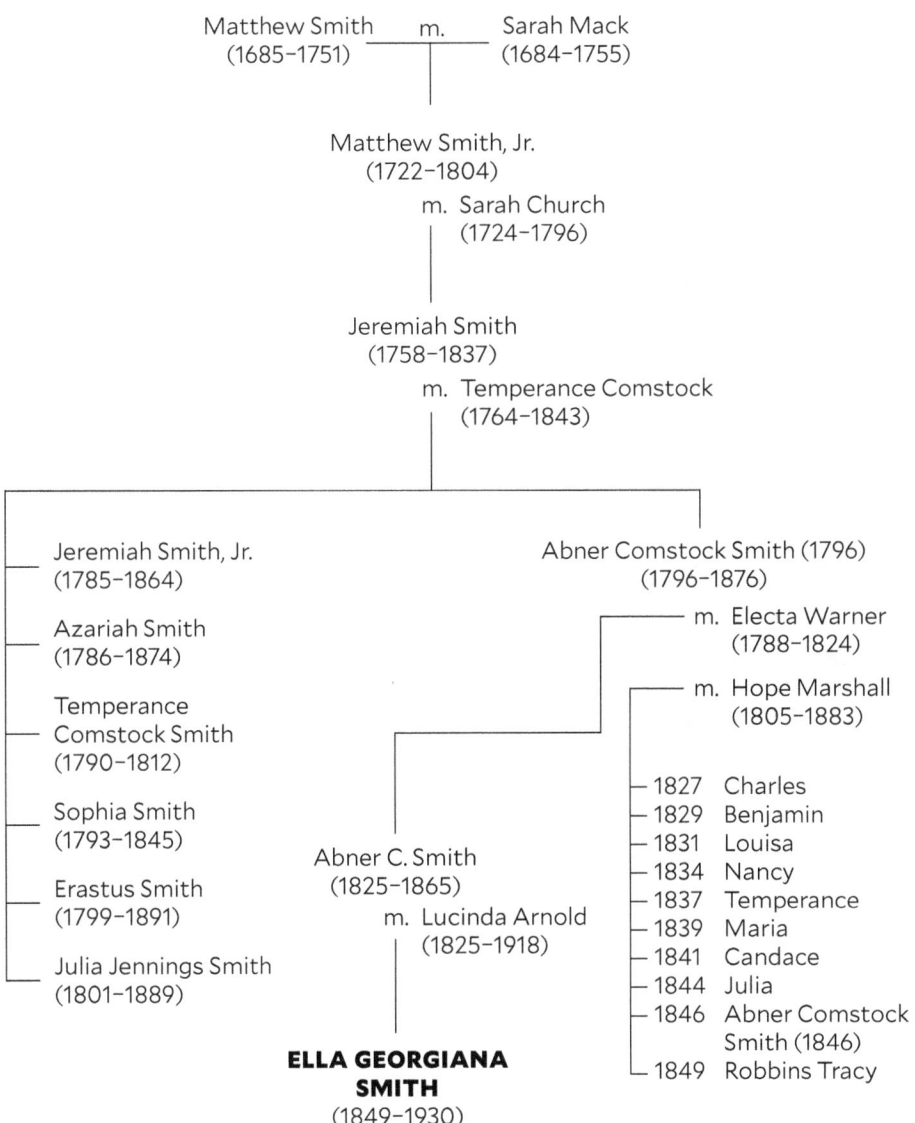

FAMILY TREES

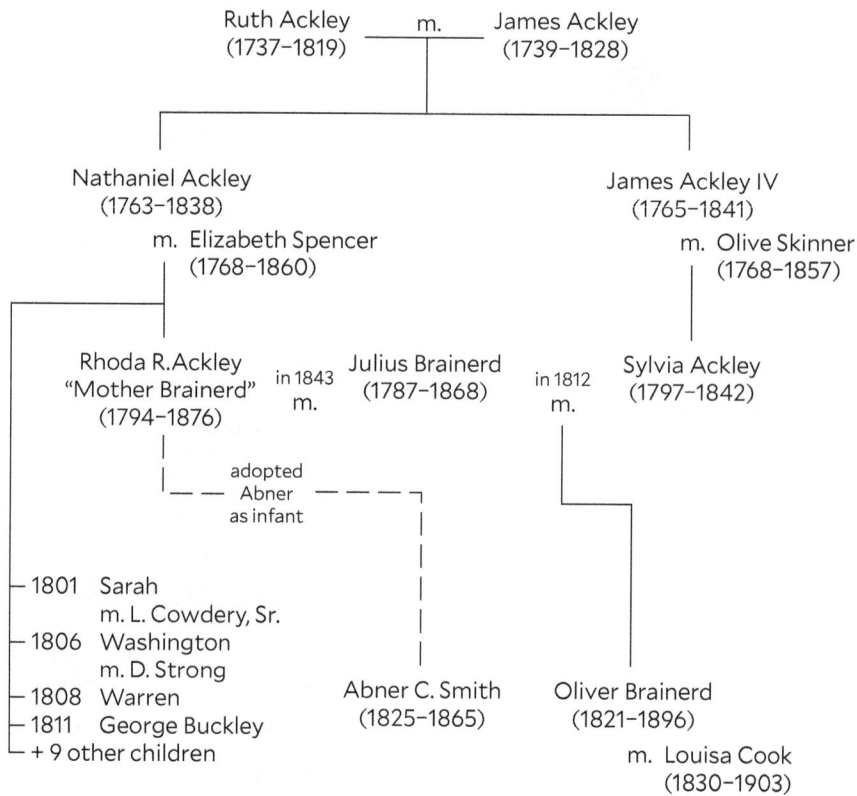

# Acknowledgements

Many people helped me enter Georgiana's world and come out with her story in this book. They gave me their expertise, encouragement, ears, opinions, patience, and their genuine curiosity.

Some helped me find records and photos. The librarians, town clerks, town historians, and historical society leaders of East Haddam, Chester, and Westbrook, Connecticut, as well as Ashley Falls, Massachusetts, made my search enjoyable. Those with special knowledge of a topic added depth and color to the facts. I give special thanks to Kandie Carle of East Haddam, the Victorian Lady and expert in Victorian life; James Clark, Connecticut Fife and Drum Corps expert, of East Hampton, Connecticut; Bruce Sievers, Moodus mill expert; Marianne Halpin of the East Haddam Historical Society; Patrick Murphy for Moodus Drum and Fife Corps and Moodus lore; Travis and Peggy Winkley of Smith Farm Gardens in East Haddam; Caryn Davis and Leif Nilsson for Chester House documents; Jim Miller from the Sheffield, Massachusetts, Historical Society and the Dewey Research Center; Mia Parker of Ashley Falls; Priscilla Hall Reuter of Ashley Falls; Fred Smith, who provided boxes of Smith family ephemera, photos and stories from the Ashley Falls years; and Gail Colby, expert on West Beach in Westbrook. Thank you. I hope as you read these pages, you see how your contributions added to the sculpting of Georgiana.

For the invaluable Civil War letters written by Georgiana's father, the thank-you goes to Don Smith of Pennsylvania for continuing to preserve the original letters of Abner C. Smith and for his insights and interest; and to Kerry Bryan who had meticulously examined the letters and allowed me to use her insightful thesis and transcriptions.

Some individuals unknowingly became models for how I visualized the characters in the book, such as Aunt Deedee (Sarah Smith Sermersheim) as the amiable aunt, Uncle Jay (Jay B. Smith) as the fun-loving uncle, my three daughters (Sarah, Annie, and Hayley) as 14-year-old girls, and Billy Demiris and Jonah LaVoie as young Smith boys.

Some unknowingly gave me material. To all the friends and family who visited our porch — for each time they rocked in the rockers, or called the porch their "happy place," or sang out loud to the music, or honked with laughter, or played word games, or enjoyed the fireworks and dancing in the street on the Fourth of July, and for each time they swung the door open under the GEORGIANA sign — thank you for bringing the spirit of Georgiana to life for me.

Many friends listened to my excitement at finding a new fact and my frustrations with time. Thank you to my West Beach friends, my book club friends, my morning walking buddies, my texting friends, my Harvey Wallbanger friends, and hairstylist Duane Brown, who heard about this book every five weeks for five years.

As for the daunting craft of writing, the Shoreline Writers — Debbie Mandel, Mary Reynolds, and Dianne Hearne — were with me from the first word, listening to me read every Civil War letter and every chapter, every rewritten chapter, every re-rewritten chapter. I thank them for their encouragement, honesty, wordsmithing, and their interest in Georgiana and women of her era. Wow, could they come up with great questions!

The keen eye and clear-headedness of copy editor Debbie Mandel, author of *All Write* (Stillwater River Publication, 2021), saved me from foggy sentences which were based on foggy notions. I learned the value of an excellent copy editor from working with Debbie.

Others helped me, too, with reading and copy editing at various stages, such as Nancy Anthony and Susan Hall. Their fresh questions made the book better. I was lucky to find Russell Shaddox to work with, who is not only an expert in book publishing and mapmaking, but literally wrote the definitive book about East Haddam *(Images of America: East Haddam,* Arcadia Publishing, 2019).

I cannot end without thanking my daughters — Sarah, Annie, and Hayley — for giving me a 21st century woman's filter. And baby Claire, my new granddaughter, who I hope will pass this book on to Smith women of the 22nd century.

Most of all, I thank Peter — patient Peter.

# Prologue

Eventually, anyone who sits on our front porch spots the old sign that reads GEORGIANA above the front door. The sign is from an old wooden boat. Let's just say that the sign has character — it's more than a hundred years old, and it looks it. But it's a hearty sign that sits quietly and securely above the well-seasoned porch door of this seaside house that used to be a summer cottage and still acts like one. Sometimes, I think the sign smiles down on the constant banging of the door beneath it.

After a bit of pondering, a newcomer asks: "Georgiana? Who is that?"

"She was the first Smith in our family to own this house. It was her summer cottage."

"How long ago was that?"

"Well, she and this house go back to 1882."

"And the house stayed in the Smith family all these years?"

"Yup. It was the family summer cottage for generations of Smiths after her."

"Who was she? Do you know anything about her?"

"Well, we know she came from East Haddam. And we know her father was in the Civil War — "

That is when the curiosity and the questions, like heads watching a tennis match, snap away from Georgiana and turn to her father and the Civil War. Georgiana is then forgotten until the next first-time porch visitor.

## MY CURIOSITY ABOUT GEORGIANA

When I married Peter Smith in 1985, I moved into his Westbrook, Connecticut, home where the GEORGIANA sign had unpretentiously hung for about a hundred years. Georgiana was Peter's great-grandaunt, someone who died long before he was born. In 1972, Peter had purchased the summer cottage from Georgiana's estate, which had never been settled after her death in 1930. By the time I moved in, he had turned it into a year-round home. At this writing, we've lived in what used to be Georgiana's summer cottage for more than thirty-five years.

Over the years, my curiosity about Georgiana grew. I learned that she and I were born a century apart — exactly. She was born in 1849; I was born in 1949. Between her lifetime and mine, so much had changed for women. I wondered what life was like for her, a woman who lived a hundred years before me in the same house.

I walk in her rooms. I park my car in her horse barn. I rock on her porch. I hear the same tides lapping in and out. I see the same sandy beach change from small to large, or vice versa, every six hours and 12½ minutes. I look at the same Long Island Sound, and the same Long Island, Duck Island, Menunketesuck Island, and Salt Island in clear view. I see the same moonbeam streaming on the water at night, and the same sun rising faster than you would think possible over the horizon in the morning. And I see the same glitter that the sun magically drops on the water each autumn.[1]

I've wondered over the years if Georgiana is the spirit in the house who keeps it feeling like a summer cottage, which is not the color-coordinated ideal shown in catalogs, or the perfectly-worded, cozy, comfy, cuddly calm found in beach novels. But — in her day, and now in mine — is the wonderful imperfection of wet towels with clashing colors hanging on anything that resembles a hook; Yankee and Red Sox baseball caps staring each other down from rocking chair posts; forgotten drinks making rings on window sills; sand on bathroom floors, sand around shower drains, sand mixed with spilled chowder on the kitchen floor, little boy handprints on glass doors; friends' lost shoes; playing cards scattered on a table; and the sounds of pre-beach whines of impatient children, after-beach screeching of overtired children, and voices from one to ninety-one shouting over the too-loud music.

I wanted to get to know the woman who first managed this house as a summer cottage, the woman who was the first to experience the same wonderful chaos, the woman who walked a hundred years ago under the same ceilings I do today, the woman whose family photos still hang on the walls, the woman no one in the family knew much about.

But would I be able to find enough information about her in the century-old records? Like nearly all women of her time, Georgiana was hardly mentioned in historical records, identified only by her relationship to the men in her life: she was the daughter of a Civil War soldier; she was the sister of a popular innkeeper; she was the local doctor's wife. Georgiana was born at a time when, with rare exceptions, only men fought the wars, had the professions, ran the businesses, owned the properties, made the laws, voted for the men who made the laws, and penned what was published. A time when only men had their stories recorded, and women did not.

Which made my curiosity even stronger.

### RECORDING GEORGIANA

The family had letters from her father written during the Civil War, a wonderful resource, but written when Georgiana was a child. I began digging for information for her as an adult, and found some official documents that bore her name, a few photographs, and a bit of ephemera. Ancestry.com provided me with facts for her intricate family tree, of which she was one small leaf.

I wanted to go beyond the presentation of mere facts. I wanted to capture the essence of a woman who lived during her era, to understand what she saw and heard during her lifetime; to determine if she was an ordinary or extraordinary woman. I learned quickly that most of her story had to be pried from the records of the men in her life or inferred from the men-owned-and-operated newspapers of her era. Words like *probably, likely,* and *perhaps* became friends who overstayed their welcome, as I *assumed, presumed,* and *guessed* my way through her story.

With those caveats, Georgiana's life is now recorded.

> *Men have had every advantage of us in telling their own story. Education has been theirs in so much higher a degree; the pen has been in their hands.*
>
> JANE AUSTEN, *PERSUASION* (1818)

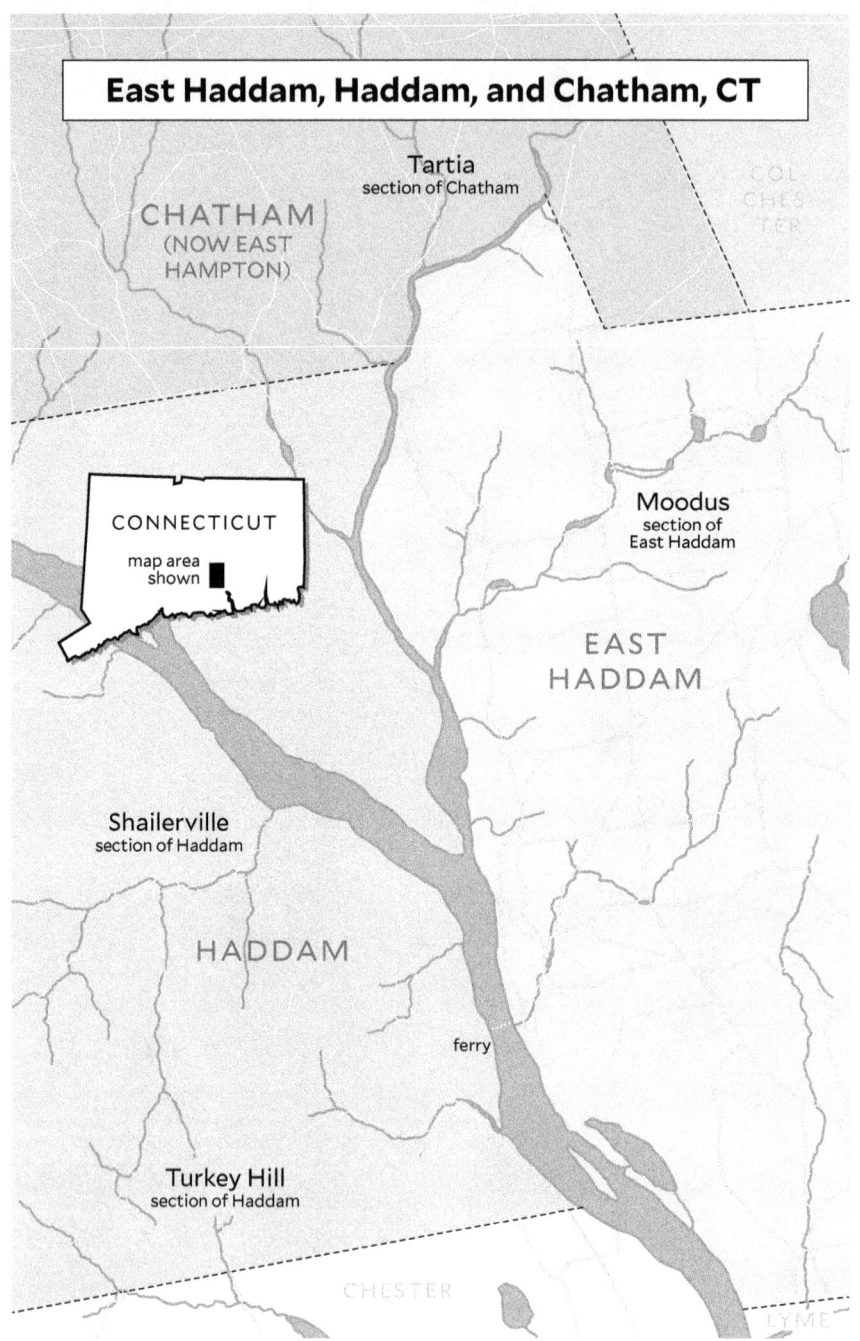

*The Connecticut River between Haddam and East Haddam, Connecticut. No bridge existed until 1913. Before then, ferries were used to cross the river.*

CHAPTER 1

# Connecticut to the Core
## Georgiana's Ancestry

The roots of Georgiana's family tree are the second deepest in Connecticut, second only to those of Native Americans. Her mother's family dates back to the first English settlers of Haddam in the mid-seventeenth century. Her father's family dates back to the first English settlers of East Haddam, eight miles away. For many generations, the families of the earliest English settlers married one another, so the marriage of her mother and father seems unsurprising, until you consider that they were separated by a major river. And there was no bridge.

In 1825, Georgiana's mother, Lucinda, was born into Haddam's **Arnold** family on the west side of the mighty Connecticut River, and her father, Abner, was born into the **Smith** family on the east side. In their youth, a primary way to cross the river was by rudimentary ferries powered by men with oars or poles or sails, and only with the New England weather cooperating. (People could also cross at will in their own boats, or by walking over ice.) But cross the river they did. When Lucinda was twenty-one and Abner was three weeks shy of twenty-one, they married.

### GEORGIANA'S MOTHER'S SIDE — THE ARNOLD FAMILY

Anyone who explores Haddam history hears of the Arnold family. Joseph Arnold (1625–1691) was one of the original twenty-eight men who settled Haddam in 1662. Wives were right there with the men, and did their share of the settling, too, but historians, who were men, recorded only the men. Married women did not appear on the early land records, as they were prevented by law from owning property. That law changed in 1877 when Connecticut's Married Women's Property Act enabled a married woman to control her own property.

The Arnold family is well-documented in two key books of Middlesex County history, both published by Beers & Company: the *History of Middlesex County, Connecticut,* published in 1884,[2] and the *Commemorative Biographical Record of Middlesex County, Connecticut,* published in 1903.[3] These sources will hereafter be referred to as *Beers 1884* and *Beers 1903.*

Joseph Arnold and Elizabeth (born Wakeman) Arnold (1630–1691) formed the trunk of a family tree that has sprouted Arnolds in Haddam, many in the Turkey Hill section, for more than three hundred years. Land in Haddam was passed down through the Arnold generations from Arnold son to Arnold son. In 1812, sixteen-year-old **Horace Tyler Arnold** (1796–1884) inherited a plot of land in the Turkey Hill section of Haddam.[4] A few years later, Horace married **Sylvia White** (1793–1881) from another well-rooted Haddam family, and they produced another generation of Arnolds. Horace and Sylvia Arnold were married for sixty-three years and are buried side by side in Haddam's Turkey Hill Cemetery. They were **Georgiana's maternal grandparents**.

### GEORGIANA'S ARNOLD GRANDPARENTS

Georgiana's grandfather, Horace Tyler Arnold, was described in *Beers 1903* as a "man of fine physique, being over six feet tall, and weighing, in his prime, more than 200 pounds," whose death "robbed the community of one of its most respected citizens." He was eighty-eight when he died. Georgiana's grandmother, Sylvia, was not a fragile flower either. She also lived to age eighty-eight, "her death occurring quite suddenly, for she was apparently in the best of health, never having been ill, or taken a dose of medicine in her life, and so vigorous that she did all of the housework until the date of her death."[5]

Horace and Sylvia had eight children — five girls and three boys — the seventh generation of Arnolds in Haddam. Their first child was a girl, Elizabeth. Their second was a boy, Horace (1819–1819), who lived only six hours. Infant death was not unusual in the 1800s, when women gave birth at home without a doctor's care. Nor was it unusual for a woman to bear eight children. This was especially true for farmers' wives, which Sylvia Arnold was, because children were needed to help on the farms that sustained their nineteenth-century families. The lack of reliable birth control also kept the babies coming. The average number of children in an American family in the nineteenth century was seven. The average in 2020 was two.

### GEORGIANA'S MOTHER

**Lucinda Arnold** (1825–1918), **Georgiana's mother**, was the fourth surviving child and fourth daughter of Horace and Sylvia. Lucinda was born in 1825. Her three older sisters were Elizabeth (1818–1831), Jerusha (1820–1862), and Sylvia (1822–1853). When Lucinda was two, a new brother Horace — Horace Edgar (1827–1897) — was born. It had been eight years since the death of the firstborn infant son of the same name. Another boy, Davis Tyler (1829–1908), was born when Lucinda was four. When Lucinda was six, her eldest sister Elizabeth, the firstborn child of the family, died at age thirteen. The next year, a new sister Elizabeth (1832–1864) was born. Childhood death was a sad reality of the 1800s. Naming a newborn after a child who had died — as Horace and Sylvia did with the second Horace and second Elizabeth — was a common practice.

> **Wondering if Lucinda Arnold is related to Thankful Arnold?**
>
> People familiar with Connecticut history know of Haddam's Thankful Arnold House, a historic Connecticut house/museum at 14

Hayden Hill Road in Haddam, Connecticut. It is one of the stops on the Connecticut Women's Heritage Trail.

**Thankful** was a woman. Female virtue names, like Thankful, Mindful, Temperance, Comfort, Patience, Obedience, Silence, Submit, and Lowly were common for baby girls' names in 1776 when Thankful was born. Today's popular baby girl names of Grace and Faith are leftovers from the virtue-name days.

**Arnold** was Thankful's married name; her maiden name was Clarke.

The Thankful Arnold House narrative is a story about women. Tour guides describe how the house was cared for by four generations of Arnold women, starting with Thankful Arnold (1776–1849), who had twelve children and was widowed at age forty-seven. The other three women were her never-married daughter, her widowed granddaughter, and her great-granddaughter. Each cared for and improved the house through the generations. Hats off to the Haddam Historical Society (and to the Arnold family who gave the house to them) for preserving and promoting women's history.

The house is set up exactly the way Thankful Arnold kept her house in the 1820s, around the time Georgiana's mother, Lucinda Arnold, was born (1825) a couple miles down the road.

The answer is **YES**. Lucinda and Thankful were related.[6] Thankful's husband, Joseph Arnold, and Lucinda Arnold were each descended from Joseph Arnold, one of the original proprietors of Haddam in the 1600s. Thankful was fifty years older than Lucinda. When Thankful died at age seventy-four in 1849, Lucinda was twenty-four and had just given birth to Georgiana.

If you're wondering if the Arnolds of Haddam are related to traitor Benedict Arnold, born in 1741 in not-so-far-away Norwich, Connecticut, the answer is **NO**. It's interesting to note that despite so many boys born into the large Haddam Arnold family after Benedict Arnold's famous act of treason in 1780, never has one been named Benedict.

Lucinda and her three sisters and two brothers attended the one-room Turkey Hill School, which is still standing today as a private home in Haddam. Like most farm girls of her time, Lucinda did not go to school beyond the eighth grade. But she did not stay a farm girl for very long after she graduated.

In the late 1830s, when Lucinda was fourteen and finishing her schooling in Haddam, textile mills were springing up in towns across New England and luring young single girls from family farms for their workforce. Across the river from Haddam, in the town of East Haddam, the village of Moodus was on the cutting edge of the new industry with state-of-the-art mills. Moodus was making clever use of dams and waterwheels on their small Moodus River and was able to supply enough waterpower to operate a dozen mills along a three-mile stretch. The mills operated in Moodus for decades, until the 1920s. They specialized in the manufacture of cotton yarn, duck (a fabric used for sailcloth on tall ships), fishing nets, and twine. The mills were so successful that the village of Moodus in East Haddam, Connecticut, was dubbed the *Twine Capital of America.*

Lucinda joined the large number of young Yankee women who left farm life to work in the mills. According to the 1840 census, Lucinda, at age fifteen, was still living with her parents in Haddam. But she soon left home to work in Moodus in the Davison factory,[7] a mill owned by Roswell Davison, where spool cotton and cotton twine were manufactured. Most mill girls worked for only a few years to save money until they married, at which point their new husbands would provide the financial support for them and their future children. It looks like Lucinda was like most mill girls.

While she worked in Moodus, Lucinda could not have lived in Turkey Hill. Crossing the river each day would have been too much of an ordeal. A bridge would not connect the east and west shores of the Connecticut River in that area for seventy more years, when the iconic bridge near the Goodspeed Opera House was built in 1913. In Moodus, Lucinda likely lived in a boarding house provided by the mill owner. Well, not exactly "provided by": $1.00 to $3.00 a month was deducted from a worker's wages for room and board. Lucinda's monthly pay, before the room and board were deducted, was probably around $14.00 [about $414 in 2020]. She may have worked up to sixty hours a week, as many mill girls did. The mills in Moodus were open ten hours a day, six days a week, closing only on Sundays, the Fourth of July, Thanksgiving, and Christmas.

## Mill Girls

In 1814, eleven years before Georgiana's mother, Lucinda, was born, Mr. Francis Cabot Lowell of Massachusetts invented a textile loom that could run from the power of local waterways. It didn't take long for him to turn his new idea into a prosperous and valuable business in his hometown, a town that grew to be the second largest in Massachusetts and was eventually named Lowell, in honor of him. It also didn't take long for others to adopt his idea and build textile mills in other parts of New England, including in Moodus, Connecticut, 120 miles away. The first mill in Moodus was built in 1819. The Industrial Revolution in the United States was underway. Towns would grow; farms would shrink.

When newspapers and word of mouth carried the story to the Yankee farms that these new mills were offering jobs to women, the farm girls were interested. The mill owners knew female workers were cheap labor. Women were paid half the wages of men doing the same job. The Equal Pay Act requiring equal wages for men and women doing equal work wasn't passed until (gasp) 1963. The gender pay gap still exists today. In 2020, women made 81 cents for each dollar men made.[8] Less, if they were single mothers or women of color. (Do you think the delay in enacting an Equal Pay Act had anything to do with the fact the lawmakers were all male? To be fair, in 1963, the United States Congress was not all male—only 97 percent were. Since then, more and more women have been elected as representatives and senators. In 2020, only 73 percent of Congress was male. Did I just say only?)

The mills offered farm girls their first taste of economic and social independence—a new slice of life for women. The young women were attracted by cash wages, accommodations in boarding houses, educational and social opportunities, and by the camaraderie of other young people. The boarding houses offered safe and family-style living with responsible females as overseers. Choosing responsible women to run the boarding houses was a smart decision by the mill owners—they wanted to help quell the reluctance of parents who were tentative about letting their teenage girls leave home before marrying.

By the mid-1830s, many New England mill workers, who were 75 percent women, were working long hours in unhealthy conditions for low wages. In the large mills in Lowell, Massachusetts, which by then employed eight thousand women, the first union of women workers was formed. They wanted a reduction in their workweek—the mills were open eighty-four hours a week (5:00 a.m. to 7:00 p.m., six days a week) and the average workweek for a mill girl was seventy-three hours. They wanted healthier working conditions. Eighty women would work in one room with poor ventilation, blaring noises, extreme heat, and low standards of cleanliness. And they wanted fairer wages. Labor protests followed. Improvements followed protests.

During and after the mid-1840s Great Famine in Ireland, sometimes called the Irish Potato Famine, the mills attracted male and female immigrants from Ireland in large numbers. Soon immigrants from other countries came too. Still, in the 1880s, a large number of the laborers at the mills in Moodus and New England were the Yankee farm girls.

A mill girl did not usually work in the mills for more than three or four years. Most worked only until they married. *A woman's place is in the home* was a belief held by most men and women. Once married, husbands made the income and the decisions for their wives. A woman who worked after marriage was required BY LAW to give her wages, as well as any property she owned, to her husband. This law was one of the many reasons women were starting to ruffle the feathers of the American eagle in the mid-1800s.

Moodus never experienced the tensions that developed over working conditions between mill owners and mill operatives (the skilled and unskilled males and females who operated the equipment) that occurred at the larger New England mills, like those in Lowell, Massachusetts. Those conflicts, which exposed the nation to the unfair treatment of women, happened about forty years after Lucinda worked in the mills. According to Bruce R. Sievers in his book, *Mills along the River*,[9] the Moodus mill owners and operatives lived in harmony with one another. In fact, in the 1880s, when owners and workers ran into conflict nationally, the Knights of Labor — the nation's first successful labor union — came to Moodus and ended up functioning less as an organization for the protection of workers and more as a social organization for dances and entertainment. Sievers writes: "The owners, supervisors, and workers were all local residents who seem to have been well aware that cooperation was more advantageous than strife."

Lucinda was the first member of her family to move away from farm life in Haddam. We might conclude that young Lucinda showed some modern spunk when she left farm life, crossed the river, and never came back. How ya gonna keep 'em down on the farm, after they've seen Moodus?

---

### How Ya Gonna Keep 'Em Down on the Farm?

*How ya gonna keep 'em down on the farm*
*After they've seen Paree?*
*How ya gonna keep 'em away from Broadway*
*Jazzin' around and paintin' the town*
*How ya gonna keep 'em away from harm, that's a mystery*
*They'll never want to see a rake or plow*
*And who the deuce can parlezvous a cow?*
*How ya gonna keep 'em down on the farm*
*After they've seen Paree?* [10]

MUSIC BY WALTER DONALDSON,
LYRICS BY JOE YOUNG AND SAM M. LEWIS, 1919

> The lyrics of this song were meant to be comical, but they weren't funny for American farming families. The song mocked a very real question that American farmers had been asking themselves since the mid-1800s, when waves of rural residents were moving to towns and cities for jobs in industries like Moodus's mills. At the start of the 1800s, hardly any Americans lived and worked in a city. By 1880, almost 30 percent of Americans lived in cities. By 1900, 40 percent.[11] By 1919, when this song came out, it was 50 percent, and the trend was not slowing. The urban-rural balance had tipped upside down forever. American farmers lost in this trend and would not be sharing in America's new prosperity.
>
> "How Ya Gonna Keep 'Em Down on the Farm?" was a hit song introduced in vaudeville by Sophie Tucker in 1919, after the end of World War I. The song became popular again during and after World War II. During both wars, many farmers became soldiers. The lyrics exposed a concern that soldiers who had seen the glitter of city life in Europe might not want to return to their less-than-glamorous farm life.
>
> (The answer to the song's question? "Ya can't.")

### GEORGIANA'S FATHER'S SIDE — THE SMITH FAMILY

**Georgiana's father** was **Abner C. Smith** (1825–1865). *Beers 1903* offers two explanations of who the parents of Abner C. Smith were. In one place, it reads that Abner C. Smith "was the only child of his parents, and was born November 9, 1825, in East Hampton [formerly Chatham], where he resided until he was about nineteen."[12] Note the clever wording of this entry. The source for this information didn't know, or was concealing, the identity of Abner C. Smith's mother and father. The source was not Abner C. Smith himself — he had died thirty-eight years before *Beers 1903* was published. The second explanation reports that Abner C. Smith was the son of Abner Smith, who "lived and died at Millington, Connecticut and was engaged in farming."[13]

Millington is a village in the town of East Haddam. So Abner C. Smith was born in East Hampton and lived there until age nineteen, but his father lived in a different town, East Haddam? The names of the towns are similar. Was this a typo? No.

Who were Abner C. Smith's parents? This has been a popular Smith family question for generations, one that could be relied on for a good hour of lively porch conversation with seriously-repeated theories and mischievously-repeated snickers, always circling back to the same starting question. I gathered new information in writing this book and have come closer to the answer.

Let's start with Abner C. Smith's official birth records. There are none. The birthdate recorded as November 9, 1825, appears only in documents written when he was an adult, when he would have provided the date himself. Towns did not record births or issue birth certificates in those days. Churches, however, recorded baptisms, which were performed any time after birth, sometimes months or years later. Lucinda Arnold's baptism, for example, was entered into Haddam's First Congregational Church records[14] as "Lucinda Arnold, daughter of Horace, baptized October 2, 1825." Her birthdate, according to *Beers 1903* and other records, was June 12, 1825. Abner's baptism is not in any preserved church records of Chatham/East Hampton or East Haddam.

### GEORGIANA'S GRANDFATHER SMITH — IT'S COMPLICATED

Confirming the *Beers 1903* entry which stated that Abner C. Smith's father was Abner Smith of Millington in East Haddam began easily enough. Abner C. Smith signed an 1850 document to purchase a house in Moodus as "Abner C. Smith, Jr." And the 1860 census and Civil War records of the 1860s record him as "Abner C. Smith, 2nd." So it seemed simple to conclude that his father was **Abner Comstock Smith** (1796–1876), a Millington resident, who would have been twenty-nine when his son was born. The names work. The dates work. The place works.

But some facts didn't line up:

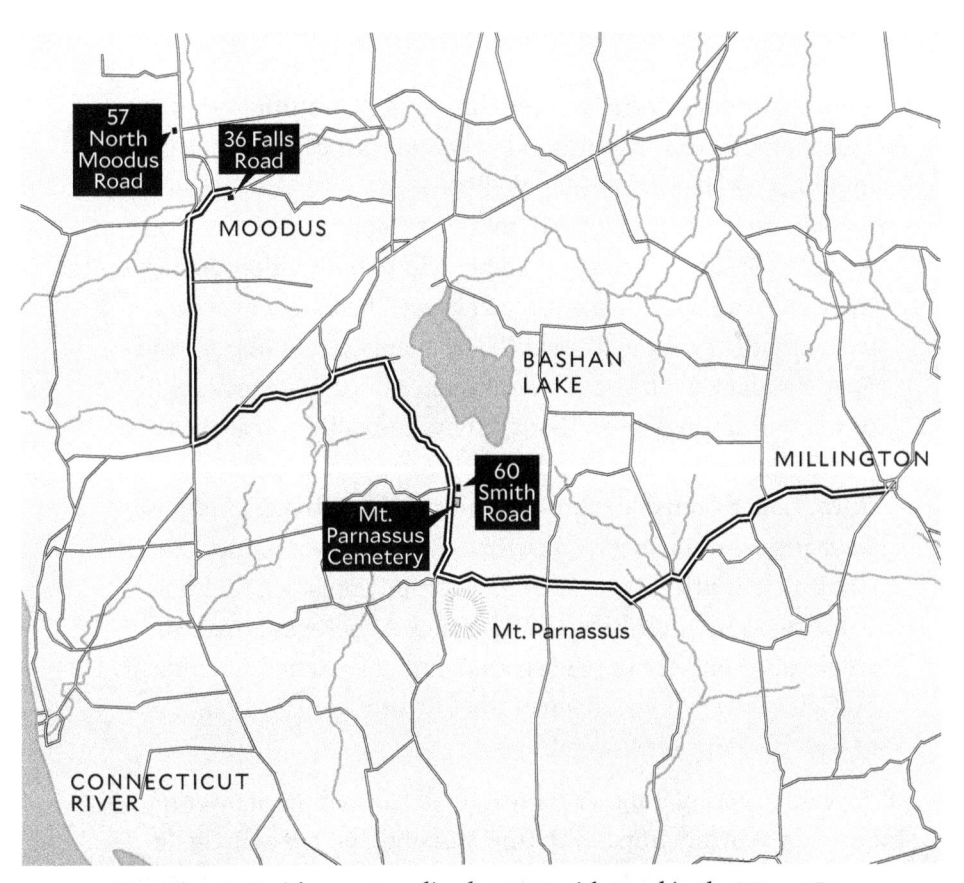

*Georgiana's Smith ancestors lived at 60 Smith Road in the Mount Parnassus section of East Haddam, Connecticut, what is today Smith Farm Gardens. It was a four-mile trip to Moodus.*

- First, an entry in the book, *Mack Genealogy*, published in 1905, reports that Abner Comstock Smith had ten children with Hope Marshall, listing each child by name and birthdate. There is no mention of a son named Abner C. Smith born in 1825, before he married Hope Marshall. His first child in *Mack Genealogy* is Charles Belden Smith, born in 1827. Point to ponder: A firstborn son was often named after the father, and this book records Charles as the first child. Is that because Abner Comstock Smith already had a firstborn son named after him?
- Second, there is no record that spells out Abner C. Smith's middle name. He never used Comstock or any middle name. He always used *C*.

- Third, why does *Beers 1903* say that Abner C. Smith lived in East Hampton until adulthood, when his father lived in Millington, East Haddam his whole life?
- Fourth, nowhere in the 113 letters that Georgiana's father, Abner C. Smith, wrote home to her and to her mother during the Civil War, does he mention a father. The letters overflow with names of people from both Chatham/East Hampton and East Haddam, yet he never mentioned Abner Comstock Smith, or ten half siblings, even though they were all living at the time within four miles of each other.
- Fifth, Abner Comstock Smith's ninth child on the list in *Mack Genealogy* is a son, born on October 30, 1846, and named Abner Comstock Smith (1846–1920). Did Abner Comstock Smith name two sons after himself? This new Abner was born two weeks after our Abner (Georgiana's father) married Lucinda on October 18, 1846, and a week before our Abner's twenty-first birthday on November 9.

After years of speculating, a DNA test finally locked the answer in stone. Peter Worthington Smith (my husband), who is a direct descendant of Georgiana's father, had his DNA tested by Ancestry.com. The results confirm that Abner Comstock Smith (1796–1876) was Abner C. Smith's biological father—Georgiana's biological grandfather.

For clarity's sake, in the rest of this book I will refer to:

- **Georgiana's father as "Abner C. Smith,"**
- **Georgiana's grandfather as "Abner Comstock Smith (1796),"**
- **Georgiana's uncle, her father's half-brother with the same name, as "Abner Comstock Smith (1846)."**

The gravestone of Georgiana's grandfather Abner Comstock Smith (1796) stands proudly upon a SMITH pedestal in the Mount Parnassus Cemetery, sometimes called Mount Parnassus Burying Ground, in East Haddam. He is one of many Smith descendants of Matthew Smith (1685–1751) and Sarah (born Mack) Smith (1684–1765), the first Smiths to settle in East Haddam when

Connecticut was still a colony of England. Some gravestones in the cemetery have the words *Revolutionary War* etched on them. Some are made of now-fragile brownstone, decoratively engraved with death heads. Some stand permanently cockeyed. Some have fallen over. Several tiny old gravestones engraved with angels can be found by scraping the grass away.

For many generations, Smiths owned and farmed and ran a tanning business on the land next to this burying ground. The Millington village center, which used to be a main hub for East Haddam and is now preserved as the Millington Historic District, is only four miles to the east. About four miles from the burying ground in the other direction is Moodus. The old, but well-maintained, road on which the Mount Parnassus Cemetery is located continues north for over a mile, goes past Bashan Lake, then cuts to the west toward Moodus. The name of the old road? Smith Road!

The old Smith homestead sat on a hill directly next to what became the burying ground. Matthew Smith of Lyme had purchased the land in 1706 when he married Sarah Mack, also of Lyme. He built a dwelling house on it for his family. In 1718, he bought more land in "Haddam on the East side [of] the Great River" in the "Coloney of Connecticut, in New-England," as the deed to the property reads.[15] When he died in 1751, he left the house and property to his son Matthew (1722–1804). In 1778, after serving in the American Revolution in the Lexington Alarm, this second Matthew built a larger house, described in one historical record as "a tall and stately mansion — overlooking all the dwellings of the plain."[16] Today this house is part of Smith Farm Gardens, an elegant fifteen-acre estate located at 60 Smith Road. The large white home is beautifully restored, and the grounds are perfectly manicured, for which the new owners deserve the credit. Tours of the homestead, which can be booked for weddings and other private events, are available and include a bit of Smith family history. It is worth seeing, even if you are not a Smith.

Abner Comstock Smith (1796) grew up in the "mansion" on the estate. His father, Jeremiah Smith (1758–1837) had inherited the property in 1804 from his father, the second Matthew Smith, whose 1792 Last Will and Testament reads:

> Item — I give to my beloved wife Sarah one-third part of my moveable estate and the use or improvement of one-third part of all my lands and buildings during her natural life.
>
> Item — I give to my son Matthew ninety pounds, my great Bible, a red chest, the first volume of Locke on Human Understanding, a large pair of tongs and one-third part of my wearing apparel.
>
> Item — I give to my son Calvin, above what he has already received, the second volume of Locke on Human Understanding, one-third of my wearing apparel and thirty pounds, to be paid in stock or country produce.
>
> Item — I give to my daughter Sarah fifty pounds, a loom and all the tackline, and the privilege of occupying the north room in my dwelling so long as she shall remain single, and the privilege of keeping one cow and ten sheep on my favor, from year to year, so long as she shall remain in single life.
>
> Item — I give to my son Jeremiah my dwelling house and barn and out-houses, and all my land, goods and chattels, including all my estate, both real and personal, subject to the encumbrance and legacies above named, and which shall remain after my debts and funeral charges shall be paid.

Lucky Jeremiah. Lucky Temperance Comstock Smith (1764–1843), his wife. Lucky Abner Comstock Smith (1796), their son. As an adult, Abner Comstock Smith (1796) owned forty acres of the Smith property and lived "a few rods [a rod is five-and-a-half yards] south of the old homestead."[17]

Moodus is only four miles from the Smith farm. Without too much effort, Georgiana could have made a day trip to the Smith homestead to visit her grandfather. She could have visited with her many (there were many!) Smith relatives. She could have attended her grandfather's burial when she was twenty-seven. She could have. Maybe. Perhaps. Possibly.

### GEORGIANA'S GRANDMOTHER ON THE SMITH SIDE — IT'S EVEN MORE COMPLICATED

So while I am certain that Georgiana's grandfather on the Smith side was Abner Comstock Smith (1796), her foundation still has a hairline crack of uncertainty when it comes to her grandmother on the Smith side (Abner C. Smith's mother). Who was she? DNA results have not revealed clues yet, so I've tried to pull answers out of these facts from historical records, mostly from *Beers 1903*:

- In 1820, Abner Comstock Smith (1796) married Electa Warner (1798–1824).
- From 1820 to 1824, no children were born of Abner and Electa.
- In April 1824, Electa died at age twenty-six.
- In February 1825, the woman who would become baby Abner C. Smith's biological mother became pregnant by Abner Comstock Smith (1796).
- On November 9, 1825, baby Abner C. Smith entered the world.
- At some point, likely at birth in 1825, baby Abner C. Smith was given to Rhoda Ackley of the Ackley family in the Tartia section of Chatham/East Hampton, which is just over the East Haddam line.
- In April 1826, Abner Comstock Smith (1796) married Hope Marshall.
- From 1827 to 1849, Abner Comstock Smith (1796) and Hope had ten children.

I considered that **Rhoda Ackley** (1794–1876), the woman who took baby Abner C. Smith to raise and the woman he called "Mother," might have been his biological mother. She was a single thirty-one-year-old woman living with her Ackley family in the

Tartia section of Chatham/East Hampton, where she lived her entire life. She was two years older than the baby's father, Abner Comstock Smith (1796). How and why and exactly when baby Abner C. Smith came into Rhoda's life is a mystery. Why did Abner Comstock Smith (1796) choose her to raise his first and at the time only son? Rhoda was not related to him, although you will read on that Ackleys and Smiths had some seriously tangled family tree branches. An easy explanation would be that Rhoda became pregnant by Abner Comstock Smith (1796) after his first wife died, and he chose not to marry her. Instead, he went on to a new life with a new wife, without Rhoda and without his firstborn namesake son.

There is little doubt that Abner C. Smith considered Rhoda his mother and the Ackleys his family. Rhoda raised Abner as her own and treated him as a son his entire childhood and his entire adulthood. She remained single until Abner was eighteen, when she, at age forty-eight in 1843, married her close neighbor, Julius Brainerd (1787–1868). The year before, Julius had lost his wife Sylvia (born Ackley), who was Rhoda's first cousin.

When Abner and Lucinda married in 1846, they made their home in Tartia amid many Ackley families. Tartia was where Georgiana was born in 1849. In the 1850 census, Abner, Lucinda, and one-year-old Georgiana still lived there. Next door was Rhoda's brother Warren Ackley (1808–1883) and his family, including his eighty-two-year-old mother, Elizabeth Ackley (1768–1860), widow of Captain Nathaniel Ackley (1763–1838). Living in the next house was another brother, George Buckley Ackley (1811–1858), with his large family. (Remember George's name!) Rhoda, married to Julius Brainerd in 1850, lived only two houses away from George.

Later in the year 1850, Abner, Lucinda and Georgiana moved to Moodus, about four miles away, to a new home with Abner's own shoemaking shop, but the close relationship with the Ackleys continued. On the first page of Abner's business account book from the 1850s, the names and shoe measurements of six Ackley girls, all nieces of Rhoda, are written alongside his own daughter Georgiana's, suggesting a special familial bond.

More than ten years later, in Abner's 1862–1865 Civil War letters, he often mentions the Ackleys in Tartia, referring to Rhoda's brothers as uncles and her sisters as aunts. Rhoda's nephew Delos Ackley (1837–1905), Warren's son, who was twelve years younger than Abner, often wrote letters and sent newspapers to Abner during the Civil War. He referred to Rhoda as "Mother" in his letters. Rhoda was, I believe, as maternal as any mother could be. She was a faithful letter writer to Abner during the war. That feels like something a mother would do.

But was she his biological mother? I think not.

### MY BEST GUESS ABOUT ABNER C. SMITH'S BIOLOGICAL MOTHER

My conclusion for the biological mother of Abner C. Smith is **Electa Brainerd (born Warner) Smith**, the first wife of Abner Comstock Smith (1796). The recorded dates make Electa an impossibility, as she is recorded as dying in April 1824, a year and a half before Abner C. Smith was born in November 1825. But I think Abner C. Smith's birthdate is wrong: he probably did not know his exact date or year of birth, which was not so unusual for the times. In the early 1800s, some people guessed their birthdates from a bit of family lore and deduction when required to record a legal document as an adult. Those looking through American family history records of the nineteenth century will tell you they find many differences in birth days and birth years recorded by ancestors. A study of the 1900 census, the first to record both a person's age and their birth date, found a large number of cases where the ages reported did not match birthdates reported.[18] (Genealogy is messy.)

My guess is that Abner C. Smith was born just before his mother Electa died on April 24, 1824. Childbirth was the number one cause of death for young women in the nineteenth century. When Electa died, she was twenty-six, had been married for four years, and had no recorded children.

Here's what I think happened: Electa and Abner Comstock Smith (1796) married. When they had their first child, they gave him the name of his father. Electa died soon after the birth and Abner needed someone to care for his son. In those days, men infrequently raised a child without the help of a woman. He chose Rhoda Ackley in Chatham/East Hampton for some reason. The Ackley, the Smith and the Warner families had several connections over the many years of living in the same East Haddam area. It's probable that Abner Comstock Smith (1796) paid her to care for his son. When Abner Comstock Smith (1796) married his second wife, they went on to raise ten children in East Haddam, while his firstborn namesake son was well cared for and well loved in Chatham/East Hampton.

Electa was buried in East Haddam's Warner Cemetery (located on Town Street in East Haddam, not far from the East Haddam Historical Society) where her parents, in their mid-sixties at the time of her death, were later buried.

I don't think Abner C. Smith was the illegitimate son of Rhoda Ackley. I don't think his father would have named a child after himself if that were the case.

Someday, more DNA results, or better scrutinized DNA results, may confirm that the unfortunate Electa is Georgiana's biological grandmother. As for Georgiana, there is no evidence that she had a strong relationship with the families of Abner Comstock Smith (1796) or Electa Warner. There is ample evidence that she, her father, and her family enjoyed a close relationship with the Ackleys in Tartia.

If you read Abner C. Smith's kind, confident, sometimes sentimental Civil War letters (found in *The Civil War Letters of Abner C. Smith*, a companion to this book), you, too, will be convinced that he was brought up in a loving family by a loving woman whom he considered his mother. And for that reason, I will hereafter refer to Electa Warner Smith as Abner C. Smith's biological mother, whom he never knew but knew of, and Rhoda Ackley Brainerd as Abner C. Smith's mother and Georgiana's grandmother.

# Meet The Smackleys: The Smiths and the Ackleys in Georgiana's Foundation

Genealogy is messy. Stories of past generations are full of ragged patches of assumptions. New hard facts leave long-established theories in crumbles. Missing information leaves unfillable gaps. Add adoption, formal or informal, to the stories, and a genealogist's mind and desk get even messier.

Georgiana's father, Abner C. Smith, was informally adopted as a baby in 1825 by Miss Rhoda Ackley. I tried to find a blood relationship between Abner's Smiths and Rhoda's Ackleys and learned there wasn't one. But in the trying, I bumped into the name Ackley in the Smith records many times. That is not surprising given that the Smiths and the Ackleys were two of the first families to settle East Haddam and Chatham/East Hampton, and their sons and sons' sons and sons' sons' sons stayed in the neighborhood, married neighborhood women, and passed their last name down, down, down through the generations.

Abner Comstock Smith (1796), Abner C. Smith's father and Georgiana's grandfather, could count five Ackleys as his relatives during his lifetime — a brother, sister, uncle, aunt, and cousin all married Ackleys.

- His brother Azariah Smith married Ruth Ackley.
- His sister Temperance Comstock Smith married Joseph Osborne Ackley.
- His uncle Matthew Smith married Thankfull (spelled with two *L*s) Ackley.
- His aunt Elizabeth Smith married Oliver Ackley.
- His cousin Matthew Smith married Fluvia Ackley.

Yet, none of these Ackleys linked to Rhoda Ackley. The reason why Rhoda chose, or was chosen, to bring up Abner Comstock Smith (1796)'s son is currently an unfilled gap in Georgiana's foundation, a gap that a reader may be able to fill.

### YOU NEED TO TALK WITH ANITA BALLEK

Everyone I talked to in East Haddam about Ackley history gave me the same advice: "You need to talk with Anita Ballek." Oh, were they right!

Anita (born Ackley) Ballek is a beloved East Haddam historian and a descendant of the first Ackleys of East Haddam. She is the keeper of Ackley genealogy and treasured lore. As of 2020, Anita, at age ninety, lives on the original Isaac Ackley farm of the 1700s, home to the popular Ballek's Garden Center on 90 Maple Avenue in East Haddam.

When I visited Anita, she told me several stories, including many colorful ones, about the Ackleys of East Haddam. She had documents at her fingertips, and she had an organized book with a unique way of sorting out the generations (which she did not need to refer to!). She drew a map for me on the back of a folder to illustrate where families lived in early East Haddam. Anita was familiar with every family name I brought up, including the Smiths of early East Haddam and Chatham/East Hampton.

The Smith story that most intrigued me was about an early-nineteenth-century adoption of a Smith boy by an Ackley. Anita had the legal document for this adoption. Genealogy gold! She generously gave me a copy so I could determine if this was the Abner/Rhoda story. Of course, it was not. (Genealogy miners experience disappointment in the same way Gold Rush "forty-niners" did.) But, of course, the document gave me new information about the Smiths related to Georgiana. (Genealogy miners also frequently find other interesting nuggets.) This is how genealogy gets messy.

The story is worth telling.

### THE CURIOUS CASE OF AN ACKLEY ADOPTING A SMITH

It seems that Ackleys liked to adopt Smiths. Fifteen years after Rhoda Ackley unofficially adopted baby Abner C. Smith from his father, Abner Comstock Smith (1796), another Ackley-adopts-Smith event took place. This time the adoption was legally recorded. Here goes:

- In 1803, Abner Comstock Smith (1796)'s first cousin Asa Smith (1781–1858) had a son and named him **Watrous Beckwith Smith (1803–1866)**.

- In 1826, at age twenty-three, Watrous B. Smith married **Sarah Hill Rogers (1809–1894),** and they soon had children. In 1827, a daughter. In 1831, a namesake son, **Watrous B. Smith, Jr.** In 1833, an infant who died. In 1834, a son. Followed by two more daughters and two more sons.
- The son born in 1834 was given the name **Isaac Ackley Smith.** Curiously, the boy was named after a prominent and wealthy East Haddam man **Isaac Ackley (1789–1880).**
- This prominent Isaac Ackley had married Rebekah Cone (1796–1859) in 1833 when he was forty-four and Rebekah was thirty-seven.
- By 1839, Rebekah Ackley had given birth to several children, but only one survived — a daughter.
- On April 14, 1840, forty-three-year-old Rebekah gave birth to another daughter. Isaac wanted a son. Without a son, Isaac's property would be inherited by a daughter, and if the daughter was married or married later, her property would be owned solely by her husband. In 1840, a married woman in Connecticut could not own property. A single woman could, but when she married, her property automatically became her husband's on her wedding day. (Remember, the Married Women's Property Act was not enacted until 1877.) Isaac Ackley feared that his large estate would be inherited by a daughter and then turned over to a son-in-law. Isaac wanted a son to ensure the Ackley property remained Ackley-owned.
- Fourteen days after the birth of his second daughter, the disappointed and sonless **Isaac Ackley signed papers to adopt Watrous B. Smith's six-year-old son Isaac Ackley Smith and change his new son's name "by legislative enactment" to Isaac Ackley, Jr.**
- The document recording Isaac Ackley's adoption of Watrous B. Smith's son, dated April 28, 1840, reads:

This Indenture, made between **Isaac Ackley,** on the one part, and **Watrous B. Smith,** on the other part (both of

East Haddam, in the County of Middlesex and the State of Connecticut), witnesseth:

*That whereas, the said **Isaac**, being moved by an extraordinary good will, affection and regard for the son of the said **Watrous B. Smith**, to-wit, **ISAAC ACKLEY SMITH,** hereby solemnly covenants and engages faithfully to keep and perform the following duties and obligations, namely: He, the said **Isaac Ackley**, by these presents binds himself to receive, adopt and affiliate the said **Isaac Ackley Smith,** and to extend to him all such rights, privileges and immunities as he would be entitled to receive if he were truly, properly and legally that said **Isaac Ackley's** own son and heir, by affording him, the said **Isaac Ackley Smith**, all needful and proper assistance, comfort and support, in sickness and in health, from the day of the date hereof, until he, the said **Isaac Ackley Smith,** shall have attained the age of twenty-one years. And the said **Isaac Ackley** further covenants and engages to make due provision for the proper education of the said **Isaac Ackley Smith**, and in all respects to treat him, the said **Isaac Ackley Smith,** as if he were the lawful issue of his, the said **Isaac Ackley's** own body.*

*And the said **Watrous B. Smith**, of the second part, hereby renounces and surrenders to the said **Isaac Ackley,** all the rights and powers which he, the said **Watrous B.** enjoys by virtue of the parental relation to him, the said **Isaac Ackley Smith** (except the right of love and homage from him, the said **Isaac Ackley Smith**), so long as he, the said **Isaac Ackley,** shall on his part well and truly keep and observe the covenant herein made and declared. And further, the said **Watrous B.** hereby consents and allows that the name of said **Isaac Ackley Smith** be changed by legislative enactment from **Isaac Ackley Smith**, to the name of **ISAAC ACKLEY, JR.***

A word about the mothers in this transaction: The fact is—there are no words about the mothers. Women had no legal rights concerning their children in the early nineteenth century. A father could give their children up for adoption without the mother's consent.

This story does not end well. Isaac Ackley legally disinherited Isaac Ackley, Jr. prior to Junior turning twenty-one. Junior moved to Kentucky before age twenty-two and married a Kentucky woman. They raised a family of seven children. Although Isaac Ackley, Jr. never changed his last name back to Smith, he dropped the Jr. He also named four of his seven children after his biological Watrous B. Smith family, including his second son whom he named Watrous. He did not name any of his children after his adoption-on/adoption-off Isaac Ackley family. And his gravestone is engraved as Isaac Ackley, without a Junior.

Why did Watrous B. Smith name his son Isaac Ackley in the first place? Was the adoption planned when the baby was born? Were Watrous B. Smith and Isaac Ackley close friends? Children born during this time in America were sometimes given the full name of a good friend, but family names were the most common choice.

- First sons were usually named after the father. Second sons were often named after the mother's father. Subsequent sons were given names from both the father's and mother's families. Was Isaac Ackley related to Mrs. Watrous B. Smith, Sarah Hill (born Rogers) Smith? No.
- Was Isaac Ackley related to Watrous B. Smith? Yes. They were cousins, but only through marriage. Isaac Ackley's sister Ruth had married Azariah Smith, who was a first-cousin-once-removed of Watrous B. Smith. By the way, Azariah was the brother of Abner Comstock Smith (1796), ergo Georgiana's great-uncle.

And just to make the records of the Smiths and the Ackleys even messier, Azariah Smith and his wife Ruth (whose brother and father were both named Isaac Ackley) named their second son, who died within a year, and then their third son, who survived—Isaac Ackley Smith.

There are just too many Smackleys in Georgiana's foundation to stack them neatly. Genealogy is messy.

## BACK TO GEORGIANA'S FATHER, ABNER C. SMITH

Abner C. Smith grew up in Chatham/East Hampton with the Ackleys and went to the town's one-room schoolhouse until at least age fourteen. He was at the top of the class. We know this because in one of his letters sent home during the Civil War, he wrote to his oldest son, Edgar: "You are now twelve years old. Just think of it. When I was of your age, I read in the first class … could read anywhere and anything, studied arithmetic, geography and grammar."[19]

Most children born in the early nineteenth century, as Abner and Lucinda were, received a basic education in reading and writing through the eighth grade. At that time, America boasted the highest literacy rate in the world. One international authority wrote in 1812:

> In America, a great number of people read the Bible, and all the people read a newspaper. The fathers read aloud to their children, while breakfast is being prepared—a task which occupies the mothers for three-quarters of an hour every morning. And as the newspapers of the United States are filled with all sorts of narratives—comments on agriculture, the arts, travel, navigation; and also extracts from all the best books in America and Europe—they disseminate an enormous amount of information.[20]

As an adult, Lucinda, who was born the same year as Abner and attended the same level of school, did not read and write as well as Abner. (Perhaps she lost practice because she was occupied preparing breakfast.)

## ABNER AND LUCINDA

When he was nineteen in 1844, Abner traveled to nearby Moodus Village in East Haddam to work in a shoe factory that made shoe lasts (lasts are molds on which shoes are constructed) owned by Mr. Hyde. There he learned the trade of shoemaker.[21] Hyde's factory was in the center of the village where nineteen-year-old Lucinda Arnold worked at the time.

Whenever there are single nineteen-year-olds around, you can be sure they will find ways to meet. Abner and Lucinda met somehow, likely in downtown Moodus, which was full of working young men and women. They also could have met through Lucinda's brother Horace, who may have also worked with Abner in the Hyde factory. When Abner ran his own shoe business in Moodus in the 1850s, he employed Horace. However, I couldn't determine whom Abner met first in the 1840s, Lucinda or her brother Horace.

### Thanksgiving in 1846?

Georgiana's Aunt Jerusha was married on November 26, 1846, the last Thursday in November. Did she get married on Thanksgiving Day? Yes. November 26 was an annual Thanksgiving holiday for the state of Connecticut. Thanksgiving was not celebrated in every state in the country, and if it was celebrated, it wasn't necessarily on the same day. In 1846, individual states chose if and when they would appoint a day for fasting and prayer to celebrate good fortune and bountiful crops. Connecticut had declared a Thanksgiving Day each year since the early 1800s.

However, 1846 was an important year in Thanksgiving history. It marked the start of a long campaign to make Thanksgiving the third national holiday of the United States. (Washington's Birthday and Independence Day were already national holidays.) **That year, Sarah Josepha Hale (1788-1879),**[22] who incidentally had written one of America's favorite poems, "Mary Had a Little Lamb," sixteen years earlier, wrote her first letter to a president of the United States asking him to declare a national holiday of Thanksgiving. She was advocating that the country designate one official day a year for all states to celebrate a day of Thanksgiving together as a nation.

Sarah Josepha Hale was editress—she liked the title editress over editor—of *The American Ladies' Magazine*. When *American Ladies* merged with *Godey's Lady's Book*, Sarah Hale continued as

> editress, turning it into the magazine that almost single-handedly defined American taste for a generation. Year after year, president after president, editress Hale persisted for the Thanksgiving Day cause with speeches and editorials and letters to five different presidents.
>
> It was finally Abraham Lincoln who made Thanksgiving Day a national holiday. He had been convinced by one of Sarah Josepha Hale's letters that the holiday would help unify the country, which was embroiled in the heat of the Civil War. Lincoln proclaimed Thanksgiving Day to be observed on the last Thursday in November 1863, two years before the war ended. Every president after Lincoln annually proclaimed a national Thanksgiving Day, until 1941, when the fourth Thursday (not always the last Thursday) in November became a permanent national holiday.[23]
>
> So we can thank a woman, Sarah Josepha Hale, for Thanksgiving as we know it today.
>
> But we can't thank her for women's rights as we know them today. Sarah Hale did not support women's suffrage. She believed in the "secret, silent influence of women" to sway male voters. (Come on, Sarah!) When she died in 1879, male voters hadn't swayed yet. A few were starting to lean, but it took forty more years for women to get the right to vote, and it surely wasn't because they were silent.

Lucinda and Abner married on Sunday, October 18, 1846, at her parents' home in Turkey Hill, Haddam. In mid-nineteenth-century New England, most weddings took place in the home of the bride's parents. The Haddam Town Marriage Record[24] reads: "Arnold, Lucinda, of Haddam, m. Abner C. Smith, of East Haddam." Note that Abner C. Smith is from East Haddam, not Chatham/East Hampton, meaning that Abner did not live in the Tartia section of Chatham/East Hampton with the Ackleys that year.

Abner and Lucinda were not married by the minister of the Arnolds' Congregational church in Haddam, as Lucinda's sister Sylvia had been four years prior when she married a Haddam-rooted Brainerd. Abner and Lucinda were married by a forty-nine-year-old Baptist minister who lived near Turkey Hill — the Reverend Simon Shailer[25] (1776–1864). Rev. Shailer also performed the marriage of another of Lucinda's sisters, Jerusha, to a Haddam-rooted Dickinson a month later, on November 26. Why did Lucinda and Jerusha choose a Baptist minister to perform their weddings when their parents were active and longtime members of the prominent Congregational Church of Haddam? Perhaps the Arnolds chose Rev. Shailer because he was a distantly-related, longtime family friend. Or because he was simply a close convenient neighbor. He lived in Shailerville — yes, named after his family — a village close to Turkey Hill in Haddam.

Exactly two years after their wedding, in October 1848, Lucinda became pregnant with their first child, who would be Georgiana.

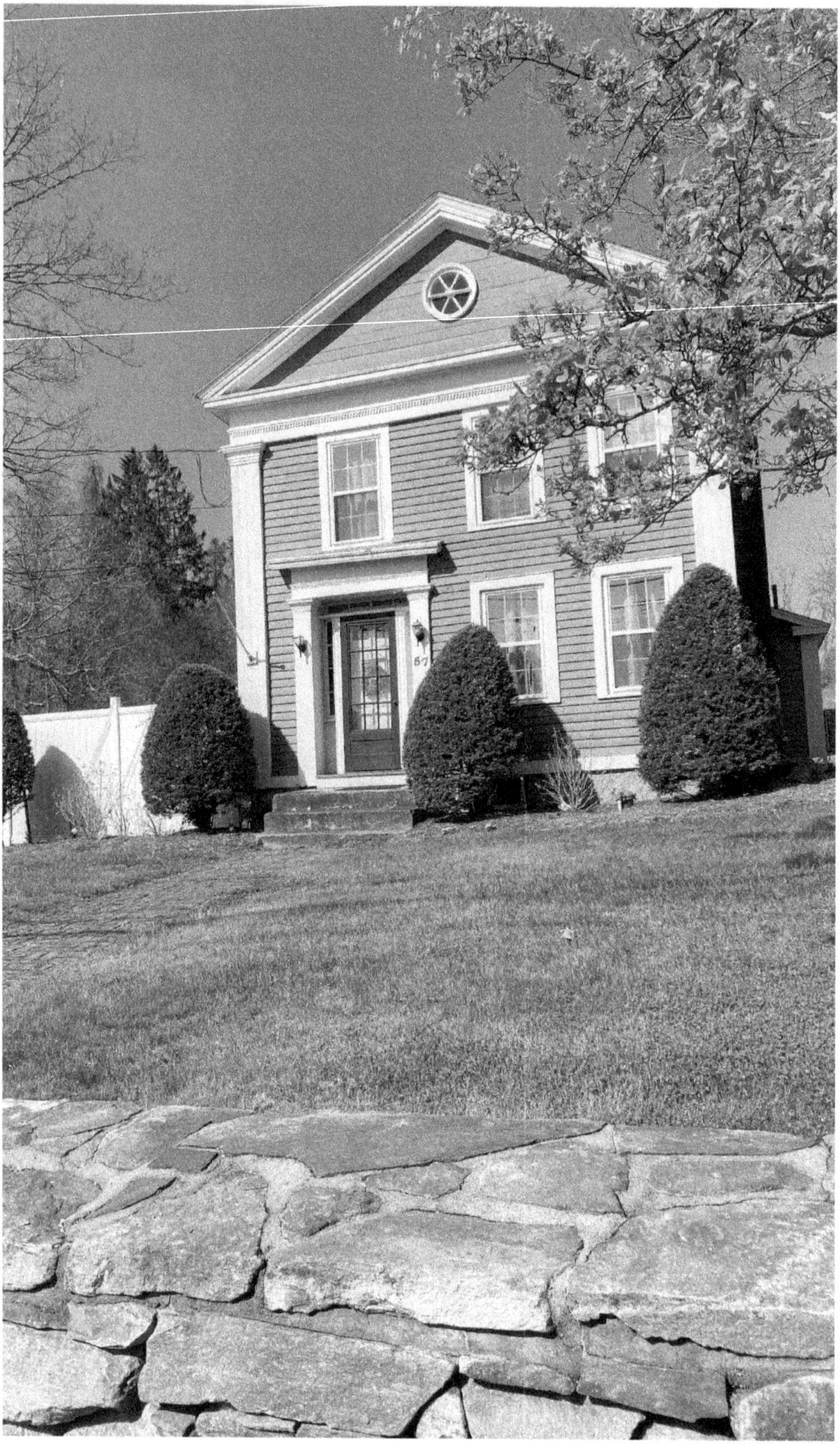

CHAPTER 2
# Little Girl
## Georgiana from Birth to Eleven
## 1849–1861

They named her Ella Georgiana Smith. She was Abner and Lucinda Smith's first child, born on July 1, 1849, in Chatham/East Hampton, Connecticut. She didn't die and her mother didn't die, for which her father would have ardently thanked God.

Death in childbirth for both babies and mothers happened with alarming frequency in mid-nineteenth-century America, when an estimated 21.7 percent of newborns died at birth or within the first year. The comparable number today is less than 1 percent — six deaths per thousand births.[26] It was also estimated that mid-nineteenth-century American women died in pregnancy or childbirth at a rate of six hundred per hundred thousand live births. Today, that number is twenty-four.[27] The word *estimated* gives overly generous credit to the nineteenth-century bean-counters, on whose numbers these statistics are based. Most historians believe that the deaths were severely underreported.

When Georgiana was born in 1849, mothers gave birth at home with midwives assisting. Even fifty years later, only 5 percent of births took place in a hospital. Pregnant mothers, miscarrying mothers, delivering mothers, and newborn babies received little or no attention from physicians, who were all men and considered it obscene to be present at a birth. All physicians in the United

OPPOSITE: *Georgiana's childhood home was at 57 North Moodus Road in Moodus, Connecticut. Photo taken 2022.*

States were male until the year Georgiana was born, when Elizabeth Blackwell (1821–1910) became the first woman to receive a medical degree in the United States.

Death would have been on Lucinda's mind during her pregnancy with her first baby. She knew that her mother's firstborn son, the infant Horace, had lived only six hours. When Lucinda was six, her oldest sister, Elizabeth, died at age thirteen. On the other hand, Lucinda knew that her older sister Sylvia (born Arnold) Brainerd had given birth to three healthy children: Louisa Fidelia Brainerd in 1843, Charles Edgar Brainerd in 1846, and Juliette Brainerd in August 1848. Lucinda's other older sister Jerusha (born Arnold) Dickinson had also fortunately had a successful birth with her first baby, Edwin A. Dickinson, in November 1848.

Baby Georgiana's twenty-four-year-old parents, her two Arnold grandparents, as well as her Arnold uncles and aunts and four young cousins were all in good health when she was born on July 1. But in September, her Aunt Sylvia Brainerd tragically lost three members of her family. Sylvia's sixty-eight-year-old father-in-law, Captain Aaron Brainerd, her twenty-eight-year-old husband, Charles Smith Brainerd, and her three-year-old son, Charles Edgar Brainerd, died in the span of three weeks. They died from dysentery, likely contracted from contaminated water or cow's milk. Georgiana's Aunt Sylvia became a twenty-seven-year-old widow with two young daughters — a pitiable situation for any nineteenth-century woman who had few options to provide for a family. At least Sylvia lived in Haddam near her mother and father who could give her comfort and provide her with necessities. After a socially acceptable one year of widowhood, Sylvia married her twenty-five-year-old neighbor Warren Washington Pardee and gave her daughters, six-year-old Louisa and two-year-old Juliette, a new father.

## Death and Disease Near Baby Georgiana

The following chart gives some insight into the state of health care in the world Georgiana was born into. It lists the combined causes of death during the first year of her life in Chatham, where she was born, and in East Haddam, the abutting town.

In 1850, for the first time in the United States, information on deaths was collected as part of the federal census. During the door-to-door census taking, residents—or whoever answered the door when enumerators knocked—were asked if anyone in their household had died in the previous twelve months, and, if so, the cause of the death. There are many reasons why the data might be unreliable and incomplete: not every census taker was diligent in the collecting process; people had moved away; and sometimes people who had died left no one to report their deaths. Given the state of maternity care and the lack of antibiotics, historians agree that there are too few infants reported on these records. And stillborn children were not recorded at all.

Note that 40 percent of the deaths recorded are children. Note that no child under four months old is listed. Note that the reason for death is sometimes a symptom (like fever or fits) and not an identified disease. Note that cancer is not listed as a cause of death in these two towns. In 1850, cancer was identified as fatal in only sixty-one of ten thousand deaths in the United States.[28] Today, cancer is the second leading cause of death after heart disease. The causes of death today do not include many of the causes of death in Georgiana's first year of life, reflecting the advancements in medicine since 1850 in diagnosing, preventing, and wiping out many diseases, especially for children.

**DISEASES OR CAUSES OF DEATH
FOR RESIDENTS WHO DIED IN CHATHAM
(POP. 1,525) AND EAST HADDAM (POP. 2,610)
JUNE 1, 1849–MAY 31, 1850**

(This chart uses data from the United States Federal Census Mortality Schedule of 1850.)

| Disease or Cause of Death (Italics are my words.) | Number of People | Children Who Are Included in Number Of People |
|---|---|---|
| Consumption (*tuberculosis*) | 10 | 1 five-month-old boy |
| Old Age | 7 | |
| Dropsy and Dropsy Head (*edema — swelling from fluid accumulation; heart failure*) | 6 | 6 children aged from five months to eight years old |
| Fever | 5 | |
| Brain Disease/Affliction of Brain | 3 | 1 five-year-old girl 1 seven-year-old boy |
| Lung Fever | 2 | 1 two-year-old girl 1 one-year-old boy |
| Measles | 2 | 1 four-year-old boy 1 five-year-old boy |
| Dysentery (*infection in the intestines*) | 2 | |
| Fits | 2 | |
| Colic | 1 | 1 eight-year-old boy |
| Typhoid | 1 | |
| Tumor Throat | 1 | |
| Whooping Cough | 1 | 1 five-month-old girl |
| Marasmus (*undernourishment causing a child's weight to be significantly low for their age*) | 1 | 1 five-month-old boy |

| | | |
|---|---|---|
| Mumps | 1 | 1 nine-year-old boy |
| Liver Complaint | 1 | |
| Croupe *(virus marked by a low-pitched cough)* | 1 | |
| Debility *(weakness; infirmity)* | 1 | 1 four-month-old girl |
| Asylum Hartford | 1 | |
| Froze to death by exposure from intoxication | 1 | 1 fifteen-year-old colored boy *(This term, now dated and offensive, was used in 1850 to describe people of a race other than white, especially African Americans.)* |
| Unknown | 5 | 3 children: a nine-month-old boy, a one-year-old boy, and a five-year-old girl |
| Total | 55 | **22 Total Children (39 East Haddam; 16 Chatham)** |

### A LIFETIME OF IMPROVEMENTS IN HEALTH CARE

Georgiana entered a world in the process of developing vaccinations, medical treatments, and cleanliness standards to prevent the spread of disease. Smallpox vaccinations were in place (although not compulsory), but other fatal and contagious diseases, like malaria, were still taking the lives of adults and children. Good hygiene, proper nutrition, fresh air, and cleanliness were not acknowledged as measures to prevent the spread of deadly diseases for another ten years. In 1859, Englishwoman Florence Nightingale

(1820–1910) wrote her *Notes on Nursing: What It Is, What It Is Not* and established her highly respected nursing school for women in London. Her ideas were considered revolutionary at the time and ultimately brought profound changes to health care. Cleanliness in the operating room and the use of antiseptics to clean wounds and instruments would not be embraced for another eight years, in 1867. The ideas that something called *germs* were transmitting diseases and that doctors should wash their hands between patients weren't put forth until 1870, when Georgiana was twenty.

The discovery that mosquitoes transmitted malaria, the discovery that vitamins were essential to health, and the invention of vaccines for cholera, rabies, diphtheria, tetanus, whooping cough, and tuberculosis were all conceived and implemented during Georgiana's lifetime. In 1928, two years before Georgiana died, Sir Alexander Fleming (1881–1955) discovered the wonder drug penicillin, which was finally successfully mass-produced in 1942 and went on to save millions of lives.[29] By the time Georgiana left the world, advancements in health care had spiked to never-before-seen levels, and yearly death rates had plummeted. (How interesting that this dramatic change coincides with women entering the medical profession.)

### A LIFETIME OF IMPROVEMENTS IN WOMEN'S RIGHTS

Georgiana's lifetime, 1849 to 1930, ran in tandem with the the American women's struggle to win the right to vote. She was born precisely one year after the July 1848 birth of the women's suffrage movement. American women would finally win the right to vote in 1920, when Georgiana was seventy-one.

The women's suffrage movement in the United States was born in the industrial village of Seneca Falls in upstate New York in July 1848. It happened when Lucretia Mott, a famed Quaker orator, traveled to the Seneca Falls area with her husband to visit relatives and deliver speeches advocating an equal voice for women. Seneca Falls was the hometown of Lucretia's friend Elizabeth Cady Stanton (1815–1902). The two women had met in London eight years earlier while attending the World Anti-Slavery Convention, at which they sat fuming together in a special section provided for women. Women were not allowed to sit with men or to vote during the convention.

In Seneca Falls that July 1848, Mott and Stanton and three other women met for tea, where they vented their long-held opinions about women's subservience in society. At the tea, they decided to hold a small convention to address women's rights before Lucretia Mott left the area. They planned it for ten days later, calling it "a start." (Ten days to pull off a convention? These women were good organizers!) The convention would be held at the Wesleyan Methodist Chapel in Seneca Falls. Word of mouth and a small notice in the local newspaper were the extent of publicity. On July 20, 1848, before three hundred women and men, Stanton read a document she and the other women had prepared — the Declaration of Sentiments. It was written in the style of the Declaration of Independence but declared the rights of American women. This convention was the first Women's Rights Convention in the United States and was the first step in the nation's women's suffrage movement advocating women's right to vote. Seneca Falls is now the site of the Women's Rights National Historical Park.

Did the young suffrage movement affect or influence the young Georgiana? No. News about the earliest days of women's suffrage activities was scant and unpopular. It took until 1869, when Georgiana was twenty, for Connecticut women to form the Connecticut Woman Suffrage Association (CWSA), which continued its work for the next fifty-two years.

# The Most Shocking and Unnatural Incident Ever Recorded in the History of Womanity

In 1848, at the nation's first Women's Rights Convention in Seneca Falls, New York, a **Declaration of Sentiments,** written by Elizabeth Cady Stanton, was presented and debated. The Declaration was modeled after the Declaration of Independence, with two important words — "and women" — added to the core line. It read: **"We hold these truths to be self-evident: that all men <u>and women</u> are created equal."**

The document included a list of sixteen facts as proof of "repeated injuries and usurpations on the part of man toward woman."

Here are the facts, word for word. (Readers – get ready to shudder!)

- He has never permitted her to exercise her inalienable right to the elective franchise.
- He has compelled her to submit to laws, in the formation of which she had no voice.
- He has withheld from her rights which are given to the most ignorant and degraded men — both natives and foreigners.
- Having deprived her of this first right of a citizen, the elective franchise, thereby leaving her without representation in the halls of legislation, he has oppressed her on all sides.
- He has made her, if married, in the eye of the law, civilly dead.
- He has taken from her all right in property, even to the wages she earns.
- He has made her, morally, an irresponsible being, as she can commit many crimes with impunity, provided they be done in the presence of her husband. In the covenant of marriage, she is compelled to promise obedience to her husband, he becoming, to all intents and purposes, her master — the law giving him power to deprive her of her liberty, and to administer chastisement.
- He has so framed the laws of divorce, as to what shall be the proper causes of divorce; in case of separation, to whom the

- guardianship of the children shall be given; as to be wholly regardless of the happiness of the women — the law, in all cases, going upon the false supposition of the supremacy of man, and giving all the power into his hands.
- After depriving her of all rights as a married woman, if single and the owner of property, he has taxed her to support a government which recognizes her only when her property can be made profitable to it.
- He has monopolized nearly all the profitable employments, and from those she is permitted to follow, she receives but a scanty remuneration.
- He closes against her all the avenues to wealth and distinction, which he considers most honorable to himself. As a teacher of theology, medicine, or law, she is not known.
- He has denied her the facilities for obtaining a thorough education — all colleges being closed to her.
- He allows her in church as well as State, but a subordinate position, claiming Apostolic authority for her exclusion from the ministry, and, with some exceptions, from any public participation in the affairs of the Church.
- He has created a false public sentiment by giving to the world a different code of morals for men and women, by which moral delinquencies which exclude women from society are not only tolerated but deemed of little account in man.
- He has usurped the prerogative of Jehovah himself, claiming it as his right to assign for her a sphere of action, when that belongs to her conscience and her God.
- He has endeavored, in every way that he could, to destroy her confidence in her own powers, to lessen her self-respect, and to make her willing to lead a dependent and abject life.

One hundred of the attendees (sixty-eight women and thirty-two men) dared to sign the Declaration of Sentiments. It became the blueprint for the nationwide women's suffrage movement but was not embraced by many. Some of the signers took steps to remove their signatures after the criticism started.

> The *Oneida Whig,* a newspaper in Oneida County, New York, about seventy miles east of Seneca Falls, published a letter from an anonymous author who was in disbelief, reflecting the sentiments of many. He (it is clear it is a man) aligned the gathering as a "bolt," as in a "bolt from the blue," meaning that the notion of women voting was a complete surprise, something totally unexpected. **"This bolt is the most shocking and unnatural incident ever recorded in the history of womanity. If our ladies will insist on voting and legislating, where, gentlemen, will be our dinners and our elbows? Where our domestic firesides and the holes in our stockings?"**[30]
>
> (Womanity—what a great word! We should bring that word back!)

## MOODUS BECOMES HOME

When the three Brainerds died from dysentery in Haddam in September 1849, three-month-old Georgiana was living safely across the river in the Tartia section of Chatham. The family of three—Abner, Lucinda, and Georgiana—stayed in Chatham for over a year, then moved to an almost brand new (built in 1846) house on North Moodus Road in Moodus.

In 1850, Abner bought this Moodus property—a house and a barn on a half-acre of land—for $1,360 [about $45,000 in 2020] with a $300 down payment and a $1,060 mortgage from the seller Frank Emmons. Frank Emmons, twelve years older than Abner, was a builder who came from a longtime East Haddam family with roots near the Smiths in Millington.

A footprint of the North Moodus Road home on an 1874 map shows a small section attached to the back of the house. According to a document compiled in 2010 by East Haddam Municipal Historian Karl P. Stofko, "the rear ell of the house is one story and appears to have been added as a carpenter shop for Frank Emmons' wood mill working business. Abner probably used the rear ell as a shoemaker shop." Abner's shoe business records show that he made shoes and shoe lasts for Silliman's Shoe Shop in Moodus.

Within six years, Abner paid off the mortgage. In the 1860 census, the real estate had increased slightly in value to $1,500 [about $47,500 in 2020] and was mortgage-free. In 2020, the original house and property, long gone from Smith family ownership, is located at 57 North Moodus Road. In 2016, the house and property sold for $225,000.

One rough edge in this otherwise smooth home purchase story: Moodus property records show that Abner purchased the property in March 1850. But the November 1850 census says that Abner, Lucinda, and one-and-a-half-year-old Georgiana still lived in Chatham. Why hadn't they moved to the house when Abner bought it? I don't know, except it appears that Lucinda's brother and his new wife were living in it. I conclude this because in the November 1850 census, Horace Edgar Arnold, also a shoemaker, and his wife Susan lived on North Moodus Road next to neighbors identical to those of Abner and Lucinda's in 1860. Perhaps Horace and Susan used or rented the house for a while before Abner moved in? Whatever the reason, I believe it's a hint that Abner had a good relationship with his brother-in-law Horace Arnold.

At two years old, Georgiana was living with her mother and father in their new home on North Moodus Road. I know this because her first baby brother was born there in October 1851. Georgiana had turned two in July. She would have heard some frightening and some wonderful sounds of her mother giving birth in the house — the slam of doors as women rushed around with buckets and rags and water and firewood; the clunks and whooshes of the water pump; the firm words of a midwife; the moans and screams of her mother; the squawk of a newborn; then the quiet coo of everyone in the house. Three times before she was nine, Georgiana heard these sounds. Three times, she experienced a household of emotions from a new baby as she became the big sister to little brothers: Charles Edgar Smith (1851–1928) arrived when she was two; Franklin Pierce Smith (1854–1938), when she was four; and Frederick C. Smith (1857–1863), when she was eight. Georgiana was the only daughter of Abner and Lucinda. (The only daughter and first in birth order — I wonder what *Psychology Today* would have to say about this in shaping a personality.)

### NAMING THE CHILDREN

Why did Abner and Lucinda name their first child "Ella Georgiana?" Neither "Ella" nor "Georgiana" were popular names at the time.[31] Even if the names were popular, Abner and Lucinda would not have selected them for that reason alone. The predominant naming protocol of Georgiana's generation and of the generations before her was the naming of children after family members. Lucinda's parents, Horace Arnold and Sylvia (born White) Arnold, named seven of their eight children after people in their families: they gave Jerusha the name of Horace's grandmother; they gave Davis Tyler two family names; they named the two Elizabeths after Sylvia's sister, Elizabeth (born White) Doane; and they named the two Horaces and Sylvia after themselves. As for Lucinda, their fourth daughter, it looks like Horace and Sylvia ran out of family names they liked. Lucinda is the only Arnold sibling whose name is not on the family tree.

Did Lucinda and her Arnold siblings carry on the tradition of recycling family names for the next generation? Not as much. Altogether, Horace and Sylvia's children gave them fifteen grandchildren, including Lucinda's four. Of the fifteen, only seven were given family names.

No one in the Arnold or Smith family tree had the name Ella or Georgiana. Yet, when Abner and Lucinda named their boys, they chose family names or names to honor someone.

- **Charles Edgar Smith**, their first son, was named after Charles Edgar Brainerd, Lucinda's sister Sylvia's three-year-old son who had died two years prior. Charles Edgar Smith went by his middle name; his school and adult records often say Edgar C. Smith. Isn't it interesting that Abner did not name his first son after himself, as was the custom?

- **Franklin Pierce Smith**, their second son, was named after the president of the United States. Franklin Pierce (1804–1869), from New Hampshire, served as president from March 1853 to March 1857. Frank was born in 1854. Naming a child after the president of the United States or a popular hero was a trend of the Victorian era (1840s to 1890s).
- **Frederick C. Smith**, their third son and last of four children, was referred to as "Little Freddy." He was named Frederick because — well, I'm not sure. But here's a stretchy possibility, one of the few hints that Abner C. Smith had a good relationship with his Mount Parnassus biological relatives. Little Freddy may have been named after the nephew of Abner's biological and deceased mother, Electa (born Warner) Smith. The nephew's name was Frederick Warner (1823–1896). He was son of Electa's brother Oliver Warner (1795–1853). Oliver Warner and Abner Comstock Smith (1796) were the same age and likely good friends as they grew up in the Mount Parnassus area of East Haddam. They would have become even closer when Abner Comstock Smith (1796) married his sister, Electa. Oliver's son Frederick Warner and Abner C. Smith were first cousins close in age and perhaps close in acquaintance through adulthood. When Little Freddy was born in 1857 in Moodus in East Haddam, Frederick Warner was thirty-three and had just married Phoebe E. Moseley (1830–1906) from East Haddam's Moseley family in the Mount Parnassus area. (I am mentioning the Moseley family because the name comes up later in Georgiana's story.) The middle C in Little Freddy's name was likely because of his father's middle C. Like Abner C. Smith, Little Freddy's middle initial was never spelled out. I wish I was certain of the reason for the choice of the name Frederick, because the name has been passed down through future Smith generations.

So I feel confident that **Ella Georgiana,** Abner and Lucinda's first child, was named after someone in their family. I have a guess that the name Ella was chosen for Abner C. Smith's deceased biological mother, Electa. Perhaps Abner grew up with adult relatives, including his Uncle Oliver Warner, referring to Electa as "El" or "Ella," or perhaps he and Lucinda wanted to use an adaptation of the name. As for the name Georgiana, my guess is that it was chosen to honor George Ackley. Remember him? He was Abner's Uncle George, the brother of Abner's (adoptive) mother, Rhoda Ackley. George was fourteen years old when baby Abner arrived in Tartia. They may have lived in the same house. George may have even taken on a big brother role. When, more than twenty years later, Georgiana was born in Tartia, George and his wife and their eight children (seven girls and one boy) lived one house away. I believe George and Abner were close, as it was George's daughters' names and shoe sizes that were noted in Abner's account book along with Georgiana's. A firmer rationale for the name choices of Ella or Georgiana may surface someday.

Georgiana went by both Ella and Georgiana in her elementary school days. Her father, in his many Civil War letters to her when she was a teen, used with an affectionate inconsistency, the names of Ella, Georgiana, Ella G, Georgia, or (my favorite) Georgie. The Smith family has always referred to her as Georgiana.

### GEORGIANA'S SCHOOL DAYS

School Days, school days
Dear old Golden Rule days.
Reading and 'Riting and 'Rithmetic,
Taught to the tune of a hick'ry stick.[32]

WRITTEN BY WILL D. COBB AND GUS EDWARDS, 1907

These are the opening lyrics from a popular American song written in 1907, when Georgiana was fifty-eight. The words reflect an older couple reminiscing about their elementary school days, which were during the same time period as Georgiana's.

The lyrics give an accurate peek into Georgiana's educational experience. In the mid-nineteenth century, children were taught the "three R's" and the Golden Rule in the classroom. Some people say that children were really taught "four R's": reading, 'riting, 'rithmetic, and religion. The hickory stick? It was indeed used to discipline naughty children. Although I doubt it was ever used on Georgiana, as I doubt she was ever naughty in school. (I could be wrong, of course.)

Like the majority of Connecticut children in the 1850s, Georgiana attended a one-room schoolhouse near her home. Some children were as young as three when they entered school. Georgiana was four when she began the winter term in November 1853. In East Haddam, winter terms ran from November to mid-March, followed by a six-week break. Summer terms ran from May to mid-September, followed by another six-week break. A school week was five-and-a-half days — full days Monday to Friday, plus Saturday mornings. During Georgiana's school years, boys and girls attended both terms. In her mother's years, girls attended only the summer terms and boys only the winter terms, for the practical reason that the boys were needed to carry firewood into the classroom for heat in the winter and were needed to work on the farms in the summer.

Georgiana's school was a common school, or public school. By the 1850s, Connecticut had organized a system of common schools throughout the state; by the end of the century, public-supported systems of common schools were nationwide and a cornerstone of the American way of life.[33] During Georgiana's school years (1853–1865), East Haddam had seventeen to nineteen common school districts, each with a one-room schoolhouse.[34]

Georgiana attended East Haddam's Fourth District School, sometimes called the Uptown District School. East Haddam was growing fast, and some of the one-room schoolhouses were overcrowded. In Georgiana's first term of school, there were sixty-two enrolled "scholars" — as pupils were called in the 1850s — thirty-one boys and thirty-one girls. The records also note that the average attendance in a classroom was forty-four children.

At the Connecticut State Library, in East Haddam's school records of 1853–1858, I found Georgiana's name when she was age four to eight. There she was, with a nearly perfect attendance record and never marked tardy, which is something that can't be said for many of the other children. During one month, only eight of the forty-seven scholars had perfect attendance, and Georgiana was one of them. Nearly-perfect and on-time attendance were, of course, due to the diligence of her mother and father. But it was also due to her good health and to the proximity of the school which was right on North Moodus Road. Her teacher was the young Nathaniel O. Chapman (1833–1881), who lived with his parents and his Percival grandmother across the street from the Smiths. Nathaniel had started teaching when he was seventeen.

Schools cost money. The common school movement, advocating free education for children, had been active in the United States since the 1830s. But during Georgiana's school years in the 1850s, the expenses of her town's schools were funded by a combination of payments from parents or guardians of the students and taxes collected from citizens of the town. Georgiana's father was chosen as one of the town's trusted collectors of school taxes. He used his 1856 personal account book for the tax records. An account book in the nineteenth century was the everyday man's bookkeeping system, a method of documenting financial transactions and customer names. Abner used his account book for recording income and expenses and bartering facts of his shoe business and his home farm. He also had a section dedicated to tax collection, where he recorded in handsome handwriting, the names of payers in the fourth school district and the amounts they paid. The records show:

1. A section entitled "School Tax of the 4th School District of East Haddam for 1 cent per day for the summer term ending Sept 26, 1856," in which he entered the names of twenty-seven parents/guardians along with the number

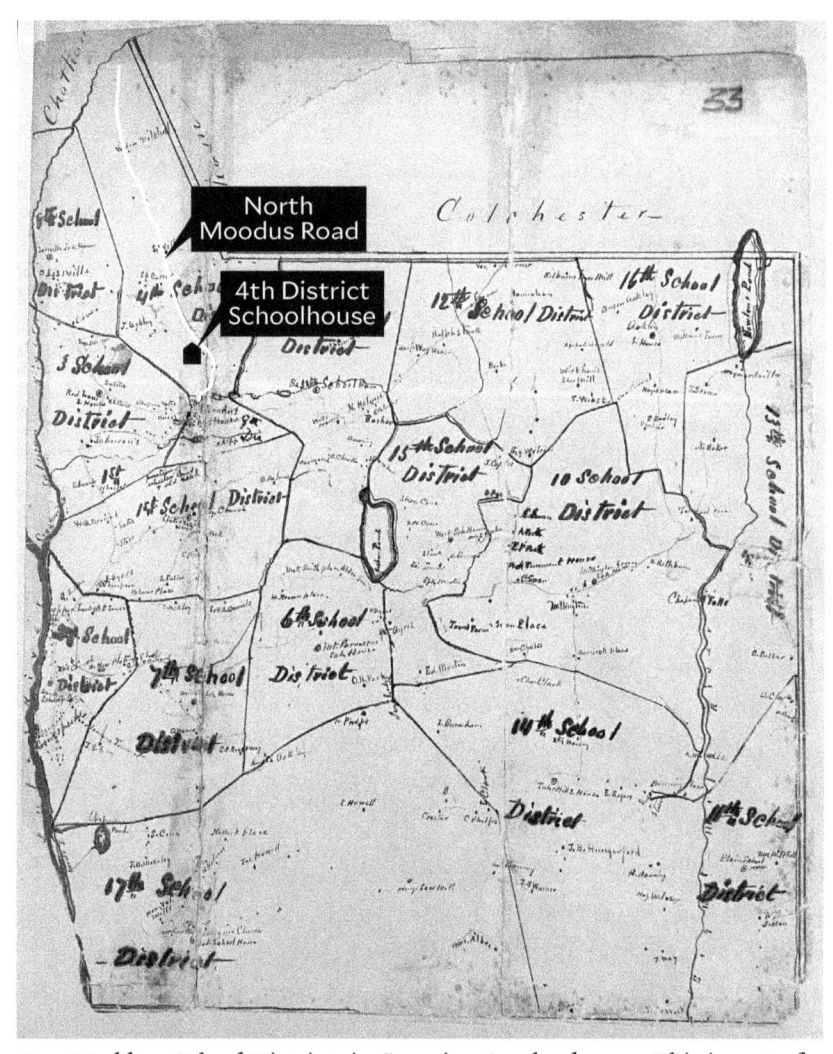

*East Haddam School Districts in Georgiana's school years. This is part of a map of school districts in East Haddam during Georgiana's school years. Georgiana was in the fourth school district. Running through the center of the district is North Moodus Road where Georgiana lived and where the schoolhouse, to the north, was located. This map can be found in the East Haddam Town Hall, One Plains Road, East Haddam, Connecticut.*

of days of school attended by their children and the dollar amount paid.

- He recorded himself as Abner C. Smith, Jr. paying $1.49 [about $45 in 2020] for 149 days of school. That represents two children, approximately seventy-five days of school each for Georgiana (age seven) and Edgar (age four).

2. A section entitled "Rate Bill of the 4th School District of East Haddam of 15 per cent on Levy 1856." (A levy was the amount a citizen was taxed by the town.) All payers of levies, regardless of whether they had children in school, had to pay an additional 15 percent of their levy as a school tax. Into this section, Abner entered 256 names, in alphabetical order, of East Haddam townspeople in the Fourth District. All except a few were men. Next to the taxpayer's name, he entered the amount of the yearly levy; in the next column, he entered an amount computed as 15 percent of the levy. The school tax dollar amounts vary, of course, but most people paid less than $10 [about $308 in 2020].

Georgiana's father was obviously good at math.

Was Georgiana? Did she learn arithmetic in school? I'm not sure. A count of the number of children (not the names) who took each subject at her school is on record for 1854. Remember that the sixty-two scholars ranged in age from three to fourteen, and not all subjects were available to the younger scholars.

Every child was taught reading and spelling, but only half were taught arithmetic. Was that because only older children were taught the subject? Or was

| Subject | Number of Scholars |
| --- | --- |
| Reading | 62 |
| Spelling | 62 |
| Arithmetic | 31 |
| Grammar | 16 |
| Geography | 13 |
| History | 5 |
| Philosophy | 5 |

it because girls were not taught math yet in East Haddam? Math was a boys-only subject until the first part of the nineteenth century. Whether East Haddam was instructing girls in math by the 1850s, I don't know. I find it curious that the number of scholars taught arithmetic is exactly half — equal to the number of boys in the school. My guess is that Georgiana learned basic arithmetic, a subject unavailable to her mother, from her father, if not from school.

For reading and spelling, Georgiana's textbook was likely the *Blue-backed Speller*. Was she aware that this important book, so named because of its blue cover, was written by Connecticut's Noah Webster (1758–1843) who had lived about thirty-five miles away? And that the book was used by children in every state to learn to spell and read and pronounce words? This little Connecticut-born book, first published in 1783, would teach five generations of American children and inspire the name for the twenty-first-century shopping center, Blue Back Square, in West Hartford, Connecticut.

Georgiana lived in a state that was a nationwide leader in education, and not only because of Noah Webster. Connecticut was home to some of the country's best colleges, like Wesleyan, Trinity, and Yale, in the cities of Middletown, Hartford, and New Haven, not far away from Georgiana. She probably heard about local ministers who had graduated from these prestigious schools. She also may have heard about boys who went, or wanted to go, to one of these colleges. I doubt she ever questioned why girls couldn't attend, as it was accepted that girls' education took a back seat to boys' education.

Some women in the nation tried to shrink the gap between girls' and boys' education. One of the most vocal and influential was Catharine Beecher in Hartford. She had been working on reforming girls' education since the 1820s and was at the height of influence during Georgiana's school years.

I wonder if Georgiana and her girlfriends knew about Catharine Beecher.

## Thank You, Catharine Beecher

One of the most influential Americans to take up the cause of educational reform for girls was Hartford's **Catharine Beecher (1800–1878),** sister of famed abolitionist and author Harriet (born Beecher) Stowe (1811–1896). In 1823, Catharine opened one of the first private girls' schools in America—the Hartford Female Seminary. At the time, the term seminary was used to denote girls-only schools that prepared women for teaching; the term later denoted a place for men (and now for any gender) to prepare for religious leadership. Moving female education initiatives forward took Beecher-level (like Kennedy-level in the twentieth century) money and power. Catharine Beecher exercised all her advantages—a powerful father and brother, money, encouragement from her family, a bright mind, a mighty pen, and well-connected friends—to set up institutions for and influence decisions made about the education of girls and women and, particularly, to promote the idea of women as teachers. One key talking point in her campaign was that poorly trained female teachers were not able to produce valuable male citizens for the country. (Catharine Beecher had good marketing skills too.)

Catharine Beecher had been leading the national movement for the education of females for more than twenty years when Georgiana began her education in the 1850s. And progress had been made:

- Girls had begun to study math, a subject previously available only to boys. A geometry exam was given to an American girl for the first time in 1829.
- Girls had begun to study theology and philosophy, subjects previously limited to boys.
- The first college to accept women, Oberlin College, had been founded in Ohio.
- Female seminaries had been opened in all states of the United States.
- A woman had founded the all-female Mount Holyoke Female Seminary,[35] which later became Mount Holyoke College in South Hadley, Massachusetts, the first of the all-female prestigious colleges known as the "Seven Sisters."

> Perhaps the most powerful change, the one that affected the greatest number of American women in the nineteenth century, was the development of two-year normal schools designed to prepare unmarried middle-class women to be teachers. The first normal school in the nation was Framingham Normal School in Massachusetts which opened in 1839, and the number of normal schools continued to rise during Georgiana's lifetime. By 1900, the well-trained women who graduated from normal schools made up most of the public school teachers.
>
> (Women can thank Catharine Beecher for a lot, but they cannot thank her for the right to vote. Unlike her sister Isabella Beecher Hooker, Catharine Beecher was opposed to, and campaigned against, women's suffrage.)

### GEORGIANA'S SCHOOLMATES

No surprise, Georgiana's schoolmates were the children from her North Moodus Road neighborhood. For example, the large Wheeler family, who lived across the street, had five children in the school when Georgiana attended. The Wheeler children (there were nine) will pop up in Georgiana's life story from time to time, as will other classmates with the familiar East Haddam last names of Chapman, Silliman, Cone, Brainerd, Brainard, and Fowler.

Did Georgiana have a set of girlfriends to confide in and giggle with? Almost certainly. I guess this because she was a spirited young girl, with three likely annoying little brothers in the days when boys played with boys and girls played with girls. I guess this, too, because she had many women friends as an adult. Did she have one best friend — one "bosom friend" as *Anne with an "E"* had? (*Anne with an "E"* is a television series based on the eponymous, bright young girl in *Anne of Green Gables*, a novel by Lucy Maud Montgomery written in 1908 but set in the late nineteenth century.) It may have been Lucy Fuller (1849–1890) who was Georgiana's age, her classmate at the Fourth District School, and who lived up the street next to the school.

There was one surprise for me in the Fourth District School records of the 1850s: three children of Abner Comstock Smith (1796) attended Georgiana's school from 1854 to 1856. His other seven children were too old or too young for school. So Georgiana, as a young school girl from age five to seven, saw her half-aunts and half-uncles — the much older Candace and Julia Smith; the slightly older Abner Comstock Smith (1846); and the same-age Robbins T. Smith — in the schoolroom every day. That is, every day that they went. Their attendance was not great. By the time the winter term started in November 1857, there were only two Smiths attending the Fourth District School. One was six-year-old Edgar C. Smith, Georgiana's brother. The other was eight-year-old Ella G. Smith, who had been newly assigned to the "Ladies Section." I can feel the pride bursting from an eight-year-old Georgiana as she moved up to the older girls' section. I can also picture a confident and spunky Georgiana insisting she should now go by her proper first name, Ella. Until this year, she was *Georgiana with an "N."* I don't know how long she stuck with Ella. The school records, which incidentally recorded her one time as Ellen G. Smith, only go back to 1858. In her adult life, she went by Georgiana with one "n." Most of the time. (Genealogy is messy.)

In May 1858, three-year-old Frank Smith started the new summer term. Then there were three Smiths in the Fourth District School — Georgiana, Edgar, and Frank, all children of Abner C. Smith without a suffix.

Back to Abner Comstock Smith (1796) for a moment. Why did his children attend the Fourth District School from 1854 to 1856? In the 1850 census, he was recorded as a farmer living on the Smith land in the Mount Parnassus section of East Haddam, which was in the sixth school district. He and his family must have moved to the fourth district in the early 1850s. It looks like they came to live near the Moodus mills. In the 1860 census, Abner Comstock Smith (1796) lived with his wife and their three youngest children — Julia (sixteen); Abner Comstock Smith (1846) (thirteen); and Robbins T. Smith (ten) — in a dwelling that Abner

Comstock Smith (1796) did not own. It may have been a boarding house. Seven other boarders, aged fourteen to twenty-seven, lived in the same house. Each was labeled as a laborer, the occupation entered for those working in the mills. Even his wife, Hope, and his three children were labeled as laborers.

Did you just read that a ten-year-old and a thirteen-year-old worked in the mills? Yes. During the 1860s, children were considered employable as early as the age of ten. Connecticut had become the first state in the nation to enact a child labor law in 1813, but the law did not address a minimum age. It did require, however, that employers provide children with free schooling in reading, writing, and mathematics, and that all working children engage in religious worship. Mill owners were fined if they did not comply. For the rest of the nineteenth century, reformers in Connecticut and other states pushed for better child labor laws.[36] By 1900, Connecticut set the minimum age for non-agricultural jobs at fourteen and strictly limited the working hours of those sixteen and under.

The Moodus mills enjoyed the profits made from the low wages paid to children. But there was also a unique second benefit to having a child employee: their tiny fingers could reach places in the looms that adult hands couldn't. The East Haddam Historical Society has one of the original machines used in the Moodus mills, on which they demonstrate where the little fingers went.

In the Moodus census of 1860, Georgiana's Smith household had six Smiths — Abner, Lucinda, Georgiana who was almost eleven, and her three brothers who were eight, six, and four. Also listed as living in their home was a twenty-one-year-old boarder and laborer named Chester Sheppard. Accommodating a boarder to provide extra income for the homeowner was a common living arrangement of the 1800s. I mention Chester for another reason though. His teenage sisters, Eunice and Abby Sheppard, were two of the laborers living in Abner Comstock Smith (1796)'s house, providing a rare link between Georgiana and her father's biological family. Except for one curious real estate transaction by Lucinda much later (thirty-two years after this census), which I will explain later, there are no other connections between Georgiana and the Abner Comstock Smith (1796) family.

### ACROSS THE RIVER IN HADDAM

During Georgiana's childhood, her Arnold grandparents remained on their Turkey Hill farm, surrounded by Dickinsons, Tylers, and Whites. Georgiana would have traveled on the ferry with her mother and family to visit them. Not every trip was a happy occasion. There were a few tragedies for the Arnold clan in Haddam as Georgiana was growing up.

Poor Aunt Sylvia, Lucinda's sister who had lost her son, husband, and father-in-law in 1849 and had become Mrs. Warren Pardee in 1850, died in 1853. She was only thirty-one. It is a good assumption that she died of puerperal fever (also called "childbed fever," an infection contracted in childbirth) after the birth of her first child with her new husband. A daughter was born on September 12, and Sylvia died on October 16. The baby, Harriett Ellen Pardee, survived, but her father died in 1854, and she was raised by her father's Pardee family in Plymouth, Connecticut, about forty miles away. Plymouth was too far to have frequent contact with her Arnold relatives. Sylvia's two orphaned children from her first husband, Louisa (nine) and Juliette (five) Brainerd, were taken in and raised on the Turkey Hill farm by their Arnold grandparents, Horace and Sylvia, then ages fifty-seven and sixty.

Georgiana's cousins Louisa and Juliette had difficult childhoods. Their father and little brother had died when Louisa was five and Juliette was one. Their mother had died when they were nine and five. Then, in 1858, when Louisa was fifteen, Juliette died at age eleven. Louisa, as a young teen, was left with no parents and no siblings. Her hardy and hearty grandparents, however, took care of her and would live to see her marry and have children. Georgiana, six years younger than Louisa, likely looked up to her older cousin. Louisa may have envied Georgiana's healthy nuclear family of two parents, three sons, and a daughter.

## WORKING AT HOME

Georgiana's father continued to provide for his family as a shoemaker, a trade that was lucrative enough for him to be able to pay off the mortgage on his house in six years. The Smiths also managed a home farm for family use and for income, with cows, pigs, other livestock, fruit trees, and a vegetable garden. Lucinda managed the housework, the gardening, the food, the making of butter, the child-rearing, the fires, the washing, the ironing, the making and mending of clothes, and the outdoor privy. Georgiana, the only daughter, would have helped with this "woman's work."

## PRAYING AND PLAYING IN THE NEIGHBORHOOD

The social life of Abner and Lucinda's family revolved around their North Moodus Road neighborhood, including the neighborhood church. Most people of mid-nineteenth-century New England practiced religion by attending worship services. Protestant children attended Sabbath school, sometimes called Sunday school. Churches also provided social outlets with family picnics, women's groups, and children's activities. During Georgiana's childhood, there were only Protestant churches in Moodus. It wasn't until 1868 that a Catholic church opened in Moodus, and not until 1910 that a Jewish congregation formed in town. Lucinda and Abner and their children attended the Moodus Methodist Episcopal Church. Some local Moodus history buffs quip that people simply joined the church that was the easiest to walk to. The history buffs may be right. Abner and Lucinda and the children could hop, skip, and jump to Moodus Methodist Episcopal Church on North Moodus Road.

    Hymns at church services provided families with some of the best, and often only, exposure to good music. Adults had their favorite hymns; the good singers (and sometimes not-so-good singers) sang in the choir; and children quickly learned tunes and words by heart. Many hymns that continue to be sung in churches today were written and became popular when Georgiana was a little girl. She would have been among the first to hear and sing the well-known Christmas hymns, "It Came upon a Midnight Clear," "We Three Kings of Orient Are," "O Holy Night," and "Angels We Have Heard on High." No doubt, the melodies and the words of Christmas and other church hymns were etched in Georgiana's memory her whole life.

Almost certainly more entertaining than church music for Georgiana and her brothers was the thundering music that came from the house across the street. The Smiths lived across from Hezekiah Percival (1801–1888), well-known in Moodus for his exceptional drumming skills. Mr. Percival, who had been drumming since the 1820s, gave drum lessons to many men and boys of Moodus. He and his brother Orville, also a musician, would gather these drummers for the simple joy of drumming together, forming what would eventually become the first Moodus Drum and Fife Corps. Georgiana could not have missed the sounds of their Revolutionary War-era drumming, a style designed to be louder than the footsteps of an army of marching men. From her front yard on North Moodus Road, she probably watched and waved to the jolly men and boys carrying drumsticks as they traveled to and from the Percival house.

### AN UPBEAT GEORGIANA IN AN UPBEAT VILLAGE IN AN UPBEAT TOWN

The town of East Haddam was marching to an upbeat rhythm in the spring of 1861 when Georgiana was eleven. In the village of Moodus, the mills were humming, horses were keeping a steady clip-clopping to and from a busy downtown, and the mail stage with its four prancing horses was appearing on a rhythmic schedule. On the Connecticut River, steamboats were whistling their arrival and departure, the oysters were multiplying, and the shad were biting. In the countryside, the orchards were full of fruit, the lakes were full of fish, and the farms were full of produce and animals. All were marching to the strong beat of the American dream, led by a new — as of March 1861 — president of the United States by the name of Abraham Lincoln.

*Georgiana's father, Abner C. Smith, in his Civil War uniform, 1862.*

*Georgiana's mother, Lucinda (born Arnold) Smith, 1862.*

CHAPTER 3

# Little Woman

## Georgiana from Eleven to Fifteen
## 1861–1865

**BOOM!** On April 12, 1861, the march of prosperity in the United States of America came to a crashing halt when a loud boom thundered from South Carolina. The Southern Confederate Army had crushed the United States Army at Fort Sumter. The Rebellion, later called the Civil War, had begun. Georgiana, who had lived her full eleven, almost twelve, years in Connecticut, "The Land of Steady Habits," was about to find her steady-as-a-rock family, village, and state holding on for dear life as the land suffered a nationquake.

Within three days of the boom, President Lincoln called for seventy-five thousand volunteers to serve three months in the United States Army to stop the uprising in the South. Two weeks later, he called for forty-two thousand more men, this time for three years. Two months later, in July 1861, the month Georgiana turned twelve, he asked for five hundred thousand additional volunteers. And he got them. Men enlisted faster than their supplies — clothing, shoes, blankets, knapsacks, canteens, military manuals, and rifles — could be provided. The northern states were so loyal to the union of the nation that citizens stopped business as usual and offered themselves to the cause. When the proud volunteers of Moodus left for the war, they were given emotionally-packed, celebratory send-offs. Town leaders bellowed out passionate speeches. Crowds shouted cheers. And loudest of all were thundering drums and piercing fifes.

By the time Georgiana turned thirteen a year later, in July 1862, the war had split the country in two: North vs. South, Blue against Grey, Union opposed to Confederacy. Like many men before him, Georgiana's thirty-six-year-old father, Abner C. Smith, was motivated by patriotism and enticed by pay to volunteer. He signed up for a three-year term, although he and most citizens at the time did not think the war would last that long. In late August, he was called to duty in New Haven. On August 28, 1862, he wrote his first letter to his wife and children — Georgiana (thirteen), Edgar (ten), Frank (eight), and Little Freddy (five). Note the optimism in his PS.

[Letter to Lucinda and Children]

*New Haven, Connecticut*
*August 28, 1862*

*Good Morning Lucinda and all of the children,*

*I will drop you a few lines to let you know where I am. This morning finds me in New Haven in a Hartford Company, Captain Henry C. Smith of Hartford and Lieutenant* [Oliver R.] *Post of Deep River, the same company the Turkey Hill boys are in. It belongs to the 20th Regiment.*

*About 33 of us were transferred into this company Tuesday afternoon. Came down here yesterday afternoon. Arrived about 5 o'clock PM, about two miles out of the city down beside the water, a very pleasant place. I can't tell you when I shall come home.*

*From your husband,*
*A.C. Smith*

*PS If you should write before I come home, direct to New Haven, Camp Buckingham, 20 Regt. C, in care of Capt. Henry C. Smith.*

Georgiana's father and twenty other men from East Haddam had been mustered into Company C of the 20th Regiment of Connecticut Volunteers. In less than two weeks, the hundred men of Company C were prepared to go south. On September 9, two days before they boarded the train to leave Connecticut, Abner wrote his second letter home. For the two-and-a-half years that Abner served in the Civil War, in state after state and camp after camp and battle after battle, he faithfully wrote to his wife and children. Lucinda saved his letters.

## Abner C. Smith's Civil War Letters

One hundred and thirteen letters, spanning two-and-a-half years, written by Abner C. Smith to his wife and children during his Civil War service (1862–1865) are carefully preserved along with their addressed envelopes. They are under the loving care of Abner C. Smith's great-great-grandson Donald U. Smith III in Pennsylvania.

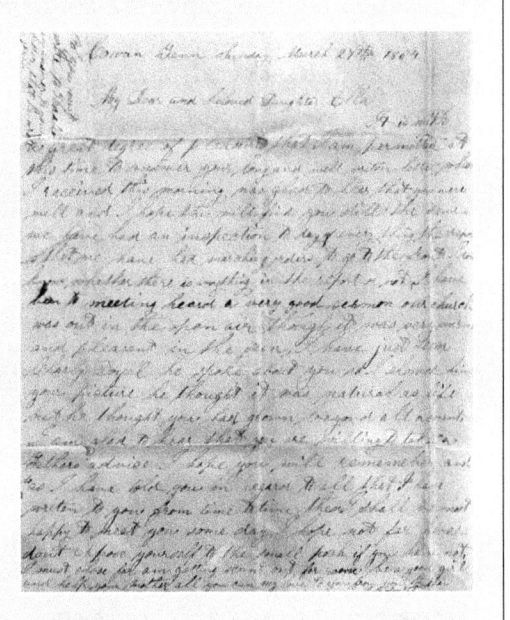

You can read the transcriptions of these letters in the companion to this book, *The Civil War Letters of Abner C. Smith*, in which most of the spelling and grammar errors are captured as Abner wrote them. In this book, as I quote some of the letters, I have sometimes altered the spelling and grammar for easier readability.

Abner C. Smith wrote about, or to, Georgiana many times in his letters. He used variations of her name and affectionate salutations like the above letter's "My Dear and beloved Daughter Ella."

LITTLE WOMAN 75

Lucinda rhythmically returned letters to her husband. Georgiana helped her mother write the letters and often added words of her own. Sometimes Georgiana inserted her own letter. The boys, who were not fans of sitting still and writing, would occasionally add lines to their mother's letters, and occasionally, after prodding by their father, would write their own. The letters written to Abner were not saved. Wars cannot accommodate extra baggage. I know that letters were mailed from Moodus continuously for the two-and-a-half years, because in nearly every one of Abner C. Smith's letters home, he references a letter from Lucinda or Georgiana.

There are no photographs of Georgiana during these years, but her father's letters capture glimpses of her and supply a running narrative of her life as a young teen. Along with descriptions of his daily life as a soldier, his pragmatic instructions to his wife, and his playful and stern messages to his sons, Abner's letters are filled with words of affection for his daughter. Often with a sense of humor, sometimes with frustration, and always with love, his letters document the range of emotions of an adolescent Georgiana: she was one day, a sweet little girl; another day, a defiant little challenge; and another day, a maturing little woman.

### THIRTEEN

In many ways, Georgiana was a nonfiction version of Jo March, the spirited main character in *Little Women*.[37] This beloved American novel, written in 1868 by Louisa May Alcott (1832–1888), tells the story of Jo and her three sisters in Massachusetts whose father went south to serve in the Civil War. Like Jo, Georgiana had just become a teenager when her father departed. Like Jo, Georgiana's mother was left to raise their four children alone while struggling with the full management of the household, a role women were not accustomed to.

Jo, based on the story in *Little Women*, and Georgiana, based on her father's letters, had the same mix-up of desires. They both wanted to be dutiful daughters, but more so, they wanted to find their own personalities and maneuver their own lives. Like Jo, Georgiana had a yearning to be somewhere other than home. This sentence from *Little Women* gave the book its title: "'I'll try and be what he loves to call me, a little woman, and not be rough and wild, but do my duty here instead of wanting to be somewhere else,' said Jo, thinking that keeping her temper at home was a much harder task than facing a rebel or two down South."

Like Jo, Georgiana was acutely naïve about the contrast between her father's problems of "facing a rebel or two down South" and the problems of her young teenage life. While Georgiana was eating cake, her father was eating hardtack. While she was asking for new clothes, he had but one set of clothes throughout the war. While she complained of a sore finger that prevented her from writing him a letter, he sat on icy ground in frigid wind, trying to control a drippy nose, juggling a bottle of ink and a frustratingly poor pen, as he scratched a letter to her using his knees as a desk, with "balls and shells whizzing and howling over our heads and around our ears a good share of the time." When Georgiana was walking on the streets of Moodus to and from school, her father was slogging through deep, thick mud with forty-five pounds of gear on his back, watching some of his fellow soldiers collapse and die on the side of the road. While she slept in her warm house, he slept crammed with other soldiers in a flimsy tent, or outside in the rain without cover, or, if he was lucky, in a hut he had built from trees he had cut down himself. While Georgiana attended a supper with a boy, her father ate next to dead soldiers whose arms stuck out of the ground from their crude graves.

Thirteen-year-old girls can be clever, or try to be. In the excerpt below, my guess is that Georgiana had used the excuse of a sore finger for not writing to her father. In his letter below, it looks like Abner saw right through her.

[Excerpt from Letter to Lucinda]

*Camp near Maryland Heights, Virginia*
*October 9, 1862*

*Well, Georgiana, I received your letter with mother's [Lucinda's]. Was glad to hear from you that you are well and that your finger has got well. You must still continue to be a good girl and help your mother all you can, so that I shall hear a good report from her when she writes to me again. Then I shall feel as though I had got a beautiful girl at home, whilst I am out here in defense of the stars and stripes, the pride of our nation.*

Sometimes Abner would write directly to his daughter instead of including a message to her in letters to Lucinda. The excerpt below is from a letter which tenderly began: "To Ella G Smith, my ever dear and affectionate daughter," and includes some fatherly advice.

[Excerpt from Letter to Georgiana]

*Camp near Maryland Heights, Virginia*
*October 15, 1862*

*Well, Georgia, I am off from duty again. Have just been to dinner. I think you would not like to board here with me, for you would not be likely to get so much frosted cake as you talk of having at home. Sometimes when you are finding fault at home, sometimes about what you have to eat, remember how much better you fare than a great many others that I could mention. Be contented with your lot.*

Was thirteen-year-old Georgiana starting to lose some of her sugar and spice? Maybe. But her father would set her straight. Maybe.

[Excerpt from Letter to Lucinda]

> *Camp near Harpers Ferry, Virginia*
> *December 9, 1862*
>
> *Good afternoon, Georgia. I must write a few words to you, my dear girl. I am very sorry to hear such a report from your dear mother in regards to you being such a naughty girl. It gives me a great deal of pain to think that my only daughter should be guilty of such conduct, and I hope the next time I hear from home, it will be better news. I hope your mother can say Georgia is a good girl. And you must write to me and always remember that it is for your own good to obey your parents in all things.*
>
> *From your dear Father,*
> *A.C. Smith*

Georgiana's misbehavior aside, her father was proud of her and her bright mind, as seen in this excerpt from an early January 1863 letter from her father to her mother.

[Excerpt from Letter to Lucinda]

> *Fairfax Station, Virginia*
> *January 3, 1863*
>
> *I had* [received] *a letter from Horace* [Lucinda's brother and Georgiana's uncle, Horace Arnold, who was also fighting in the Civil War]. *He said that he was better pleased reading Georgia's letter than any he had ever had from any of his relations.*

Georgiana's penmanship and command of the English language were superior to her mother's, and she often penned the letters

LITTLE WOMAN

for her. The following letter is to Lucinda, in which Abner has to balance his praise for his daughter without insulting his wife.

[Excerpt from Letter to Lucinda]

> *Fairfax Station, Virginia*
> *January 11, 1863*
>
> When I commenced reading your last letter, I thought you had improved very much in writing and telling, but before I finished it, I found that your and my own darling daughter, Ella G, had the honor of performing the penmanship of the said article, and not my own dear Wife Lucinda.
>
> Not that I wish to say anything against your writing, Lucinda, but I want to give Georgia the praise of being a good writer. If she is amind to take a little pain, I hope she will try and improve all of her time writing and studying to get a good education while she has an opportunity.

## A HARD BLOW

Lucinda knew that every day might bring word of her husband's death or wounding, especially after she learned soon after Abner's August 1862 departure from New Haven that the young Wheeler boy across the street had been killed in the war. Seventeen-year-old Alfred Wheeler[38] (1845–1862) had died in Virginia in September. Wives and mothers of soldiers were continually on tenterhooks when mail arrived. I'm certain Lucinda was as prepared as she could be to receive a letter of bad news from a faraway state. But, as a cruel twist, it was Abner who received bad news from Lucinda.

On January 21, 1863, five-year-old Little Freddy died at home from scarlet fever.[39] Georgiana likely penned the letters for her mother that broke the news of Little Freddy's severe sickness and then his death. Abner wrote back in a letter dated January 26, 1863.

[Excerpt from Letter to Lucinda]

> *Stafford Courthouse, Virginia*
> *January 26, 1863*
>
> *I got your letter Tuesday night which brought me the sad intelligence of our Little Freddy's death. It was a hard blow. Oh, could it have been otherwise and he been spared for a comfort to us in our after years, if I should be permitted again to return to my family. But, alas, the little circle is broken. He is gone and his dear father never more permitted to see his dear little face in this world, but shall live in hopes of meeting him hereafter.*

Abner and Lucinda could only console each other through the written word.

Little Freddy's death was indeed a hard blow for all the Smiths. Lucinda had lost her youngest child. Georgiana probably bounced between giving comfort to and receiving comfort from her mother. Eleven-year-old Edgar, struggling to be the man of the house, and eight-year-old Frank had lost their little buddy. Both Lucinda and Georgiana, based on the advice of Abner, decided to wear black to mourn Little Freddy. If they followed the etiquette of the day, Georgiana wore black for six months and Lucinda for one year.

Life for the remaining four Smiths on North Moodus Road was a jumble of mourning, fear, and too many duties. They were not unlike the rest of the rattled nation, which had also been hit with hard blows. Men, many of whom were fathers, had stopped their jobs and gone to war. In Connecticut, almost half the men from ages fifteen to fifty served in the military during these years. Women, many of whom were left alone with little money to manage the homes, farms, and children, gathered to help the war effort by packaging up bedding, clothing, and medical supplies for the soldiers. Children, like Georgiana and her brothers, had to take on more chores at home. Georgiana was expected to help her mother with the woman's work. The boys reluctantly did the outdoor work: chopping and stacking and carrying wood; shoveling snow; cutting and lugging hay; feeding and cleaning up after the animals; and watering the cow, which Lucinda finally sold because the task was too often neglected.

> ## The Smiths' Money Management During the Civil War
>
> With her husband away during the Civil War, household money management was left to Lucinda. It was a challenge for her for two reasons: one, women of Lucinda's age had not been taught math; and two, money was controlled almost exclusively by men.
>
> Abner tried to manage the household money remotely, directing Lucinda through his letters. He instructed her to collect money from those who owed him from his shoemaking business prior to the war, advised her which merchants to pay, and directed her on how much to save. In some letters, he cautioned her against overspending; in other letters, he encouraged her to buy what she needed. He explained to her how to keep accounting of how much she had and how much she owed. Georgiana likely helped her mother with money matters.
>
> For income during the war, Abner received his payments directly in the field. He was paid twelve dollars [about $246 in 2020] a month. When he was promoted to corporal after a year of service, he received thirteen dollars a month. The payments did not always arrive on time. Sometimes he would receive several months of overdue payments in one lump sum. Because money was frequently stolen out of the letters soldiers sent home, Abner would send the cash to Lucinda in small amounts over a period of time.

As Abner's wife and the mother of his children, Lucinda received a monthly payment of ten dollars [about $205 in 2020] from the State of Connecticut. She also had access to "the old nest egg in the trunk," which Abner advised her to use if she needed to.

With an overwhelmed mother and in the absence of a day-to-day father, Georgiana began to direct her own life with all the maturity (sarcasm here) and resiliency of a thirteen-year-old. Within a month of Little Freddy's death, she was asking for her father's permission to go to a dancing school. On February 22, 1863, Abner wrote his disapproval to Lucinda.

[Excerpt from Letter to Lucinda]

> Stafford Courthouse, Virginia
> February 22, 1863
>
> Georgia spoke of her going to a dancing school. I do not think it advisable for her to go there, as there is no one to see to her. If I was at home to go with her, it would be another thing. I think you can understand the reason why I think so. You, yourself, must know that she is too young to go to such a place without someone to look out for her, as there are those at dances of a doubtful character. Therefore, I hope you will take my advice and keep her at home.

The next day, he wrote again and included a message directly to Georgiana.

[Excerpt from Letter to Lucinda]

> Stafford Courthouse, Virginia
> February 23, 1863
>
> Georgia, what you wrote in your last letter in regard to going to dancing school, I am sorry to say that I shall have to disappoint you in your request that I would not write anything in opposition to your wishes.
>
> Perhaps now you do not understand why I object to your going, but when you get more advanced in years, you may,

> *and be glad that I did not consent. It is because I love you and think a great deal of you that I did as I have.*

Within three weeks, Georgiana attended the dancing school.

[Excerpt from Letter to Lucinda]

> *Aquia Creek Landing, Virginia*
> *March 15, 1863*
>
> *Georgia ... If you go to the dancing school, you must try and learn all you can and behave yourself like a lady and be a good girl to your Mother.*

One month later, after the dancing school victory, Georgiana was on to the next request: to go to a select (private) school for the summer term starting May 1863. Lucinda alerted Abner that Georgiana's preference for the select school had little to do with learning. Here is his reply, which included a bit of scolding for Lucinda.

[Excerpt from Letter to Lucinda]

> *Stafford Courthouse, Virginia*
> *April 24, 1863*
>
> *Georgia wishes to go to the select school. Now, if I was sure that she would learn enough more to pay the bill* [Abner means that Georgiana needs to learn enough for the cost to be worth it], *I should be perfectly willing that she should go.*
>
> *You seemed to think that learning was not what she was after. I don't know what else there would be at such a school except only to try and learn.*
>
> *You were in favor of her going to the dancing school and I was opposed, but she went. Now I am more in favor of her going*

> to this, if she will go and behave herself and try all she can to learn. I will give my consent for her to go, but she must always go and come direct from school and not be leaving to stay away from home nights, for her place is at home.
>
> So here you have my idea on the subject. If she thinks she can abide by what I have proposed in these few lines, she can go. Other ways, she must go to the district school.

(Abner didn't know "what else there would be at such a school except only to try and learn?" Ah, the timeless power of a daughter over her father.)

Abner soon sent money for Georgiana to attend the select school for the summer term which ran from May to September. I don't know which select school it was, but it seems it was within a reasonable walking distance from her home as her father insisted she come home before nighttime. Which, evidently, she didn't.

[Excerpt from Letter to Lucinda]

> *Stafford Courthouse, Virginia*
> *May 22, 1863*
>
> Well, Georgia, I must write a few words to you and give you a few commands, which I wish you always to bare in mind whenever you get a notion in your head that you don't want to mind your Mother, but on the contrary think you can do just as you are a mind to.
>
> I have a sort of presentiment that you sometimes are a naughty girl, and it makes your dear Father feel very bad to think that his only daughter is getting to be headstrong and not want to mind her Mother but have her own way, while her Father is in an enemy's land, away from home and friend. Perhaps you may never again be permitted to see my face.

> *If you should remember what I have often wrote to you — to be a good girl and mind your Mother — you must not get it into your head that you want to go out nights, unless your Mother goes with you. It is a very bad plan for girls of your age to be out nights away from home.*
>
> *Now, remember what a loving Father says. Write when you receive this and tell me if you will try and abide by the instructions I have given here, now and before.*

Thirteen. (Ugh)

### FOURTEEN

On Georgiana's fourteenth birthday, July 1, 1863, she was attending a select school and no doubt still battling with her mother. On that same day, her father, in Pennsylvania, was fighting in the first day of the three-day Battle of Gettysburg, considered by many to be the most famous and most important Civil War battle. Abner C. Smith had started a letter, writing the date, July 1, but was interrupted. Not until July 4 was he able to pick up his pen again. He had just spent three gruesome days in battle, and he recapped them in a long letter to Lucinda. His full letter, which puts the horror of the historically important Battle of Gettysburg in an ordinary soldier's imperfect words, can be found in *The Civil War Letters of Abner C. Smith*. Here is an excerpt:

[Excerpt from Letter to Lucinda]

> *On the march, somewhere in Penn between Littlestown and Gettysburg July 1, 1863 and July 4, 1863*
>
> *A fierce fight it was. To the way the Rebs shelled us, I can tell you, was a caution* [something that astonishes or commands attention.] *They played at us, the best they know how for three*

> *hours. We was in the woods at the time and no one knew but each minute was his last. The shells flew thick and fast. They struck all around me, burst and fly in all directions. One piece struck me on the heel of my shoe. They burst amongst the trees overhead and some of the small pieces fall down onto me. The solid shot and Railroad iron howled awfully. One cannon ball struck the ground about three feet from me. It made the dirt fly a little, I tell you.*
>
> *Last night, I slept on the field of battle with dead Rebs all around me. I eat my supper and brakefast in les than a rod of one. There has been a big slaughter of Rebs at this battle and their loss in prisners was heavey.*

The Battle of Gettysburg was the deadliest battle of the Civil War.[40] Close to eight thousand soldiers died. Another forty thousand were wounded, captured, or missing. All the numbers are estimates; no one could keep count.

Abner survived Gettysburg, and in the days that followed, he survived more skirmishes. While awaiting orders to "fall in at a moment's notice," he wrote a letter to Lucinda. Ever the loving father, he included a response to his now fourteen-year-old daughter, who had decided she didn't like the select school.

[Excerpt from Letter to Lucinda]

> *Drawed up in the line of battle in a wheat field somewhere near Hagerstown, Maryland*
> *July 12, 1863*
>
> *Georgia, I was glad to receive a line from you ... You wanted to know if you could go to the district school when yours was out. If you can learn enough to pay for going, I have no objections. But while I grant your wishes, you must remember that I expect you will be a good girl and mind your Mother.*

LITTLE WOMAN

That August, as she finished her one and only term at the select school, Georgiana was campaigning to live away from home at a Mr. Semes's[41] house. Who he was and why she wanted to go there, apart from escaping her mother's discipline, is a mystery. I believe she wanted to work and make her own money, and perhaps Mr. Semes offered housekeeping work. Abner knew Mr. Semes and did not object to him, but he wrote to Lucinda about his concern for Georgiana leaving home.

[Excerpt from Letter to Lucinda]

> *Kelly's Ford, Virginia*
> *August 13, 1863*
>
> I do not quite like the idea of Georgia going away from home to live, for she is too young to go away. It is true it is close to home, but still it takes her out from under your control in part. I presume Mr. Semes is a good place as she could have to live to, but, after all, it is diferant from home. It gives her more liberty. She is out of her Mother's sight, and I think that the best place for a girl of her age is at home, as long as you are able to keep her there.
>
> If she stays to the Semes, she must not be allowed to race around nights just as she pleases. I suppose if Georgie reads this, she perhaps may feel rather bad. But she must remember that it is from a Father that loves her as he does himself, and always did, and he wants her to grow up to be a Lady that no one can say naught against.

Abner ended up consenting to Georgiana's move under the condition that she continue school, which would start again in November, and that she stay a good girl. She went to the Semes's house in August. Here is an excerpt from her father's letter to her mother in late August:

[Excerpt from Letter to Lucinda]

> *On the bank of the Rappahannock River*
> *doing picket duty, Virginia*
> *August 24, 1863*
>
> *I was glad to hear that Ella G likes to go to Mr. Semes and they like her, for if they like her, it shows that she is a good girl. I certainly have no objections to her staying there if it is going to be an improvement in her for the better.*
>
> *You are well aware that girls of her age ought not to be away from home too much, for they are apt to think that they are for themselves and they can do as they are amind to. But Georgia, I know, is not quite so olde as some of the girls of the same age that I knew of when I was at home, and I am very glad that she is not. You know very well what I mean.*
>
> *She can stay to Mr. Semes as long as you think it advisable for her, if they both like, all the fall and winter, if they will send her to school. That is, if they want her so long.*

At the forefront of Abner's mind was the fear that his fourteen-year-old daughter had reached the age when, if left unsupervised, she might not behave like a "good girl." And, to quote Abner, "you know very well what I mean."

Either Mr. Semes wasn't happy with the arrangement or Georgiana didn't abide by her parents' rules. By the beginning of the district school's winter term (November 1863 to March 1864), she was back home with her mother. And she was not happy.

[Excerpt from Letter to Lucinda]

> *Stevenson, Alabama*
> *November 20, 1863*
>
> *You said in your last letter that Georgia was mad so she was not going to write. I am sure she could not have been mad with me.*

Lucinda did not have access to the advice in the book, *I'm Not Mad, I Just Hate You! A New Understanding of Mother–Daughter Conflict*,[42] which, more than a hundred years later, was still trying to help mothers deal with tumultuous teenage daughters. But somehow Georgiana calmed down enough to pick up a pen and, in a beautiful letter, transformed her self-absorbed self into a dutiful young lady for her father. She knew that her father, even miles away, was still the decision maker about things that mattered most to her — permission to spend money and permission to go places — and the wrapping of him around her little finger would begin once again.

Three days later, he wrote her a letter full of praise.

[Excerpt from Letter to Lucinda and Children]

> Stevenson, Alabama
> November 23, 1863
>
> Georgia, what shall I say to you? I received a good long letter from you this time. I am glad that I have got such a nice girl to write to me. I got a very good idea of what the folks are doing round home from what you wrote.
>
> I was glad to see that you think something of yourself, and I hope you may never do anything that will disgrace you or bring disgrace on your parents. You must be a good girl and see how fast you can learn this winter, for you are growing older every year and by & by you will be too old to go to school. And I want you should get learning so that you can teach school, for some day you may have to earn your own living. We can't tell what will happen.
>
> I think you have got a very pretty dress — rather of better than a poor girl's like A.C. Smith's can aford in times of war, but seeing you have got it, I guess you will have to ware it. I should like to be at home to see it on you, to see which looks the

> *best — you or the dress. The old saying is "fine fethers make fine birds." I hope that will be the case with you.*
>
> *Remember my advice, Georgia, to carry yourself straight.*

Georgiana was in many ways like a headstrong and head-spinning teenage girl of the twenty-first century. She cared about clothes, dances, schools, boys, independence from her mother, being somewhere other than home, and getting her own way.

For Christmas in 1863, she sent her father her photo, which pleased him to no end. Here is his message back to her:

[Excerpt from Letter to Lucinda and Georgiana]

> *Stevenson, Alabama*
> *December 21, 1863*
>
> *Well, my dearest little Georgia, I received your present and will say that I was very well pleased with it, although I should rather see the person than the picture. But that cannot be. I will try and content myself by looking at the picture. I think it looks first rate. You have got to be a great girl in appearance, a lady and I hope you will behave as well as you look. If you can do that, I want you should always remember that it is behavior as well as looks that make a fine lady, and if you will behave as well as you look, you will do well enough.*

Abner's dearest little Georgia wasn't as dear or as little as he thought, something he would learn slowly, letter by letter, or rather, no letter by no letter.

LITTLE WOMAN

[Excerpt from Letter to Georgiana]

*Stevenson, Alabama*
*January 6, 1864*

*I hear that when you are asked to write to me, that you have nothing to write. Now it is the same with me when I write to you. I have to write the same old thing over and over again, but what of that. Write something. If it is nothing more than that you mean to try to be a good girl and try to be better every day.*

*Am sorry to hear that you run away with a notion that you shall do what you have amind to when you get to be eighteen. Why, I was perfectly astonished to hear anything of the kind from my only darling daughter, and I hope you will repent anything so rash before it get to be too late.*

*Just write to me in your next letter what you think of what I say and have said to you before. Such a nice girl as you ought not to get such notions in her head. You must try to obey your mother always. It will be for your own good. Say will you?*

That winter Lucinda and her children attended *donations,* the shortened term for *donation suppers.* Donations were fund-raising social events put on by churches to raise money for the war effort. I'm guessing the Moodus Methodist Episcopal Church organized the donations that the Smiths attended. The evening was a dress-up affair, often held in the spacious home of a wealthy family. Women in the community would cook and donate their most scrumptious dishes, of which chicken pot pie was often the favorite. The community would buy tickets for the event, and the proceeds were used to purchase and send items to soldiers. Entertainment of music and dancing often followed the supper. The event was attended by all ages. For young people, it was a party and a place for a date. Georgiana, at fourteen, was evidently invited to go with a local soldier, a point which Lucinda revealed to Abner, who wrote directly to his daughter about it.

> [Excerpt from Letter to Georgiana]
>
> *Cowan, Tennessee*
> *February 28, 1864*
>
> *I suppose you had a good time at the donation. I expect you eat one of those suppers for me. Did you not say that you went to supper the first time with Newel Stephens? Now who and what is he? I don't know anyone by that name, unless it is Jonathan Stephens' son and if it was him, all I have got to say is that you are getting into pretty high company.*

William Newell Stevens (1844–1866) was a nineteen-year-old soldier, home between terms of service. In his uniform, he would have been an important and handsome figure at the donation. He had served a three-year term already, having enlisted at age seventeen in 1861. After this February 1864 visit home, Newell returned to the war and was wounded in October. He recovered and stayed until the end of the war in 1865. After the war, he came back to Moodus where he died a year later, perhaps from war wounds. He was the son of Moodus farmer Jonathan D. Stevens (1820–1881) and Rosetta (born Banning) Stevens. Newell Stevens does not come up again in Georgiana's story, but he was likely a friend and district school classmate of Georgiana's future husband, who was the same age and from the same neighborhood.

### STILL FOURTEEN

Consistent and insistent about the importance of education for his children, Georgiana's father laid down the law when it came to her attending school beyond the eighth grade, which she had completed in March 1864. But she pushed back.

[Excerpt from Letter to Lucinda and Georgiana]

*Cowan Station, Tennessee*
*March 18, 1864*

*Georgia, you seam to have a great dislike for going to school, but I shall insist upon your going this summer notwithstanding what you may say to the contrary. You need not be afraid of getting so good an education. If you live and become a woman, you may see the time that you won't be sorry that you improved your younger days at school. So take a Father's advice and see how well you can doe.*

Three days later, he reiterated this point to Lucinda.

[Excerpt from Letter to Lucinda]

*Cowan Station, Tennessee*
*March 21, 1864*

*You say that you think Ella behaves like a lady. I am glad to hear that, and I hope you won't get disappointed, but she must not say that she won't go to school this summer, for I say she must.*

Abner C. Smith's March 27, 1864, letter to his "dear and beloved daughter Ella," shows hope for her compliance.

[Excerpt from Letter to Georgiana]

*Cowan, Tennessee*
*March 27, 1864*

*I am glad to hear you are willing to take a Father's advice. I hope you remember and do as I told you in regard to all that I*

> *have written you from time to time. Then I shall be most happy to meet you some day. I hope not far hence.*
>
> *Don't expose yourself to the small pock, if you have not.*

A week later, Abner advised Lucinda about the dreaded smallpox.

[Excerpt from Letter to Lucinda]

> *Cowan, Tennessee*
> *April 3, 1864*
>
> *I should think that the smallpox was raging considerable in Moodus. I hope you and the children will be fortunate enough to keep clear of it. We have had one case of it here in this camp lately, but it has not spread any as yet. Have all the children and yourself been vaccinated? If not, I think you had better be. Georgie says she has been three times and it had not taken. It must be that the material was not good or else it was not done right.*

Smallpox was an ugly threat at the time across the nation. In East Haddam, vaccinations were available, but were not compulsory. In 1905, the United States Supreme Court ruled that states have the authority to require vaccinations against smallpox during smallpox epidemics. I believe all the Smiths were vaccinated; none caught smallpox.

### TO MERIDEN AT FOURTEEN

That same April brought a new adventure for Georgiana. With the blessing, or perhaps the throwing up of hands, of her mother, Georgiana went to Meriden to stay with her Aunt Elizabeth (born Arnold) Ventres, who was Lucinda's youngest sister. Elizabeth had married Fisk Brainard Ventres (1829–1875) in 1852 when Georgiana was three. At this point, Elizabeth and Fisk were in their thirties and did not have children. Elizabeth had been to the Smith house on North Moodus Road many times. Fisk's brother Daniel Ventres and his wife and two young children lived two houses away, making the Smiths and the Ventreses both family and friends.

Before Georgiana went to Meriden, she had brokered with her father to buy her some new summer clothes, which he had consented to, provided that she continue her schooling in May back in Moodus. But when May came, the sweet, obedient girl who had told her father just what he'd wanted to hear did not go to school as he had commanded. She had not even come back to Moodus.

Perhaps the reason was that she was enjoying a large, more exciting town. Meriden, eighteen miles west of Moodus and over the Connecticut River, had three times the population of Moodus. It was attracting diverse manufacturing businesses and was beginning its journey to become the "Silver City of the World." Georgiana was helping her aunt and uncle[43] with cooking and housekeeping, but she also may have been introduced to a new social scene with new friends, female and male.

In May, Abner C. Smith was marching with his regiment from Tennessee to Georgia and was unreachable. He was unaware Georgiana hadn't come home from Meriden, and worse, he was unaware she hadn't started the summer term of school that month. In June he included this message to Georgiana in a letter to his wife:

[Excerpt from Letter to Lucinda]

*Somewhere in the woods in the state of Georgia*
*June 5, 1864*

*Wal, Ella, I presume you are at home by this time although I have not heard from you since I received a letter from you while you was at Meriden. I did not answer it for I was on the march and have been ever since. You must excuse me for*

> *not answering your letter. I should like to hear from you and Mother every week, but it has been a month since I heard from home. It seems a long time and it may be another month before I hear from you. I have just heard that the Rebs have captured some of our mails. If that is true, perhaps they have got some that belong to me.*

It appears that Georgiana was too busy to write. Fourteen. (Ugh)

### FIFTEEN

On July 1, 1864, Georgiana turned fifteen. In Meriden. She had been there for three months.

By mid-August, Abner had still not heard from Georgiana. He had been away from home for two years, had lost and continued to lose his friends to bullets and disease, and believed he was losing his little girl.

[Excerpt from Letter to Lucinda]

> *Camp near Atlanta, Georgia*
> *August 17, 1864*
>
> *You did not say anything about Georgie, so I don't know as she is one of the family now. I have not received but one letter from her since she went to Merriden. I guess she has forgot that she has got a Father in the army that feels an interest in her welfare, and that would like to hear from her every week, but insted of that, I have had one letter in three months.*
>
> *We are now right in front of the Rebs. Our lines are but a short ways apart. Their bullets are whistleing into our camp constantly. They are whizzing over and past my head all of the time whilst I am writing this letter. It is a very dangerous place here whare we are now. Our boys in this regiment are getting picked off almost every day.*

Then, this heartbreaking letter to Lucinda a week later:

[Excerpt from Letter to Lucinda]

> *Camp near Atlanta, Georgia*
> *August 23, 1864*
>
> *I don't see why Georgia does not write to me. I have not had but one letter from her since she left home. I don't know but she feels above writing to her dad. Perhaps she has forgot how she used to hug & kiss me sometimes when I was at home. If she has, I have not, and I wish I might see them times again.*

In September, Lucinda paid a visit to Meriden. I presume it was to convince Georgiana to come back to Moodus. After the visit, Abner received a letter from Georgiana. And one from Elizabeth ("Elib") too. A frustrated and discouraged Abner wrote to Lucinda.

[Excerpt from Letter to Lucinda]

> *Atlanta, Georgia*
> *September 13, 1864*
>
> *I answered Elib's & Ella's letters. I presume you have got Ella's before this time, for I directed it to Moodus because she wrote that she thought she should go home with you. But I received another from her day before yesterday and found her still in Meriden.*

She's coming back home. She's not coming back home. Georgiana did not leave Meriden. Instead, she asked to stay and attend school there. Perhaps she wanted to study to become a teacher as her father wanted. Were these fifteen-year-old-girl-decision-making moves or telling-a-father-what-he-wants-to-hear moves?

Her patient father replied to her.

[Letter to Georgiana]

*Atlanta, Georgia*
*September 22, 1864*

*Beloved Daughter Ella,*

*You said that you were very much disappointed when Aunt Elib's letter came not to find anything in it addressed to you. I am sorry that it happened so, but the reason was you wrote that you thought you should go home with Mother, so I thought there would be no use in writing to you there* [Meriden]. *I therefore wrote to you and directed it to Moodus, and I hope you have got it before this time.*

*You wanted to know in your first letter if Fred Chapman had recovered from his wound. That I am unable to tell you. I have not heard anything from him since the 23rd of July. He was taken prisoner at the time and has not been heard from since. So you see that we know not whether he is dead or alive, and the picture that you wanted from him, I guess you will have to waite a while for.* [Fred Chapman was not seen or heard from again after he was taken prisoner by the Confederacy on July 23, 1864.]

*And you wanted me to send you my photograph. I would like to please you by so doing but, in the first place there is no chance to have it taken here, and if there was, I have no money to pay for having it taken. In that case, I don't see but you will have to go without it for a while.*

*I should like to have been in Meriden and took supper with you at the time you wished so I could taste of your victuals that you cooked. But as that could not be, I must be satisfied to stay where I am and live on what is provided for me by the government. I have no doubt but you are a good cook and I live in hopes that the time will come soon when I can come and eat with you and enjoy your company.*

> *Now, Georgie, about your going to school in Meriden. I do not think it best for you to do it this winter. I do not feel able to send you away to school while I am in the army. Wait till I come home and then I will see what can be done for you. I want you should be a good girl and mind your mother and behave like a lady. Set a good example for your brothers.*
>
> *I must close. So good day. My love to you, dear daughter.*
>
> *From your Father,*
>
> *A.C. Smith*

Were it not for the Civil War, Georgiana may have attended normal school. Her father, with his value for education and his wish for his daughter to become a teacher, may have found a way to afford it. But in the current turmoil of war, normal school was completely out of the question for Georgiana.

The only Connecticut normal school at the time was the State Normal School in New Britain, thirty-five miles away from Moodus. It had been founded the year Georgiana was born, the sixth training school for teachers in the nation. The school stayed open during the Civil War but closed afterwards for two years. Much later, this school became Central Connecticut State University.

Abner C. Smith was trying desperately to hold onto the reins of his daughter from afar. He was a good father. A prudent father who asked her not to spend money on clothes and bonnets. (She got them anyway.) A try-to-be-strict father who explained to her that she was too young at age thirteen to go to dancing school and stay out late. (She went anyway.) A patient father with a sense of humor who wondered, with loving snickers you can feel through his letters, why he was being asked for advice when she didn't take it. (He continued to give advice; she rarely took it.) A proud and unselfish father who hardly ever complained to her about his hardships, but consoled her about her sore throat, her dizzy head, her school, her restrictions. (She had a list.) A sentimental father who marveled at the photo of his only daughter, grown tall and into a young lady, and who longed for the attention she had given him when she was younger. (She was oblivious.) A smart father who insisted that education be her priority and encouraged her to become a teacher. (She didn't.) And a worried father who repeatedly advised his daughter to be "a girl that no one can say naught against" and "a good girl." (Was she?)

By November 1864, Georgiana had still not come home to Moodus. She had been in Meriden for seven months. Abner and Lucinda's family was falling apart. Their only daughter would not stay home and would not go to school. Edgar, at twelve, did not like much about his life; he bounced between working, which he did not like, and school, which he did not like; he lived at home, which he did not like, or on the farms of family members and neighbors, whom he did not like, and who would (or were supposed to) provide him with clothing and schooling in exchange for farm work, which he did not like. Frank, at ten, was often the only one at home to help his mother with chores, but he was not doing well in school.

A discouraged Abner wrote to his wife.

[Excerpt from Letter to Lucinda]

*Atlanta, Georgia*
*November 8, 1864*

*It seems that Ella did not come home when she calculated to, but I presume she is at home before this time. If so, I want her to go to school this winter and be a good girl and see how fast she can learn as she has not been to school through the summer.*

*And Edgar, also, if he stays at home this winter, must go to school and learn beyond all account to make up for some of the lost time he has had.*

> *And that Frank of mine — if he don't learn faster, I don't know what I shall do to him when I come home, but I guess I shall take his ears off. He must learn to write. He is plenty old to begin to write. When I was his age, I could write a good hand, and if he never begins, he will never learn. That's what the matter is. So you just git him some paper and set him about it.*

A week after this letter was written, on November 16, 1864, Aunt Elizabeth died. She was only thirty-two years old. Elizabeth may have died in childbirth. That's merely a guess, because in the 1860s, most deaths of women her age were due to complications in childbirth. There is no record of the cause of Elizabeth's death, nor a record of a child's birth or death.

On the same day of Elizabeth's passing, Abner was one day into the march that became known as Sherman's "March to the Sea." Union General William Sherman led sixty-two thousand soldiers on a destructive 285-mile march in Georgia, from Atlanta, in the northwest corner of the state to Savannah, on the Atlantic coast. The march lasted from November 15 to December 21, 1864. It was the beginning of the end. The Civil War would be over in four months.

After Elizabeth died, Georgiana finally came home to her mother in Moodus and returned to the district school. Together again, mother and daughter wrote letters to Abner, which he received in a bunch when he reached Savannah. Georgiana wrote to him on Thanksgiving Day, giving him news that must have warmed his heart: the family had spent the day in Tartia with the Ackleys and Mother Brainerd. On Christmas Eve in Savannah, Abner wrote a letter home. He didn't mention Christmas.

In the three weeks following Christmas, an exhausted Abner and his exhausted regiment marched another twenty miles from Savannah, Georgia, to Hardeeville, South Carolina, slogging through unrelenting rain and mud at the end of the trip.

Georgiana, who had traveled on her own crooked and bumpy path for two years (although never to be compared to the path of her father) was finally walking on the straight and narrow path her father so desperately wanted her to find. Edgar walked next to her. Frank lagged behind with a pet pig.

[Excerpts in Letter to Georgiana]

> *Hardeeville, South Carolina*
> *January 23, 1865*
>
> *Wal, Ella, I received your letter with Mother's yesterday … I am glad to hear from you at school and hope that you will improve all of your time over your school books and not have a moment wasted in idelness.*
>
> *Wal, Edgar, I am glad to hear a better report of you. I hear that you are a very good boy and that you learn more this winter than you used to. That I am very glad to hear. I thank you for your love and send you mine in return, and I want you should write me a good long letter.*
>
> *Frank, I am glad to hear that you are a good boy, but they say you do not learn very well. That I am sorry to hear. I want you should try to learn. Now is the time for you, if you ever expect to know anything. I hear you have got a pig. You must take good care of him and make him grow.*

Good for Georgiana, Edgar, and Frank — all back in school! Good for Lucinda! Great for Abner, who needed good news and the satisfaction that his long-distance fathering had mattered. Optimism was in the air. A few days later, Abner wrote to Lucinda with new hope that he'd be coming home soon.

[Excerpt from Letter to Lucinda]

> *Hardeeville, South Carolina*
> *January 28, 1865*
>
> *I am at the same place that I was the last time I wrote to you, but we expect to march either tomorrow or next day. I don't know where we shall fetch up, but hope in some good place. I hope I shall fetch up in Moodus in the course of 7 or 8 months.*

The Smiths could sense a change. Newspapers reported that the Union was winning. Abner's letters home said the same. The Smith household was on firm ground. At the start of 1865, the three Smith children — Georgiana at fifteen, Edgar at thirteen, and Frank at ten — were together, living at home with their mother, with good reason to feel a new and unfamiliar optimism that their world would stop shifting.

Abner C. Smith was a survivor. God had given him a body to withstand hardtack and hardships. He had survived bloody battles in Gettysburg, Chancellorsville, Atlanta, and Savannah. He had survived the dysentery and diseases that took the lives of more soldiers than bullets did. His powerful body had withstood the abuse of sickening filth, putrid stench, fierce drenching, extreme cold, extreme heat, swarming flies, and poor nutrition, which could hardly be called nutrition. He had survived the madness of being pressed together with so many other soldiers in a train's cattle car that when one man wanted to turn over, all men had to turn over. For two-and-a-half years, his strong legs had marched south, west, and east. Then they carried him for the exhausting six weeks of Sherman's March to the Sea at the end of 1864, and north again to South Carolina to start 1865.

After his January 28, 1865, letter from Hardeeville, South Carolina, there were no letters from Abner until March. He had been tramping to North Carolina.

On March 19, 1865, in the Battle of Bentonville in North Carolina, a bullet struck Abner in the leg. Lucinda, Georgiana, Edgar, and Frank learned about it in a March 23 letter. This letter from Abner, although in his own words, was in someone else's handwriting.

[Letter to Lucinda]

> Hospital near Goldsboro, North Carolina
> March 23, 1865
>
> My Dear Wife,
>
> It is under rather peculiar circumstances I cause this letter to be wrote, but while some has been cut down, I am still living minus one leg. Feeling thankfull that I am so well as I am. It was on the 19th when the accident happened and we have had to be brought here on an ambulance thus far, but I don't expect to be long here and you nead not write to me till you hear from me again.
>
> The right leg is cut off above the knee and the wound is doing first rate. You need not worry about me. I will write you again soon. I think with some care, I may be permitted to come home before long, for I no doubt but we shall be sent to our respective states when we are able to stand it. We have everything in our favor. The weather is fine and pleasant, and we have no flys to bother us now what there is in summer.
>
> We have lost some sixty in our regiment since the 12th — 6 killed, the rest wounded.
>
> Dear children, I would say a word to you. I am thankful to God that I am so well as I am. I would have you be good children till I see you again, of which I hope won't be long.
>
> May God, in his mercy, spare us all to meet again once more in the flesh.
>
> From your ever affectionate husband and father,
> Abner C. Smith

Horatio D. Chapman, Abner's close friend since the first day they left East Haddam and tentmates throughout the war, wrote this in his diary on March 21, 1865:

[Excerpt from the Diary of Horatio D. Chapman]

> *March 21, 1865*
>
> *My dear comrade, Abner Smith, than whom there was no better or courageous soldier, who had marched by my side from the commencement of our enlistment in '62, almost three years, and had been in every general engagement in which the regiment had been engaged, and had been my tentmate all the time — just as the battle closed, was wounded.*
>
> *I received permission to help carry him to the rear about one and a half miles to our field hospital. A minie-ball* [bullet] *had entered his right leg near the thigh and passed down and came out on the opposite side just above the knee, and shattering the bone all to pieces.*

A week later, a letter addressed to Lucinda arrived from the army chaplain.

[Letter to Mrs. Abner C. Smith, 2nd]

> *Goldsboro, North Carolina*
> *March 29, 1865*
>
> *Dear Madam,*
>
> *You have already been informed that your husband was seriously wounded in the battle of the 19th inst. You have been told that it was needful for him to submit to an amputation of the leg.*
>
> *The wound appeared to do well, and we had hoped that he would recover from the shock. But he was very much exhausted by the long ride from the hospital near to the battlefield to this place. And he never fully recovered himself. All was done which*

could have been under the circumstances. But it was in vain. He continued to fail till the morning of the 28th when he was taken from this scene of pain and sorrow to another world. He died from exhaustion, for one doctor told me that his wound was appearing finely.

Thus we have lost another good soldier and man, and you have lost a kind and loving husband. We feel our loss but you must feel yours more shurrly — no friend on earth was so dear to you as your husband. I know that your heart bleeds under the afflictive stroke of God's providence. You have my sincere sympathy. While my prayer is that from this sorrow, you may derive rich spiritual benefit, and find, from a most unhappy experience, that God is good to those in sorrow. May the fountain of all consolation be opened to you that your love may be refreshed therein.

I saw your husband when he was brought from the field and frequently after that, till the day of his death. All speak of him as being a good and faithful soldier, always ready to perform his duty.

He will be buried in a strange part of the land. [Abner was buried in Goldsboro, North Carolina. His remains were later moved to the Raleigh, North Carolina, National Cemetery, Section 7, Grave 279.] Yet the ever-watchful eye of our Heavenly Father will ever care for him. I was with him his last hours. He was weak and wandering in his mind. But let us hope that God prepared him for that world where no one will say any more I am sick.

God bless you in this keen sorrow.

With Christian sympathy,

Yours truly,

Chas. N. Lyman Chaplain 20th C.V.

## THE END

The quake that had been shaking the country since 1861, that had swallowed over six hundred thousand soldiers, that had stolen limbs, eyes, ears, innards, and sanity from another one-and-a-half million soldiers, and that had sent tremors to homes around the nation for four years, took Georgiana's father twelve days before the rumbling stopped.

Abner C. Smith died on March 28, 1865.

Twelve days later, Robert E. Lee surrendered to Ulysses S. Grant.

Six days after that, Abraham Lincoln was assassinated.

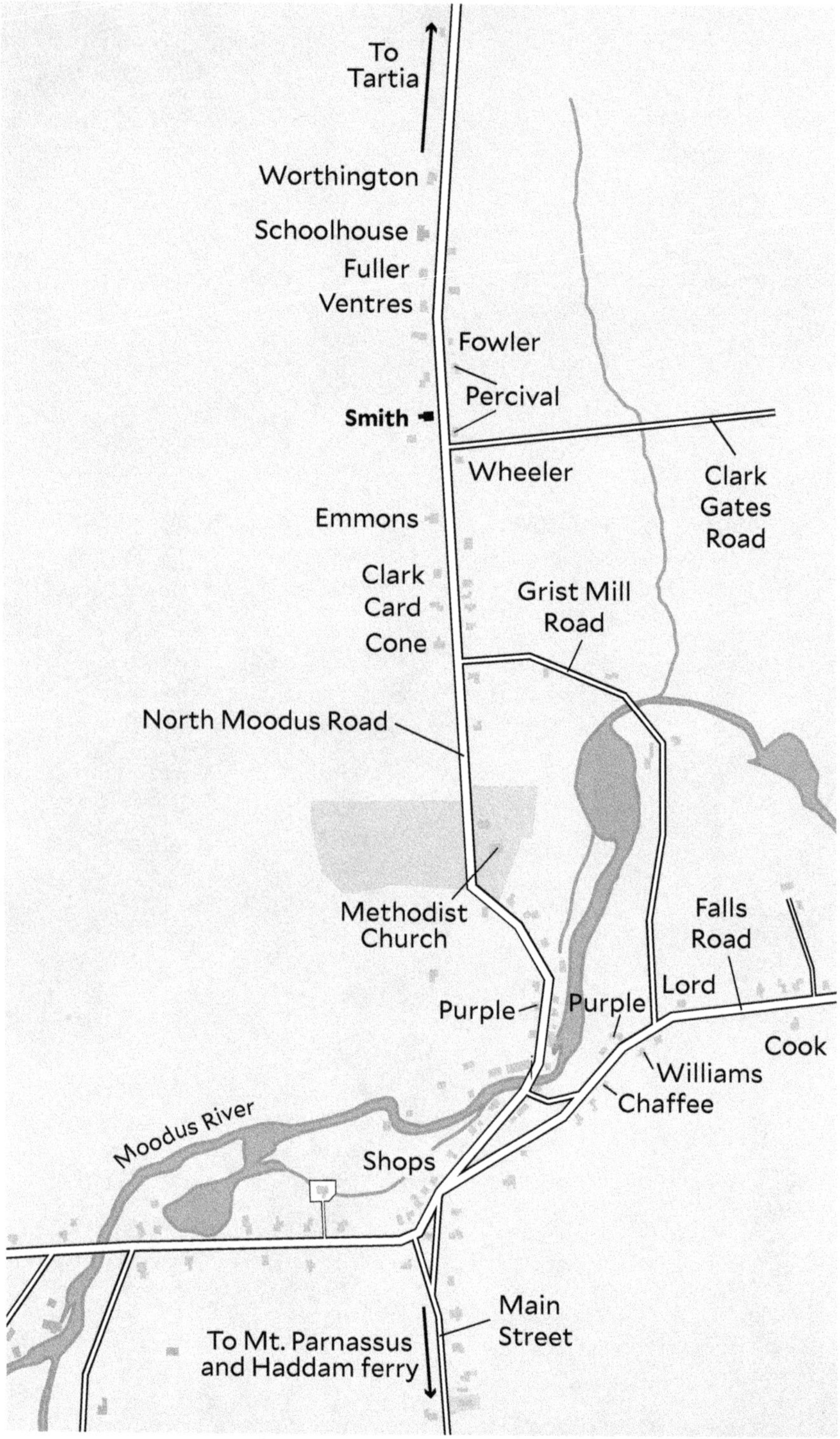

To Tartia
Worthington
Schoolhouse
Fuller
Ventres
Fowler
Percival
Smith
Wheeler
Clark Gates Road
Emmons
Clark
Card
Cone
Grist Mill Road
North Moodus Road
Methodist Church
Falls Road
Lord
Purple
Purple
Cook
Williams
Chaffee
Moodus River
Shops
Main Street
To Mt. Parnassus and Haddam ferry

CHAPTER 4

# Marching On
## Georgiana from Fifteen to Eighteen
## 1865–1868

Word of Abner C. Smith's death on March 28, 1865, would have sped up North Moodus Road from neighbor to neighbor — from the Percivals, to the Fowlers, to the Ventreses, to the Fullers, through the schoolhouse, to the Worthingtons, then over the East Haddam line to Tartia in Chatham, where Mother Brainerd and the Ackleys may have heard the news before Lucinda could break it to them. At the same speed and at the same time, the news would have tumbled down North Moodus Road — from the Wheelers, to the Emmonses, to the Clarks, to the Cards, to the Cones, through the Methodist church, down the hill to the Purples, over the Moodus River, then in one direction to the Chaffees and the Williamses and more Purples and the Lords and the Cooks, and in the other direction to the shops in Moodus center, where it would be carried by horse and buggy to Mount Parnassus and by ferry to Haddam.

Abner C. Smith was one of thirty-five soldiers from East Haddam to die in the Civil War. The surviving East Haddam soldiers, battered and tattered and scattered around the country, were on their way home by June 1865. They returned, some without the same bodies or minds, to tend to their farms or their fishing or their businesses and to head up their families again. The Moodus mills restarted, the Moodus shops restocked, the villagers of

OPPOSITE: *Moodus, Connecticut, at the time of the Civil War*

Moodus reassembled, and Moodus reentered the march toward prosperity that they'd had to abandon at the start of the war.

The women of East Haddam, like other women throughout the nation, had proven their worth as independent managers of life during the war years. Since age thirteen, Georgiana had watched her mother manage a household and a farm on her own. She had watched her mother follow the practical instructions in her father's letters. She had read her father's words of respect for his wife's judgment in his absence. But Georgiana would have also noticed that even with her father's words of help and encouragement, it was difficult for a woman to manage a farm and a home alone.

### LUCINDA MARCHES ON

During and after the Civil War, it was not uncommon to see black dresses in East Haddam. Widows, mothers, sisters, and daughters of the town's fallen soldiers were wearing them in 1865 when Lucinda put hers back on, only two years after wearing it for Little Freddy in 1863. Civil War widows wore black for two to two-and-a-half years; daughters wore black for six months. In the black months that followed Abner's death, Lucinda would have been helped and comforted by many — by the pastor and members of the Moodus Methodist Episcopal Church, by Abner's Ackley family in Tartia, by neighbors, and by the presence of her three children.

But Lucinda's Arnold family in Haddam could not provide a support system for her in East Haddam. The wide river separated them in the days before a bridge or a phone connected the two towns. Lucinda's parents, Sylvia and Horace Tyler Arnold, were in their early seventies and lived at the Arnold homestead. During the war, Lucinda's last two sisters, the older Jerusha and the younger Elizabeth, had died. Of Lucinda's seven siblings, only her two brothers, Horace Edgar Arnold and Davis Tyler Arnold, were alive when Abner died. Horace's wife had left him, and Davis's wife had died. Both sons lived on Arnold land near their parents. For a bit of good Arnold news, in the spring of 1862, Louisa, the orphaned daughter of Lucinda's late sister Sylvia, had married Henry Clarke, a nearby Haddam farmer with substantial means. During the war, Louisa and Henry had a son and a daughter, blessing the Arnold family with the first two children of the next generation.

Lucinda was thirty-nine when Abner died. In addition to grief, she had to deal with how to provide for herself and her children. In August 1865, she applied for a Civil War widow's pension. The pension took more than two years to process. In August 1867, she received a lump sum for the retroactive payments and then began receiving $12 [about $210 in 2020] a month. Lucinda's monthly $12 represented $8 for her and $2 each to support Edgar and Frank, who were both under sixteen. No money was provided for children sixteen and over, and Georgiana had turned sixteen three months after her father's death. Lucinda received the Civil War widow's pension monthly (the amount increased over the years) for the rest of her life.

Lucinda's house was paid for, she was exempt from taxes because she was a war widow, and she made extra income from the home farm, but it would still have been hard for her to make ends meet. Her pension of $12 a month was less than the $15.50 monthly wage of the average farm laborer, which was one of the lowest paying jobs. If Lucinda wanted more income, she'd have to remarry (which she never did) or take a job herself. She was not afraid of work. Before marriage she had worked in the mills earning about $12 a month. Lucinda had wanted to work when Abner was at war, apparently against his wishes. In a June 1864 letter, Abner wrote to his wife:

> *You say that there is a number of people that wants you to take care of them by and by. I have told you before what you had better do, but you can act on your own judgement about such matters. If you should go to either of those places, you must not*

MARCHING ON

> ***leave things at loose ends at home.*** [Georgiana had just moved to Meriden at age fourteen, Edgar was twelve, and Frank had just turned ten.] ***I am glad you did not go to Jones*** [a local merchant and hotel owner] ***to work.***

Did Lucinda go to work in 1864 after receiving this letter? I don't know. Perhaps she was able to make enough extra income from her home farm on North Moodus Road to stay at home with the children.

What about her home on North Moodus Road? After Abner died, could Lucinda and her children continue to live there? With the help of a Connecticut law and a good neighbor, Lucinda was able to keep her house. Well, it wasn't technically *her* house while her husband was alive — married women could not own property in Connecticut until 1877. But as a widow, she could own property, and she was entitled to dower rights, meaning she was legally entitled to one third of her late husband's home and property. In August 1866, a year and five months after Abner died, his estate was settled at the East Haddam Probate Court. Lucinda's dower was described in the court records (Vol. 3, pages 603–605) as "all of the first floor of the house, excepting the front parlor and the hall; one third of the cellar and garret with the privilege of access to the same; one third of the barn; one third of the land; and privilege of the privy located in the barn." As for the other two thirds of the property, Abner's three children were entitled to split it. One of the requirements in the probate process was that Lucinda had to apply for guardianship of her (own!) minor children. On August 9, 1866, the court awarded her the guardianship[44] of Georgiana, Edgar, and Frank, who were seventeen, fourteen, and twelve.

Lucinda, as administrator of Abner's estate, was also responsible for his debts pending at the time of his death. In his letters during the war, money was a recurring topic. He kept track of the income and expenses for his household, noting his bills to be paid and who owed him money. When Abner died, there were pending bills from his former shoemaking business, from farm transactions, and from expenses Lucinda had incurred during the war years. As part of the settlement of Abner's estate, the East Haddam Probate Court ordered Lucinda to sell real estate to pay off the net debt of $299.67 [about $4,865 in 2020]. Lucinda complied. She sold her portion of the house and property to neighbor Edward Worthington. Mr. Worthington gave Lucinda $304.67 to settle her debts and to pay the $5 "incidental charges" also ordered by the court. In exchange, Lucinda granted him the title to an "undescribed third" of the North Moodus Road home and property (East Haddam Land Records, Vol. 31, page 443).

Edward Worthington, old enough to be Lucinda's father, was a well-off farmer, businessman, and trusted neighbor, who lived with his wife and some of his adult children near the schoolhouse on North Moodus Road. Abner had sometimes advised Lucinda in his letters to seek help from Mr. Worthington for financial transactions. Basically, in this August 1866 transaction, Mr. Worthington gave Lucinda money to pay off Abner's debts, took title on paper only to "one undescribed third" of the property, then allowed Lucinda and her family to continue living there. There is no record of the transfer of the property back to Lucinda from Mr. Worthington, but she regained ownership of it before 1870. Lucinda and her children maintained ownership of the house for forty more years — even after she moved out in 1881. They owned it all the way until June 1910, when Lucinda and her three children sold it for $1,000 [about $27,300 in 2020]. Abner had paid $1,300 for the property — a half-acre parcel of land, a house, and a barn — sixty years earlier, in 1850.

### GEORGIANA'S BROTHERS MARCH ON

After the war, Georgiana's brothers quickly grew into little men. Edgar, who was thirteen when his father died in March 1865, finished school when he was fourteen. He likely continued living with his mother after he graduated and may have provided some income for the household for a couple years. At some point, Edgar moved to Middletown where, I speculate, he completed an apprenticeship as a joiner. In the 1870 census, at age nineteen, he was living in Middletown in an all-male boarding house managed by a couple who formerly lived in East Haddam. Of the ten men boarding there, Edgar was one of the youngest. He was not listed as an apprentice as the other young men were. He was listed as a joiner, his apprenticeship presumably completed.

Frank was ten, almost eleven, when his father died. He had not seen his father since he was seven. According to Frank's biography in *Beers 1903*, he "attended the district schools in his native town until he attained the age of fourteen [1868], although he had begun to support himself when only ten [1865], at the time of his father's death. The brave little fellow worked for the farmers in the vicinity in the summer, attending school in the winter."

### GEORGIANA MARCHES ON

Through my rose-colored glasses, I envision Georgiana in the three years following her father's death as bravely marching on as the supportive daughter — living at home and helping her mother emotionally and financially. Through these lenses, I can see her as a schoolteacher, or working in a milliner's shop, or assisting a dressmaker. But take the glasses off, and the vision is not so rosy: she is a not-so-angelic daughter, working as a housekeeper at someone else's home or as an operative in the Moodus mills. She was still a teenager, only fifteen when her father died. I don't know where she worked after she finished school, but I'm certain she earned income in some way.

Few opportunities were available for women to earn their own income at this time. Like most teenage girls in postbellum America, Georgiana knew her future was marriage, and she would have invested most of her free time in attracting a husband. Not that Georgiana would have found that activity distasteful. I believe that 16-year-old Georgiana, after a socially-appropriate six months of mourning her father, spent her free time with 20-year-old Silas Cook.

### SILAS

Silas Cook (1845–1925) was exactly what Georgiana needed to help her march out of the black and blue and grey Civil War years into a colorful life. Four years older than Georgiana, Silas had grown up within walking distance of her home in Moodus.

Like the Smiths and the Ackleys, Silas's family was part of the local history. Generations of Cooks (his father's family) and Stricklands (his mother's family) had lived and died in the area since the time of the earliest settlers. The hats of the Cooks and the Stricklands and the Smiths and the Ackleys would have been routinely tipped to one another for years as they bounced along in their buggies in Chatham and East Haddam and on the roads in between. Silas was born slightly over the East Haddam line, in the nine-mile-long, three-mile-wide, western portion of Chatham that had adopted the name of Portland four years before he was born. His father, Dr. Henry Evelyn Cook (1809–1874), was a respected physician in Chatham-turned-Portland and in Moodus, where he brought his family to live when Silas was nine weeks old. Unlike Georgiana, Silas did not grow up in a household that worried about money. The Cooks lived in a home with more than one hundred acres of land near the center of Moodus.

In his earliest school years, Silas attended the district school in downtown Moodus. At nine, he entered a private academy in Essex, Connecticut, about fifteen miles south and across the Connecticut River. Hills Academy, now the Essex Historical Society building at 22 Prospect Street, was a coeducational school for ages nine and older. Boys boarded next door to the school in a separate building that has since been demolished. I don't know if or where girls boarded. Silas began attending in August 1854.

In 1857, at age twelve, Silas met Georgiana, age eight. I know *when* he met Georgiana because of a document he signed when he was nineteen, which I will explain later. But *how* did he meet her? At twelve, Silas was taking drum lessons from master drummer Hezekiah Percival who lived across the street from the Smiths. My best guess as to how Georgiana met Silas is that he met the whole Smith family, including the born-in-July Little Freddy, on North Moodus Road when he walked to and from Hezekiah Percival's for his drum lessons.

As children and adolescents, Silas and Georgiana would have walked on the same Moodus roads and have attended many of the same village events. In 1860, when Silas was fourteen, Hezekiah Percival and his brother Orville Percival pulled together a group of drummers and fifers to play music for fun. Silas was a drummer. His father was a fifer. According to many Moodus historical records, this informal group was soon a favorite at local community events. No doubt, in the crowd in 1860, stepping to the time of the music, were Mr. and Mrs. Abner C. Smith with their four children, ranging in age from eleven-year-old Georgiana to three-year-old Little Freddy.

In the fall of 1860, Silas, at age fifteen, entered his first of four years at Wesleyan Academy, a coeducational college preparatory school in Wilbraham, Massachusetts, where, according to *Beers 1903*, he "devoted much time to boisterous play, and frequently astonished the teachers by his unexpected methods of relieving his pent up feelings." This little nugget is a perfect example of how a genealogist can use the records of a man to gain insight into a record-lean woman's personality. According to this entry, Silas was a bit of a prankster — a bit devilish. Georgiana was attracted to him, from which I conclude that Georgiana was not an angel.

Silas's years of attendance at Wesleyan Academy are presumptions on my part, relying on his age and piecing together other events in his life. But I believe he was there when the Civil War broke out in April 1861. In August 1862, when Georgiana's father left Moodus for the war, Silas was likely home between school terms. I think it's a fair assumption that the just-turned-seventeen Silas played with the group of Moodus drummers and fifers at the

August 1862 send-off for the departing Abner C. Smith and other East Haddam men. It's an even better assumption that thirteen-year-old Georgiana was at her father's send-off, where she may have paid more attention to the handsome young snare drummer than to her father waving goodbye from the train.

Silas was likely in Wilbraham and not in Moodus when, six months later in February 1863, the Smiths lost Little Freddy. And he was likely not in Moodus when Georgiana was having her fourteen-year-old dramas later in 1863 and 1864 — when she lived in Meriden, and when her father was begging her to be a good (you know very well what I mean) girl.

### SETTLING DOWN

In November 1864, when Georgiana returned to Moodus from Meriden, Silas was living with his parents in their Falls Road home and settling into his medical apprenticeship under his father. He had graduated from Wesleyan Academy and chosen to be a physician like this father. Georgiana settled down in the North Moodus Road home with her mother and brothers and went back to school. Silas turned nineteen in August; Georgiana was fifteen.

Were Georgiana and Silas a *couple* when word came of Georgiana's father's death in March 1865? I think so. I think a relationship between Silas and Georgiana had begun by this time, because, five months later in August 1865, Silas served as an official witness on Lucinda's "Widow's Application for Pension." Here is an excerpt from the application:

> ALSO, PERSONALLY APPEARED Henry C. Harris and S.U. Cook residents of East Haddam, in the State of Connecticut, persons whom I certify to be respectable and entitled to credit, and who, being by me duly sworn, say that they were present and saw Lucinda Smith sign her name in the foregoing declaration, and they further swear that they have

> every reason to believe, from the appearance of the applicant and their acquaintances with her, that she is the identical person she represents herself to be, and that they have no interest in the prosecution of this claim. Also that they know the said Lucinda Smith is the widow of the within named Abner C. Smith, who performed the military service mentioned in the declaration, from a personal acquaintance with her of about 8 years, and with her said husband of about 8 years before his death. That they lived together, and were reputed to be husband and wife, and that she has remained a widow since his death and that the said Abner C. Smith left two children under 16 years of age, Edgar C, aged 13, and Frank P, aged 11 years.
>
> That they reside as aforesaid, and that their means of knowledge of all these facts are derived from a personal acquaintance with the family for the period of time above mentioned.
>
> [SIGNATURE] Henry C. Harris
>
> [SIGNATURE] S. U. Cook
>
> Notarized by Judge Julius Attwood of the East Haddam Probate Court, August 8, 1865.

**S. U. Cook** was Silas. Georgiana may have asked the older, college-educated Silas to help her and her mother with this application and other paperwork. He may have been by the sides of Georgiana and Lucinda as they made their way through the probate court process.

By the way, when Silas recorded in this document that he knew Lucinda "from a personal acquaintance with her of about eight years," and "a personal acquaintance with the family for the period of time above mentioned," he was reporting that he had known her since 1857, when he was twelve. Thus my earlier conclusion that he was twelve when he met Georgiana.

The second witness, **Henry C. Harris** (1818–?) was a forty-seven-year-old Moodus resident who lived close to Silas and was the father of four daughters. The youngest daughter, Rosie, may have been a friend of Georgiana's. She was Georgiana's age and attended the Fourth District School. Henry C. Harris would have known Georgiana's father through Abner's role as the Fourth District School's tax collector.

Two weeks after Silas signed this document, he turned twenty. Georgiana had turned sixteen in July. Both were growing into promising young adults.

U.S.

The first year after the Civil War was an emotional time for many in America. Intense waves of patriotism crashed over the nation, striving to rinse away the residue from gunshots and blood spatter. People coped by pouring their hearts and minds into honoring the sacrifices of the soldiers. Poets like Walt Whitman and Emily Dickinson sought to find meaning in patriotism, war, and death. *Harper's New Monthly Magazine* published articles advocating national cemeteries for the thousands of dead soldiers, whose bodies, one of which was Georgiana's father, were scattered across the South in makeshift graves. War veterans carefully folded their battle-worn flags for preservation. Towns flew new flags with crisp reds, whites, and blues. Mothers, widows, children, grandchildren, and townspeople decorated the graves of their Civil War heroes with flowers and flags. Committees, many led by and made up of women, formed and planned permanent monuments lest future generations forget the Civil War, which the village of Moodus never did.

Silas Cook was swept up by the waves. So much so that he changed his name to **Ulysses S. Cook.** The name Ulysses was rarely used before the Civil War, but it rose in popularity because of Union General Ulysses S. Grant, who had become a national hero. The popularity of the name lasted about twenty years after the war, although the name never made it to the most popular list.

An interesting piece of trivia about Ulysses S. Grant: he had also changed his name. Grant was born Hiram Ulysses Grant, but when he started at West Point, he was erroneously registered as Ulysses S. Grant. After trying to get it corrected and failing, he officially took the name of Ulysses S. Grant, forever quipping that the *S* stood for nothing. Some historians report that Grant preferred the initials "U. S." because it stood for "United States." Silas Cook would have known this story. In 1866, following in his hero's footsteps, Silas changed his name at age twenty-one to Ulysses. He dropped the name of Silas and became Ulysses S. Cook, aka U. S. Cook. I have viewed more than a hundred documents and articles with the name Ulysses S. Cook and I found only one with the middle S spelled out: the name Silas appears as his middle name on his marriage license. For the rest, it's simply S.

### DRUM ROLL

When exactly Georgiana and Ulysses became a couple, I don't know. When Ulysses helped Lucinda with her pension application in August 1865, Georgiana would have been in her fifth month of mourning for her father. According to the custom for the daughter of a slain soldier, she would have worn black and attended no social events for six months. My guess is that in the fall of 1865, Ulysses brought the color back into Georgiana's life in the same way he brightened up the village of Moodus with his music.

That fall, the group of drummers and fifers, who had informally played together through the war years at recruitments and rallies, formalized and officially became the soon-to-be-famous Moodus Drum and Fife Corps, and Ulysses was elected its first music director. I'm surmising that Georgiana spent the rest of age sixteen and the next two years attending patriotic celebrations, cheering on the sidelines of parades, gliding in and out of her circles of friends at social gatherings, and dancing in the arms of Ulysses, who would soon ask her to be Mrs. U. S. Cook.

## Georgiana, Ulysses and Drum Corps Make Three

Georgiana did not play a drum or a fife, but few people were closer to the Moodus Drum and Fife Corps. From the day the corps was born, Georgiana was a part of its life, and it was a part of Georgiana's.

The loud booms of drums and high shrills of fifes had serenaded Georgiana since she was a toddler on North Moodus Road. She lived directly across the street from Hezekiah Percival who played both instruments. She was eleven, in 1860, when Hezekiah and his brother Orville, a drummer, began to gather fifers and drummers to play together as a group, and when Georgiana's immediate neighborhood became the birthplace of what would become the famous Moodus Drum and Fife Corps.

The year that the Moodus Drum and Fife Corps was founded is not always reported as 1860, but that is the year recognized by the corps itself. Its big and seasoned bass drum is proudly imprinted with 1860; its 150th anniversary was celebrated in 2010, and the Percival brothers' story with the 1860 start has been hardwired into East Haddam's history.

In the fall of 1865, after playing together informally through the Civil War years, Percival's group took action to formalize. Francis Brainard, who also lived across the street from Georgiana, spearheaded the initiative, and her neighborhood continued its active participation.

The Moodus Drum and Fife Corps's start is recorded in Francis Hubert Parker's *Contributions to the History of the Town of East Haddam, Connecticut*, a compilation of newspaper articles written from 1914 to 1927 and originally published in the *Connecticut Valley Advertiser*. (I will hereafter refer to this compilation as *Parker's*.) Parker created his collection in 1938. Here is an excerpt from *Parker's* about the start of the corps:

> With the Civil War came a revival of interest in martial music, and a few old time drummers and fifers living in Moodus and the vicinity brought out their musical instruments

and provided music at Fourth of July celebrations and on the occasions of Union victories. Among these drummers were Orville Percival, Alfred Silliman, Thomas Silliman, William Silliman, Daniel W. Ventres and DeWitt C. Williams. The fifers included William Brown, Dr. Henry Evelyn Cook [father of Ulysses] and Hezekiah W. Percival.

Hezekiah W. Percival and his fife [across the street from the Smiths on North Moodus Road], Francis W. Brainard with a snare drum [also across the street from the Smiths], Daniel W. Ventres with a bass drum [the Ventreses lived two houses away from the Smiths and were connected to the Smiths through the marriage of Lucinda's sister] and perhaps others, whose names have not been preserved, furnished music for a Fourth of July celebration on the Plain [currently Plains Road] near the Baptist church in 1865. The possibility of forming a drum and fife corps was mooted [broached] as a sequence to the popular approval of their musical program, and not long thereafter Francis W. Brainard invited a number of men to meet at his house and consider the matter.

At that meeting, in the fall of 1865, Francis W. Brainard, Wilbur S. Comstock, Ulysses S. Cook [who still went by Silas Cook in 1865, but this article was written after he had changed his name to Ulysses], William S. Purple, Thaddeus R. Spencer, and Daniel Lamond Williams, snare drummers; John S. Ackley, David O. Chapman, and Emory Lewis, bass drummers; and William Brown, George Rinaldo Buell, Dr. Henry Evelyn Cook, and Hezekiah W. Percival, fifers informally enlisted in the enterprise, though it was understood that Mr. Brown and Dr. Cook [Ulysses's father] were to act only until other fifers could be trained.

Dr. U. S. Cook was musical director of the corps from the beginning.

A few years after the 1865 organization of the Moodus Drum and Fife Corps, Georgiana married its musical director.

And the three lived happily ever after.

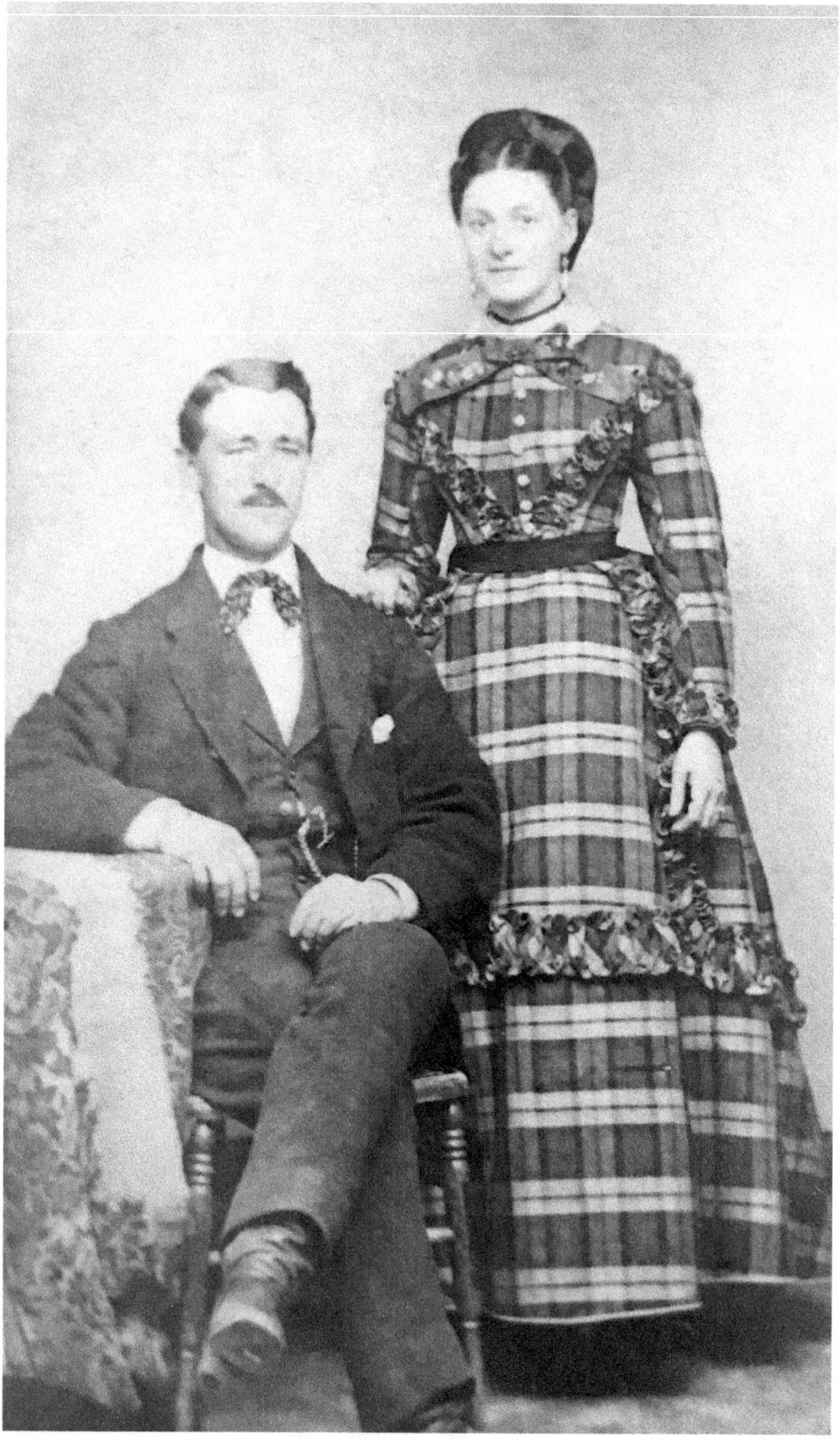

CHAPTER 5

# Start the Music
## Georgiana from Eighteen to Twenty-one 1868–1870

Ella Georgiana Smith became Mrs. Ulysses S. Cook on April 9, 1868. She was eighteen. He was twenty-two. It was a Thursday morning. They adhered to the nineteenth-century custom of holding weddings on weekday mornings. But they did not follow the custom of getting married at the bride's home. The wedding took place at the parsonage of the Congregational church in Little Haddam. The church is East Haddam's First Church of Christ Congregational Church, the large white edifice located at 499 Town Street. Ulysses's parents had been attending this church for over twenty years, since their move from Portland to Moodus. The Reverend Silas W. Robbins performed the marriage ceremony. He had been with the church for twelve years and likely knew the Cooks well.

No particulars were recorded about this event, as was customary for the time. Most weddings were small private affairs. Georgiana and Ulysses's marriage would have been formally announced to the church congregation at the following Sunday's church service, another wedding custom of the times.

Wedding customs in 1868 America were on the cusp of change — moving from the antebellum days of informal, simple events to formal, extravagant affairs. The change was sparked by the 1840 wedding of Queen Victoria. It was then fueled in the 1850s by articles in *Godey's Lady's Book,* the bible of etiquette for

OPPOSITE: *The new Mr. and Mrs. Ulysses S. Cook, 1868.*

nineteenth-century America that women of all classes flipped through with delight (and perhaps with a touch of envy for its famously illustrated fashions). And the change was further fueled by the new popular novels in the 1850s that included lavish wedding ceremonies as settings in their plots. But the Civil War (1861–1865) put a pause on lavish anything. It was not until after the war that America's new wedding customs — white dresses and veils for brides, wedding cakes, wedding presents, attendants, formal invitations, afternoon weddings, receptions with music and dancing, and wedding announcements in newspapers — became the norm for the upper class in cities. And not for another few years, that the new style of wedding trickled down to the middle classes in small towns. I don't think it had reached Moodus by 1868.

Here are my guesses about the details of Georgiana's wedding:

- Georgiana's mother and Ulysses's parents would have attended. But few others. Maybe her brothers, Edgar (sixteen) and Frank (thirteen).
- Ulysses would have given Georgiana a gold wedding ring, but wedding rings for grooms were not yet a custom.
- No reception. They perhaps had a small *wedding breakfast* at the parsonage after the ceremony.
- No *honeymoon*. Honeymoons weren't a custom until the 1900s.
- Georgiana would have felt the emptiness of her father's absence. She knew he would have been bursting with pride for his only daughter. Whether anyone took his place to *give her away*, I don't know. The custom of the time was for a friend to replace a deceased father. Perhaps it was Horatio Chapman, her father's tentmate; there are some indications that, after the war, Mr. Chapman watched out for Georgiana as a daughter.
- The Cooks probably funded the whole event, including the wedding clothes and a trousseau for Georgiana.
- Her wedding clothes? She would have worn a new dress or outfit. Not a wear-only-one-time wedding dress, but something new she could use again for special occasions after she was married.

## THE HEIGHT OF FASHION

It is possible that the plaid dress Georgiana is wearing in the photograph at the beginning of this chapter was the dress she wore for her wedding.

I consulted Victorian era expert and actress Ms. Kandie Carle of Kandie Carle Victorian Lady[45] about the photograph and Georgiana's clothing. She shared the following insights with me:

> The date of the photo is between 1868 and 1871. The photo was a studio picture, possibly the 'couple' picture to give to family and friends as the new Mr. and Mrs. Cook. Plaid garments were very fashionable. The fabric could have been cotton or wool. Sashes like hers and the very large necktie/bow at her neck were the height of fashion at the time. The outfit is a skirt and bodice; the sash covers the waistband. She has a lovely white lace collar and a choker necklace, both of which were, again, the height of fashion at the time. Under her skirt would have been an elliptical crinoline petticoat, which was shorter and flatter in front and elongated in the back.

The height of fashion! So happy I asked an expert — I would have never guessed this about plaid.

## NEWLYWEDS WITH THE IN-LAWS

The young newlyweds moved in with Ulysses's parents, Dr. Henry Evelyn Cook and Mrs. Elizabeth (born Strickland) Cook, on Falls Road in Moodus. The Cooks had moved to Falls Road from Portland in 1845 with their twelve-year-old daughter, Sarah, and new baby Silas. Sarah had died in Moodus at age sixteen in 1849, the year Georgiana was born, when Silas was four and the Cooks were in their early forties.

Dr. and Mrs. Cook were in their early sixties when their son married Georgiana. I'm assuming that Elizabeth Cook welcomed a bright, young daughter-in-law into her life and home. She probably had her dressmaker make Georgiana's wedding outfit and trousseau. Georgiana likely found the Cook family and their house a comfort, and her new free-from-money-problems life exciting.

Dr. Henry Evelyn Cook, who sometimes went by his middle name, was a well-established physician and one of the most affluent people in East Haddam. Of the 673 heads of households in the East Haddam 1870 census, there were only twenty with more wealth. Of the twenty, ten were land-rich farmers or widows of land-rich farmers, seven were Moodus mill owners, one was a banker, and the top two wealthiest (by far) were Luther Boardman (1812–1887), a spoon manufacturer, and William Goodspeed[46] (1816–1882), a shipbuilder. The other doctors in East Haddam — there were seven — were not as wealthy as Georgiana's father-in-law.

Perhaps one of the reasons Dr. Henry Evelyn Cook did well financially was that he "practiced as a cancer curer."[47] He specialized in Thomsonian Medicine, a treatment for cancer and other physical maladies, developed by American herbalist and botanist Samuel Thomson (1769–1843). This alternative system of medicine utilized steam baths and the ingestion of cayenne pepper and natural laxatives for the purpose of opening the paths of elimination of toxins. The methods were sometimes controversial but were becoming more popular at this time for people suffering from all sorts of ailments. Those seeking a cure for cancer would likely pay quite a bit for care from Dr. Cook.

Dr. Cook's medical office was attached to his home. This is where Ulysses trained to be a Thomsonian physician like his father. Apprenticeship with an established physician was a common path for medical education and training in the 1860s. Before going into practice for himself, Ulysses spent several years studying and gaining clinical experience under his father's tutelage. This included traveling to patients' homes in a horse and buggy, sometimes over long distances. In June 1870, at age twenty-four, two years after marrying Georgiana, Ulysses was not identified as a physician in the census — his occupation was left blank. He was still apprenticing.

*Ulysses S. Cook and Ella Georgiana Cook (standing). Dr. Henry Evelyn Cook and Mrs. Elizabeth Cook (seated).*

## Ulysses's Parents

Ulysses's parents, Henry Evelyn Cook (1809–1874) and Elizabeth (born Strickland) Cook (1808–1880) came from long lines of Connecticut families in the Chatham-turned-Portland area. They married in 1830 in the Chatham Congregational Church.

Ulysses's mother, Elizabeth, was one of six children born to Noah Strickland (1776–1859) and Phebe (born Bement) Strickland (1780–1865) of Chatham. Elizabeth may have inherited money or valuable goods from her parents, because in the 1870 Moodus census, at age sixty-two, she is one of the few married women with her own personal estate value. She is recorded as having $3,000 (about

$59,110 in 2020) of personal estate value. She has zero in real estate value, as married women could not own property in 1870.

Ulysses's father, Dr. Henry Evelyn Cook, was the first of four sons of Selden Cook (1774–1867) and Sarah/Sally (born Clarke) Cook (1790–1849) of Chatham. Selden Cook owned a good amount of land in Chatham, Portland, and Moodus. In his will, written in 1861 when he was seventy-one, Selden Cook bequeathed money to each of his four sons and bequeathed his real estate to his youngest son. Was he favoring his youngest son? No. Selden Cook had already distributed portions of his land to his three older sons (the oldest being Ulysses's father) before he wrote his will. In the 1840s, he had given his son Dr. Henry Evelyn Cook the property on Falls Road in Moodus. In 1845, Falls Road became Dr. Henry Evelyn Cook's home and medical office, which later became the same for Ulysses.

### A FEW WOMEN KEEP THE WOMEN'S SUFFRAGE BALL ROLLING WHILE MOST WOMEN "KEEP HOUSE"

In the 1870 census, the one in which the occupation for Ulysses was left blank, twenty-year-old Georgiana Cook's occupation was recorded as *Keep House*. Those are the same two words entered for her mother-in-law in the same house. And the same two words entered for Georgiana's forty-five-year-old mother, Lucinda, who lived alone less than a mile away in her house on North Moodus Road. And the same two words used for nearly every married woman in that year's census. Recognizing housework as an official occupation represented progress for women. In previous censuses, the occupation column for most women was left blank and the only females with occupations listed were the young mill girls, a few teachers, and the rare milliner or dressmaker. (I wish I could have witnessed the men of the 1870 census committee as they discussed the proposal to add "Keep House" as a job worthy enough to be classified as an occupation.) Small improvements in the status of women were starting to happen after the Civil War. Women were starting to be heard.

When Georgiana and Ulysses became husband and wife in 1868, twenty years had passed since the first women's rights convention in Seneca Falls. During those years, more women in the United States had become emboldened to fight for rights, especially after the Fourteenth Amendment was passed in 1868. That amendment granted citizenship to "all persons born or naturalized in the United States" and included recently freed slaves. But the amendment excluded women. Georgiana may have read about this; Moodus men and women may have talked about it. But the conversations about women's rights had not reached many ordinary Americans at this point and wouldn't reach great numbers until the 1900s.

While women's rights issues were probably not on Georgiana's priority list in 1868, her first year of marriage, a growing number of women around the nation were getting involved. *The Revolution*, the first newspaper focusing on women's rights, hit the presses in 1868. It was published by women activists in New York who felt that the mainstream newspapers covered women's issues with bias, if they covered them at all. These women did *not* support the newly proposed Fifteenth Amendment, which stated that "the right of citizens of the United States to vote shall not be denied or abridged by the United States or by any State on account of race, color, or previous condition of servitude." The women were against the amendment because they wanted the word *sex* to be added after the word *color*. (The amendment was later passed — without the addition.)

I wonder if Georgiana knew anything about the 1868 Women's Suffrage Convention in Washington, D.C. It was at this convention that Elizabeth Cady Stanton delivered her scathing "The Destructive Male" speech in which she slammed men outright, but also added "I do not wish to be understood to say that all men are hard, selfish, and brutal, for many of the most beautiful spirits the world has known have been clothed with manhood." I'm not sure the eighteen-year-old newlywed Georgiana paid much attention to Mrs. Stanton and the national women's suffrage issue.

Closer to home, in 1869, two bold women from Hartford, Connecticut, Frances Ellen Burr (1831–1923) and Isabella (born Beecher) Hooker[48] (1822–1907), formed the Connecticut Women's Suffrage Association (CWSA). They started with only 138 members and did not reach a substantial number of members until the 1910s, when Katharine Martha Houghton Hepburn (1878–1951), mother of actress Katharine Hepburn (1907–2003), assumed the leadership and grew the membership to over 32,000. By the way, Isabella Hooker was the sister of education-for-women advocate Catharine Beecher. The Beecher sisters were on opposite sides of the women's suffrage issue: Isabella promoted a women's right to vote, and Catharine campaigned against it. Harriet (born Beecher) Stowe, a third sister, a social justice advocate famous for her 1852 book *Uncle Tom's Cabin,* initially took both of her sisters' points of view into account when writing about women's suffrage, eventually supporting women's right to vote.[49] Like the Beecher sisters, women in Connecticut were not all of one voice: some were pro-suffrage, some anti-suffrage, and most were thinking, thinking, thinking about the pros and cons.

One woman who (surprising to me) fought against women's suffrage was Old Lyme's Florence Griswold (1850–1937) of Lyme Art Colony fame, whose life spanned almost the same years as Georgiana's. Ms. Griswold became a leader in the local *Connecticut Association Opposed to Woman Suffrage*, a group that eventually had chapters in nearly every Connecticut town. Women in individual towns of Connecticut formed local chapters of both the pro-suffrage and anti-suffrage groups.

Georgiana, I believe, was in the large group of women who were thinking, thinking, thinking. I did not uncover any clues about her stance on women's right to vote. However, I can infer that she leaned toward supporting it — from her confident (read headstrong) personality during her teen years as revealed through her father's letters, from her choice of a spirited husband, and from her friends who supported women's suffrage efforts. I think Ulysses supported women's suffrage too. I believe he possessed one of the "beautiful spirits" that Elizabeth Cady Stanton spoke of.

My guess is that Georgiana, like so many women of her era, would not have invested time in her early years of marriage in activism for or against the women's suffrage issue. Her days would have been filled with the many chores of keeping house, being a dutiful daughter-in-law, helping her widowed mother, shopping (in a way she never could before marriage!), supporting her husband's activities as a doctor in training, and, perhaps the most time-consuming task of all, supporting him as a musician.

One certainty in Georgiana's first year of marriage: she heard her husband beat the drum for candidate-for-president Ulysses S. Grant. Ulysses S. Grant won the election in November 1868 and became president of the United States in March 1869, at which point Ulysses S. Cook probably staged one heck of a party with his drum corps buddies.

### MUSIC AND PARADES IN MOODUS

From the inception of the Moodus Drum and Fife Corps, Ulysses was the musical director, a position he held for over forty years, until his legs couldn't march any more. This role involved hours of selecting and providing music for the group, teaching the new arrangements to the players, giving drum lessons to new members, and arranging their performances. His leadership played no small part in the success of the group, which grew with great speed in the number of members, performances, requests to perform, newspaper articles about them, and buttons burst from pride.

According to *Parker's*, the Moodus Drum and Fife Corps in the late 1860s "commenced appearing on public occasions in Moodus, East Haddam and Goodspeed's Landings, Hadlyme, East Hampton, Colchester and other nearby places. Its music met with popular approval and its local reputation was soon firmly established."[50] Georgiana likely organized the social aspects of her husband's passion, such as post-parade events, fund-raising events, and visits to their home from fellow musicians and their families. From what I've learned about Georgiana, she loved her role, and she loved being Mrs. Ulysses S. Cook, wife of the town's music man.

## The Music Man

I like to call Ulysses the Music Man of Moodus. Like Broadway's *Music Man,* invented by Meredith Willson, Ulysses was the colorful leader of the musical group that was the pride of the village.

*The Music Man* debuted as a Broadway musical in 1957 and was later adapted to film and television. Ever a favorite with professional theater companies, it was produced by East Haddam's Goodspeed Musicals at the Goodspeed Opera House in 2019.

If you have ever seen *The Music Man* performed, you have seen the fictionalized and glamorized world of Ulysses and Georgiana and Moodus. The show takes place in the early 1900s in the small town of River City, with train-traveling salesmen, a library with an unmarried woman as a librarian, pianos in homes, patriotic speeches from town leaders, town picnics, gossiping townswomen, men singing in barbershop quartets, unanimous awe for John Philip Sousa, and parades. And like Professor Harold Hill, the main character in *The Music Man,* Ulysses gave music lessons to the local boys and inspired them to become members of a marching band with bright new uniforms.

The similarities only go so far, however. Ulysses was not a con man like Professor Harold Hill, who pretended to be professor and a musician. Fake credentials were not uncommon in 1900, even in Moodus, but Ulysses was a real doctor and a real musician.

There is one more parallel between the fictional narrative of *The Music Man* and the nonfiction story of Georgiana and Ulysses: the wonderful love stories between the main characters. Professor Harold Hill and Marian the Librarian fell in love, just as Dr. Ulysses Cook and Georgiana did. The final duet in *The Music Man* captures them perfectly: "There were bells on a hill, but I never heard them ringing. No, I never heard them at all, till there was you."[51]

Few parades were more meaningful to Georgiana and Ulysses than the Decoration Day parades, which began two years after they married. In 1868, May 30th was established by the Grand Army of the Republic (GAR)[52] as Decoration Day, an annual day to commemorate the fallen soldiers of the Civil War and decorate their graves with flowers. This was the predecessor of today's Memorial Day. East Haddam's first publicly observed Decoration Day took place in 1870. The town held three separate parades — one in Moodus, one at East Haddam Landing, and one at Goodspeed's Landing. The three parades converged at the Little Haddam Cemetery (next to the Congregational church and the parsonage where Georgiana was married), where townspeople decorated the soldiers' graves with flags and flowers, and listened to an address given by the Moodus Methodist Episcopal Church pastor. The united procession, headed by the Moodus Drum and Fife Corps, then marched to the Moodus Cemetery. Georgiana and Ulysses, I'm sure, were active participants in the town's first Decoration Day festivities and every year thereafter.

I envision Georgiana at these Decoration Day parades dressed in smart clothing, wearing a new bonnet, standing in a favorite spot on the Moodus parade route, thinking of her father, putting an arm around her mother, attending to Ulysses's parents, chitchatting with the other Moodus Drum and Fife Corps wives, waving the American flag, and smiling with pride as her husband and the music marched by.

## NEW BEATS, NEW TUNES

Georgiana and Ulysses and American music entered these lively years together. American music, like Georgiana, left the weight of the Civil War years behind. The heavy hymns that were so prevalent in those years, such as "The Battle Hymn of the Republic" with lyrics written by Julia Ward Howe (1819–1910) during the war, would be replaced by light, snappy songs. Right around the corner were the John Philip Sousa years, the vaudeville years, and the years of hometown orchestras, outdoor bandstands, and family sing-alongs around the player piano. Americans were ready for upbeat music.

Music would surround Georgiana for the rest of her life. My guess is she enjoyed the music — to listen to it, or dance to it. But not to sing it or play it. I have a hunch that her musically gifted husband asked her with sweet affection to be an official listener. I have not met many Smiths who can carry a tune!

DO YOU TAKE THE EAST HADDAM ADVERTISER?

## Our National Anniversary!

# GRAND CELEBRATION IN MOODUS,

## TUESDAY, JULY 4TH, 1871.

A NOVEL PROCESSION NEARLY ONE MILE IN LENGTH!

### Dramatic Entertainment.

### Ringing of Bells.

## BOARDMAN'S CORNET BAND.

## FUN FOR THE MILLION!!

Among other attractive features of the day will be an exciting

# TUB RACE,

OPEN TO ALL COMPETITORS.

READING OF THE DECLARATION OF INDEPENDENCE.

## ORATION.    MUSIC.

The EVENING ENTERTAINMENT will consist of the

### Great Moral Drama in 5 Acts, entitled

# VICE AND VIRTUE,

performed by the

*(margin: Now is the time to subscribe. Issued weekly, for 1871-2. To be the leading paper in Middlesex county. enterprise.)*

CHAPTER 6
# High Notes and Low Notes
Georgiana in Her Twenties
1870–1880

In love, in their twenties, in their hometown, in peacetime, and in step with the grand entrance of the Gilded Age, Georgiana and Ulysses entered the 1870s.

The Gilded Age would last three decades, until 1900 when Georgiana was in her fifties. During these years, a burst of major achievements would change the lives of Georgiana and Americans forever. In these years, America had its Golden Age of Innovation and became the world's preeminent industrial nation. The post-Civil War boom in railroads fueled new industries and a rise in employment, which brought a rise in disposable income, which brought a rise in mass-produced goods, which went by train to cities with new department stores and to towns with small shops, where they would ultimately be carried off in buggies to everyday homes.

A rise in education brought a fall in illiteracy, which fed a rising wave of new and varied readers and writers. From books that later became identified as American literature, to magazines, to newspapers, to the introduction of the affordable dime novels, America was reading. A new optimism in the arts became the foundation for magnificent museums and grand libraries. New amusements and entertainments popped up: horse racing, pro-

OPPOSITE: *The top half of a newspaper advertisement promoting a July 4, 1871, Moodus celebration. Found in the archives in the Rathbun Free Memorial Library, East Haddam, Connecticut.*

fessional baseball teams, croquet, amusement parks, live theater, band concerts on town greens, musicals, circuses, medicine shows, Wild West shows, and vaudeville. A distinctly American music emerged, prompting the formations of amateur orchestras and openings of public dance halls in nearly every town. Popular Tin Pan Alley songs captured the era and were pumped out of the newly invented player pianos in saloons and home parlors. And, perhaps best of all, the Gilded Age brought the luxuries of the telephone, electricity, and indoor plumbing into homes.

With the new intricate web of trains in postbellum America, people and goods could travel farther and faster than ever before — from New York to California and from small town to small town. Early in the 1870s, a Chicago man named Aaron Montgomery Ward saw the financial possibilities inherent in the new rail system and introduced the nation's first mail-order business. His venture had been delayed a bit when the Great Chicago Fire destroyed most of his merchandise in 1871, but by the time the Gilded Age ended, the Montgomery Ward catalog[53] was one thousand pages thick and a staple in American homes. Housewives around the nation with the ability to spend money — Georgiana was one of them — were said to be seduced by it. Commonly known as the "Wish List," the catalog offered a variety of clothing from wool socks to corsets to hoop skirts, as well as items from butter molds to cellos to the newfangled bicycles.

The catalogs and the merchandise were delivered using the nation's rail and mail system. In Moodus, until late in the nineteenth century when free home delivery by the United States Postal Service reached rural areas, most residents went to the post office to pick up their mail and parcels. Some residents paid a fee to have their mail delivered. It was an exciting day in the American home when the new Montgomery Ward catalog was carried in, and the old one was relegated to the outhouse.

Of the many new rail lines in Connecticut, Georgiana would have been most familiar with the Connecticut Valley Railroad. The trains of the Valley Railroad, as it came to be called, carried passengers and goods back and forth between Hartford and Old Saybrook ten times a day on the west side of the Connecticut River. The Valley Railroad officially opened on August 24, 1871, when twelve railcars, each filled with dignitaries, made the forty-five-mile ceremonial trip from Hartford to Old Saybrook, stopping at each of the seventeen stations on the route, where they were greeted by bands playing and crowds cheering. The closest station to Georgiana and others in East Haddam was Goodspeed's Station across the Connecticut River in Tylerville, a village in Haddam.[54] For Georgiana, the opening of the Valley Railroad marked the beginning of an exciting new way to travel. For East Haddam, it marked the beginning of the railroad replacing the Connecticut River as the area's major transportation artery, forever changing the future of the town.

The iron horses on the west side of the river were one impossible hurdle away from the town of East Haddam, which had prospered when the river ruled the economy. For the next forty years, to board a train, East Haddamites had to take a ferry across the Connecticut River to the west-side-of-the-river towns of Haddam or Chester. There were no tracks on the east side of the river, and the bridge connecting east to west did not open until 1913. By that time, towns on the west side of the river, such as Middletown, had reaped the economic benefits from direct access to the railroad. The population numbers tell the story: Between 1870 and 1890, while the population of Connecticut grew by 39 percent, the towns on the west side of the river grew at high rates too — Middletown by 37 percent, Essex and Old Saybrook by 22 percent each, and Chester by 16 percent. But East Haddam, on the east side of the river, lost 14 percent of its residents.[55]

Even so, East Haddam managed to remain prosperous and active during the Gilded Age with twine manufacturing in Moodus, other industries, new retail stores, attractive residential and rural areas, new steamship lines on the river, and, importantly, the construction of the Goodspeed Opera House by East Haddam native William Goodspeed. This majestic five-story Victorian building on the bank of the Connecticut River has thankfully been preserved in its Gilded Age glory. A prominent "1876," the year of its construction, still proudly remains engraved in stone high above the entrance doors on the central tower.

Goodspeed Opera House officially opened on October 24, 1877. Georgiana was twenty-eight. I like to think that she and Ulysses made the five-mile trip from Moodus down to the river in a stylish horse-drawn carriage for the lavish opening night, which was attended by six hundred people.

The Goodspeed Opera House was not a venue for operas as its name suggests. Rather, it was a theater for professional comedic plays. As people looked to get away from the frenzied pace of American progress in overcrowded, smoggy cities where railroads and industries puffed away, the Goodspeed on the Connecticut River offered a refreshing change. Audiences came from all over Connecticut and from other states as well, helping East Haddam begin its evolution into an entertainment and vacation destination.

The village of Moodus, particularly, began a long transformation that would leave behind its nineteenth-century, mill-dominated identity as the "Twine Capital of America" and move into its twentieth-century, resort-dominated identity as the "Catskills of Connecticut."

America's progress and the unfettered spending at the top level of society provided the sparkle for the Gilded Age. But there was another side, a dark side, in the form of imbalanced wealth and political scandals. Mark Twain, who lived in Connecticut during the Gilded Age, and who displayed quite a bit of glitter himself (have you seen his 1874 Hartford house?), coined the term *Gilded Age* in 1873 with his satirical novel, *The Gilded Age, a Tale of Today*. Georgiana and Ulysses would not come close to the Mark Twain-level of wealth, but they did lead a pretty nice life within their own circle.

### A HOME OF THEIR OWN

In the early 1870s, after living with Ulysses's parents since their wedding in 1868, Georgiana and Ulysses moved into a home of

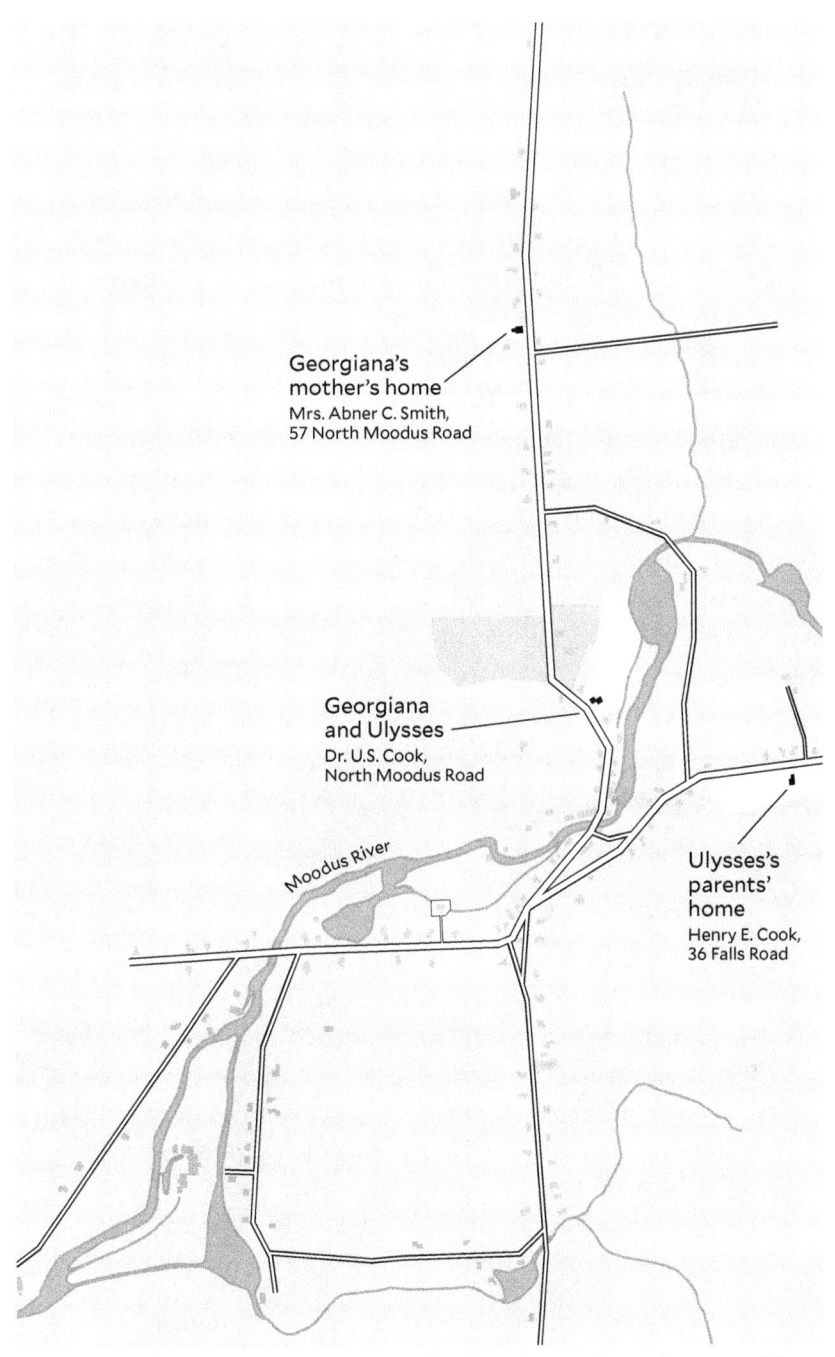

*Moodus, 1874. Georgiana and Ulysses lived within walking distance of her mother and his parents.*

their own, the first home in which Georgiana would be the lady of the house. On an 1874 map of Moodus, their house is located on North Moodus Road, halfway between Georgiana's mother up the road and Ulysses's parents down the road.

Before they moved, Ulysses had successfully completed his apprenticeship with his father and had opened an infirmary, sometimes referred to as a sanitarium, for cancer treatments. I have not been able to determine where the infirmary was located. At the bottom of an 1880 map of Moodus, thirty-six buildings are listed by name. One is "Dr. Cook's Infirmary," but the location of the infirmary and the locations of most buildings listed are not pinpointed on the map. In *Beers 1903*, the biographical entry about Ulysses implies that the infirmary was a separate facility from his medical office, which presumably was in his home. The entry reads: "Returning home [from school] he began the study of medicine under his father, and devoted much time to a special course in the treatment of cancer. Upon his father's death [1874] he succeeded to the entire practice, which he has greatly extended. At present Dr. Cook conducts a sanitarium, as he did for many years prior to his father's death."

## What Was Dr. Cook's Treatment for Cancer?

Dr. Ulysses S. Cook specialized in the treatment of cancer from the early 1870s to 1909 in Moodus, Connecticut. Ulysses treated his patients with Thomsonian Medicine, a system of medicine developed by botanist Dr. Samuel Thomson (1769–1843), whose methods were both popular and controversial in the nineteenth century. In 1822, Thomson published his *New Guide to Health, or, Botanic Family Physician*,[56] which served as a guide to physicians.

Here is how Dr. Thomson explains his theory for treating cancer:

> Heat is life. Cold, or the loss of heat, is the universal cause of disease and death. Whatever will increase internal heat, remove obstructions from the system, restore the digestive

powers of the stomach, and produce a natural perspiration is universally applicable in all cases of disease, and therefore may be considered as a general remedy.

In his book, he guides physicians to take these five steps with patients:

1. A hot-air or vapour bath.
2. An emetic [something to induce vomiting], prepared and administered according to the direction hereafter given.
3. An injection to evacuate the bowels.
4. After the operation of the emetic, the vapour bath is again applied, to restore a natural warmth to the system.
5. Light nourishment is to be given after the emetic operates.

Dr. Thomson's manual has over five hundred pages of explicitly detailed directions, as well as recipes with herbs, roots, tonics, oils, eggs, hops, vegetables, fruits, and other substances for the treatment of all types of diseases. Here are a few verbatim extracts from the long section on the treatment for breast cancer:

- The constitutional treatment for cancer should consist of employment of such means as are best adapted to improve the condition of the general health. There are no specific remedies for the cure of cancer.
- An occasional hot air bath and an emetic; the use of the No. 3 pills to prevent the mucous membranes from coating with unhealthy secretions, taking as many as 6 or 8 of the pills about the middle of the forenoon and afternoon; and occasionally from one to three or four of the compound lobelia [a plant that induces vomiting] pills, constitute the remedies best suited for regulating the constitutional health.
- If there be acidity of the stomach, and the bowels costive [constipated], pulverized charcoal will be beneficial. It may be taken prepared in water, composition or spice bitters tea. The dose of the charcoal is a large teaspoonful; to be repeated two or three times a day, before meals.

- When a violent paroxysm of pain comes on, it may be mitigated by the use of the warm foot bath, or of the vapour bath, and the use of enemas composed of some mild stimulant, such as composition of pennyroyal tea, with the addition of from a half of a teaspoon of lobelia, either the powder, tincture [alcoholic extract] or third preparation. Difficulty in breathing will be relieved by the treatment above described.
- Applications to the tumour before the skin is broken: During the early periods of cancerous tumour, [the tumours] should be kept warm and the skin in a perspiration, by the application of some simple kind of salve spread on silk oil-cloth, or by wearing a piece of rabbit skin with the fur side to the breast. Poultices are to be applied when the tumour softens and the skin becomes inflamed. The poultice may be made of elm, ginger and cracker [high-fiber crackers were part of an American health craze of the 1820s[57]] or any soft emollient substance, adding a portion of lobelia powder, say a tablespoonful to each poultice.

(I hope the infirmary was not in Georgiana's home!)

## KEEPING HOUSE

Georgiana and Ulysses lived in their North Moodus Road home for the rest of the 1870s and the early 1880s. Keeping house at this time was not an easy job with no indoor plumbing, no electricity, and no refrigeration. But it may have been easier for Georgiana than most, as she had a live-in servant. According to the East Haddam June 1880 census of 504 families, only twenty-one families had a domestic servant. The households on this list read like an 1880 *Who's Who List* for East Haddam, with the prominent and wealthy families of Attwood, Boardman, Johnson, Mitchell, Purple, and Goodspeed included.

Georgiana, at age thirty at the time of the 1880 census, was the youngest wife in East Haddam to have a servant in her household. Nellie B. Skinner was her name. She was nineteen and may have been related to Georgiana's father's Civil War tentmate, Horatio

Chapman, whose wife was born Rosanna Skinner from Skinnerville in Chatham. However, lest we think Georgiana and Ulysses were part of the elite set of East Haddam (they weren't), there may be an explanation for why the Cooks had a servant: If Ulysses's medical office was in his North Moodus Road home, and his infirmary was on the property, Nellie may have been responsible for housekeeping of the rooms used by patients in both facilities. Quite a bit of cleanup would have been necessary after Dr. Cook's Thomsonian purging treatments.

As in the 1870 census, Georgiana's occupation on the 1880 census, like the occupation of nearly every married woman in that census with or without a servant, was entered as "Keeping House." If and how Georgiana and Nellie Skinner divided tasks, I don't know. What I do know is that there were many tasks to be done.

Like households everywhere in America until the end of the nineteenth century, one major time-consuming chore was water management, which often fell into the women's sphere. With no indoor plumbing, women would have pumped well water into buckets, carried the buckets inside, filled the kettles and the pots for cooking, filled the pitchers for drinking, filled the basins for washing clothes and housecleaning, and filled the washstand pitchers sitting in the bowls in the bedroom. No indoor plumbing also meant outhouses and chamber pots, which needed routine attention. Filling a big tub with heated water for baths was a weekly chore. And let's not forget the job of emptying all that dirty water outside.

Fires were another arduous responsibility for the women of this era. With no electricity, the tending of fires was a constant requirement for light, heat, and cooking. Candles and oil lamps, maintained by the housewife, were used for light. Wood was essential for heat and cooking. It was the man's job to chop and stack the wood, but it was the woman's job to keep the fireplaces and the stove lit and fed. Georgiana, in her first years of marriage, probably had a cast-iron stove fueled by wood.

During the 1870s, the wealthiest homes began to use coal. Some called it the *fuel of the fashionable*,[58] partly because of the cosmetic appeal of the new, intricately decorated cast-iron stoves. By the end of the Gilded Age at the turn of the century, coal would be in the average home. Whether using wood or coal, in addition to starting and maintaining a fire in the stove, it was also the woman's job to remove the ashes and adjust the flue and damper at least twice daily. Some estimate that a housewife spent four hours each day tending to the stove. Fire prevention was foremost in the mind of the nineteenth-century housewife whose long, highly flammable skirts, shawls, and hair came within inches of flames many times a day.

And there was no electric refrigeration in the 1870s. Georgiana would have had perishables, such as butter and milk, delivered often to her doorstep. The essential, and strong, local iceman would have made frequent visits, loading a large block of ice onto his back and lugging it to an outbuilding. There the perishables could lean against it, and chips of ice could be carved away when needed. Georgiana may have been one of the lucky housewives to have access to the newly invented indoor wooden ice box inside her home. This ice box had a drip tray beneath it to catch melting ice. The tray needed to be emptied often, also a housewife's task.

Managing a garden and food was another layer of responsibility. Beans in a pot, bread in the oven, eggs and poultry, apples from the orchard, fresh vegetables from the backyard garden, and root vegetables stored in a root cellar during the off-season were the likely staples of the Cook household.

Georgiana was in her twenties in the 1870s (she turned thirty in July 1879) and would have easily managed to keep up with her occupation, but, as much as she liked home, she also liked to go out. She hadn't been a homebody as a teenage girl, nor would she be as a middle-aged woman, so I doubt she spent all her time keeping house when she was a young wife. I imagine Georgiana in her first years of marriage frequently leaving the house to walk downtown for errands or to visit friends for local gossip. I picture her walking with her back straight, wearing a long dress with a high neck, holding her head up, and donning a stylish hat. Victorian style, the fashion of the Gilded Age,[59] dictated that her long hair would have been pinned up in public, and that a tightly laced corset would have straightened her back and cinched her waist.

### SEPARATE SPHERES AND COMMON INTERESTS

When it came to work, women and men operated in separate spheres in the nineteenth century, and it looks like Georgiana stayed in hers. The 1924 newspaper article about her and Ulysses's fifty-sixth wedding anniversary reported that Georgiana was "an ideal companion and home-maker." She would have stayed out of the sphere of her husband, who somehow successfully harmonized the somber notes of treating sick cancer patients with the merry notes of playing in the hearty drum corps. A married woman's place was in the home — not in her husband's office, and definitely not in the testosterone-powered Moodus Drum and Fife Corps.

The Moodus Drum and Fife Corps made a name for themselves in the 1870s. Early in the decade, they increased their local activities, playing in East Haddam's parades, at political campaigns, and other celebrations. By the middle of the decade, word about the talented musicians from the little village of Moodus had spread beyond East Haddam. They were invited to perform at parades and events across Connecticut, and in 1875, at the Boston, Massachusetts, centennial celebration of the famous 1775 Battle of Bunker Hill. *Parker's* records that the "period of greatest activity" for the Moodus Drum and Fife Corps was 1876 to 1900.[60] These were the years that Ulysses was the musical director at the core of the corps.

After their performance in Boston, for which they wore borrowed uniforms, the corps began the expensive and time-consuming initiative to invest in its own uniforms. They continued to borrow uniforms for performances until 1877, when they donned their new uniforms at the state drummers' convention and took first prize. It was the first of many awards. On June 19, 1878, the corps hosted "Moodus Day," a gala celebration that attracted other Connecticut fife and drum corps and a prestigious corps from

New York. Businesses closed, buildings were decorated, and banners were hung. According to *Parker's,* "Perhaps the village never saw at any other time so large an assembly of people there," and goes on to say that "a bountiful banquet was served by the ladies in Music Hall."[61] Moodus's Music Hall, in downtown Moodus, was used for dances, concerts, celebrations, and musical groups. You can bet that the Music Hall was a familiar place of Georgiana and Ulysses, and that Georgiana, at age twenty-eight, was one of the "ladies" who served at the banquet. She and Ulysses wouldn't have missed one minute of the "Moodus Day" event.

The Moodus Drum and Fife Corps in their Continental uniforms. Ulysses is second from left. Photo courtesy of the East Haddam Museum and Historical Society.

## Ulysses and the Uniforms

(Much of the information below about the uniforms of the Moodus Drum and Fife Corps is from the blog "Ancient History Unraveled, Part 2: How the Ancients Got their Uniforms," retrieved July 1, 2020, from *historyoftheancients.wordpress.com.* This blog is dedicated to preserving the historical facts and lore about Connecticut's Fife and Drum Corps. The blog's authors give credit to the Moodus Drum and Fife Corps for influencing the adoption of continental uniforms by the "ancients," the many individual corps of the Connecticut Ancient Fife and Drum Corps.)

For their first seventeen years (1860–1877), the members of the Moodus Drum and Fife Corps did not have uniforms. They performed in street clothes or in uniforms borrowed from other corps. As their reputation for outstanding music grew, and invitations to perform started to come in from more Connecticut towns and other states, they wanted their own uniforms. By 1877, they had them.

The uniforms were, in a word, stunning. They were the visual equivalent of the patriotic, loud, colorful, and historically authentic music played by the corps. As replicas of the one-hundred-year-old uniforms used by George Washington's Continental Army, they were a perfect match for the corps' one-hundred-year-old Revolutionary War-era drumming style.

The uniform initiative began in 1875, when the corps was fifteen, Ulysses was thirty, and the United States of America was ninety-nine. The Moodus Drum and Fife Corps, because of its excellence in music and its Revolutionary War-era drumming perfection for which Ulysses's strictness can take credit, was invited to play at the centennial celebration of the famous 1775 Battle of Bunker Hill in Boston, Massachusetts. For this event, the men borrowed uniforms. And it was at this event they saw the striking uniforms of Hartford's illustrious Putnam Phalanx.

The Phalanx, founded to commemorate the American Revolution, was a private militia made up of prominent, rich, and politically powerful Hartford men. All members of the Phalanx wore facsimiles of a major general's uniform from the Revolutionary War's Continental Army. The drum corps of the Phalanx also wore the uniform, but without the officer rank insignias of epaulets, sword belts, swords, and sashes. The drummers did, however, wear the same handsome brass-buttoned and red-trimmed navy coats, tan vests and trousers, tricornered hats, and fancy boot tops. The uniforms of the Phalanx had been replicated with historical precision; some of the Phalanx's members (with connections!) had literally borrowed the uniform worn by George Washington from the federal government in Washington, D.C. and brought it to Hartford to have a replica made.

Ulysses and his fellow Moodus corps members were convinced that the Phalanx uniforms were perfect for their group. It took a couple of years, but, in 1877, the men of the Moodus Drum and Fife Corps appeared for a Connecticut drumming contest, for which they won first prize, in bright new uniforms that wowed the crowd. According to the "Ancient History Unraveled, Part 2" blog, "As late as 1879, press reports continued to comment favorably on the new 'Continentals' sported by the 'gentleman drummers of Moodus.'"

Ulysses was as particular and protective of the corps' uniform style as he was of their style of drumming. He had been taught to drum by the Moodus drum corps' founder, Hezekiah Percival, who had been taught and certified by militia drummer Samuel B. Wilcox, a drum major in Connecticut's militia. Ulysses became a stickler for preserving his master's style. With strict teaching and possibly a bit of stubbornness, he kept the historical veracity of the ancient militia drumming style alive for the next generation and, as it turns out, for all future generations. Moodus Drum and Fife Corps members have passed these unique drumming techniques, now called "Moodus style," through the generations into the twenty-first century. James Clark writes in *Connecticut's Fife & Drum Tradition*,[62] a book which uses a photo of the nineteenth-century Moodus Drum and Fife Corps on its cover, and which includes praise for the Moodus Drum and Fife Corps' significant part in Connecticut's fife and drum history, "The Moodus style is an astonishingly accurate preservation of early martial music." Clark adds that the authentic ancient militia fife and drum sound can be disturbing: "The Moodus musicians generally make a lot of noise, they march very slowly and nothing is prettified: the drummers don't hold back, and the fifers do not add sweetening harmonies. The music is heavy and purposive."[63] This is the kind of music George Washington and his troops

> would have heard. To this day, the Moodus Drum and Fife Corps plays the authentic continental music and wears continentals, just as Ulysses did.
>
> The Moodus uniforms soon became the model for other Connecticut fife and drum corps. But Ulysses held the design close to the vest. One story tells about the determination of the Mattatuck Drum Band, formed in Connecticut in 1881, to obtain the original Moodus uniform design from Ulysses: "Some leader of their group came to see Dr. U. S. Cook, drum major for the Moodus Corps, and wanted to borrow one of their new uniforms. Dr. Cook was reluctant to let him have it, so he thought if he asked him for a deposit of $50 [about $1,265 in 2020], this man would refuse to pay and leave. But evidently the man came prepared and immediately 'peeled off' the bills and gave the deposit." In the end, the Mattatuck Drum Band copied Moodus's uniforms.
>
> Through this uniform story, we get a glimpse of Georgiana's husband, Ulysses — a proud, practical, productive, protective, persistent, and passionate patriot.

Would Georgiana have gone to the out-of-town events of the corps? There are no references to wives in the minutes of the corps, which could mean that wives did not accompany their husbands to out-of-town events. On the other hand, it could be that wives, who were not members of the corps, were simply not mentioned when recording the corps's official business. To help answer the question, I consulted James Clark, the author of the book *Connecticut's Fife and Drum Tradition*. He believes that Georgiana and other wives might have joined their husbands on out-of-town trips when a social event followed a performance. Perhaps Georgiana made the trip to New York City in February 1879, when the corps played for an audience of three thousand in an elaborate fife and drum corps competition and, after the show, joined the other corps members at the banquet and ball.

One event I feel confident Georgiana would have attended was the *Battle Flag Day* parade in Hartford. The Moodus Drum and Fife Corps was one of the many groups from around the state who proudly marched in the one-time parade. It was held on September 17, 1879, to honor the state's veterans of the Civil War, the conflict that had taken the life of Georgiana's father. Civil War veterans grouped into their old regiments and marched while holding what was left of the regiment and national flags they had carried in battles.

The war had ended fourteen years earlier, but one hundred thousand spectators[64] watched as eight thousand Connecticut Civil War veterans, still passionate about the flag that fifty-five thousand men of the state had fought for and that fifty-five hundred had died for and that some uncountable number had been maimed for, marched with their former regiments. Some limped. Some had empty sleeves pinned up. Some could not walk and rode in carriages.

Georgiana would have been in the crowd to applaud the men of the 20th Connecticut Volunteer Regiment, her father's fellow soldiers. She and Ulysses and many others from the patriotic towns of East Haddam and Chatham would have taken the one-and-a-half-hour train ride on the Connecticut Valley Railroad to Hartford. Perhaps Georgiana's mother and brothers went with her. Perhaps she stood with other wives from the Moodus Drum and Fife Corps. Or perhaps she stood with the family of Horatio Chapman, who marched in the parade and whose heart and mind were certainly filled with memories of his tentmate, the comrade he had marched next to for hundreds of long miles over two-and-a-half long years.

The veterans ended their march at the new-in-January Connecticut State Capitol building in Hartford, placing their flags in specially-made cases to be preserved. The flags remain on display to this day in the Capitol's Hall of Flags.

## A FUN-LOVING COUPLE

Parades, all more joyful than the Battle Flag Day parade, were high notes of the world that Georgiana and Ulysses delighted in together, as were other celebrations, social events, dances, and musical and dramatic performances. In the historical room records of the Rathbun Free Memorial Library in East Haddam, I found a full-page advertisement in the *East Haddam Advertiser* for the July 4, 1871, GRAND CELEBRATION OF MODUS.

This was the kind of fun Georgiana and Ulysses, then twenty-two and twenty-five, and the townspeople of Moodus enjoyed in the days when all entertainment was in person and unplugged. Here are the highlights:

- A NOVEL PROCESSION NEARLY ONE MILE IN LENGTH!
- 40 HORSES.
- RINGING OF BELLS.
- BOARDMAN'S CORNET BAND.
- TUB RACE open to all competitors.
- READING OF THE DECLARATION OF INDEPENDENCE.
- A GRAND DRAMATIC MATINEE in the afternoon under a mammoth TENT of 6,000 FEET of CANVASS.
- A GREAT MORAL DRAMA IN 5 ACTS, ENTITLED "VICE AND VIRTUE" *as the evening entertainment performed by the* MOODUS DRAMATIC ASSOCIATION.

Note the last item. Guess who was in the cast of this *great moral drama!* Georgiana and Ulysses! *Vice and Virtue* was "a rip-roaring melodrama with thrills and laughter."[65] Georgiana and Ulysses played lively minor characters who flirted and danced with each other. Ulysses played two parts — *Old Johnson* and the *Bar Keeper,* and Georgiana played *Patience,* a role that involved lively dancing.

*Vice and Virtue* was also titled *The Drunkard*.[66] The show had debuted in Boston twenty-seven years earlier, in 1844. Using comedy to show the evil effects of alcohol on family life, the show became a popular *temperance play* — so popular that it helped kick-start the temperance movement in the United States, the social movement against the consumption of alcohol. *The Drunkard* continued to be performed throughout Prohibition (1920–1933), through the rest of the twentieth century, and was still being performed in 2020.

Participating in a temperance play is not to say that Georgiana and Ulysses were teetotalers. As you read on, I think you'll conclude with me that they were not.

### THE TEMPERANCE AND SUFFRAGE SISTERS

The temperance movement had gained momentum by the time Georgiana and Ulysses performed in *Vice and Virtue* in 1871. The movement was led by women. Married women — powerless to earn their own living, powerless to remove their children from a violent household, powerless to divorce, powerless to change laws because they could not vote — were often victims of husbands who drank too much. Women bound together as they never had before to support temperance. In 1873, they founded the soon-to-be-powerful Woman's Christian Temperance Union (WCTU), which quickly became the largest women's organization in the United States (and later, in the world). Women wanted to vote about alcohol laws, so temperance and the right to vote became causes that women increasingly linked.

Georgiana was in her twenties when the two movements were conceived and the shell around what would become known as the *new woman* began to crack. Inside, pecking away to get out, was a less constrained woman whose life would extend beyond her

OPPOSITE: *The bottom half of a newspaper advertisement promoting a July 4, 1871, Moodus celebration. Found in the archives in the Rathbun Free Memorial Library, East Haddam, Connecticut. Ulysses's and Georgiana's names ("U Cook" and "Mrs Cook") are highlighted.*

The EVENING ENTERTAINMENT will consist of the

# Great Moral Drama in 5 Acts, entitled
# VICE AND VIRTUE,

performed by the

## MOODUS DRAMATIC ASSOCIATION,

supported by the following Dramatis Personae:

| | |
|---|---|
| Edward Middleton, | NELSON H BOWERS |
| Lawyer Cribbs, | JOSEPH P MITCHELL |
| William Dowton, | E E JOHNSON |
| Farmer Gates, | WM CONE |
| Farmer Stevens, | EDWARD CHAFFEE |
| Old Johnson, | U COOK |
| Sam, | ED MITCHELL |
| First Loafer, | |
| Second Loafer, | |
| Mr Kincolan, | H B NILES |
| Landlord, | J G BARBER |
| Bar Keeper, | U COOK |
| Watchman, | |
| Mary Wilson, | MRS WM PURPLE |
| Agnes Dowton (Maniac) | CLARA MITCHELL |
| Mrs Wilson, | MRS BARBER |
| Patience, | MRS COOK |
| Julia, | MISS J MITCHELL |
| Miss Spindle, | MRS HOLCOMB |

Village Loafers, Watchmen, &c.

| | |
|---|---|
| Leader of Vocal Music, | JAMES ALEXANDER |
| Leader of Orchestra, | E GLADWIN |
| Business Manager, | JOHN G BARBER |

**Tickets for both Entertainments 50c.**
**Single Tickets  -  -  -  -  25c.**

be obtained at all the stores and at the Office of the *Advertiser*.

Afternoon Matinee commences at 3 o'clock,
Evening         "            "       8      "

home duties; a more vocal woman who would speak up publicly about social problems and solutions; and a resolute woman who would advocate equal rights as a citizen of the nation. It would take a long time for the *new woman* to poke her head out. She first had to break through the male-dominated newspapers that were the major source for influencing opinions in the 1870s.

For example, when women were not allowed to vote in the November 1872 presidential election, and early suffragist Susan B. Anthony (1820–1906) led a few women in New York, to cast ballots, the *New York Times* covered the brazen event with an insignificant one paragraph in the "Minor Topics" section of the paper. Anthony and her "little band of nine ladies," as the then-misogynistic *Times* phrased it, cast their ballots for incumbent Ulysses S. Grant. Georgiana was twenty-three at the time. A whopping forty-eight more years would go by before the *new woman* would fully emerge and legally vote for president, which happened in 1920 with the ratification of the Nineteenth Amendment, when Georgiana was seventy-one.

One of the nation's earliest and loudest voices for women's rights resided in Hartford, Connecticut. I have mentioned her before — Isabella Beecher Hooker, one of the founders of the Connecticut Woman Suffrage Association (CWSA). In 1877, Isabella pulled off a major win for women in the state: she convinced the all-male state legislature to pass the Connecticut Married Women's Property Act. In fairness to men, Isabella's husband, Thomas Hooker, and the other courageous men who voted to pass this law deserve credit too. But Isabella was the primary mover and shaker. Until this law, a married woman could not own property. If a woman owned property at the time of her wedding, or if she inherited property during her marriage, her husband became sole owner of it. The 1877 act allowed a married woman — and let's face it, most women in the nineteenth century were married — to retain control of property in her name. As epochal as this law was in the movement for equal rights for all married Connecticut women, only a limited number of women, predominantly rich and white such as Isabella Hooker, were involved in the state's women's rights issues during the 1870 decade.

Ulysses probably read about the 1877 act in the *Hartford Times*. According to one of Ulysses's obituaries in the 1920s, he subscribed to this paper continuously in his adult life. Georgiana, if she was like most nineteenth-century women, did not read the newspaper as regularly as her husband. Even when women read the newspapers, most did not follow political issues with the same interest as men. In small towns like East Haddam, it may be that women, including Georgiana, did not learn about this legal change in women's property rights or about the CWSA and the growing number of women interested in speaking up for a change in women's rights. (When I searched the CWSA records, I found only one member from East Haddam. The handwriting is difficult to decipher, but I believe her name was Nancy M. Bissell.) Like so many women of those early days of the women's rights movement in the 1870s, Georgiana would start to see and hear little bits of news about women wanting to change their role.

### GEORGIANA'S BROTHERS

By the end of the 1870 decade, Georgiana's brothers, Edgar and Frank, had grown into productive young men who held steady jobs. Edgar, who had been living in a Middletown boarding house and working as a joiner in 1870, at some point during the decade, landed a job with the great employer of the Gilded Age, the railroad. In 1877, when he was twenty-six, Edgar married eighteen-year-old Harriett (Hattie) Dibble (1859–1920) from the Connecticut shoreline town of Old Saybrook. They made their home with Harriett's widowed mother in Old Saybrook. Perhaps Edgar had met Harriett when his train stopped at one of the three Connecticut Valley Railroad station stops in Old Saybrook. It's possible that Edgar and Harriett were Georgiana's first connection to Westbrook, the western part of Old Saybrook that had split off to become its own town in 1840, and the shoreline town that would come to play a major role in Georgiana's life.

Georgiana's younger brother Frank took a more adventurous ride before getting married and settling down. According to *Beers 1903*, "When he was fifteen [1869], he went to Deep River, Conn., and was employed in a hotel there, by a Mr. Kellogg, as chore boy, receiving ten dollars [about $190 in 2020] a month with board and lodging." In 1869, Martin David Kellogg (1834–1919) was thirty-five and working as hotel keeper in Deep River, then called Saybrook. Mr. Kellogg had grown up in the Tartia section of Chatham, next to Abner C. Smith's uncle, Washington S. Ackley, and other Ackleys and Brainerds. I think it's fair to assume that Frank was hired based on the connections between his father's Tartia family and Mr. Kellogg.

Frank spent the next seven years living in different communities — Deep River, Hartford, New York, and northern Michigan. With the exception of northern Michigan, where, at age eighteen, he and Martin Kellogg made a failed attempt to get into the lumber business, Frank worked in hotels. At age twenty-two in 1876, after a few years' experience at the American Hotel in Hartford and at a summer hotel in Cayuga Lake, N.Y., Frank returned to live in his mother's house in Moodus. He took over management of the Barker House, a hotel in downtown Moodus, working for the widow of Charles Barker, the former proprietor. The Barker House was the beginning of Frank's successful and lifelong career in hotel management, a career that came with highs and lows for him — and for Georgiana too.

Two years after returning to Moodus, in October 1878, Frank married Sarah Jane Moody (1859–1954), a local girl. He was twenty-four; she was nineteen. Her large family (she had nine siblings) was one of the many Irish families who had fled to the United States after the Great Famine in Ireland in the 1840s and found Moodus to their liking. Sarah was four when they arrived. Her father was a farmer and her older brothers worked in the cotton mills, where many in the workforce were Irish immigrants.[67] The Moody family put down roots and remained in the area for the rest of their lives, all marrying local people as Sarah did.

## HIGH AND LOW NOTES

When Sarah and Frank married, they made their home with Lucinda in her North Moodus Road home, just up the road from Georgiana and Ulysses. Frank's marriage gave Georgiana the sister she never had and gave Ulysses the brother he never had. Georgiana was ten years older than Sarah; Ulysses was nine years older than Frank. My guess is that Frank and Sarah looked up to them. Sarah, a young newlywed joining the Smith family, would have turned to Georgiana for advice, social connections, and friendship. Frank, who had spent most of his life without a father, probably admired and sought attention, maybe even approval, from his older, wiser brother-in-law. The two couples — Ulysses and Georgiana Cook and Frank and Sarah Smith — were a close foursome for the rest of their lives. They shared property; they shared holidays, celebrations, laughs, mischief, and tragedies; and they shared love and care for Lucinda. The marriage of Frank and Sarah in 1878 was indeed one of the high notes of Georgiana's life.

On a low note during this decade, Ulysses lost both parents. In 1874, Dr. Henry Evelyn Cook died at age sixty-five. His wife, Elizabeth, lived for another six years. Across the street from the elder Cooks on Falls Road lived the Lords — Daniel Chapman Lord and his wife Elizabeth (born Gates). Four years after Elizabeth Cook lost her husband, Elizabeth Lord, who was eighteen years younger than Elizabeth Cook, lost her husband. At some point, Elizabeth Cook's health failed to the point of her needing care. In the June 1880 census, Elizabeth Cook is recorded at age seventy-one with a "nervous disability" (census language). She had a servant with her. Also living with her and probably caring for her, was the younger widow Elizabeth Lord and her three sons, ages seventeen to twenty-two. Elizabeth Strickland Cook died in November 1880 at age seventy-two at Georgiana and Ulysses's home,[68] where she was likely nursed in her final days.

Deaths of people in their sixties and seventies in the late nineteenth century were not unexpected. Life expectancy didn't move up to age sixty until the 1930s, after the breakthroughs of vaccinations and sanitation countered many causes of death. Still, the loss of both parents would have had a profound impact on Ulysses, who had spent nearly every day of his life with them or within a mile of them, and whose life had been shaped by their love, guidance, pride, professional training, and musical talent. As Ulysses and Georgiana entered the next decade, only one of their parents remained alive: Georgiana's mother, Lucinda Smith, who was in great health at age fifty-five, and whose parents, Horace and Sylvia Arnold, were hale and hearty in their eighties across the river in Haddam.

Perhaps the lowest note of the decade for Georgiana and Ulysses was the realization that they would not have children. This was a time in history when most married couples started families soon after they wed. A small number of couples may have chosen not to have children, but I don't believe Georgiana and Ulysses were among them. As I absorbed Georgiana's life for this book, I discovered a woman who had all the right stuff for motherhood and was married to a man who would have made a great father. But, by the end of the 1870s, married ten years and turning thirty, Georgiana likely lost hope in bearing a child.

How Georgiana felt when she learned the news that Frank and Sarah, married less than two years, were expecting a child is a point to ponder. My hunch is she was unselfishly delighted.

The baby arrived on October 11, 1880. It was a girl, the first child of the next generation. Frank and Sarah, with a powerful show of love and admiration for Georgiana, named the baby **Georgiana Cook Smith (1880–1942).**

Which was perhaps the highest note of the decade.

*Georgiana and Ulysses's home was at 36 Falls Road, Moodus, Connecticut. Photo taken 2022.*

CHAPTER 7
# Riding the Wave
## Georgiana in Her Thirties
## 1880–1890

Georgiana was thirty when the 1880 decade began. Some would say she was entering the prime of her life. Some would say America was too. In this decade, the nation swelled toward its crest as the greatest economic power in the world. Riding the wave of prosperity were Georgiana and Ulysses, enjoying every splash.

### A BEAUTIFULLY APPOINTED HOME IN MOODUS

This was the decade when Georgiana and Ulysses built the Moodus home they would live in for the rest of their lives together. It was the house where Ulysses would have his medical office and the house in which he would die at age eighty. It was the house where, for over forty years, Georgiana and Ulysses entertained friends with food and drink and music. And style. According to a newspaper article in 1924, "The Cook home has always been a delightful place to go, either on special occasions or to make a friendly call, a home that serves fine and generous food — the Cook kind."[69] *Beers 1903* describes Georgiana and Ulysses's home as their "beautifully appointed private home."[70]

Ulysses inherited his childhood house on Falls Road in Moodus after his mother died in November 1880. However, he and Georgiana did not move in right away. The old Cook house apparently did not suit his and Georgiana's needs, because, in 1883, Ulysses sold it "for removal," meaning the house would be lifted from its foundation and brought to another location.[71] In the late nineteenth century, it was not unusual to move a house from one location to another by horse, oxen or boat.

In this case, the Cook house was sold to Albert E. Purple. Albert (1843–1924) and Ulysses (1845–1925) lived almost identical lifespans in Moodus. The Purple family and the Cook family, each with deep roots in the East Haddam area, had been well-acquainted for several generations. The signatures of Albert, at age eighteen, and his mother appear as witnesses on the 1861 will of Ulysses's grandfather Selden Cook. When Albert E. Purple, at age forty, bought the old Cook house, he was the well-known owner of the mill across the street, the well-known merchant whose popular dry goods store in the center of Moodus carried his name, the well-loved man from the well-loved family whose three children had died at young ages, the well-respected citizen who had served as a state representative of East Haddam in his thirties and would later serve as the judge of probate, and well on his way to become the wealthiest man in town.[72]

On the vacated foundation of the old Cook house, Georgiana and Ulysses built a new house with accommodations for Ulysses's medical practice and, I'm guessing, according to Georgiana's tastes. Today the house is located on Connecticut Route 149 at 36 Falls Road, directly next to the Moodus Post Office. Over the last hundred years, the house has been updated and enlarged, but if you look at a current photograph of the lovely yellow house, you can see the original façade of the home from Georgiana's time: a farmhouse style home with two stories, an attic, and a generous front porch. I'd like to think that the ocular attic window that gives the house a faintly Greek Revival air and the Victorian gingerbread-trimmed porch were there in Georgiana's day as well.

Ulysses also inherited 110 acres of land. Over his lifetime, he sold or gifted all but the three acres of land surrounding the house. When he died in 1925, his property in Moodus was described in his will, in which he bequeathed everything to Georgiana, as "Land and buildings at Moodus, East Haddam, Conn. Three Acres more or less, frame dwelling house, garage, barn and shed." The value was $6,575 in 1925. That's about $97,000 in 2020 dollars, an amount that would represent the value of the house before additions and renovations were made after Georgiana sold it to the town of East Haddam in 1928, which led to the repurposing of the building into a twelve-room "teacherage" (a home for teachers).

Currently, the house is thirty-four hundred square feet. I believe that Georgiana and Ulysses's home was less than half that size. Today, set back from the house is a two-car garage with a large addition; this structure may be a renovation of the old barn used by Georgiana and Ulysses.

### A MYSTERIOUS GRAVEYARD IN GEORGIANA'S BACKYARD?

In the backyard of the house is a tiny cemetery that still intrigues East Haddam history lovers. It dates back to the days of Ulysses's father, Dr. Henry Evelyn Cook. Was this a Cook family cemetery? Probably not. Whose then?

I will turn this part of the story over to East Haddam Municipal Historian, Dr. Karl P. Stofko, who researched this old graveyard and, on November 10, 1999, delivered this speech to the East Haddam Historical Society as part IX of his East Haddam Mysteries series:

> **Who's Buried in the Graveyard behind the Dr. Cook Place in Moodus?**
>
> When I first came to East Haddam in 1965 and became interested in its history and cemeteries, the late Bertha Pear told me of an old graveyard, which is located out behind the former teacherage on Falls Road in Moodus, not far from the post office. Bertha, herself a teacher, had roomed at the teacherage in the 1930s.
>
> This small graveyard has never been listed on any map of East Haddam, recorded in any land deed, nor mentioned

by any previous writer of East Haddam's history. Since no gravestones exist in this graveyard, I put off its investigation. Recently, however, I was reminded of the cemetery by Louis and Helen Soja, who live next door to the former teacherage. With renewed interest in this mysterious cemetery, I and local archaeologist Anita Sherman did a site survey this past spring.

The cemetery definitely dates back to the early Victorian period — about 1840 to 1850. It is just 12′1″ wide by 15′10″ long and is surrounded by a fence of eight tapered granite posts, which are interconnected by three tiers of iron rods. The entrance is in the northwest corner. Probing of the ground within the cemetery's boundaries showed that ALL of the ground had been dug to a depth of at least five feet. In the 1800s, an area of 12′ x 16′ could easily accommodate six graves. Yet no evidence, such as foundation stones, could be found for any previous gravestones or monuments.

Is anyone still buried in this old cemetery or were its occupants disinterred and moved to another East Haddam cemetery many years ago? Hopefully, a history of the teacherage property would reveal the answer.

Dr. Henry Evelyn Cook [Ulysses's father] of Portland, Connecticut, removed to Moodus in 1845 with his wife Elizabeth, daughter Sarah, and infant son Ulysses [named Silas at the time]. The following year he built a house on land purchased from shoemaker Nelson Richmond. There Dr. Cook practiced botanic medicine or herbal medicine as we would call it today. After pursuing general practice for several years, he turned his attention principally to the treatment of cancer without resorting to surgical methods and achieved a marked degree of success according to local historian Francis H. Parker.

Sarah, the doctor's daughter, died in 1849 at the age of sixteen. It is possible that Dr. Cook set aside a small plot of land in his back yard as a small family cemetery at the time of Sarah's death, but there are no records to prove this. Dr. Henry E. Cook died in 1874 and his wife Elizabeth in November 1880, just one month before burial records were started here in East Haddam. While it is possible that Henry, Elizabeth, and Sarah may have initially been buried in this small cemetery, it is rather doubtful. The entire Cook family is actually buried in the Moodus Cemetery on North Moodus Road. However, the Moodus Cemetery Association has no records as to exactly when Henry, Elizabeth, and Sarah were laid to rest there.

The house of Dr. Henry Cook passed to his son Dr. Ulysses S. Cook, who was also a physician in the treatment of cancer. Ulysses had his father's house removed and then built the present house, later known as the teacherage, in 1883, upon the same foundation. If Ulysses's parents and sister were moved from this family cemetery to the Moodus Cemetery, it would have been logical for Ulysses to remove the fence from around the old family graveyard and use the land as an herb garden. But he did not. This would imply that the small cemetery still contained human remains. Dr. Ulysses Cook died in 1925 and his wife [Georgiana] in 1930. They had no children. Both are buried in the Cook family lot in Moodus Cemetery. The town of East Haddam purchased the house from Ulysses's widow for the use as a teacherage in 1928.

Just as Bertha Pear had been told that people WERE buried in this small Victorian period cemetery, Helen Soja was also told a very similar story. Helen even went so far as to forbid her three sons from playing in this old graveyard out of respect for the dead.

Since 1880, when town burial records were first started, no burials have taken place in this graveyard. If, indeed, six persons are buried there, they were probably interred by Dr. Henry E. Cook, himself, between 1845 [when he moved there] and 1874 [when he died].

Many persons suffering from cancer in those days in the mid-1800s sold all they had and came to a clinic like the one run by Dr. Henry Cook in the hope of being cured of that dread disease. Despite his apparent success in treating cancers with herbal medicine, a goodly number of Dr. Cook's patients probably still died of the disease, perhaps even some of these at his clinic. It is possible that Dr. Cook buried some of these patients who were without family and/or money in this small cemetery as a gesture of the deep sympathy he had for them. No other possibility can be found for the continued existence of this small graveyard and the stories passed down by others to both Bertha Pear and Helen Soja.

Only a full scale archaeological dig could definitely prove if any people are actually still buried in this cemetery and exactly how many. Even then, the mystery as to the identities of these individuals would continue on. Unless, that is, the medical records of Dr. Henry E. Cook are eventually found.

Georgiana lived with a graveyard in her back yard and an infirmary giving Thomsonian Medicine treatments to cancer patients in her house? Yes. Yet, as you will continue to see, she and her husband and her home were full of life.

### IN THE MIDDLE OF THE BELLS

Picture the towns in the popular 1950s television westerns, and you can imagine Moodus's village center in the 1880s. It had a dirt road, wooden sidewalks, hitching posts, the blacksmith and livery, the bank, the town green, the office of the local newspaper, the music hall, general stores, the post office, taverns, saloons, hotels, and a one-room schoolhouse. Georgiana and Ulysses lived their entire fifty-seven years of married life within a short walking distance of the center of Moodus. They experienced firsthand the changes to the village downtown — the wonderful changes from progress, such as

# Moodus Mills in Georgiana's Day

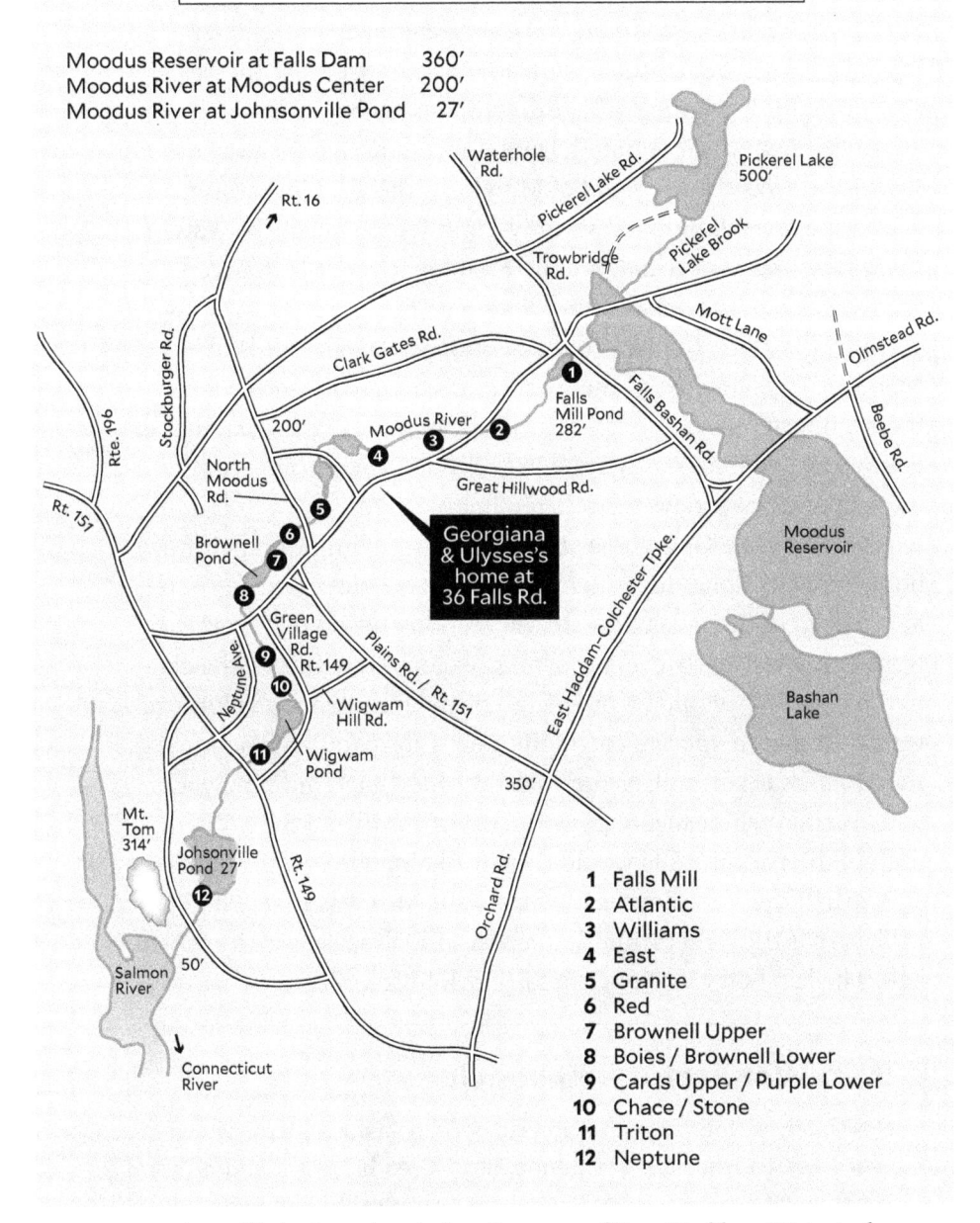

Moodus Reservoir at Falls Dam      360'
Moodus River at Moodus Center      200'
Moodus River at Johnsonville Pond   27'

1 Falls Mill
2 Atlantic
3 Williams
4 East
5 Granite
6 Red
7 Brownell Upper
8 Boies / Brownell Lower
9 Cards Upper / Purple Lower
10 Chace / Stone
11 Triton
12 Neptune

*Moodus mills in Georgiana's day. Courtesy of East Haddam Historical Society.*

RIDING THE WAVE

the first telephone poles in 1882, as well as the tragic changes, such as the devastating fire in 1906. They lived in their Falls Road home until 1925, when Ulysses died and Georgiana, at age seventy-six, moved away permanently. That year, Moodus lost eyewitnesses to, and participants in, their village downtown history.

To the right of Georgiana's front door, about a mile away on Falls Road, was the lifeblood of Moodus — the almighty water. There, a waterfall plunged seventy-eight feet to begin the water's three hundred-foot trip down the Moodus River, which urged the water on with a descending riverbed, giving power to twelve cotton mills along the way to the Salmon River. The mills of Moodus — so symbolic of the Northeast's industrialization with their modern production methods and their increasing number of European, predominantly Irish in the 1880s, immigrant employees — operated six days a week, ten hours a day.

In 1883, while Georgiana and Ulysses were building their new home on Falls Road, the mill owners were building a strong gate at the head of the falls to create the Moodus Reservoir. After that was completed, early every morning, except on Sundays, the gate to the reservoir would be opened to release the precise volume of water needed to operate each mill. The water would gush down the Moodus River, and, as the water reached each mill, the water wheels and turbines were powered up, one mill at a time. Then each of the twelve mills would ring its distinctive bell in succession to call their employees to work. Falls Mill was first. The East Mill, across the street from Georgiana and Ulysses, was the fourth bell. The last bell was Neptune Mill in Johnsonville.

### It's a Wonderful Johnsonville

How many of you remember Johnsonville in East Haddam? Whenever I ask this question in Connecticut, eyes brighten, and arms shoot up. "It was wonderful." "We went every year." "Remember the covered bridge?" "I loved the paddlewheel riverboat on the pond!"

"The lights during the holidays were unbelievable!" These happy memories are from the Johnsonville of the 1960s to the 1990s when it was owned by Raymond Schmitt, who had affectionately transplanted authentic vintage buildings and antiques from other towns in Connecticut, as well as from out-of-state, to recreate a charming Victorian-era (1837–1901) village.

Georgiana, born in 1849, over a hundred years before Schmitt's wonderful re-creation, lived during the original nineteenth-century Victorian-era Johnsonville. Then, it was a little hamlet in Moodus — the thriving mill community and home to the towering Neptune Twine and Cord Mill. Neptune Mill, built in 1832, was the farthest mill west on the three-mile strip of mills in Moodus. Stanton Card, one of its owners, built a beautiful home for himself and his family next to the mill in 1842. The tall, impressive Neptune Mill, with its large bell tower, and the Card homestead, with its Victorian charm, were part of the landscape of Georgiana's world.

In 1868, newlyweds Georgiana and Ulysses would have heard through the news and through the Moodus grapevine that the ownership of the Neptune Mill and its property had passed to Emory Johnson (1817–1896). Stanton Card had died in 1867, and Emory Johnson, Card's son-in-law and business partner, acquired possession of the Neptune Mill, the homestead, and the property. Stanton Card had no sons to inherit his property; he had two daughters, one of whom had married Emory Johnson. Emory Johnson was deeply involved in Moodus mill businesses. He was the industrious owner of the equally impressive Triton Mill built near Neptune Mill five years earlier, at the start of the Civil War.

Emory Johnson and his wife moved into the homestead. The little Moodus community that developed around Johnson's mills and his home became known as Johnsonville. It included housing for the mill operatives, its own post office, and a library. The mills were eventually lost to fires, but the Neptune Mill office building and the Johnsons' picturesque Victorian home, now privately owned, still stand today.[73]

> Georgiana and Ulysses knew the Johnson family well. Mr. and Mrs. Emory Johnson were faithful members of the Moodus Methodist Episcopal Church that Georgiana attended. Their son, E. Emory Johnson (1841–1905), was a contemporary of Georgiana and Ulysses. He was four years older than Ulysses and had attended the Moodus district schools. He had also attended the same Wesleyan Academy in Wilbraham, Massachusetts, that Ulysses attended. Like Georgiana and Ulysses, Mr. and Mrs. E. Emory Johnson lived in Moodus their entire lives and were active citizens of the village. Often the couples' lives and interests interwove, as they did as members of the Moodus Dramatic Association.
>
> Was Johnsonville in East Haddam like Pottersville in Bedford Falls, the fictional village in the movie *It's a Wonderful Life?* Yes, in some ways it was. Johnsonville was named after Mr. Johnson and Pottersville was named after Mr. Potter. Both men were wealthy and powerful citizens of their towns. But the real Mr. Johnson was not a bitter money grabber as the fictional Mr. Potter was. According to *Beers 1884*, the elder Emory Johnson "not only established a reputation for honest productions, but in all his dealings with his fellow men, he has kept in view the Golden Rule. Outside of his business affairs, his tastes and inclinations have led him to engage in works of charity and benevolence."[74] His son, E. Emory Johnson, who co-authored (with Hosford B. Niles) the "Town of East Haddam" section of *Beers 1884* in which this entry appears, was also a generous man. According to *Beers 1903*, E. Emory Johnson was "very liberal in his donations, believing that workingmen can improve themselves and that they should be given the opportunity of doing so, and provided mill workers a fine free library and reading room."[75]
>
> Both generations of Johnsons and their families are buried in the Moodus Cemetery. I imagine the Neptune and Triton Mill bells rang out over the town for their funerals. I wonder if some angels got their wings.

Six mills were within eyeshot of Georgiana: two to the left and four to the right. All twelve mills were within earshot. Mill bells were extra loud — they were also used as fire alarms for the village. Despite the volume, the bells had a pleasant sound, at least to some, like mill owner Crary Brownell, who likened the early morning ritual to the harmonious sound of a carillon, a musical instrument with bells.

Bruce R. Sievers provided me with these descriptions of the Moodus mills. As author of *Mills along the River,* he interviewed Crary Brownell, the last surviving mill owner.[76] Sievers dedicated his book "to the men and women of the nineteenth and twentieth centuries who worked in the Moodus River cotton mills, and to Mr. Crary Brownell." Mr. Sievers is also a featured speaker about the Moodus mills in the documentary film series, *Saving Land, Saving History*, a collaborative project between the East Haddam Historical Society and the East Haddam Land Trust, produced in 2021 by Ken Simon.[77]

In 1880, the Moodus mills employed about five hundred people, which was 17 percent of East Haddam's population. The mills, the housing for workers, and the homes of the mill owners themselves were concentrated within a three-mile stretch along the Moodus River, with Johnsonville to the west, Main Street in the center, and Falls Road to the east. During the summer, Georgiana would have watched the mill operatives — the men, women, teens, and a few younger children — walk to and from the stifling hot mills. She would have watched as wagon wheels and horse hooves churned up the dry dust from the road, coating the sweat-drenched clothing and hair and skin of the workers. She would have been thankful for the advantages that kept her cool — the occasional breeze through her windows, the cold, clean water from her well, the iceman's delivery, and her handheld fan, which, I'm sure, was a fashionable one.

### GEORGIANA'S FAMILY MATRIARCH DIES

Early in the decade, on January 2, 1881, Georgiana's hale and hearty and healthy-to-the-last-day-of-her-life grandmother Sylvia White Arnold died at age eighty-seven at her Arnold homestead in the

Turkey Hill section of Haddam. She had lived there for sixty-three years, since marrying Horace Arnold, who now survived her.

Sylvia had never lived without the comfort and company of family surrounding her. The 1880 census counts twenty-two families in the Turkey Hill section of Haddam. Six were Arnolds, seven were Dickinsons (some of whom had married Arnolds), and two were Whites from Sylvia's side of the family. Of Sylvia and Horace's eight children, five had died before Sylvia. Two sons and one daughter remained. Their son Horace Edgar Arnold and his wife lived with them. Their other son, Davis Tyler Arnold, lived in a nearby house with his fourteen-year-old son, Eudell. Davis's first wife, Eudell's mother, Esther Dickinson, had died when Eudell was four. The one surviving daughter of Sylvia and Horace was Georgiana's mother, Lucinda, who had left Haddam in her teens, crossed the river to make her life in Moodus, and was still living there at age fifty-five when her mother died.

Although not shocking, the death of Sylvia Arnold would have been a major event for her family members, including Sylvia's numerous Arnold and White relatives, many of whom lived in Haddam or the bordering towns. Sylvia had been the eldest of the family — a great-grandmother, grandmother, mother, sister, grandaunt, aunt, cousin, second cousin, and more to so many. The family would have mourned their matriarch. They would have attended the funeral service together and helped the aging Horace deal with the emotions and practicalities of his wife's death. The members of the First Congregational Church of Haddam, where the Arnolds were longtime members, would have mourned too. There was likely a big turnout for the funeral and the burial at the Turkey Hill Cemetery. Sylvia Arnold was buried next to her daughter Elizabeth Arnold who had died fifty years earlier at age thirteen. A few graves away was Sylvia's brother William White, who had died ten years earlier.

It was perhaps at the early 1881 family gatherings for this sad event that thirty-one-year-old Georgiana took a special interest in Lillie Belle White (1874–1956), her six-year-old second cousin. (Genealogy is sometimes too messy for words. The best way to understand how Lillie and Georgiana are related is to flip to the family tree titled "How Georgiana is Related to Lillie White" at the start of this book.) Lillie's father had died in 1879. Lillie's mother, Louisa (born Clark) White (1834–?), had been a widow with five young children for two years at the time of Sylvia's funeral. Louisa and her children lived in Chester, the town abutting Haddam to the south, not far from Arnold territory. Sylvia would have known the unfortunate Louisa and her children. She would have known that husband-less meant income-less, and that a widow with young children would not have the means to support a family. Sylvia had probably helped the overwhelmed Louisa with food, provisions, money, wisdom, love, and, perhaps, child care. Georgiana, who was in a better position to assist than most, may have been encouraged by her grandmother Sylvia to help. And help she did. Georgiana and Ulysses took little Lillie Belle White into their home as their child.

### LILLIE, LOVED INMATE OF THE FAMILY

When exactly Lillie came to live with Georgiana and Ulysses, I don't know. It was definitely after the 1880 Chester census that lists five-year-old Lillie living with her widowed mother and four siblings. This 1880 record shows that Lillie had two brothers, ages two and eleven, and two sisters, ages seven and sixteen. Her sixteen-year-old sister, Jennie L. White, was handicapped in some way. After her name on the census, there is a checkmark in the column titled "maimed, crippled, bedridden, or otherwise disabled."

My best guess for the year that Lillie left Chester and arrived in Moodus to be raised by Georgiana and Ulysses is 1881. This was before they moved to Falls Road, which was in 1884. Lillie turned seven in July 1881. I know she came to the Cooks at an early age because of this entry in *Beers 1903*: "Dr. and Mrs. Cook have no children of their own, but they have tenderly reared one who is now a young lady, and a loved inmate of the family."[78] At the time of this entry in 1903, Lillie was twenty-nine years old and had lived with Georgiana and Ulysses since they had taken her into their home as a child.

Adoptions without legal formalities were accepted in America during the 1880s. It wasn't until the mid-twentieth century that all states instituted formal adoption laws and had the resources to administer them. In the 1880s, when young widows like Lillie's mother found themselves unable to provide financially for all their offspring, they would allow children to be taken and raised by relatives, trusted friends, or even strangers. The children often kept their born-with last names, as Lillie White did.

Turning thirty-two in 1881, Georgiana probably wanted a child. Nearly every woman her age had children. Perhaps her maternal instincts were awakened by the two recent deaths of mothers in her family — Ulysses's mother, Elizabeth Cook, in November 1880 and her own grandmother Sylvia Arnold in January 1881. Perhaps Georgiana's grandmother had been trying to orchestrate an adoption for her widowed niece's children and appealed to Georgiana. Or perhaps Georgiana was feeling family-deprived because 1881 was also the year her mother and brother and his family moved out of Moodus.

In mid-1881, Frank, Sarah, and their baby Georgia (from now on, I will refer to Frank's firstborn daughter as Georgia, not Georgiana) moved across the river to Chester to live in the Chester House where Frank had secured the position of proprietor. Lucinda went with them. This meant that Georgiana was the only member of her immediate family left in Moodus. Were Georgiana's feelings hurt when her mother chose to live with Frank and Sarah? Had Georgiana invited her mother to stay in Moodus and live with her instead? Georgiana had lived her full life with her family within daily walking and chatting distance, and now, with telephones still in their primitive days, she would have felt the gap.

Whatever the reason for wanting a child, Georgiana and Ulysses brought Lillie into their home and their lives. The "rearing" of Lillie White seems to have been a blessing for everyone involved. With the Cooks, Lillie was able to live a secure life — in fact, a charmed life. Under their wing, she lived in a beautiful home, had fashionable clothes, summered at the shore, and enjoyed a life free of financial concerns.

 A bonus for Lillie was her new family's love of music and entertaining. I found an old, tattered newspaper clipping about Lillie at the time of her thirteenth birthday in July 1887. It read: "Lillie White gave a birthday [missing word] to a number of her young [missing word]."[79] Perhaps the first missing word was *concert* and the second was *friends*. Lillie had learned to play the piano, a privilege only a limited number of families could afford at the time. The Cooks were one of the few households in East Haddam to own musical instruments. The tax records of 1887 show that only 50 out of 744 East Haddam households owned a piano or musical instrument.

 In the late 1880s, the affordable upright piano was on the cusp of replacing grand pianos; in another decade, many households would own them. I assume Lillie took piano lessons from a teacher who came to their home. It was probably Georgiana who had the unpopular task of making Lillie practice daily, but it was probably the disciplined musician Ulysses who stood over Lillie helping her perfect her posture, perfect her wrist positions, perfect the curl of her fingers, perfect her timing, perfect her scales, perfect her *fortissimos* and *pianissimos,* and, by his example, teaching her to love music.

 On top of all the material advantages Lillie enjoyed was the genuine love and affection she received from Georgiana and Ulysses, confirmed by the *Beers 1903* entry reporting that Lillie had been raised "tenderly" by the Cooks and had become "a loved inmate of the family."

### GEORGIANA, A NINETEENTH-CENTURY WIFE

As I sculpt Georgiana from the small number of records that bear her name, a home-loving and family-loving woman is taking shape, one who "kept house," raised a child, and first and foremost, fulfilled her role as a wife. Every indication is that she was content with the role of a nineteenth-century wife. This was a time when husbands controlled their wives in a world where women were not legally permitted to vote for changes in the laws they were forced to abide by. Well, maybe husbands didn't control every aspect of their wives' lives, but a husband controlled her money, property, children, and last name. Many wives, like Georgiana, with kind, generous, industrious, and honest husbands may not have minded this arrangement. In fact, they may have liked it.

As a wife, Georgiana was responsible for the home duties. Her week in the 1880s would have followed the schedule adhered to by many American wives in the Victorian Age: "Wash on Monday, Iron on Tuesday, Mend on Wednesday, Market on Thursday, Clean on Friday, Bake on Saturday, Rest on Sunday." These once-a-week chores were in addition to the daily chores of tending the fires and the water, making beds, cooking meals, doing dishes, and keeping up a steady supply of fresh cloth cleaning rags, as paper towels were not invented until 1931.

While Georgiana had Nellie Skinner living in her home as a servant, I don't know how many years Nellie or any other servant stayed. I only know that twenty years later, in 1900, there was no servant living in the Cooks' household. The 1890 census records for East Haddam and most other towns were lost in a 1921 fire in Washington, D.C., a tragedy (or at least a *darn it* moment) for many genealogists. At some point between 1880 and 1900, Georgiana likely replaced a live-in servant with helpers who didn't live in her home.

A laundress, for instance, probably did the washing, a task that required a strong back and strong arms to carry the tubs of water to and from the stove and to operate the hand-cranked washers. The laundress would have scrubbed with bar soap until the new ready-made washing powders invented in Chicago during this decade were available. And she would have starched many items, a routine step in the laundry process of the 1880s. For drying, clotheslines were used along with wooden clothes pegs or with the new spring-actuated clothespins invented in Vermont during this decade. A laundress may have also done the ironing. She would have used a flat iron base (with a detachable wooden handle) which had been heated on the stove, pressing the clothes and linens on the newly invented ironing tables we now call ironing boards. Washing, drying, ironing, and folding was a weekly two-day ordeal.

I can picture Georgiana and Lillie, who turned fifteen in 1889, sitting together at work on the mending and sewing chores. They may have used the treadle sewing machine designed for at-home use introduced in 1885 by Singer, the American company that would become the largest sewing machine company in the world.

Cooking would have consumed a lot of Georgiana's time. Did she bake her own bread? Probably. Or perhaps she purchased her bread from a local bread wagon or local baker. Commercially baked bread on store shelves had not become commonplace yet, and the "best thing since sliced bread" was years away — not sold to consumers until 1928.

Bread aside, Georgiana would have enjoyed a cornucopia of new foods in the 1880s thanks to the advancements in food preservation, mass production, and the railroad's speedy delivery. There was a proliferation of new cookbooks and new magazines which regularly featured new recipes. In the pages of *Ladies' Home Journal*, launched in 1883, or in *Good Housekeeping*, launched in 1885, and in the newspapers, Georgiana would have read the first advertisements for new brands of food we still buy today, like Royal Baking Powder, Bell's Poultry Seasoning, Quaker Oats, Dr. Pepper, and Coca Cola. I have a feeling that Georgiana would have enjoyed trying new recipes with the new products. She was likely a frequent customer at Purples and the other local grocers.

Georgiana's family dinners would have included poultry dishes, like chicken pot pies, or beef, pork or mutton, probably from Beebe's Meat Market. And, because of easy access to boats and fishermen and fish markets and fishmongers, seafood. Several items we consider luxuries today were everyday foods for Georgiana: shad, fresh from the Connecticut River in April and

May; fish and oysters fresh from Long Island Sound year-round; and clams, also from the sound, so abundant they were often served before the main meal. Georgiana was likely comfortable with clams — eating them raw, steaming or roasting them in their shells, mincing them for clam cakes, and making Connecticut Clam Chowder. According to *A History of Connecticut Food* by Eric D. Lehman and Amy Nawrocki published in 2012,[80] Connecticut Clam Chowder originated in New London and was a clear broth chowder made with steamed clams, salt pork, onions, and potatoes. In this book, which includes delicious information and recipes, the authors explain that Connecticut Clam Chowder, because its broth is thickened by potatoes rather than milk, is richer and creamier than the New England clam chowder we are familiar with today. (Take that, Massachusetts!)

Molasses, a staple in kitchens in the late nineteenth century, was a common and favorite sweetener, good for making pies, cakes, or cookies — and baked beans. In many New England homes, baked beans prepared with molasses and a chunk of salt pork (they sure did like their salt pork in the nineteenth century!) were cooked in a bean pot for at least six hours on Saturdays in preparation for the ritualistic Saturday night baked bean supper. Georgiana and other housewives may have squinted with suspicion outwardly, but smiled inwardly, when they saw America's first convenience food[81] — precooked pork and beans in a tin can — on store shelves in the 1880s. She probably jumped on the easy-to-cook hotdog bandwagon in the 1880s, the decade that hotdogs became popular and a new standard of the Saturday night baked bean supper. When hotdogs were served in America's baseball parks a decade later, in the 1890s, they made their way into American culture, as permanently and as iconically as baseball and apple pie.

All-American apple pies! Georgiana surely made them. She and Ulysses had three acres of apple trees — 140 trees — on their land, which also included seven acres of hay, an acre of potatoes, two horses, and a milk cow. For the apple picking, farm work, and care of the animals, they hired farm workers. Georgiana had never liked farming. I don't think anyone in her family liked it. Even Lucinda, who used to make her own butter, was living a cow-free life in Chester. Georgiana likely enjoyed buying her butter, poultry, eggs, honey, corn, cranberries, fresh fruits, and fresh vegetables from farmers nearby.

Based on the photos of the portly Ulysses Cook in middle age, I can surmise that Georgiana was a good cook.

### GEORGIANA AND CHURCH (CHURCH SOCIALS, THAT IS)

A woman's social outlet in New England in the nineteenth century often involved church social activities, even if the woman was not a member of the church. Official membership in a Protestant church in Georgiana's day (this is still true today) required either baptism at the church, usually done within a year of birth, and confirmation, usually done at age fourteen, or "by letter" from another church confirming a previous official membership. Nonmembers could, and did, attend church services and could, and did, join the church's social groups. Georgiana fell into the category of those who were not members of the Moodus Methodist Episcopal Church.

The story of Georgiana's religious life is blurry and is filled with gaps. To tell it I need to insert several *maybes.* Here's my fragile summary: Georgiana was never baptized as a baby. At least there is no record of her baptism. Nor are there baptismal records for her brothers. According to her father's Civil War letters, Georgiana and her family had, in the past, attended services at the convenient Moodus Methodist Episcopal Church. Georgiana and her brothers had gone to Sunday school there. In her teen years, when her father was at war, she and her mother went to church and participated in activities there. But no one from the Abner C. Smith family was ever an official member of the church. When Georgiana married at age eighteen, in 1868, her wedding was held in the First Congregational Church in East Haddam where Ulysses's parents were members.

Did Georgiana attend church after marriage? Maybe. Maybe she went with her in-laws to the First Congregational Church in East Haddam. Maybe she went to the Moodus Methodist Episcopal Church with her mother, who maybe continued going there until she moved out of Moodus in 1881. It's all *maybes* when it comes to Georgiana participating in church services after marriage.

In June 1881, Georgiana, although not a member of the Moodus Methodist Episcopal Church, joined its Ladies Benevolent Society. The Ladies Benevolent Society was a social group that raised money for community charities and for major items for the church itself, such as a carpet. The ladies of the society included several wives of drum corps members, certainly friends of Georgiana. Some were women from prominent Moodus families. One of the ladies who joined the society on the same day that Georgiana joined in June 1881 was Mrs. E. Emory Johnson, whose Johnson in-laws were some of the most active leaders in the church.

The ladies met at one another's homes to socialize and to plan their activities. I found records of the society in the Connecticut State Library and found Georgiana's name entered as a new member in 1881. The society's social events during Georgiana's years as a member were also recorded. In addition to their main event, the popular Strawberry Festival held each June in Moodus, there were also chicken suppers, art exhibits, *penny socials*, and *butterfly socials*. It's interesting to me that Georgiana did not hold any meetings in her home, because, as you will discover as you read on, she often opened her home to guests. Georgiana stayed with the group for nine years, until 1890, but never took an officer position. Nor did she officially join the church.

Maybe Georgiana became active with the church social group during these years because Lillie had come into her life. The years of Georgiana's membership in the Ladies Benevolent Society coincide with the years she was raising Lillie — from Lillie's arrival in 1881, when Lillie was seven, to 1890, when Lillie turned sixteen. Georgiana likely brought Lillie to Sunday school and to the social events that the *Juniors* (the youth) of the church attended. The society's minutes show that Lillie joined the Ladies Benevolent Society in 1896, when she was twenty-two, five years after Georgiana had dropped out. It looks like Lillie was a one-year-only member, and, like Georgiana, never officially joined the church.

---

### Church Socials

Georgiana's Ladies Benevolent Society of the Moodus Methodist Episcopal Church put on socials to provide nonreligious, lighthearted, and alcohol-free amusement for the community as well as to raise money for a cause or for the church. The get-togethers usually involved food, music, and a game or group activity. The events were often attended by both men and women; some events were for the Juniors of the church.

Below are the guides for two of the socials Georgiana's group held while she was a member. These descriptions were printed in the book, *Social Evenings: A Collection of Pleasant Entertainments for Christian Endeavor Societies and the Home Circle:*[82]

- **A Butterfly Social:**
  A form of social that will delight the Juniors is the butterfly social. Slight refreshments are to be served, and the waiters are to be dressed with butterfly wings made from delicately colored paper. The napkins on the table should be folded in butterfly designs. In a room nearby, paper articles may be for sale, the attendants at the table and the Juniors everywhere, so far as possible, being arrayed in butterfly costumes. A musicale programme with songs by the Juniors will fill out a very pleasant evening.

- **A Penny Social:**
  Use may be made of a penny for an enlivening Christian Endeavor social. Charge at the door an admission fee of twenty-five cents. Give each person a penny in change. The twenty-four cents are for the supper. The one cent is for the following game.

  After supper, distribute cards bearing this list. The participants are to find all these things on their pennies: [This is a sampling; I've put the answers are in brackets.]

> - find a name of an animal [hair]
> - name of a fruit [date]
> - name of a flower [tulips]
> - a place of worship: [temple]
> - things you like to receive [letters]
>
> An appropriate motto for this card would be "A Penny for Your Thoughts." Give twenty minutes to the questions, and then require each member to write his name on the card and to have the ushers collect both cards and pennies. Prizes are awarded by the committee, who after examination of the cards, gives to the owner of the best set of answers a scent-bottle filled with perfumery.

### THE CELEBRATED MOODUS DRUM AND FIFE CORPS IN THE 1880S

Ulysses was never active in church life. His *Beers 1903* commemorative biographical record reads: "Although not associated with any religious denomination, Dr. Cook recognized the need for such, and is a firm believer in the religion promulgated." More to Ulysses's liking than church activities, and I believe more to Georgiana's as well, were the happenings of the Moodus Drum and Fife Corps, which reached peak success in the 1880s.

The reputation of the corps had risen to the top among drum corps in Connecticut, becoming famous for its musical precision and for the fine figures the musicians cut in their distinguished and colorful uniforms. During this decade, the corps furnished the music for most of East Haddam's patriotic commemorations, parades, and political rallies for both parties. It also marched in notable Connecticut parades in Chatham, Essex, Chester, Hartford, New Haven, Bridgeport, New Milford, and Danbury. The press contributed to the elevation of the corps's status with flattering descriptions like "the celebrated Moodus Drum and Fife Corps with sixteen expert performers."[83]

In 1881, the deeply patriotic corps went to New London, Connecticut, for the 100th anniversary of Benedict Arnold's infamous burning of the city in 1781. Parades with townspeople carrying and publicly burning an effigy of Arnold had begun in 1782 and continued annually until the Civil War. This 1881 parade was likely a one-time revival of the tradition to mark the hundred years since Arnold's attempt to destroy New London. In 2013, annual revivals of the tradition began — the two-faced effigy is still paraded, the effigy is still burned to cheers of the crowd, and drum corps in Revolutionary War uniforms still perform.

The corps also traveled out of Connecticut quite often in the 1880s — to New York, Maine, Massachusetts, and Washington, D.C. Georgiana likely stayed home with Lillie and enjoyed some drum free evenings when Ulysses traveled long distances.

The peak of pride for Ulysses and the corps came in 1885, the year Ulysses turned forty. In February, the corps traveled to Washington, D.C., for the dedication of the Washington Monument. While there, members were invited to give a private performance for President Chester A. Arthur. *Parker's* reports:

> The day was so intensely cold that brass bands were practically silenced, and the musical honors of the day fell to the Moodus Drum and Fife Corps. At the suggestion of Senator Joseph R. Hawley, the United States senator from Connecticut 1881–1905, President Arthur invited the corps to visit the White House. The corps accepted the invitation and serenaded the president. The president personally came outside and invited the band to come into the White House and play within its portals. After playing two or three times, they were invited in the East Room, where each member of the corps was presented to the president and other prominent officials who were in the receiving line.[84]

James Clark writes in his book that "the thunder of the drums cracked the plaster of the wall" in the East Room.[85] Clark was not using a metaphor — the loud Moodus drums literally cracked the

White House plaster. Perhaps, because this was such a special trip, Georgiana attended and joined Ulysses in the White House. If she was there, I wonder whether she was horrified or had to hold back a little laugh as the plaster came tumbling down.

Locally, drum corps wives joined their husbands for the social events. Like Ulysses, many of the "gentlemen drummers" of the Moodus Drum and Fife Corps in the 1880s were married and in their thirties and forties. I imagine Georgiana developed strong friendships, even best friendships, among the drum corps wives. Georgiana, as the wife of the drum corps leader, would have been one of the leading ladies. She would have entertained the members and wives at her home year-round, providing good food, good company, and good times.

## The Gentlemen Drummers and Their Ladies

Below are listed many members of the Moodus Drum and Fife Corps in 1888 in order of age. The source for the names of members in this chart is the book entitled *Records of the Moodus Drum and Fife Corps, December 31, 1887, to October 3, 1892,* which was reproduced in 1974 from the original records of the Moodus Drum and Fife Corp. The book is held at the East Haddam Historical Society. The source for age, occupation and wife's name is U.S. Census Bureau records of 1880 and 1900, accessed through Ancestry.com.

| Member | Age in 1888 | Profession | Wife's Name |
| --- | --- | --- | --- |
| W. E. Odber | 46 | Jailer | Mattie |
| D. L. Williams | 46 | Hardware Dealer | Rosa (1895) |
| U. S. Cook | 43 | Physician | Georgiana |
| G. R. Buell | 40 | Tinsmith | Rebecca |
| W. A. Cone | 40 | Insurance Agent | Flora |
| W. S. Comstock | 38 | Reporter; Insurance Agent | (single) |

| M. E. Wetherall | 37 | Cotton Mill Overseer | Abby |
| D. J. Treat | 31 | Barber | (unknown) |
| W. W. Beckwith | 31 | Merchant | Ellen |
| G. Bowers | 29 | Merchant | Florilla |
| S. E. Ackley | 25 | Farmer | Harriett |
| E. J. Grundshaw | 23 | Cigarmaker | (single) |

### DECORATION DAY — A BIG DAY FOR GEORGIANA, ULYSSES, AND AMERICA

In the 1880s, the gravestones of Civil War veterans were still among the newest in cemeteries across the nation. Fifteen years had not diminished the zeal for remembering the slain soldiers on Decoration Day, the holiday established soon after the war. East Haddam and Moodus had celebrated Decoration Day every year since its inception with a parade. Early in the 1880s, the parades were solemn processions, followed by a cemetery ceremony at which drums beat slowly in funereal rhythm, then stopped, leaving an emotionally packed silence in the air, as gathered townspeople awaited the prayers of ministers and speeches by members of the community.

Horatio Chapman, the tentmate of Georgiana's father and an eloquent speaker, was often asked to read pages from his Civil War diary at the East Haddam Decoration Day exercises. He may have read, for all to hear, his poignant entry about carrying his wounded friend Abner Smith to the field hospital in North Carolina at the end of the war, setting off trembles in the chin of Georgiana, who was certainly among those who gathered. Let us not forget that for Georgiana, Decoration Day did not include decorating her father's grave. Her father's remains were miles away in North Carolina, a sad truth that Georgiana would have had to face every year on Decoration Day.

The attendance at Decoration Day events continued to grow in East Haddam throughout the 1880s. During the decade, while the quiet cemetery ceremonies remained unchanged, the crowds grew larger, the parades grew louder, and the after-parade picnics grew livelier with the addition of games and food for the community.

East Haddam's parade on Decoration Day of May 1887 was its largest to date, with veterans from the neighboring town of Colchester joining in. The Moodus Drum and Fife Corps, along with the newly formed Moodus Cornet Band that Ulysses had helped create, led the large parade to the Moodus Cemetery. At the front of the parade was thirty-seven-year-old Ulysses, leading the procession as the proud and colorful drum major. For many years following, whether it was the Moodus Drum and Fife Corps or the Moodus Cornet Band or both who furnished music for Decoration Days in Moodus, Ulysses was there. He was clearly overflowing with patriotism and with reverence for the Civil War veterans. I think he was also overflowing with love for his wife, to whom Decoration Day meant so much.

I can imagine Georgiana and Ulysses at the Decoration Day after-parade picnic in 1887 — he in his striking uniform, and she in the latest fashion — each bursting with pride for the other.

### NEW WAVES OF ENTERTAINMENT

The 1880s brought a new wave of entertainment to America, including to Georgiana, who had the financial means, the energy, the sociability, and the lively husband needed to enjoy it.

William H. Goodspeed's Opera House in East Haddam had become one of Connecticut's most glamourous entertainment venues since it had opened in 1877. By the time the 1880s began, full Broadway shows, with accomplished actors, actresses, performers, and extravagant costumes, props, and scenery, were traveling by steamboat up the Connecticut River to East Haddam, sometimes for a one-night performance. The busy Goodspeed offered entertainment of all kinds: popular melodramas, comedies,

*The Goodspeed Opera House in the 1880s.*

*The Music Hall Building in Moodus during Georgiana's days.*

concerts, minstrel shows, humorists, vaudeville shows, and costume balls. But the heart of the theater stopped when the heart of its brainchild-owner-producer-financier William H. Goodspeed, stopped on New Year's Day, 1882.

After his death, the Opera House was no longer used for professional shows. Instead, it was used for performances by amateur entertainers, including the East Haddam Drama Club, and for local dinners, readings, and dances. It never regained its initial glory, but it did stay open until 1920 when it closed completely as a venue for entertainment. The Goodspeed was given a second life through the generosity and diligence of the Goodspeed Opera House Foundation, which restored the building to its original splendor and reopened it as an entertainment venue in 1963.[86] Today it is living in glory again as a popular musical theater venue owned and managed by Goodspeed Musicals.

In the forty-three years of the Opera House's initial run, I think Georgiana and Ulysses would have been in the audience many times. Attending an event at the Goodspeed was probably as enchanting for Georgiana and Ulysses as it is for us today.

Closer to Georgiana, situated within easy walking distance for her on Main Street in Moodus, was the more modest Moodus

Music Hall, which held multiple gatherings year-round. Georgiana may have seen the legendary P. T. Barnum (1810–1891) when he performed there.[87] The date of P. T. Barnum's Moodus Music Hall performance is uncertain, but it was likely in the 1870s or 1880s when Barnum was promoting his new circus as the "Greatest Show on Earth." Moodus's Music Hall was a familiar place for Georgiana, a lover of dancing, and for Ulysses, a lover of music. They likely went to all the major events held there, including a Grand Ball, hosted by the Knights of Labor in January 1887, which a large number of guests attended.[88] Something tells me Georgiana and Ulysses would have loved a ball and would have made a handsome couple on the dance floor.

Whist parties were popular social events of the 1880s. Whist — think bridge — was an intense card game, sometimes with gambling, played by a foursome. Did Georgiana and Ulysses play whist? Did they go to, or host, *drive whist parties* — the term used in the 1880s for prestigious social events where progressive whist games were played? The *Connecticut Valley Advertiser* reported on local whist parties, and, in November 1887, included this mention: "A drive whist party was given at the home of Mr. and Mrs. David Purple." These Purples — there were many Purples in Moodus — lived a few houses away from Georgiana and Ulysses on Falls Road. They were older than Georgiana and Ulysses by a generation. David Purple (1823–1892) had been postmaster in Moodus during the Civil War. After the war, he and his younger-by-twenty-years nephew Albert E. Purple (the one who would become the wealthiest man in East Haddam) ran Purple's general store in downtown Moodus. After David died in 1892, Albert partnered with Arthur Silliman, and renamed the store, Purple and Silliman. Although Georgiana and Ulysses were well-acquainted with the David Purples, I doubt they attended the Purples whist parties, or any whist party. I don't think whist fit their profile. Whist takes time to study and master, and I don't think Georgiana and Ulysses wanted to spend their time that way. Also, whist is a quiet game, and they were not quiet people.

## How Wealthy Were the Cooks?

Georgiana and Ulysses lived well, but they were:

- not as wealthy as the New York Joneses (the ones people tried to keep up with), whose Gilded Age lifestyle was revealed by the pen of their daughter, Edith Jones Wharton, in her book, *Age of Innocence,* for which she became in 1921 the first woman to earn a Pulitzer Prize in Literature;
- not as wealthy as Connecticut's Isabella Beecher Hooker, whose old money and spirit allowed her to lead the women's suffrage movement in the state and across the country;
- not as wealthy as East Haddam's top 1 percent, like the Boardmans who mastered the silversmith trade;
- not as wealthy as Moodus's wealthiest resident, Judge Albert E. Purple.

Georgiana and Ulysses did, however, squeak into the top 10 percent of the wealthiest in East Haddam. The 1887 Grand List (list of taxable property) of East Haddam recorded Ulysses S. Cook as one of the top East Haddam residents in terms of assets (i.e., value owned). Income was not recorded, taxed, or used as a measure of wealth in Ulysses's lifetime.

In 1887, assets were recorded in a man's name, except for widows and a very few single women, whose names were prefaced with *Miss*. Married women were rarely acknowledged in the grand list. When a married woman was included, her name did not appear; rather, the two words *and wife* were tacked onto her husband's entry. Like most wives, Georgiana was not acknowledged as owning any assets.

Ulysses's taxable assets in 1887 totaled $2,645 (about $72,000 in 2020). The categories of assets on the grand list offer some insight into what was valued in the 1880s, as well as insight into Georgiana's lifestyle.

- **Real estate** was the first category listed and had the majority of assets. Ulysses's real estate, much of which he inherited from his parents, totaled $2,150. He had 110 acres of land worth $950. He also had a dwelling house, barns, and sheds worth $1,200.

- **Horses** were valuable and expensive. Only 43 percent of taxpayers had a horse. Ulysses owned a horse valued at $75. A horse would have been a necessity for a traveling doctor.
- **Vehicles/Coaches** (horse-drawn carriages) were owned by only 17 percent of taxpayers. Ulysses owned two vehicles/coaches worth $60 in total. Another necessity for his doctor visits.
- **Bank or stock:** Ulysses had $300.
- **Pianoforte and Other Musical Instruments** was its own category. A pianoforte was simply an early piano. Musical instruments in 1887 were luxuries. Only fifty households on the tax records (6.7 percent of all taxpayers) had an entry in this category. Values ranged from $10, which Ulysses had, to $225 for William Goodspeed. Could $10 in value in 1887 represent a piano in addition to the drums that Ulysses owned? I doubt it. Yet I am certain that Georgiana and Ulysses had a piano in their parlor because Lillie, their adopted daughter, learned to play the piano during the 1880s as a young girl.
- **Clocks, Watches, Timepieces, and Jewelry** accounted for the last $50 of Ulysses's assets. He was one of the few (6.5 percent of taxpayers) who owned anything in this category. This probably represents a combination of inherited items, such as a pocket watch from his father, and, I like to imagine, lovely jewelry for Georgiana from his mother.

Only 9 percent (67 of 730) of East Haddam taxpayers had more assets than Ulysses. Among those were five *big money* East Haddamites who owned ten to twenty times more than Ulysses: the Boardmans of Britannia Silversmith fame; the Goodspeeds of Goodspeed Landing and Opera House fame; Judge Albert E. Purple of largest-mill-owner-and-leader-of-almost-everything-in-Moodus fame; Emory Johnson of Johnsonville fame; and Frank C. Fowler of a fame you will soon read about.

## GEORGIANA, ULYSSES, AND CONNECTICUT DISCOVER THE SEASHORE

Finding relief from the summer heat of New England was an annual challenge, but a new breeze of opportunity came whistling through Connecticut in the 1880s. Thanks to the new (begun in 1871) railroad which chugged between Hartford and Old Saybrook, central Connecticut residents now had easy access to the Connecticut shoreline with its cool salt air and cold ocean waters for boating and *bathing,* the nineteenth-century word for swimming or dabbling in the water. The state's beaches became a destination for the wealthier inland residents who could afford to stay in the seasonal cottages or in the hotels that dotted the coast. In summer, the Connecticut Valley Railroad filled its cars daily with people and luggage from Hartford and other Connecticut River towns, heading for Old Saybrook where the river empties into Long Island Sound.

Old Saybrook had three stations: Saybrook Junction, where the current train station stands; Saybrook Point; and Fenwick. Most people would disembark at the first two stations; a small group of the ultra-wealthy from Hartford would stay aboard to travel on a private half-mile track to the Fenwick section of town. At Saybrook Junction, some people would switch trains and board the elegant, larger lines that whistled and stopped at other shoreline towns up and down the coast between New York and Boston.

On the shoreline track heading west from Old Saybrook, the first station stop was Westbrook, fewer than five miles away. By the 1880s, the little town of Westbrook had been discovered as a summer haven. Westbrook's permanent population in 1880 was only nine hundred, smaller than Old Saybrook's thirteen hundred, about a third the size of East Haddam's three thousand, and a small fraction the size of Middletown's twelve thousand. *Beers 1884* touted Westbrook as a summer resort: "The unsurpassed fishing and bathing of its bay have drawn to Westbrook a new population, which during the summer months nearly doubles its census. The sound front is being rapidly covered with cottages, which now number about one hundred, erected and occupied during the summer months by families abroad."[89]

With the means to pay, and for the love of a good time that seemed to define their lives, Georgiana and Ulysses joined the crowds of the fortunate. On June 29, 1882, in time for the summer season, Ulysses bought "a parcel of land with one half of a cottage" on West Beach in Westbrook. Buying half of a cottage was not unusual at the time. There were many *doubles,* the nineteenth-century term for two-family summer cottages with two sides, usually east and west, along the Connecticut shoreline. A common wall without a door separated the halves of the cottages. The owner of one half did not necessarily know the owner of the other half.

Typical of all doubles, Georgiana and Ulysses's half had its own front and back entrance, and its own upstairs and downstairs verandas. Today we would use the word *porch* instead of veranda, but in nineteenth-century vernacular, a porch was only a small stoop. A cottage half would also have its own front room, into which some cottagers like the Cooks squeezed a piano against a wall; its own kitchen with its own stove and a stovepipe connecting it to its own chimney; and its own staircase leading to three upstairs bedrooms. Each half of the cottage was only 750 square feet, but the open-air verandas (called *sleeping porch*es starting in 1915) offered additional space for sitting, hammocking or sleeping. And luxury upon luxury, each half had its own private outhouse a few feet from the back door.

Ulysses bought the western half of the cottage in 1882 for $550 [$14,000 in 2020] from "William E. Odber and Mattie C. Odber (wife)."[90] Ulysses knew William Odber (1842–1921) through the Moodus Drum and Fife Corps, in which Odber was a drummer. Well known to residents of Middlesex County as the county jailer in Haddam, Odber held that position, not without controversy, for twenty-four years, starting in 1877. The Odbers had acquired the half-cottage as a new structure only three months before they sold it to Ulysses. I don't know why the Odbers bought it,

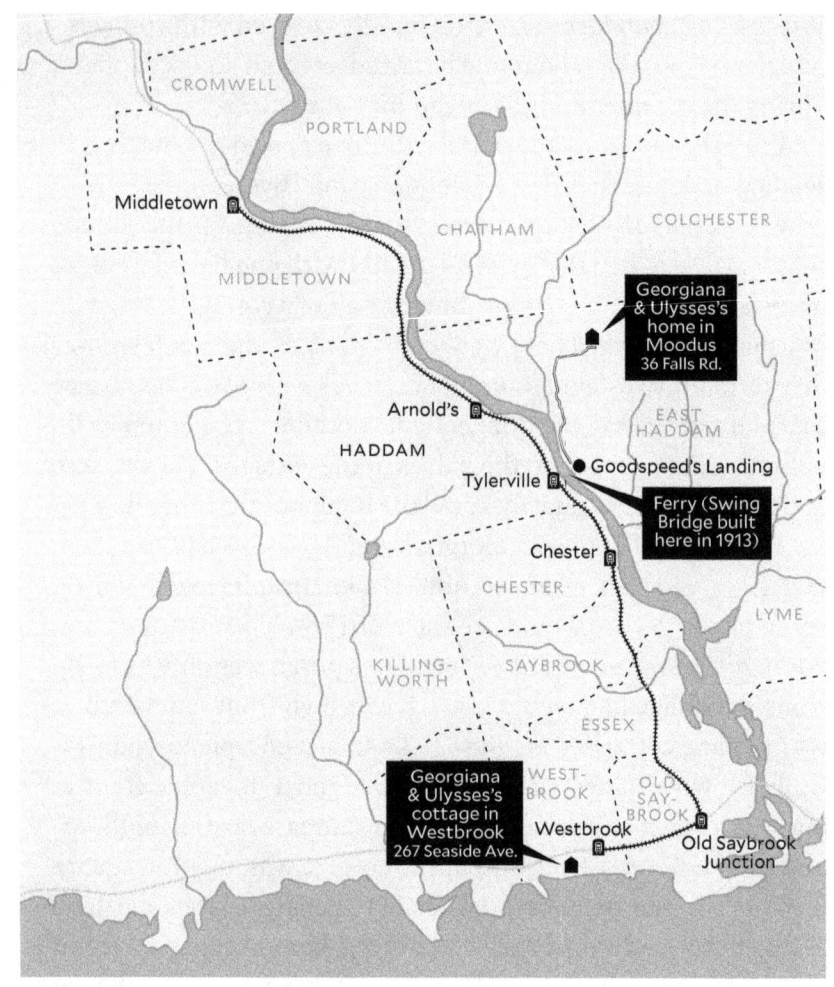

*The trip from East Haddam to Westbrook. Georgiana and Ulysses traveled about twenty miles by horse-drawn carriage, train, or automobile from Moodus to Westbrook, Connecticut, to reach their summer cottage. (Rand McNally map, Middlesex County, Connecticut, 1911)*

then immediately sold it (an investment perhaps?), but when Georgiana and Ulysses learned it was for sale, they grabbed it and never let it go.

Starting in the summer of 1882, Georgiana and Ulysses along with their family and friends began their summers of fun at the West Beach half-cottage.

*The Westbrook, Connecticut, summer cottage in the late 1880s, when Ulysses and Georgiana owned the western half (with tree in front) only. Note the two chimneys. In photo, from left to right are: Ulysses, Georgiana, Lucy Bishop of Guilford, Connecticut, dog, Mrs. James Cronin of Middletown, Conn., and Miss Margaret Welch of Middletown, Connecticut. Is Georgiana holding a puppy?*

### GEORGIANA, THE AMIABLE HOSTESS

"The amiable hostess." This is how Georgiana was described in the minutes of the Moodus Drum and Fife Corps after she and Ulysses entertained the members at their Westbrook cottage. Here is the entry from August 25, 1888:

> Upon invitation from Dr. U. S. Cook, our Corps went to Westbrook and were well entertained. The genial host and the amiable hostess were untiring to make everyone comfortable and happy, for which they have our Thanks. It was the night of the Illumination [this refers to Westbrook's annual Grand Illumination] and the Essex Cornet Band played at the Beach. Most of the members remained over Sunday.

The *Hartford Courant* wrote about the event on August 27, 1888, closing the story by saying that the Moodus Drum and Fife Corps's "music was well received by the cottagers and they, themselves, [the members and wives of the corps] had a good time."

Georgiana knew how to throw a party.

## The Grand Illuminations At West Beach

In 1884, when Georgiana and Ulysses were in their first years of summering in their new Westbrook cottage at West Beach, then called "Westbrook Beach," their neighborhood began to hold an annual Grand Illumination—a night when shoreline residents lit up their cottages as brilliantly as they could for a unified display of light. It was a celebration of summer, held on a Saturday in the dog days of August. Illuminations began before electric streetlights, when only hotels and a few cottages had outdoor oil lamps dotting the dirt road that ran along the water on Seaside Avenue, then called Bay Shore Road. When the sun set on the night of the Illumination, the row of cottages lit up the entire street. And the cottagers did it all without electricity!

*Poster courtesy of Karen Heagle*

Within three years, the annual Grand Illumination at West Beach was attracting thousands. See this newspaper clip, published two days after the event in 1887:

> [*Hartford Courant,* Tuesday, August 23, 1887]
> The ninety-two summer cottages at Westbrook beach were illuminated with Chinese lanterns, etc., Saturday evening. There was a good display of fireworks and the illumination was witnessed by thousands of people from Westbrook and

surrounding towns. Excellent music was furnished by the Essex Band.

Cottages and their porches were illuminated inside and out with candles, lanterns, oil lamps, kerosene lamps, and roaring fireplaces. Chinese lanterns, semi-translucent paper lanterns with candles inside, became the traditional must-have for this event. These decorative pastel lanterns dripped from the cottages' gingerbread trims and bobbed from temporary ropes strung like clotheslines across the front of cottage verandas. Red, white, and star-spangled blue cloth swathed the facades and flowed down the porch columns. Semicircles of bunting hung in swags under windows. On the beach, firecrackers arched over the water, roman candles shot into the dark sky, and fire balloons floated out to sea.

Families promenaded from house to house, admiring the cottage decorations and the brilliant show in the night sky. Bands and drum corps paraded and played. Ulysses's drum corps had the honors in 1888, when Georgiana was the "amiable hostess." People sang. Children danced and twirled their thin, fragrant, slow-burning *joss stick* sparklers. Grandparents rocked on the front porches and worried about fires.

The event was a way for cottagers of all ages to celebrate summer together. The partying started in the afternoon with picnic lunches, swimming, foot races, boat races, baseball games, and indoor whist parties. To the delight of everyone, the Cooley House, a hotel built in 1891 amidst the family cottages and tall elms that lined the road, sold bricks of ice cream in paper cups. At dusk, the popcorn man came down the street pushing his red-trimmed, lit-up, glass-sided wagon from which the distinctive, mouthwatering smell of toasted corn wafted. He would stop along the way to pop, salt, and butter popcorn, an irresistible temptation for a salivating child or adult who then bought a warm, buttery bag for five or ten cents.

Families prepared for this event for weeks. Pressing and hanging the cloth bunting, rigging the ropes, and stringing the Chinese lanterns took hours. It was a labor of love that involved the adults and children of the household, guests included. When the day came,

> everyone dressed up. Despite the heat of August, women wore long white linen dresses with long sleeves, older men wore jackets and ties, young men wore long sleeve shirts and ties, boys wore sailor suits, and girls wore frilly dresses and big bows in their hair. It was the grandest party of the summer.
>
> The Illumination drew people from nearby towns for the stroll and for the fireworks. To the Cook cottage, the Westbrook Grand Illumination drew an overflow of family members and guests who crammed into any available space — including the horse barn in the backyard — for an overnight stay. Other beach communities in the United States also held Illuminations. To this day, Martha's Vineyard, Massachusetts, which lit itself up for the first time in 1869, continues to have a Grand Illumination in Oak Bluffs every August.
>
> West Beach's Illuminations continued, not annually but regularly, for over fifty years, until Westbrook's shoreline was devastated by the Hurricane of 1938, the deadliest and costliest storm in Connecticut's history (which Georgiana's cottage survived). In the early 1980s, a group of neighbors at West Beach held an Illumination Centennial celebration, during which the houses were lit up and decorated as they had been a hundred years before. Georgiana's cottage was center stage.

Georgiana and Ulysses were not alone in their love of the beach. Americans were discovering summer vacations at the shore, a trend that went full steam ahead with the advent of trains, then accelerated with automobiles. West Beach in Westbrook became a popular family cottage destination, which it still is. Today, Georgiana and Ulysses's original cottage is part of a larger, year-round home (my home) at 267 Seaside Avenue. It is still a cedarwood shingle house with rocking chairs on the downstairs porch. It retains the original roofline, the original beadboard ceilings, the center ceiling beam that used to split the east and west sides, traces of a second indoor stairway that was removed, loud creaks when the nor'easters blow, and the spirits of the Smith summer cottagers through the generations, of which Georgiana was the first.

## GEORGIANA, THE AMIABLE AUNT

Imagine having an amiable aunt and jocular uncle with a summer cottage at the beach who welcomed you to visit with open arms! Georgiana and Ulysses were aunt and uncle to two young nieces and two young nephews in the 1880s. All four were the children of Frank and Sarah who resided in Chester. In the last summer of the decade, in 1889, Georgiana's namesake niece Georgia was nine; Frederick Abner Smith (1883–1951) was five; Donald Ulysses Smith (1885–1962) was almost four; and Kittie Louise (1888–1906) was one. What fun they must have had.

I suppose it's questionable whether Lillie had a great time in Westbrook during these first years at the cottage. She would have been going through her preteen and early teen years in the second half of this decade, turning fifteen in 1889 — mature enough to babysit her younger cousins and immature enough to pout about it. The two families, Georgiana and Ulysses with Lillie in Moodus, and Frank and Sarah with their four children plus Lucinda in Chester, were together quite a bit. They would travel back and forth between Moodus and Chester for holidays and visits, and the Westbrook cottage became the family summer vacation spot for all.

Frank and Sarah's children loved, respected, and cared for Aunt Georgiana through her lifetime. They also loved and cared for her Westbrook cottage after she died, keeping it in the Smith family, which it has never left. Frederick Abner, who learned to love the beach at his Aunt Georgiana's cottage, would become my husband's grandfather.

### THE EVENT-FILLED EIGHTIES END

Westbrook summer fun with family and friends, Moodus Drum and Fife Corps marches, Moodus Cornet Band performances, fund-raising fairs for both organizations, parades, picnics, dances, church socials, Ladies Benevolent Society Strawberry Festivals, Moodus Music Hall events, Goodspeed performances, events with

Lillie, visits to Chester, entertaining friends and family in their Moodus home — all added up to an active social life for Georgiana and Ulysses in the 1880 decade. I wonder how Georgiana, Ulysses, and Lillie managed several days alone in their home in March 1888, when everything in Moodus — from the mills, to the drum corps rehearsals, to the horses, to Lillie's piano lessons, to Ulysses's infirmary treatments, to Georgiana's hospitality — came to a halt, silenced by the snow that piled to fifty inches during the Great Blizzard of 1888. Maybe they learned to play whist. My guess is they were restless and eager to get on with the active lives they enjoyed so much.

The decade of the 1880s closed with Georgiana and Ulysses riding the waves of good health and prosperity. As you read more, you will come to admire how steady and seaworthy Georgiana and Ulysses were as they splashed through the next American decade — the Gay Nineties.

*Menunketesuck Point in Westbrook, Connecticut, was a peninsula a half mile from Georgiana's front porch. Today it is known as Menunketesuck Island. Photo taken by Wm. J. Neidlinger, Westbrook, Connecticut.*

CHAPTER 8
# The Splashy Nineties
## Georgiana in Her Forties
## 1890–1900

Like the swelling of a great wave, Georgiana's life continued to rise to the crest of her life in the 1890s. The first half of her life had gradually risen toward this splashy decade and the second half would gradually subside from it. She couldn't have picked a better time to peak, as America's Gay Nineties made its mark on American history.

Georgiana entered 1890 at age forty. She was old enough to appreciate the contrast between this decade and the decade of her childhood during the Civil War, and young enough to fully enjoy the decade that came to be known for its merriment. Fun-loving, music-loving, dance-loving, seashore-loving, life-loving, and fashion-loving — am I describing Georgiana or the 1890s? The answer is both.

Although I have no records to prove it, I'm confident that Georgiana swirled around in the breakers that surged and spilled over the United States during these years. There are no photos of her in this dazzling decade. There are no letters. There is not even an 1890 census record, because of the 1921 fire in Washington D.C. To gain insights into Georgiana's life during these years, I resorted to the limited number of newspaper clippings that included her name, to events that took place near her, to the actions of the men in her life (whose lives, unlike women's, are well-documented), and to the woman I've come to know in writing this book — all viewed, unapologetically, through my rose-colored glasses.

## WHAT A DECADE!

The 1890s were an iconic time for America. Nicknamed the "Gay Nineties" or "Naughty Nineties" retrospectively in the 1920s, the decade is still remembered as one of the happiest in America. The history of these ten years has been preserved with depictions of well-dressed, self-satisfied, playful people: couples dancing the waltz; little boys in knickerbockers rolling hoops; little girls in ruffled pantaloons jumping rope; young lovers strolling together in a park but hardly touching; handsome men tipping their skimmer hats to pretty women who are coyly averting their eyes; red-uniformed brass band members sliding shiny trombones; women posing in the first bathing costumes (later called bathing suits); men pinching their handlebar mustaches; friends singing around an upright player piano; circus strongmen lifting barbells; and well-dressed men clinking beer glasses, toasting the good times.

Having fun became a major activity in America, with musical theater, baseball, horse races, bicycles, boating, beach fun, popcorn wagons, the first comics, the first moving pictures, and waves of new enjoyments. A perfect representative of the decade was the 1893 Chicago world's fair, the World's Columbian Exposition, which attracted more than twenty-seven million visitors, who saw everything new in America, including new foods like Cracker Jacks and Juicy Fruit gum, a Woman's Building, designed by a female architect, and a giant amusement ride that could carry more than two thousand people at one time — the newly invented "Ferris Wheel."

Lest we forget, it is mostly the upper-class Americans who are depicted in these nostalgic images of fashion, fairs, and fun. There were plenty of people who did not have a joyful decade: the lower class lived in poverty; and a serious economic depression from 1893 to 1897 brought runs on banks, high unemployment, and bankruptcies. And at the end of the decade, Americans fought and died in the Spanish-American War. But American history has chosen to depict the 1890s in much the same way the 1950s are depicted in the television sitcom *Happy Days*.

For the Cooks in the 1890s, life was good. Ulysses continued his medical practice and his musical life without missing a beat. Lillie turned sixteen in 1890, in the same decade that James Thornton's sentimental ballad "When You Were Sweet Sixteen" topped the charts. Lillie lived with Georgiana and Ulysses the entire decade and enjoyed their 1890 lifestyle with them. As for Georgiana, she gave her full share to making happy days for Ulysses and Lillie, as well as for guests, at the cottage in Westbrook and at her home in Moodus.

This was the decade when electricity came into homes, lighting the rooms and lightening the work for women. The Cook home was one of the first in Moodus to get electricity. According to *Parker's*, "[in 1892] wires for electric lighting were soon carried to the center of the village [of Moodus], as far east as the office of the New York Net and Twine Company and the house of Dr. Ulysses S. Cook."[91] With electricity came light — light without the mess, light without the danger of fire, and light without labor of the housewife.

## WHAT A DECADE FOR WOMEN!

The invention of electricity sparked a thirty-year stream of inventions that would reduce the labor and time women needed to put into their household duties. Think of Georgiana turning lights on and off without having to struggle with kerosene lamps, lanterns, or candles. Think of her ironing with an electric iron instead of heating and reheating a flat piece of metal on the coal stove. Think of her plugging in an electric fan and letting the breeze cool her down while she used her hands for something other than fanning herself. Think of her pushing around an electric vacuum cleaner, beating cake batter with a standing mixer, and hearing her clothes slosh in a washing machine. Don't think of her using a clothes dryer — dryers were not around in her lifetime. For drying, she would have hung clothes on clotheslines in both her Moodus and Westbrook backyards. Then pause and think of her delight in discovering she had leisure time, a new concept for women.

With the advent of leisure time, like many women of the 1890s, Georgiana had more time for social activities, which meant more occasions to wear *going out* clothes. A new style in American women's clothing got its kick start in this decade, putting the long skirts and long sleeves of all previous generations solidly in the past. From the practical day dresses to the fanciest evening attire, women's outfits began to allow more ease of movement, a welcome change from the many-layered, voluminous, restricting, bustle-rigged, takes-an-hour-to-get-on dresses women were used to.

Laces were finally starting to loosen. But the corset — the very symbol of restriction for women, the painful vice that women wore to comply with society's expectations of the female figure, and a target for women suffragists — persisted. Georgiana wore a corset her whole adult life. Despite the more forgiving corsets designed for sporting women, and despite some physicians speaking out against the crushing harm of corsets on women's bodies, in the 1890s, women of every class continued to wear corsets (including under their new bathing costumes) to forcibly mold themselves into the ideal "hourglass figure." Even when, two decades later, the United States issued a patent in 1914 for a *brassiere* (which, by the way, was to a woman, Caresse Crosby, the former Mary Phelps Jacobs), corsets didn't die in great numbers until the 1940s when the steel used in corsets' stays was needed for World War II supplies. Georgiana did not live to see the days without corsets.

In my view, few images are more iconic of the 1890s than the tiny waists and distinctive fashion of women's clothing of these years: pinching belts; high-neck collars; *leg-of-mutton sleeves* with their giant puffs from shoulder to elbow; long A-line shaped skirts with a kick; high-buttoned shoes with sturdy heels; wintertime's formfitting jackets with securely fastened, ornate buttons; summertime's white cotton eyelet dresses trimmed with lace; and pretty, but not-just-for-looks, parasols.

A distinctive hairstyle also defined the decade. Long hair was pinned up and swirled into artistic designs, often with the help of faux hair pieces. Short curly bangs were perfectly coiffed. And perched on the top of heads, secured with fashionable pins, and tilted just so, sat massive and magnificent hats — hats with ribbons, flowers, feathers, fake fruit, and the kitchen sink.

*Sketched by L. Durie.*

Did Georgiana dress like this? Given that much of her life involved social events, and that she had a husband who could afford the latest fashions, I think the answer is yes. But she would not have dressed like the high society women in *Harper's Bazar*, the American women's fashion magazine first published in 1867 that catered to the middle and upper classes. (An interesting aside: *Harper's Bazar* did not spell Bazaar with three *A*'s until 1929.) Nor would Georgiana have dressed like the women in *Vogue*, the new magazine for the elite in New York City. Georgiana was a small-town Connecticut woman, who would have dressed in modest versions of the new styles.

Georgiana could have purchased ready-made clothing in stores by the 1890s, but she likely hired a dressmaker for her special occasion dresses. For hats, she and Lillie may have shopped in Moodus at Elliott J. Rogers on Main Street, which advertised a "Full Line of Millinery, Dry and Fancy Goods."[92] (The term *fancy goods* was a common nineteenth-century catchall term for nonessential, often ornamental accessories such as gloves, parasols, buttons, hairpins, mirrors, ribbons, and handkerchiefs.) After seeing sketches of the latest women's fashions in Hartford newspapers, Georgiana and Lillie may have taken the train to Hartford. There, G. Fox was growing into a large, fashionable department store and offering delivery of purchases to customers' homes if they spent enough money, and if their home was within fifty miles. Georgiana lived within delivery distance!

## G. FOX & CO.

### Free Delivery.

We deliver without charge within a radius of 50 miles all goods (excepting furniture) amounting to $5.00 or more, thus affording our many out of town friends an opportunity of purchasing goods at our store with the same advantages that city people have.

### Ladies' Sweaters.

For Bicycle Riders and Lawn Tennis, button on the shoulder or lace front. High sleeves or coat sleeves. Colors, white, tan, black, cardinal and navy.

*Advertisement from the* Hartford Courant, *April 5, 1895.*

# Daisy Changes to a Bicycle Built for One

*Daisy, Daisy,*
*Give me your answer do!*
*I'm half crazy*
*All for the love of you!*
*It won't be a stylish marriage,*
*I can't afford a carriage.*
*But you'll look sweet on the seat*
*Of a bicycle built for two!* [93]

LYRICS AND MUSIC BY HARRY DACRE
1892

This well-known song was written in 1892 when America was on the cusp of a bicycle craze. It became an instant hit, one of the many waltz songs of the 1890s that depicted courtships of American men and women.

Early in the decade, bicycles built for two were rare. They were expensive and downright difficult to operate, especially for the person on the back seat who pedaled for two. Rare also in 1892 were women who rode bicycles. Within a couple years, though, large numbers of American women took to cycling. And they rode bicycles built for one. At the start of the decade, the country produced forty thousand bicycles a year — at the end, a million a year. Americans went crazy for bicycles.

Sales of bicycles had boomed in the late 1880s after the invention of "safety bicycles." This new style of bicycle, unlike its utterly awkward predecessors, had brakes, cushioned tires, and wheels of the same size. Today's bicycles are the same basic style. Factories for safety bicycles opened around the nation. Leading the way was Pope Manufacturing Company in Hartford, Connecticut, where Albert A. Pope produced his Columbia Safeties. Until 1896, Pope was the top producer of bicycles in the country. For those who know Hartford — yes, Pope Park is named after him. He donated the property to the city for a public park in 1895.

*Advertisement from the* Hartford Courant, *July 27, 1895. One hundred dollars is the equivalent of about $3,100 in 2020.*

The bicycle craze in America was driven by urban upper- and middle-class men and women. Businessmen found bicycles an affordable, comfortable, and efficient alternative to horses, carriages, streetcars, and trains. They enjoyed the freedom of not having to tend to horses, the control over their own schedules, the private commuting time, the money saved, and the time saved.

Both men and women loved bicycles as a new form of recreation. Bicycle clubs and wheel clubs (the terms *wheel* and *bicycle* were used interchangeably) sprung up in towns and villages across the country. Bicycle parties became fashionable. Bicycle tours became great escapes. Bicycle language entered the vocabulary. Newspapers published regular bicycle columns and bicycle advertisements. And bicycle racing became as popular a sport as baseball.

Women found the new bicycles easy to ride, especially the new *ladies' bicycle* with its drop frame to accommodate long skirts. Women also found new freedoms with bicycles — freedom from dependence on a man to hitch horses to a carriage, freedom to self-schedule, freedom to select whom to ride with, freedom to ride alone. Along with the bicycle craze came a rational dress movement enabling women to pedal without fear of their clothing getting entangled in the wheels. The change in fashion to accommodate women's ability to ride a bicycle resuscitated divided skirts and bloomers, which had been rejected in women's fashion for decades. Shorter skirts and trousers for women were introduced. And so that women could move and breathe on a bicycle, the rational dress movement crushed the bones of the vicious corset monster, sending corsets on their first steps down the path toward extinction.[94]

The bicycle could easily be considered one of the famous American feminists. It symbolized the spirit of change in American women of the 1890s as they emerged on their path to self-reliance. Susan B. Anthony, perhaps the most famous American feminist, would agree. At age seventy-six, in 1896, she wrote, "Let me tell you what I think of bicycling. I think it has done more to emancipate women than anything else in the world. It gives women a feeling of freedom and self-reliance. I stand and rejoice every time I see a woman ride by on a wheel … the picture of free untrammeled womanhood."[95]

*Advertisement for Ferris' Good Sense Waist for Bicycle Wear, 1987 (National Museum of American History).*

## NEW WOMAN

Looking back, we can see that the new leisure time, new fashions, and new bicycles all paved the way for an emerging *new woman*, or maybe it was the other way around. The *new woman* represented the change in women from those who were interested in homemaking, educated for homemaking, and active in homemaking to those interested in careers, educated for diverse occupations, and active in sports. And a change from women reliant on men for government and submissive to men in marriage, to self-reliant women who wanted a voice equal to men's in government and in marriage.

A small number of women had set the stage for the *new woman* at the start of Georgiana's life. By the 1890s, Georgiana was most likely aware of the term, or at least the concept. I wonder what she thought of the changing role of women. She wouldn't have known that she was at the midpoint of an historic change in the country's social order. Both Georgiana and the United States women's suffrage movement were at the halfway mark of their lives in the 1890s. Georgiana lived from 1849 to 1930; the women's suffrage movement lived from 1848 to 1920, when it achieved its major goal — passage of the Nineteenth Amendment, which gave women the right to vote.

In the 1890s, Georgiana could not have foreseen the major changes for women that would take place in the second half of her life. She may have noticed some articles about the women suffragists in the national news. She may have chatted with other women about voting. She may have read about the sharply criticized publications written in the 1890s by women authors about women's issues, such as Charlotte Perkins Gilman's short story, "The Yellow Wallpaper," in 1892, or Kate Chopin's book, *The Awakening*, in 1899. She may have sensed a change coming.

Would Georgiana have initiated discussions about women's rights with Lillie and her nieces? At the end of the decade, Lillie was twenty-five, and Georgiana's nieces, Georgia and Kittie, were twenty and eleven. Maybe these young ladies of the new generation brought the issues to her attention! I hope they did, and I hope they had lively conversations!

> ## Conversations in the 1890s
>
> In the 1890s, women and men stayed primarily within their separate spheres for conversation. Most women, and I presume Georgiana was one of them, were casual newspaper readers. They scanned the headlines and browsed a weekly column dedicated to topics the newspaper editors felt would attract women readers. (Topics were often fashion.) Women's conversations with one another were less about national or state affairs, and more about events and relationships close to home, with word of mouth as their main source for news.
>
> Men like Ulysses were avid newspaper readers and would talk with one another about current events, sports, and politics. I picture Ulysses with his male friends in early 1891 blustering out opinions about why the U.S. Navy team crushed the U.S. Army team in football with a score of 24-0 in November 1890 (the first Army–Navy game), what really happened at Wounded Knee in South Dakota in December 1890, the unlikelihood of automobiles replacing horses, the improbability of escalators working properly, the flaws in the roads, the flaws with President Harrison, the flaws with the voting process in Connecticut's gubernatorial race in the November 1890 election, the flaws of legislators for not yet resolving the problem, the flaws with all politicians, and the certainty that the split between Democrats and Republicans in Connecticut was irreconcilable.
>
> What was all the talk about the flawed November 1890 election? In the early months of 1891, the main topic of conversation in the men's sphere in Connecticut was the continuing delay in naming the winner of the November election for governor. Due to ballot irregularities, the interpretation of the voting laws, and the formula for computing a majority, the state had been unable to declare a new governor to take office in 1891. As it turns out, they were never able to. The former governor, East-Haddam-born Morgan Gardner

> Bulkeley (1837–1922) had not run for reelection in November 1890, but with the gridlock in declaring a new governor, he refused to leave office and in an unprecedented, unresolved, and unbelievable controversy, served as *de facto* governor for the full 1891–1893 term. The issue dominated the news and conversations in Connecticut until a new governor was elected in November 1892.
>
> I picture Georgiana with her friends in the women's sphere during these years, asserting opinions on the new fashions for lady bicycle riders, the difficulty of learning to ride a bicycle, the beautiful new Episcopal church and its need for a bell tower, the new Haviland china patterns, Frank Fowler's new mansion, the disgrace of Frank Fowler's business, the ridiculous price of a pound of butter, the flaws with the school system, the flaws with the new minister, the flaws with the new minister's wife, the flaws with the grocer, the flaws with the laundress, and the flaws with the government men who couldn't even count votes.

## A DECADE OF JOLLIFICATIONS

[jollification, noun. jol·li·fi·ca·tion | \ jä-li-fə-'kā-shən \

*A nineteenth-century word that hardly needs a dictionary definition, but is defined in Merriam-Webster as festivity, merrymaking.*]

It was a musical time for the nation, metaphorically and literally. Live music ruled the day. Military marching music, the favorite of Ulysses and many Americans, reached its pinnacle through the brilliance of John Philip Sousa (1854–1932), who formed his famous Sousa Band in 1892. In New York City, where bright streetlights made the streets safer, and trolleys made transportation easier, family-friendly entertainment blossomed and prostitution wilted. Musical comedies were performed by the hundreds on Broadway. Carnegie Hall opened in 1891 and became the performance destination for classical and popular musicians worldwide.

In America's small towns, local bands and orchestras increased in popularity, providing music for parades, picnics, political rallies, celebrations, fairs, dances, and Sunday afternoon outdoor concerts on town greens.

Recorded music was in its infancy but had made its debut with discs that could record and play music on new inventions called phonographs and gramophones. Now Americans could listen to Sousa's band in their home parlors.

## Sousamania

"When the sale of seats for John Philip Sousa's appearance opened this morning, there was a lively rush of purchasers. The man is omnipresent. It is Sousa in the military camp, Sousa in the ballroom, Sousa in the concert hall; everywhere it is Sousa. The urchin in the street blithely whistles his stirring marches; the sweet girl graduate electrifies her friends with his stirring strains. It is Sousa in the phonograph, Sousa in the hand organ, Sousa in the music box; and for the next week it will be Sousa in every part of Waterbury. Sale opened this morning: prices 50, 75 cents and $1."

This excerpt from Connecticut's *Naugatuck Daily News,* April 29, 1899, describes the *Sousamania* that had captured America. During the 1890s, John Philip Sousa was a superstar, perhaps the first American superstar. Patriotic marching music was a favorite of Americans at this time, much like rock 'n' roll would be in future decades. And the king of marching music was Sousa; Americans were wild to see him.

Known as "The March King," Sousa composed and conducted America's famous patriotic marching music. He formed his Sousa Band in 1892. Through the 1890s and for thirty more years, Sousa conducted his band in more than fifteen thousand live performances nationally and internationally. Connecticut towns, including Hartford, New Haven, Waterbury, and Meriden, were on Sousa's annual touring schedule. Fans came from across the state to see the master of the bandmasters.

*This is not Ulysses. This is John Philip Sousa.*

At the same time, gramophones and phonographs were debuting, improving, and entering American homes. As was the recording industry. Sousa's marches were among the first and most popular recordings. Although Sousa felt that the new *mechanical music* might harm the experience of music (if you listen to the early recordings, you will hear why he thought this), by 1897 he had become a recording star.

Sousa composed over 130 marches. In 1896, he wrote his masterpiece, "The Stars and Stripes Forever." It has been, and is still, played by thousands of musicians. In 1987, the song was adopted as the National March of the United States.

Sousa died in a hotel room in Pennsylvania a day after guest-conducting a rehearsal of the "The Stars and Stripes Forever" with a community band. He was seventy-seven, the same age as Mick Jagger was in 2020.

During this decade, Americans also became enthralled with Tin Pan Alley songs and sang them everywhere — from the Broadway stage to corner barbershops. In the evenings, home parlors would find family and friends leaning over the piano player, reading the lyrics from the latest popular sheet music, and singing their hearts out — often with a favorite uncle singing loudly, happily, and obliviously off-key.

Pianos were sold by the millions in the 1890s. For the first time, pianos were affordable to the growing middle class, due largely to the innovation of monthly installment payment plans. When Singer introduced the new installment payment plans for sewing machine purchases, piano companies latched onto them. Piano sheet music of popular songs became a new commodity. Millions of copies were sold, reaching homes everywhere in the nation, including a house on Falls Road in Moodus, Connecticut, where I envision a parlor with musical notes, musical staffs, G clefs, and colorful covers on every surface, jammed into the piano bench, and piled on the floor.

### Tin Pan Alley Songs

Tin Pan Alley songs dominated the American popular music scene in the 1890s. They were first published in the form of sheet music at a time when live performances and at-home pianos were the only ways for most Americans to hear popular songs. For four decades, both Tin Pan Alley sheet music and pianos couldn't be produced fast enough. It wasn't until the 1930s that phonographs and radios, both of which increased exponentially in quality and accessibility, upstaged sheet music as the music industry's main product.

Tin Pan Alley was not an alley. It was a district in New York City's Manhattan borough on West 28th Street, between Broadway and Sixth Avenue, renowned for its large number of music publishers' headquarters and its music stores. Eventually, the biggest music companies in the nation established themselves there with their own printing companies to print their own sheet music.

*Sketched by L. Durie.*

And Tin Pan Alley did not sell tin pans. Some say the name Tin Pan Alley was coined by a New York newspaper writer, Monroe Rosenfeld, who likened the din of composers demonstrating their new songs on cheap upright pianos to the sound of someone banging on tin pans. There are other versions of the name's origin, but they all connect back to the tinny sounds produced on cheap pianos.

Tin Pan Alley's goal was sales, and sappy songs sold. The lyrics of Tin Pan Alley songs were often tearjerkers, stories that contribute considerably to the sentimental images we have today of the 1890s. The biggest hits included tunes and lyrics that are still known to many now. I bet you can sing a line or two from some of these:

- "After the Ball" (Charles K. Harris, 1892)
- "The Sidewalks of New York" (Charles B. Lawlor and James W. Blake, 1894)
- "And the Band Played On" (Charles B. Ward and John F. Palmer, 1895)

- "There'll Be a Hot Time in the Old Town Tonight" (Joe Hayden and Theodore Mertz, 1896)
- "On the Banks of the Wabash, Far Away" (Paul Dresser, 1897)
- "Hello Ma Baby (Hello Ma Ragtime Gal)" (Joseph E. Howard and Ida Emerson, 1899)
- "A Bird in a Gilded Cage" (Harry Von Tilzer, 1900)
- "In the Good Old Summertime" (Ron Shields and George Evans, 1902)
- "Bill Bailey, Won't You Please Come Home" (Huey Cannon, 1902)
- "Give My Regards to Broadway" (George M. Cohan, 1904)
- "In the Shade of the Old Apple Tree" (Harry Williams and Egbert Van Alstyne, 1905)
- "Take Me Out to the Ball Game" (Albert Von Tilzer and Jack Norworth, 1908)
- "By the Light of the Silvery Moon" (Gus Edwards and Edward Madden, 1909)
- "Down by the Old Mill Stream" (Tell Taylor, 1910)
- "Let Me Call You Sweetheart" (Beth Slater Whitson and Leo Friedman, 1910)
- "God Bless America" (Irving Berlin, 1918)

*Two sources provided much of the information for this section; (1) "Tin Pan Alley Music Genre Overview," allmusic.com and (2) Wikipedia's "Tin Pan Alley" entry.*[96]

With music and Sousa marches so prominent in American life, Ulysses was probably one of the happiest of men in the 1890s. I might even dub him the "Metronome of Moodus," given that much of the rhythm of Moodus's musical life marched to Ulysses's beat. He continued beating the snare drum for the drum corps and continued as drum major for the Moodus Cornet Band. For Georgiana, Ulysses's musical group connections offered her social events and friends.

## The Moodus Cornet Band: Filled with Friends of the Cooks

Cornet bands were not unusual in the 1890s. Even little East Haddam had two. What were they? Did only cornets, similar to but smaller than trumpets, play? These bands were full of cornets, yes, but they were also full of other instruments.

The Moodus Cornet Band was also filled with friends of Georgiana and Ulysses—friends whose names come up in Georgiana's story repeatedly and some of them, their closest friends.

To show the variety of instruments and the familiar names, I have included this list of the members of the original band from 1886 as it appeared in *Parker's* (143b).

| Name/Title | Instrument |
|---|---|
| Thaddeus R. Spencer, President | Cornet |
| Charles H. Rogers, Secretary | Clarinet |
| William J. Thomas, Treasurer | Trombone |
| Joseph A. Cone, Leader | Cornet |
| Dr. Ulysses S. Cook, Property Manager | Drum Major |
| J. Wilbert Chapman, Property Manager | |
| Frank C. Fowler, Property Manager | |
| Edward J. Grundshaw | Cornet |
| G. P. LeCrenier | Cornet |
| Harold F. Chapman | Clarinet |
| Dr. E. E. Williams | Clarinet |
| Louis G. Mitchell | Alto (Saxophone) |
| Charles H. Moshier | Alto (Saxophone) |
| J. Herbert Cone | Alto (Saxophone) |
| Thomas H. Carroll | Trombone |
| George W. Rich | Baritone(Saxophone) |
| Jeremiah O'Connell | Bass drum |
| Michael J. Barry | Snare drum |
| James Edward Clevonshire | Cymbals |

> Ulysses served as drum major from the start of the band in 1886 until 1905 when the original group suspended activities. The group reorganized in 1916, but Ulysses did not rejoin.
>
> Wives of the band members are not mentioned in *Parker's*, even in the article about the band's popular annual picnic and dance, which reads: "The Moodus Cornet Band held a picnic with a dance in a pavilion in Lord's grove for several years, which soon came to be anticipated as an enjoyable social event." This event was surely run by the wives of members, Georgiana included.

As if two active musical groups weren't enough, Ulysses founded a third. He formed his own orchestra, and this time he played the violin. *Parker's* reports:

> In 1893 Dr. Ulysses S. Cook organized an orchestra in Moodus, which for a number of years [about twenty!] furnished music for dances, receptions, and other social functions, not only in East Haddam, but in several other towns.[97]

The violin? The violin was a household fixture in many homes in America, and had been since America's birth. Not everyone could master it, but Ulysses did. Perhaps Ulysses studied the violin because the famous John Philip Sousa, no doubt his idol, was an accomplished violinist. Or perhaps he did so to please Georgiana, who would have enjoyed the orchestra-type events that often included dancing. As for Ulysses's skill with the violin, a line in his obituary in the *Hartford Courant* (November 19, 1925) reads: "Dr. Cook was a musician of unusual ability on the violin."

Ulysses's orchestra consisted of five musicians: Ulysses, three men, and a pianist. Initially, the three men were Harold F. Chapman, J. Oldorf, and Lyman R. Sexton. Later they were (Mr.) Bernice William Talbot, Eugene B. Thomas, and Charles T. Spencer. Who was the pianist? Lillie! She was nineteen when the orchestra was created and was the pianist for its first seventeen years.

In 1910, Miss Carrie Bowers (1882–?)[98] took over the role. Miss Bowers's father was a good friend of Ulysses and a member of the Moodus Drum and Fife Corps.

Never losing first place in Ulysses's musical world, however, was his beloved Moodus Drum and Fife Corps, in which he continued as music director and wearer of many hats: head of property and fund-raising event committees, chairman pro tem at meetings, host of business meetings, and leader of practices. He and the corps were devoted to East Haddam's Decoration Day events on May 30 each year and to the political rallies for presidential candidates from both parties in 1892 and 1896. In 1892, they played at the Goodspeed Opera House for incumbent Benjamin Harrison (R) and in Marlborough for Grover Cleveland (D). They joined the Democratic Jollification at East Haddam Landing in mid-November to celebrate Cleveland's victory.

Woven into the local schedule were several out-of-town trips:

- In 1890, to Boston for the twenty-fourth annual encampment of the Grand Army.
- In August 1891, to play twice before President Benjamin Harrison — first in Bennington, Vermont, at a dedication of a monument, and later in Saratoga, New York, at the Grand Union Hotel.
- In September 1892, to Washington, D.C. for another encampment of the Grand Army.
- In 1895, to the Great Parade in Copley Square, Boston, Massachusetts, where a newspaper reported that the Moodus Drum and Fife Corps was "hailed with delight, sharing with the commandery in the plaudits of the crowd." This parade was reported to have had fifty thousand spectators with twenty-five to thirty thousand marching men who showed (according to the newspaper reporter) "great manhood."[99]
- In 1896, to New York City for the Sound Money Parade, reported as the "largest parade ever held in the United States."[100] This parade was in support of presidential candidate William F.

McKinley, whose monetary policy was labeled Sound Money.[101] Ulysses was the drum major for this parade.
- In 1897, to Hartford for the Farragut Day Parade.

The drum corps life was indeed a source of jollity for Ulysses. And for Georgiana. She and the other drum corps ladies — the wives of the gentlemen of the drum corps — ran the local social events, such as fairs, dances and picnics, to help raise funds for the corps.

### Let's Not Forget the Ladies

Five years of minutes from the business meetings of the Moodus Drum and Fife Corps have been preserved in a large, blue-covered paper document titled *Records of the Moodus Drum and Fife Corps, December 31, 1887 to October 3, 1892*. The booklet was produced in 1974 from original drum corps records and is available at the East Haddam Historical Society.

According to these minutes, the men were extraordinarily busy. In addition to their local performances, they met for weekly Monday evening business meetings, routine committee meetings, special meetings, practices with **Drum Leader and Music Director Dr. U.S. Cook,** and out-of-state trips that included hotel stays. They also enjoyed local day trips together. In September 1891 the corps sailed on the Connecticut River to Saybrook, recorded in the minutes as follows: "On invitation of Drum Major Captain W.E. Odber [the man who sold the Westbrook cottage to Ulysses], fourteen members of the corps went in uniform and with drums and fifes in his steam yacht, to Saybrook, and enjoyed a fine shore dinner at the Leonard House. The day passed pleasantly and in due time we reached home in safety." I doubt that Ulysses missed this trip, or one meeting, one practice, or one event of the corps.

Most of the drum corps activities were for men only. But a fund-raising fair in early 1892 is a good example of how Georgiana and other wives were involved. The planning for the fair began at the regular business meeting of the corps members on November 30, 1891. The minutes read: "Voted — That the corps hold a fair, duration and dates to be decided upon by the committee to be raised

THE SPLASHY NINETIES

> and that the following named persons be a Committee: C. H. Rogers, W. W. Beckwith, W. J. Comstock, **U. S. Cook** and D. J. Treat." Arrangements were made by the committee for the fair to be held in late January 1892 in Moodus's downtown Music Hall. In the minutes, this building was once referred to as Fowler's Hall because the Music Hall building was owned by Frank C. Fowler.
>
> A January indoor fair in New England? What went on? One thing I'm sure of — there was dancing. The December 1891 minutes record that George Bowers (father of the piano-playing Carrie) and Fred Hefflon were named as the committee "in full charge of dancing at fair." The event was held in late January as planned. It was successful, raising a satisfactory amount of money. At meetings held after the event, the corps voted to appoint trustees of the corps's funds. Appointed were Secretary/Treasurer W. J. Comstock, Past President W. W. Beckwith, and **U. S. Cook.**
>
> Behind the scenes of this successful event were the ladies — the wives of the drum corps gentlemen. The minutes of March 16, 1892, read: "Voted that the Secretary be authorized to write an article for local papers, extending thanks to those who made donations to our recent fair, and not forgetting the ladies." Georgiana was certainly one of these ladies. She and the other wives likely had their own form of camaraderie as they prepared for this event, busily conducting the many tasks needed for a successful social event that women from all generations know so well. [I'm so glad they weren't forgotten.]

### THE CONTINENTAL NEXT DOOR

Amid their popularity in 1892, the drum corps recognized the need for its own facility for practicing and meeting. Since the corps' inception, members had met in various places — in rooms they rented, in buildings owned by members, or in members' homes, including Georgiana and Ulysses's.

The corps's dream was to build a hall, a big hall — one not only for practices and meetings, but large enough for public entertainment. To fund it, the business heads of the corps (I'm quite sure that Ulysses was not one of them) held fund-raisers and set up a state-approved corporation, selling shares at $25 [$700 in 2020] each to members. Ideas for the grand hall were drawn up, but land was needed for the structure.

Like a parent who helps a son or daughter buy a first home, Ulysses gave the new corporation a generous gift — the perfect piece of land. Perfect as the site for the hall and perfect for him, as it was right next door to his house. Within a year, the corps had built the hall of their dreams. *Parker's* reports:

> The building was completed and furnished, ready for use in April 1893. Upon a happy suggestion of Arthur J. Silliman, it was named "Continental Hall." [Arthur J. Silliman (1855–1929) was joint owner with Albert E. Purple of Moodus's Purple and Silliman's dry goods store.] It had upon the first floor a commodious dining room, kitchen and storeroom. The hall on the second floor was 62 by 40 feet, and a dressing room under the stage. The building was admirably lighted with electric lights and provided with a cloak room and ticket office. The hall was finished in hard wood with an excellent floor for dancing. It was admirably adapted for use for musical entertainments, dramatic presentations, or public speaking.
>
> The Continental Hall was opened to the public with a concert and ball on April 19, 1893. Every seat was filled, and the occasion was at the time described as the largest social event in the history of the town. Financially it was very successful, and over $400 [about $11,000 in 2020] was realized for the benefit of the [Moodus Drum and Fife] corps.[102]

If ever Georgiana would get a stunning new dress and fancy goods to match, it would have been for this ball!

For Georgiana and Ulysses in 1893, the brand new Continental building may have been an extension of their own home. There in the Continental, the drum corps practiced, performed, and stored their instruments. There, Ulysses gave his drum lessons. There,

Ulysses's orchestra practiced and performed. There, parties were held, plays were put on, and special events took place. There, the Ladies Benevolent Society of the Moodus Methodist Episcopal Church held their annual June Strawberry Festival. There, the Decoration Day parade began, and there, the parade ended, to be followed by an evening of music and refreshments.

Imagine Georgiana enjoying this new space and new amenities for entertaining in style; imagine her secret joy at having no more drums thundering in her home; and imagine her delight with the large dance floor! All right next door.

## A DECADE OF DANCING

Georgiana, Ulysses, and Lillie dancing happily at the Continental — now, that's a picture right out of the 1890s, even if it's only in my mind. Would Georgiana have danced with others — men, women, or children — while her husband played in the orchestra? Yes, I think so. She likely attended the orchestra events and frequently acted as hostess, in charge of refreshments or greeting guests. And she probably helped Ulysses select the music for the dances. *Harper's Bazar* carried this article which describes the type of dancing Georgiana may have experienced. Here are some excerpts:

> [*Harper's Bazar*, December 22, 1896]
> It is not unusual for a dancing entertainment to be given where the order of dances for the entire evening is made up of jolly waltzes, polkas, and two-steps, danced one after the other, with about twice as many waltzes and two-steps as polkas.
>
> The two-step, which is now in full tide of popular favor, almost rivaling the waltz in the opinion of its devotees, is danced to march time, the fine spirited marches of Sousa's being the music most used to accompany it.

> To make such an entertainment thoroughly successful, however, the greatest care must be taken in the selection of the musicians who are to play the dance music. It is not necessary to have many of them, but those chosen must be well prepared. Their selections must be new and gay, the time well accentuated, but not too much so and all the pieces played with the right spirit for dancing. Each selection should last about twenty minutes, and then should come a rest of about ten minutes before the next one is begun.[103]

I imagine that Georgiana whirled her way through this decade.

### A DECADE FOR BEACH FUN

Going to the beach, made possible for many by the railroad, became a new summertime leisure activity in the 1890s. For people like Georgiana and Ulysses, who enjoyed entertaining and jollifications, few places could compare to a shoreline cottage full of family and friends. Especially in this decade, when the new *bathing costumes* encouraged men and women to cool off in the sea.

After ten years of owning one half of the cottage and falling in love with Westbrook, Ulysses bought the eastern half in July 1893. He bought "one half of a cottage by the Sea Shore" from Mary Brainard for $375 [about $11,000 in 2020].[104] Owning both halves meant that Ulysses could rent one half to friends while he, Georgiana, and Lillie stayed in the other half, or it might have meant that they could throw one heck of a party for friends and family.

After the purchase of the cottage's second half, one of the first guests of Georgiana and Ulysses was Middlesex County Sheriff Thomas S. Brown (1854–1927) and his family from Chatham/East Hampton. Sheriff Brown's wife was Elizabeth (born Chapman) Brown (1856–1931). Elizabeth was the daughter of Horatio Chapman, Georgiana's father's tentmate throughout the Civil War. Elizabeth was nine and Georgiana was fifteen when Elizabeth's father carried Georgiana's wounded and dying father to the field hospital in 1865. Horatio Chapman, I believe, watched over Georgiana after the death of her father and after the war. His daughter Elizabeth and Georgiana likely formed a special bond that continued as married women, with Georgiana's husband, Ulysses, and Elizabeth's husband, Sheriff Brown, social friends. (It was good to have a sheriff as a friend in the 1890s.)

From the newspapers of the day, we get a picture of the summertime fun at West Beach. Here are some clips:

[*Hartford Courant,* July 4, 1896]
The Cooley House[105] on West Beach run by Joseph Cooley of Hartford is enjoying its usual patronage. [The Cooley House was Cooley's Hotel, about a five-minute stroll to the east of the Cook Cottage.] Mr. Cooley is making extensive preparations for the Fourth. A special shore dinner will be served from 11 a.m. to 7 p.m. Brooks's orchestra of Chester will render selections from 11 a.m. to 12. The Deep River Drum Corps will endeavor to inspire the cottagers from 1 to 3 p.m. In the evening will be the prettiest sight of all: the illumination and fireworks. Dancing will be indulged in from 7:30 p.m. to 11 p.m.

And a month later:

[Excerpts from the *New York Herald,* August 9, 1896]
**Summer Home of Cottages**
*Connecticut's Principal Cities Represented in the Colonies of Westbrook*
WESTBROOK, CONNECTICUT

At this populous Connecticut resort, August is the liveliest month, and the cottages and hotels are fast filling with summer sojourners. At no place along the coast line of the State are there to be found so many summer cottages as here at Westbrook. There are nearly one hundred and seventy-five cottages. During August these are all occupied making the summer population more than a thousand.

Westbrook beach stretches in crescent shape from Kelsey's to Menunketesuck Point, a distance of two miles and offers a pleasant view of the Sound, with the blue hills of Long Island in the distance. A picturesque cluster of rocks half a mile off shore bears the name of Salt Island, and lends enchantment to the young folks as once having been a haunt of Captain Kidd and his band of pirates.

The centres of social activity are the two hotels. The Saturday night hops are very popular, and the hotel parlors and verandas are crowded with a gay assemblage of young persons all during the evening. Progressive whist parties and musicales are favorite diversions on cool evenings.

Tennis is a favorite pastime with some of the cottages, but in the degree of popularity, bicycling far surpasses all other forms of recreation, even bathing and yachting. Any person on the beach who does not ride a wheel is practically ostracized. The roads to Fenwick, Saybrook and Clinton are as good as cycle paths, and are more traversed by wheels than by any other conveyance. Bicycle parties to the neighboring resorts for shore dinners are everyday events. Guests of the Pochoug House [a hotel] have formed a wheel club. Half of the members are women.

The excellent opportunities for bathing and boating and the scarcity of mosquitoes have made Westbrook distinctly a family resort.

The blackfishing grounds are frequented every day by parties with hook and line, and some big catches have been made, or rather reported. [This made me chuckle.] Dr. U.S. Cooke makes a catch of a hundred or more a week.

Ulysses's blackfishing success had been reported the year before, in 1895, by another Connecticut newspaper who credited him with holding the record for the largest blackfish ever caught — twelve pounds. Was Ulysses telling fish stories? The reporter above certainly hints that it indeed was a fish story when he adds "or rather reported." The term *fish story* originated in America to describe the traditional exaggeration by fisherman of the size of their catch. Ulysses was American through and through.

And ten days later:

>[Excerpts from the *Hartford Courant,* August 19, 1896]
>
>**Westbrook Pleasures**
>
>*Sailing And Fishing Parties To Falkner's And The Race*
>
>A party of sixteen young people from West Beach sailed to Falkner's Island Saturday in Captain Myers's Sensation ... Their arrival in the bay at sundown was very manifest by the din of tin horns and whistles and the waving of flags.
>
>Monday morning Captain Fred Avery took out a West Beach party of eight in his Ada. The boat made a quick run to Fenwick and back.
>
>Not a little amusement was caused yesterday afternoon by half a dozen young and ambitious athletes on West Beach in a close and exciting four-legged race. [A four-legged race is a race of three people running in unison with the middle person's legs tied to the adjacent legs of the other two runners.]
>
>A delightful entertainment was given by St. Paul's Guild in the town hall this evening, several farces being presented. Those who took part were largely beachers. [That's an old-fashioned word I would like to see make a comeback!]
>
>"Jenkins Up" is again coming into popularity on the beach and parties are everyday occurrences. [Jenkins Up is a group game involving two teams. It is often a drinking game and is set around a table. A member from one team holds a coin in their closed hand, as the others on the team pretend to, and the opposing team tries to guess who holds the coin. Rules vary considerably.]

Georgiana, Ulysses, and Lillie did not spend their entire summers in Westbrook. I believe they went every summer in late July and in August. They acted as many of the owners of summer-only cottages still act today in Westbrook, taking day road trips in the spring to *open the cottage*, renting it to others for a week at a time in summer, using it themselves from two to four weeks in the prime time, and, in the fall, popping down for a weekend to *close down the cottage*, leaving it bundled up with shutters securely bolted to brave the winter alone.

### A DECADE OF DUBIOUS MEDICINE

Ulysses continued practicing medicine and seeing his patients in a dedicated section of their Moodus home. I believe (and hope, for Georgiana's sake) that the infirmary for his Thomsonian Medicine treatments of bloodletting, purgatives, and emetics was sufficiently separated from their personal living space.

Medicine in the 1890s was ugly. There was little regulation of treatments or drugs or physicians. In Connecticut, an act was passed in 1893 requiring physicians, for the first time, to hold a certificate of registration/license issued by the state's Board of Health. Ulysses was approved for a certificate at the first issuing in 1893. He remained a cancer specialist, sticking with his Thomsonian Medicine methods, which were respectable treatments in the 1890s. He did not perform surgery. I can confirm this because he is not identified as a surgeon in any records, as other doctors were. He was one of four doctors in the 1896 *East Haddam Directory*, in which two were listed as "Physician and Surgeon," one was listed as simply "Physician," and one, Ulysses, was listed as "Cancer Specialist."

The doctor with the title of simply "Physician" in the directory was Dr. Eugene E. Williams (1863–1924), whose office and home were located on Main Street in Moodus. According to the *Directory of Deceased American Physicians, 1804–1929*, a directory that was compiled in 1929 from handwritten 4" x 6" card files created and preserved by the American Medical Association, both Ulysses and Dr. Williams practiced "allopathy." Allopathy was a term used to describe conventional or mainstream medicinal treatment.

I think Georgiana, although thirteen years older than Dr. Williams's wife, Juliet (born Harris) Williams (1862–1940), could count Juliet as one of her many friends. I'm drawing this conclusion because they lived within walking distance of each other, they were both married to doctors and musicians, and because they served on two committees together in the 1890s.

Juliet was a member of the Daughters of the American Revolution (DAR), which was founded nationwide in 1890. To be a member of the DAR, a woman needed to prove that her ancestors fought in the Revolutionary War. Ten years after the national founding of this organization, The Nathan Hale Memorial Chapter of the DAR was organized on June 6, 1900. The date was chosen to recognize the birthday of Nathan Hale (1755–1776). The DAR attracted rich white women; many were the same women who would become the core of the women's suffrage and temperance movements. Juliet qualified for membership in the DAR because two ancestors on her father's side had served in the Revolutionary War, one who had been a minuteman in Lexington.

Georgiana never became a member of the DAR, although she clearly qualified as a "daughter," with ancestors who were Revolutionary War soldiers on both her mother's Arnold and father's Smith side. Why hadn't she joined the DAR? This is one of the questions that shifted my thinking a bit about Georgiana's interests and status. Her husband was deeply connected to the Revolutionary War with his drum corps. Georgiana had friends and neighbors who were members. Was she not confident in her ancestry? Was she reluctant to ask her Smith-side relatives for the bloodline information required for the application? Or was the DAR too upper class for her?

Juliet Harris was from a more educated and more well-to-do family than Georgiana's. Juliet's father, Dr. Nathanial Otis Harris (1823–1906), a native of Salem, Connecticut, had graduated from New York University Medical College in 1854. He had established a medical practice in East Haddam, with his office and home located next door to the prestigious Maplewood Music Seminary,[106] which opened during the Civil War at East Haddam Landing. The seminary was a boarding school for young ladies, attracting wealthy students from around the country. Dr. Harris was probably their physician. The school closed after a severe malaria epidemic hit East Haddam in 1880. Although age seventy and no longer practicing medicine in 1893, Dr. Harris received the state's certification that year, the first year that certifications began. This was the same year that his son-in-law, Dr. E. E. Williams, and Ulysses received their certifications.

### MOODUS'S PROFESSOR F. C. FOWLER AND DR. RUDOLPHE

And then there was Moodus's Frank Chester Fowler (1859–1919). I have mentioned him before as one of the wealthiest men in Moodus. He also received his medical license when the certificates first came out in 1893. Fowler was one of America's many *patent drug* salesmen of the 1890s, who unscrupulously manufactured and advertised *cure-alls* in a bottle which the American public fell for and bought. This was one of the reasons the 1890 decade earned the nickname "Naughty Nineties."

Frank Fowler advertised himself as Professor F. C. Fowler and sold "Dr. Rudolphe's Specific Remedy" as a means of "Self Cure for those suffering from the Effects of Youthful Errors, Seminal Weakness, Spermatorrhea, Lost Manhood, Nervous Debility, Early Decay, Loss of Memory, Impotence, Gonorrhea, Gleet and Premature Old Age." Think Viagra. Think STDs. Then think mail order with the promise of confidentiality from Professor F. C. Fowler who ended his advertisements with the message: "Patients will please bear in mind that all communications are regarded as strictly confidential. All letters are destroyed as soon as they are carefully read and the cases are strictly examined, consequently it will be necessary to give in each letter your full name and address."

## Moodus's Professor F.C. Fowler and Dr. Rudolphe

The photo above is the top half of the front page of a pamphlet published in 1884 by Frank C. Fowler of Moodus, when he was twenty-four years old. Claiming to be Professor F. C. Fowler, he introduced his invention, "Dr. Rudolphe's Specific Remedy," as an amazing "self cure for those [men] suffering from the effects of youthful errors ... showing clearly how anyone afflicted may speedily, cheaply and permanently restore themselves."

Take a look at the official seals of authority in the masthead, included to dismiss any notions that Professor F.C. Fowler might be a swindler. On the left, HOPE with the image of a dove and a Latin phrase. On the right, HEALTH, STRENGTH, VIGOR and MANHOOD.

The drawing of the five-story building implies it is the "Medical Office of PROF. F. C. FOWLER in Moodus, Connecticut. The four signs

240                                                              CHAPTER EIGHT

read, from top to bottom: "FOWLER'S, MEDICAL LABORATORY, DR. RUDOLPHE'S SPECIFIC REMEDY, PROF. F.C. FOWLER." Hmm. I haven't seen any photos of buildings like that in the historical archives.

What was Dr. Rudolphe's Specific Remedy? This pamphlet, which sold for $3.00 [about $79 in 2020) through the mail, begins the explanation of the "remedy" on the first page and goes on in the same grandiloquent style and in the same tiny type for three more pages, but no ingredients are given. Who was Dr. Rudolphe? In one section, Professor Fowler explains. Here's a clip:

> My preparation is called DR. RUDOLPHE'S SPECIFIC REMEDY from the fact that I procured the original formula from a celebrated chemical Professor of that name, under guarantee that should I subsequently think proper to introduce the Remedy to the public, I should do so under that title. The Remedy at that time seemed to meet every symptom and indication of these diseases, immediate and remote, but not with the rapidity and thoroughness I wished. It was then that I began to study the subject, and there is none more practically important in medicine, of special methods of medication for special diseases. Gradually, after years of studious work on the leading medical books, by means of physiological and pathological experiments, I reached that truth which is the great corner-stone of my unprecedented success.

Truth in Advertising laws had not been enacted yet!

By advertising in major newspapers around the country, Moodus's Frank Fowler amassed a fortune selling Dr. Rudolphe's Specific Remedy through the mail to customers who read his newspaper advertisements with his promise of confidentiality. One record[107] claimed he earned $300,000 a year. That's $7.7 million a year in 2020 dollars.

At the turn of the century, Professor F. C. Fowler authored and published a book titled *Life: How to Enjoy and How to Prolong It*.[108] *Professor* was a title he gave himself, as Professor Harold Hill did in *The Music Man*. I have a copy of Frank Fowler's book. It is labeled as the "twenty-first edition." Was it so popular that it had twenty-one editions? Or was that a false claim? I think the latter. The content? I'll put it this way: Men's Health.

Frank Fowler became a prominent 1890s Moodus figure. He engaged in several successful local businesses in addition to his mail-order drug business. He bought a Moodus mill. He became part owner with East Haddam's William Henry Goodspeed of a ferry line that operated four ferries, one of which was named the "F.C. Fowler," and which notoriously provided ferry service to customers of the River House, Hartford's premium upscale brothel.[109] Over the course of only a few years, Frank Fowler came to own a 110-foot yacht; a two-thousand-acre local game preserve; commercial real estate in Moodus; and his Oak Grove Stock Farm which had one of the finest harness racetracks in New England and a stable with over seventy blooded horses, some of which were expensive Kentucky race horses.[110] He also owned a large home on Plains Road opposite the Moodus town green, less than half a mile from Georgiana and Ulysses. Today the house is at 30 Plains Road, still revealing the elegant style of the Gilded Age despite its wear and tear.

In 1894, Frank Fowler purchased the *Connecticut Valley Advertiser* with a partner, Mr. Giles P. LeCrenier (1862–1926). In 1897, demonstrating his popularity, or the power of owning the press (there was no ethics code in journalism until the 1920s), or the power of corruption, or an acceptance of the patent drug business among Americans, or the naiveté among Americans, or all of the above, Frank C. Fowler was elected to the Connecticut General Assembly.

In 1901, Frank Fowler moved from his Moodus mansion to a mansion on Ocean Avenue in New London, Connecticut. He continued his patent drug business. In 1906, the United States enacted the Food and Drug Act, which attempted to stifle the patent medicine business, yet Fowler continued his business until 1916. He died an extremely wealthy man at age fifty-nine in 1919 in New London. He is buried in the Moodus Cemetery.

We can't ignore Frank C. Fowler in Georgiana's story. His life intersected with hers over and over, starting from the day he was born a few houses away from her on North Moodus Road in 1859, when Georgiana was ten, Edgar was eight, Frank was five and the youngest Smith child, Little Freddy, was two. Frank Fowler was only three when five-year-old Little Freddy died.

During the Civil War, Frank Fowler was one of the youngest children in the same district as the Smiths. He would have been educated in the same one-room schoolhouse with Frank and Edgar Smith, who were older than him by five and eight years. Miss Georgiana Smith may have been one of his instructors, as the oldest students took care of the youngest in those days.

Frank Fowler grew up with the Smiths as neighbors. At some point before he was eleven, Frank Fowler's parents divorced. His father took a new wife in Michigan, then disappeared; according to some records, he died shortly afterwards. Frank's mother and little sister went to live in Chatham with his mother's Rich family. But Frank stayed on North Moodus Road with his Fowler grandparents, whose other son, Frank's uncle William Fowler, Jr., had married another North Moodus Road neighbor, Mary Percival, the daughter of Hezekiah Percival.

Days before he turned eighteen in late 1877, Frank Fowler entered the Navy in New York. But he immediately went onto the sick list, diagnosed with "adynamia (!)". [Adynamia is weakness. The exclamation point is not mine; it is written in the official hospital records.] He was in the Naval Hospital in February 1878, still with adynamia, and was likely soon discharged. The next record of him is on the East Haddam June census of 1880, on which he is recorded at age twenty, living with his Fowler grandparents on North Moodus Road and working in a button factory. This was the same time that Georgiana and Ulysses were living a little farther down North Moodus Road, and the same time that twenty-four-year-old Frank Smith, his new wife, and new baby were living with Lucinda, close to the Fowlers. I surmise that the two Franks were friendly neighbors.

THE SPLASHY NINETIES

In 1882, the year before Georgiana and Ulysses built their new house on Falls Road, Frank Fowler started his new patent drug business less than a mile away on Main Street.[111] As the 1880s moved on, with his business, his wife (he married in the mid-1880s) and two children born in the 1880s, and his home in Moodus, Frank Fowler would often bump into the Cooks. When Professor Frank C. Fowler and "Dr. Rudolphe" became famous — and rich — in the 1890s from the lucrative growth of the patent drug business, Frank Fowler began to buy a significant amount of property in Moodus and nearby Colchester. Ulysses sold several acres of land to him. Some of the land was virtually in the Cook back yard, on which Frank developed the Oak Grove Stock Farm and a harness racetrack. Socially, Frank and Ulysses both belonged to the Moodus Gun Club. For a short time, Frank was a drum corps member and shareholder; he also rented rooms to the drum corps for its headquarters. And Frank and Ulysses were joint property managers of the Moodus Cornet Band.

I don't think that Georgiana or Ulysses, whose lives overlapped with Frank Fowler's in so many ways, considered him a close friend. Frank Fowler's first cousin, Oscar P. Fowler (1857–1936), was a local Moodus music teacher who, with his wife, was in Georgiana and Ulysses's circle of friends. But there is no evidence or hint that Georgiana became friends with either of the two Mrs. Frank Fowlers, an interesting point to ponder given that Georgiana had many lady friends in Moodus. The first Mrs. Fowler, who married Frank in the mid-1880s and gave him two sons, divorced him in April 1896. One newspaper reported that "Mrs. Frank C. Fowler of Moodus was liberated."[112] She died five months after the divorce, in September 1896, when her sons were eight and nine. The second Mrs. Fowler, whom Frank married in December of that year, raised his sons to adulthood and later separated from him.

When I reviewed the census records, there was hardly a person in Georgiana's vicinity with whom she or Ulysses did not have a personal association in some way — whether through music, drama, Westbrook visits, events, clubs, or church. As I try to glean the personality and character of Georgiana from her personal connections, the lack of social association with Frank Fowler, the boy-across-the-street when she and her brothers were children, and the man who grew to celebrity status in Georgiana's lifelong hometown, is noticeable. (You can tell a lot about a person from the friends they keep — or don't keep.)

The patent drug business reached its pinnacle in the 1890s. It looks like the beautiful waves that splashed over the nation in that decade also washed in a couple of ugly logs.

### UNDERTOW

As with all powerful swashes, there can be a dangerous undercurrent pulling the other way that will test your strength. And so there was for Georgiana during the 1890s.

On the surface, money seemed to be no problem for the Cooks. But I've come to the conclusion that Ulysses was not a great businessman. Funding for their lifestyle did not come from the income of his medical practice. It came from the sale of most of the 110 acres of property he had inherited. Between 1889 and 1900, he continually sold parcels of this land, a total of seven major land sales, three of which were to Frank Fowler.

In addition to providing for his own family, Ulysses provided for the drum corps. He had generously donated the land for Continental Hall. As for the hall building, owned by the corps, the annual expenses were to be covered by income from rentals. But the income wasn't enough. Five years after opening, in 1898, Ulysses bailed the corps out of its financially-draining building and took ownership of the hall — along with its debts.

## Whatever Happened to Moodus's Continental Hall?

Dr. Ulysses Cook nurtured and cherished Moodus's Continental Hall for its first twenty-three years, from 1893 to 1916. When he was forty-eight, in 1893, he donated the Falls Road property next door to his home to the Moodus Drum and Fife Corps as a site for their new building, which went up the same year. In 1898 the corps could not make financial ends meet and Ulysses came to the rescue, taking full ownership of the building, the property, and its debts. He allowed the corps to continue using the building as their headquarters as long as he owned it, which was for another eighteen years. When Ulysses was seventy, in 1916, he sold the property and the building to new owners.

The Continental was a well-known landmark in Moodus, but not remembered fondly by the residents who saw it in its last years. Over its lifetime, it was used by the Moodus Drum and Fife Corps and for community events: holiday concerts, Friday night whist parties, dances, grand masquerade balls, military balls, and soldier recruitments and send-offs during World War I. When Ulysses owned it, he often donated the use of the building for these special events.

In the 1920s and 1930s, which saw the deaths of Ulysses in 1925 and Georgiana in 1930 as well as the hard financial times of many, the Continental was in desperate need of repair, better sanitation facilities, and modernization. In the 1930s, when basketball games were played in the hall, two potbelly stoves supplied the only heat, and a bucket of cold water with a dipper supplied the only after-game showers.[113] In 1942, the building was condemned, and from what I've learned from someone who knew it then, it needed to be.

Today, the United States Postal Service at 34 Falls Road occupies the land on which Continental Hall stood from 1893 to 1942. Next door, at 36 Falls Road, is the house that Georgiana and Ulysses lived in.

Ulysses was more artist than businessman. I can't help but think that Jane Austen's description of Marianne Dashwood in *Sense and Sensibility* could describe Ulysses: "She was sensible and clever; but eager in everything: her sorrows, her joys, could have no moderation. She was generous, amiable, interesting: she was everything but prudent."

While Georgiana and Ulysses were using their land resources to stay afloat, underneath, currents were stirring and tugging and building strength. The tug did not pull them under; the money never ran out in their lifetimes, but there was a lot less of it when the decade came to an end.

It was the undertow from Georgiana's brother Frank that almost knocked them over, financially and emotionally. I haven't mentioned Frank much lately, but he was as strong a force in Georgiana's life as the moon is in the tide's.

The Chester House in 1898 (best guess date). In front, from left to right, unknown man, Frank Smith (44) holding the reins of two horses, Frederick Smith (14), Vernon Smith (4), Donald Smith (12) next to donkey, Lucinda Smith (72) holding hand of unknown child, unknown man. On balcony, from left to right, unknown woman seated, Georgia Smith (17) standing, Kitty Smith (10) standing. Photo courtesy of Caryn Davis and Leif Nilsson, Chester, CT.

CHAPTER 9

# Oh Brother

## Georgiana's Brother Frank in the 1880s and 1890s

While Georgiana was sailing through the end of the nineteenth century with a new house, a new summer cottage, a new little girl by her side, and a trusty husband at the helm, her brother Frank had the winds at his back too. Frank had found his niche in the hotel business. In 1881, he became proprietor of the three-and-a-half-story, twenty-room Chester Hotel in Chester, Connecticut, a landmark that dominated the center of the cozy town.

How Frank landed this choice position was a combination of good business sense, good luck, and a good sister. But to understand the whole story, we need to travel back a decade.

In 1872, a few months after the Connecticut Valley Railroad made its first run along the Connecticut River, Erastus Weaver, a forty-six-year-old hotelkeeper in Canterbury, Connecticut, bought the Chester Hotel, which had been built in the early 1840s. Erastus had foresight: Chester was on the west side of the Connecticut River and was one of the stops for the new railroad. The town would be growing, and the handsome Chester Hotel would be busier than ever with the new-to-Chester traveling businessmen brought in by the trains. As was the custom for hotelkeepers then, part of the hotel served as Erastus's home. His wife Carile (born Hosmer), their twenty-seven-year-old daughter, Roselle (pronounced Rose-a-lee), and their fourteen-year-old son, Clinton, resided there with him, although during the academic year, "Clintie" lived away from home at Phillips Academy, a prestigious prep school in Andover, Massachusetts.

The following year, 1873, Erastus continued as hotelkeeper but transferred ownership of the hotel to twenty-five-year-old Olin R. Wood of Manchester, Connecticut. The Weavers knew Olin from Manchester, where they had previously lived. Olin, who had recently been admitted to the Connecticut Bar Association, had opened a law practice in Manchester. It's possible that the hotel was given as part of a dowry; three years later, in 1876, Olin Wood married Erastus Weaver's daughter, Roselle, in Chester, but the couple made their home in Manchester.

### 1880

A few years later, in May 1880, Frank took a position as clerk in the Chester Hotel, which was still managed by Erastus Weaver and still owned by Olin Wood from Manchester. At twenty-six, Frank knew quite a bit about hotels. He had spent ten years in the business, working his way up the hotel business ladder in various positions, in various hotels, and in various states. He had most recently managed the Barker House in Moodus.

Living in Moodus with his mother and his wife, but working across the river in Chester, meant that Frank stayed in Chester most nights. When he did return home, he likely traveled on the new steam-powered Chester–Hadlyme ferry. This latest ferry had replaced the old, pole-operated Warner's Ferry that had run the route for over a hundred years. Chester was a straight shot by boat from Hadlyme, a village seven miles southwest of Moodus. Of the hundred-plus ferries that have operated on the Connecticut River, the Chester–Hadlyme ferry service is one of only two still in operation from the pre-bridge days. The other is the Rocky Hill–Glastonbury ferry, which is the nation's oldest in continuous operation.[114]

Frank was working across the river in Chester while Sarah was expecting their first baby. Sarah had stayed in Moodus with Frank's mother, Lucinda. When baby Georgia was born on October

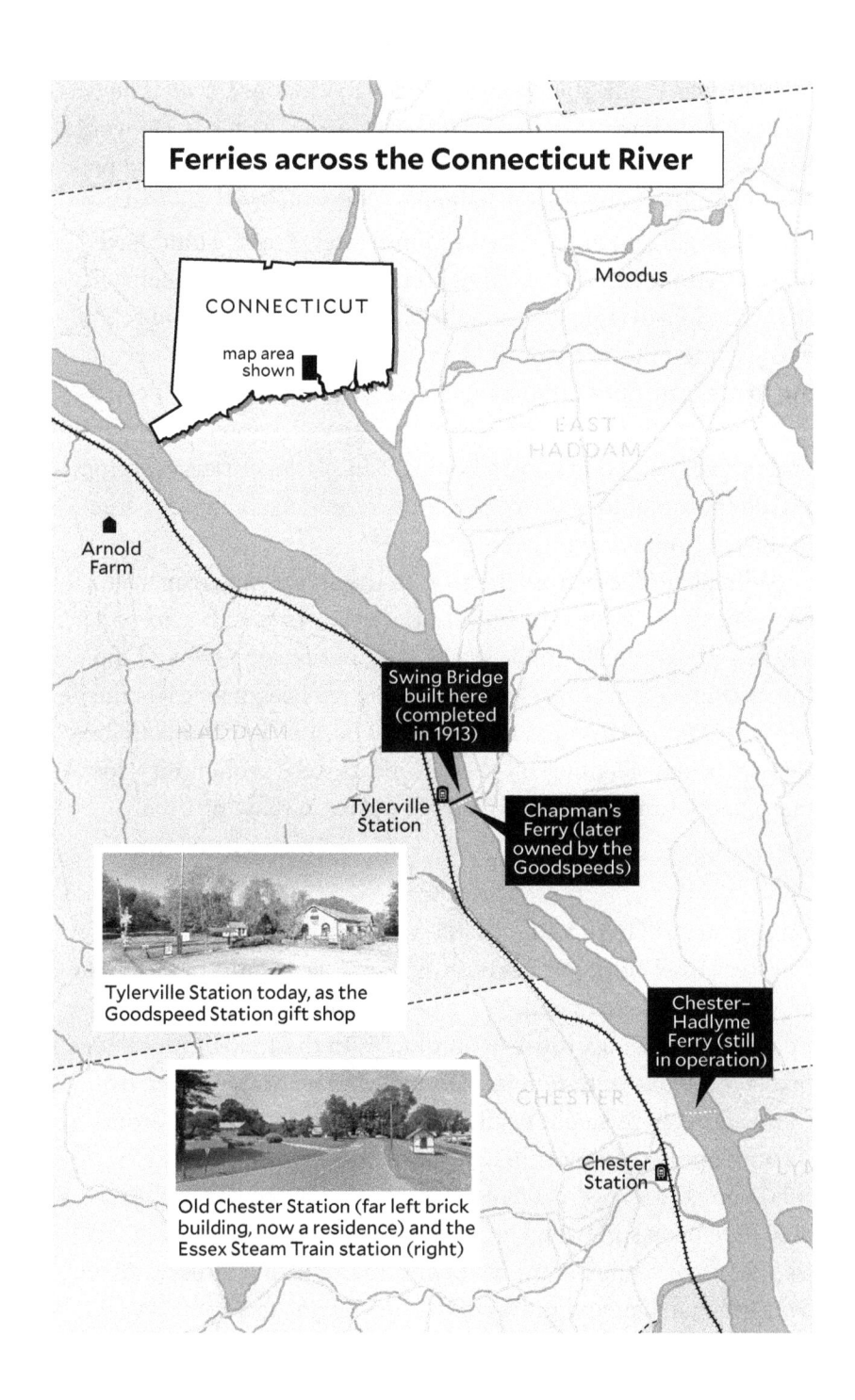

**Ferries across the Connecticut River**

CONNECTICUT
map area shown

Moodus

EAST HADDAM

Arnold Farm

Swing Bridge built here (completed in 1913)

Tylerville Station

Chapman's Ferry (later owned by the Goodspeeds)

Tylerville Station today, as the Goodspeed Station gift shop

Chester-Hadlyme Ferry (still in operation)

Chester Station

Old Chester Station (far left brick building, now a residence) and the Essex Steam Train station (right)

11, 1880, was Frank able to make it back to Moodus? Even if he was, he would not have been by Sarah's side during the birth. He would have waited and paced in another room while a midwife, and perhaps Lucinda or Georgiana, helped with the birth.

If Georgia's birth had been a month later, Frank would have had an extra tough time getting home. The river had frozen early that year, in November. When the river froze, which it did reliably every winter, the ferries shut down until the ice thawed. According to the *New Era* newspaper, which was published in Chester and covered the lower Connecticut River Valley towns, navigation on the river ceased in November 1880 and large vessels carrying fifteen thousand tons of coal were prevented from moving, stuck in the ice from the unexpected freeze.[115]

With no bridges across the river in the area, Frank may have been one of the many who crossed the river of ice with a horse or a horse-drawn sleigh. In the 1880s, the Connecticut River would freeze over so thick that sleighing parties and sleigh races on the ice between Middletown and East Haddam became popular activities. By 1900, those sleighing-on-the-ice events were prohibited — too many people and horses fell through the ice at thawing time.

## 1881

On January 20, 1881, when Frank was eight months into his new Chester Hotel clerk job, his boss, fifty-five-year-old Erastus Weaver, was found dead in bed. The cause, according to the *Hartford Courant,* was "an overdose of chloral."[116] In the 1880s, chloral was taken as a sedative to relieve insomnia and was often taken by those addicted to alcohol suffering from withdrawal symptoms. As with opium and morphia, other sedatives prescribed in the 1880s, abuse and overdoses of chloral often led to death.[117] Erastus may have been suffering with alcoholism or with other medical issues[118] for a while before he died. If Frank hadn't already taken over full management duties of the hotel prior to Erastus Weaver's death, he did then.

Running a hotel was Frank's dream job. Owning a hotel was his pipe dream—he did not have that kind of money. What he did have was an abundance of ideas, a savvy marketing sense, a charming personality, a lot of ambition, and a devoted sister with a generous husband. Dr. Ulysses Cook, with hope of a good return on investment, with confidence in Frank, and with love for Georgiana (who may have offered some convincing words), bought the Chester Hotel and its property in May 1881 for $3,500 [about $89,000 in 2020] from long-distance owner Olin Wood. Frank then speedily improved the hotel. After only three months, he ran this newspaper ad:

> [*Hartford Courant*, August 18, 1881]
> CHESTER HOUSE, Chester, Conn. – F. P. Smith, Proprietor. This well-known Hotel, having been thoroughly renovated, refitted and refurnished, is now open for accommodation of permanent and transient guests.

So, was the well-known hotel named the Chester House or the Chester Hotel? The names were interchangeable in Frank's days. Both names were used in the press, which ran articles about the establishment many times a year. Going forward, I will refer to Frank's hotel as the Chester House.

Ulysses likely provided the funds for the renovations, which included remodeling a section of the hotel as a permanent residence for Frank and his family. Frank outfitted a large private wing, with a comfortable balcony overlooking the center of Chester, as the new home for himself, Sarah, baby Georgia, and his mother, Lucinda, who all left Moodus, never to return.

For fifty-six-year-old Lucinda, moving to the west side of the river and next door to the town of Haddam may have felt like going home. She had left her parents' Arnold homestead in Haddam thirty-five years before. In Chester, she was but a seven-mile carriage ride away. Sadly though, Lucinda's mother, Sylvia Arnold, had passed away at the homestead in January. Her father, eighty-five-year-old Horace Arnold, struggling with rheumatism and with the loss of his wife of over sixty years, did not remain on the homestead once Frank and his family came to live in Chester. Horace moved into the Chester House and spent the last three years of his life surrounded with and cared for by his daughter (Lucinda), his grandson and his wife (Frank and Sarah), and his great-grandchildren. He died in the Chester House in 1884.

Yes, there were great-grandchildren — plural. Before Horace died, Sarah had given birth to a second child, 'a brother for three-year-old Georgia. Frederick Abner Smith was born in November 1883 in the Chester House. His first name was in honor of Little Freddy — the younger brother of Georgiana, Edgar, and Frank who had died at age five during the Civil War. Frederick Abner Smith was never called Freddy, always Fred. His middle name, Abner, was in honor of his grandfather Abner C. Smith.

### THE MOST SUCCESSFUL PROPRIETOR

*Kate Silliman's Chester Scrapbook*[119] is a comprehensive and charming book about the history of Chester compiled from the notes of Chester-born-and-bred Kate Silliman (1879–1959). Kate experienced Chester firsthand during the Frank Smith years. According to the book, Frank was the most successful proprietor the Chester House ever had. **Beers 1903** confirms Frank's success, reporting him as a well-known and popular proprietor who conducted the Chester House as a first-class hotel that "gained merited reputation for excellence of its cuisine and appointments, [attracting] a large patronage from the traveling public, as well as from residents of the town itself."[120]

*Frank P. Smith, proprietor of the Chester House. As printed in the Hartford Courant, February 28, 1902.*

Train-traveling salesmen were Frank's secret to success. The railroad station was one bumpy mile away from the center of

Chester, but Frank would personally meet the arriving trains. There he would greet his guests and attract new ones, promising good food, commodious rooms, kind treatment, a livery stable, a special room for display of their commercial samples, and a well-kept billiard room.

### AND A SALOON

A story about hotels and trains and traveling salesmen in Connecticut in the 1880s wouldn't be complete without including alcohol and saloons. *Saloon* was the nineteenth-century word for tavern or bar.

The 1919 Eighteenth Amendment, which prohibited alcohol in the United States, was still over three decades away. It's easy to understand why the country grew to favor Prohibition. In the years leading up to the amendment, liquor consumption was excessive. According to the 2011 PBS documentary film series *Prohibition*, directed by Ken Burns and Lynn Novick, "By 1830, the average American over fifteen years old consumed nearly seven gallons of pure alcohol a year — three times as much as we drink today."

In Connecticut, starting in the 1840s, each town decided for itself if it would allow liquor to be sold and thereby grant "licenses for the sale of spirituous liquors." Qualified citizens (meaning literate, property-owning males over twenty-one) cast ballots almost every year on whether to allow liquor licenses or not. A YES vote made the town a *license town* or a *wet town*; a NO vote made it a *dry town*.

The late nineteenth century was a time when men frequented saloons in record numbers, spending a big chunk, and sometimes all, of their pay on liquor. The cost of a beer or a whiskey (or a cigar) in a saloon in the 1880s ranged from 12 to 25 cents [about $3.00 to $6.00 in 2020], at a time when a quart of milk cost 7 cents.[121] Five to ten beers would chew up a day's salary ($1.34)[122] for the average man in 1880. Despite the price, alcohol was in high demand, which made sales high, which in turn made saloon owners quite wealthy, which in turn made liquor licenses quite precious, which in turn tempted some approvers of the licenses, the local politicians, to be corrupt.

## A ROCKY START: 1880 AND 1881

In October 1879, the town of Chester voted YES, by a margin of two votes, to make their town a license town. The next month, in November 1879, Erastus Weaver paid $100 [about $2,600 in 2020] for a one-year license "to sell and exchange intoxicating liquors at the Chester Hotel." This was six months before Frank began to work there in May 1880, at which time the saloon on the ground floor was operating profitably and legally. But when the one-year license expired on October 31, 1880, Erastus could not get a new license because the town voted NO in the October election.

Because of the NO vote in October 1880, the Chester House was not licensed to sell liquor when Ulysses bought it, and when Frank opened for business in 1881. For the rest of the 1880s, Chester most often voted NO in their yearly voting, but not always. Frank tacked his way through Chester's shifting winds of YES and NO to try to get a liquor license. It wasn't an easy sail — the temperance groups in Chester, who were getting stormier by the day, gathered in force to try to prevent the sale of alcohol.

## 1882 AND 1883

So Frank did the only thing any salty saloonkeeper in the 1880s would do when the winds were not in his favor: he sold liquor anyway — without a license — a fact that anyone who read the newspapers would not have missed. This news item appeared a year after Frank opened for business:

> [*Hartford Courant*, August 28, 1882]
> Frank Smith, proprietor of the Chester house, Chester, has been fined $140 for illegal liquor selling.

A fine of $140 [about $3,600 in 2020] was not pocket change. Frank appealed the case to the superior court. In February 1883, his case was heard in criminal court, wedged between two egregious criminal cases. Breaking the liquor law was evidently serious business. Frank was found guilty.

## Was Chester a Wet or Dry Town?

Before Prohibition became a nationwide law in 1919, each town in Connecticut had the right to prohibit the sale of alcohol within its boundary. The town's citizens could vote on whether to issue liquor licenses to local businesses or not. A YES vote meant the town would be officially a license town or colloquially, a *wet town*. Conversely, a NO vote meant the town was a *dry town*.

Between 1880 and 1903, the years when Frank Smith operated the Chester House, Chester's citizens voted nearly every year on the license question. During these years, the population of Chester ranged between 1,200 and 1,300, but only about 20 percent voted, as only men over twenty-one who met residency and literacy requirements were eligible to vote. Voting took place on the first Monday of October.

Of the twenty-two times votes were taken during those years, Chester voted YES only five times. The difference between YES and NO votes was often tiny, keeping the temperance groups—and Frank—on their toes.

In 1895, 164 of the 168 cities and towns in Connecticut voted on the license question. A new secret-ballot method, was used for the first time. *The New York Times* explained:

> [*New York Times,* October 6, 1895]
> **Connecticut Elections**
> The last [Connecticut] General Assembly, through the efforts of the temperance people, passed a law whereby the voting on the license question comes under the provision of the secret-ballot law, and an envelope will be used and a separate box provided for the license vote. Prior to this time the old style was used, and it is claimed that liquor dealers and saloon men worked the thing so that it was greatly to their advantage. It is a question whether or not the new order of things will benefit the temperance people.

For Chester, the new secret ballots used in 1895 did favor the temperance people, for this one election anyway. The NO votes won, but only by six votes; in the following year, the YES votes won by thirty-four. Not until the turn of the century did the temperance movement have a firm grip on voting levers of Chester.

## Town Of Chester, Connecticut
## Results Of Liquor Licensing Votes 1879–1903

*"Shall Any Person Be Licensed To Sell Spiritous Or Intoxicating Liquors In Chester?"* *

| Year | YES | NO | TOTAL | MARGIN |
| --- | --- | --- | --- | --- |
| 1879 | **78** | 76 | 154 | 2 |
| 1880 | 53 | **131** | 184 | 78 |
| 1881 | 47 | **95** | 142 | 48 |
| 1882 | 62 | **80** | 142 | 18 |
| 1883 | **105** | 99 | 204 | 6 |
| 1884 | 84 | **105** | 189 | 21 |
| 1886 | 103 | **117** | 220 | 14 |
| 1887 | 124 | **148** | 272 | 24 |
| 1888 | **104** | 88 | 192 | 24 |
| 1890 | 65 | **125** | 190 | 60 |
| 1891 | 96 | **104** | 200 | 8 |
| 1892 | **113** | 101 | 214 | 12 |
| 1893 | 109 | **140** | 249 | 31 |
| 1894 | 120 | **121** | 241 | 1 |
| 1895† | 136 | **142** | 278 | 6 |
| 1896 | **129** | 95 | 224 | 34 |
| 1897†† | **WON** | | | |
| 1898 | 134 | **138** | 272 | 4 |
| 1899 | 116 | **150** | 266 | 34 |

| 1900 | 127 | **149** | 276 | 22 |
| 1901 | 108 | **152** | 260 | 44 |
| 1902 | 84  | **132** | 216 | 48 |
| 1903 | 105 | **155** | 260 | 50 |

\* This was the question on the ballot from 1884 onward. The question before 1884 was "Shall the selectman make any recommendations for the granting of licenses for the sale of spirituous liquors generally, or for the sale of lager beer or wine?"

\*\* In 1885 and 1889, the question was not on the ballot.

† A new secret ballot process began in Connecticut in 1895.

†† In 1897, Chester town records show that a vote on the question was scheduled, but no results were recorded. However, a newspaper article of December 1897 reported that Chester voted YES that year.

[*Hartford Courant*, February 14, 1883]
The February criminal term of the superior court [in Middletown] opened yesterday, Judge Stoddard presiding. Robert Sullivan pleaded guilty to simple assault in slashing Ephraim Dickson with a razor on November 15th last. His sentence was 30 days imprisonment in Haddam. Frank P. Smith was found guilty of violation of the license law, and sentence was deferred until this morning. A thirteen-year-old boy will be tried today for an outrageous assault on a three-year-old girl.

I could not find a record of Frank's sentence or fine. Perhaps the court imposed a fine only and no jail time, considering that it was Frank's first offence. But the violation denied him the right to hold a license for one year. When, eight months later, the town voted YES to licensing in October 1883, and Frank applied for a license, the county commissioners refused to give him one.

By November, three more complaints had been made against Frank for selling liquor.

> [*Hartford Courant,* November 15, 1883]
> The three complaints against Frank P. Smith, charged with selling liquor in the hotel at Chester without a license, were continued until the next term of the superior court.

Georgiana was watching her brother through all this, perhaps with irritation or perhaps with sympathy. Ulysses was watching his investment. Frank needed a plan to be able to serve liquor legally. And who helped him concoct one? Ulysses. They probably worked out the plan the following week, while smoking cigars after Thanksgiving dinner. Georgiana, Ulysses, and Lillie had gone to the Chester House to celebrate Thanksgiving with Lucinda, Frank and Sarah, three-year-old Georgia, newborn Frederick Abner, and Grandfather Horace, who was in his final months.

Less than a week later, the plan went into action. On November 27, Ulysses, as owner of the Chester House, applied for a liquor license. And as you can see from the article below, many Chester residents weren't happy about this scheme and signed a remonstrance. The word *remonstrance*, which means an official protest, was a favorite word of the temperance movement. (And a word that will become old hat to you as you read Frank's story.) A month later, after Ulysses's application, the residents presented their remonstrance to the county commissioners.

> [*Hartford Courant,* Thursday, December 27, 1883]
> The county commissioners having refused a license to Frank P. Smith, landlord of the hotel at Chester, the owner of the building has applied for one. He resides in Moodus and his name is Dr. Cook. He has retained Attorney Robinson of this city to advocate his claims. [Attorney Silas Arnold Robinson (1840–1927) was an attorney in Middletown. Five years later, in 1889, he was appointed judge of the superior court in Connecticut, after serving as both mayor of Middletown and judge of probate for the district of Middletown.] A large number of residents of Chester have signed a remonstrance, which has been presented to the county

commissioners, who will hear evidence and arguments at the town hall in Chester on Friday of this week at 1 p.m.

The hearing was held on Friday, December 28. There was indeed evidence; there were indeed arguments. The following Monday, New Year's Eve, the *Hartford Courant* reported on the hearing:

> [*Hartford Courant*, December 31, 1883]
> Attorney Robinson appeared for the petitioner in the contested license application case of Dr. Cook. He said that the doctor stated in his application for a license on the 27th of November that he was on that date an occupant of the Chester hotel; that he was a suitable person to sell liquor and that the town of Chester had voted to license. [In October, the town had voted YES to licensing for the first time since 1879.] Samuel C. Silliman appeared for the remonstrants, who represented three-fourths of the taxable property of the town. [This does not mean that three-fourths of the citizens were represented. It means that a smaller number, those who owned a lot of property, were represented.] He replied that the vote in favor of license was a forced one, and had but six majority, and did not represent a majority of the voters; that Dr. Cook is a nonresident and does not make Chester his permanent home; that he would only sell through an agent; but if he has actually controlled the house since November 27th, he ought to be refused, as men have become drunk there since that date, although the place is not licensed. [Silliman] introduced two residents of Chester who testified that their sons had become drunk in the hotel since November 27th.
>
> [A note about Samuel C. Silliman (1809–1896): In 1883, he was seventy-four years old and was considered a Chester *town father*, a term used in *Kate Silliman's Chester Scrapbook* to describe the men who had become identified with the public affairs of the town since its incorporation in 1836. He served in nearly every position of trust in Chester, including as a state representative in 1862 and as a county

commissioner for ten years. According to the *Scrapbook,* "He was somewhat radical in his view of the pleasures of life and detested immorality and vice in every form. His descendants quote his oft repeated statement, 'The Silliman Blood is Pure.'"][123]

Leading citizens of the town spoke in opposition to Cook's application, and he admitted that he did not intend to move from East Haddam, but that an agent would sell for him if the license should be granted; that the present landlord of the house [Frank] would only attend to the hotel business proper, hereafter, while another person would run the bar-room. He would not say who that person would be.

The commissioners will announce their decision on Wednesday of this week.

The decision? No license for Ulysses either.

### 1884 — IN FAVOR OF THE LAW, BUT AGIN' ITS ENFORCEMENT

The town of Chester was fractured and frustrated over the question of licensing and the enforcement of the liquor laws. Even the newspapers were confused. In 1879, the *New Era* had promoted itself as an organ of the Prohibitionist Party, a national political third party that advocated the outlaw of intoxicating beverages. But the paper received too much flak from its readers in Chester and other towns, and decided, after only three months of advocating prohibition, to represent both sides of the issue from then on. In the mid-1880s, the editor of the *New Era* stated this in an editorial: "In Chester we are somewhat like the old farmer member of the legislature — when the farmer was called upon to express himself in regard to the Maine law, said he, 'Mr. Speaker, I'm in favor of the Maine law, but agin' its enforcement!'"[124]

The Maine law? At the time the *New Era* editor wrote this, the state of Maine had recently enacted, for the second time, a state law prohibiting the sale of alcoholic beverages. Thirty-three years earlier, in 1851, Maine had become the first state to prohibit the manufacture and sale of alcohol. The law didn't go well. Riots followed and the law was repealed in 1856. States tried to enact *Maine Laws,* which became the term for prohibiting alcohol for the entire state instead of town by town. But states were as split on the issue as the towns were.

### Women and Alcohol

Women could not vote in the 1880s, yet many women felt that alcohol licensing affected a woman's life as much or even more than it did a man's. Connecticut came close to giving women the right to vote on alcohol issues in 1880. In March 1880, the all-male Connecticut House of Representatives narrowly voted (one hundred to ninety-eight) in favor of a bill that "every woman over twenty-one may vote on any question relating to the sale of liquor, subject to the same restrictions to male voters, as to residence, etc." But when the bill went to the all-male Senate for approval, it didn't pass. The House tried again; the Senate rejected it again. That was the end of that idea.

Were women allowed in saloons in the nineteenth century? Legally, yes. Socially, no. In 1937, though, Connecticut passed a law making it illegal to serve alcohol to a woman at a bar or at a table within three feet of a bar. This law didn't change until the 1970s.

### "Come Home, Father" by Henry Clay Work

Henry Clay Work (1832–1884) was a well-known abolitionist and writer of Civil War songs. He also wrote many songs to help the cause of temperance.

The most famous of his temperance songs, written in 1864, was "Come Home, Father,"[125] the story of a little girl pleading with her father in a saloon to come home to the bedside of his dying little son. This tearjerker was often sung at temperance meetings. The

Woman's Christian Temperance Union eventually adopted this song as its anthem.[126]

Grab a tissue.

*Father, dear father, come home with me now!*
*The clock in the steeple strikes one.*
*You said you were coming right home from the shop,*
*As soon as your day's work was done.*

*Our fire has gone out, our house is all dark,*
*And mother's been watching since tea,*
*With poor brother Benny so sick in her arms,*
*And no one to help her but me.*

*Come home! Come home! Come home!*
*Please, father, dear father, come home.*

*[Chorus]*
*Hear the sweet voice of the child,*
*Which the night winds repeat as they roam!*
*Oh, who could resist this most plaintive of prayers?*
*"Please, father, dear father, come home!"*

*Father, dear father, come home with me now!*
*The clock in the steeple strikes two.*
*The night has grown colder and Benny is worse,*
*But he has been calling for you.*

*Indeed he is worse, Ma says he will die,*
*Perhaps before morning shall dawn;*
*And this is the message she sent me to bring:*
*"Come quickly, or he will be gone."*

*Come home! Come home! Come home!*
*Please father, dear father, come home.*

*Father, dear father, come home with me now!*
*The clock in the steeple strikes three.*
*The house is so lonely, the hours are so long,*
*For poor weeping mother and me.*

> *Yes, we are alone, poor Benny is dead,*
> *And gone with the angels of light;*
> *And these are the very last words that he said:*
> *"I'd like to kiss Papa good night."*
>
> *Come home! Come home! Come home!*
> *Please, father, dear father, come home.*
>
> LYRICS AND MUSIC BY HENRY CLAY WORK<br>1864
>
> Henry Clay Work was born in Middletown, Connecticut, where he is immortalized on a monument — a bust and a plaque — located on the Middletown Union Park Green.

In 1884, a countrywide temperance movement was gaining steam, although it would be another thirty-six years before Prohibition was enacted as a national law. That April, in Middletown, one thousand people attended a temperance meeting to hear Miss Frances E. Willard[127] (1839–1898), president of the Women's Christian Temperance Union (WCTU) and women's rights activist, who that year spoke to large crowds in every state in the United States. As luck would have it, on the same day Miss Willard addressed the crowd in Middletown about the evils of alcohol, Frank was in the Middletown courthouse. Guilty again.

> [*Hartford Courant,* April 24, 1884]
> In the superior court, Tuesday, the jury returned a verdict of guilty in the case of state vs Frank P. Smith, landlord of the Chester Hotel, who was charged with having the reputation of selling liquor contrary to law. He was fined $20 [about $500 in 2020] and costs.

You will often see the word *reputation* in nineteenth-century liquor violation records and newspaper reporting. If a sale of liquor was suspected but not witnessed firsthand (the saloon owners were often a step ahead of the enforcers in covering up the evidence), the suspected seller could be charged with "having a reputation for selling liquor."

Frank didn't stop. He didn't stop serving liquor at the Chester House. He didn't stop applying for a liquor license. And he didn't stop ignoring his opposers. Who also didn't stop.

[*Hartford Courant,* July 26, 1884]
The county commissioners at their meeting at Haddam on Friday [July 23] unanimously decided against the application of Frank P. Smith for a license at the Chester house. It was shown at the hearing before the commissioners on this application at the town hall, Chester, on Wednesday, that Smith was convicted and paid a fine at the April superior court, for violation of the license, and that his present and recent reputation was that of an illegal liquor seller. A large portion of the best citizens testified that he was an improper person for the business.

After the hearing was ended, Smith was charged, in the presence of the commissioners, with having recently put strong liquor in lemonade and distributed it among boys of ten years of age. [Connecticut did not have a minimum drinking age.] He admitted the charge, and boasted that he would do it again. [Oh, brother!]

Then Frank confidently went back to running the popular and profitable Chester House as he always had. In October, the winds again blew unfavorably: Chester voted NO.

In November 1884, all the liquor at the Chester House was seized by the authorities.

## 1885

Was the profit so great from the sale of alcohol that Frank would continue to violate the law? Yes. After running the Chester House for only four years, Frank was financially fit enough to buy it. On

August 24, 1885, Frank bought the Chester House from Ulysses for $4,500 [about $121,000 in 2020]. Ulysses had paid $3,500 for it in 1881; the other $1,000 may have been money Ulysses lent to Frank for the initial renovations or other expenses, or it may have been the return on Ulysses's investment.

Considering Frank's court cases, the resulting fines, the newspaper articles announcing his lawbreaking escapades to everyone in Georgiana and Ulysses's world, and the questionable future of licensing in Chester, Ulysses may have wanted out of the Chester House business. He may have asked Frank for his money back. Yet there is no sign of controversy between Frank and Ulysses at this time, or any other time for that matter. Quite the contrary: less than a month later, when Frank and Sarah had their third child, a son, they gave him the middle name of Ulysses. Donald Ulysses Smith was born September 19, 1885.

That same September, Frank made the news again. His name appeared on the published list of criminal cases to be heard in the next term of the superior court. Of the cases listed, three men were charged with "selling liquor contrary to law." One man was from Higganum, one was from Cromwell, and one was Frank P. Smith from Chester. The three cases were weaved into the docket with twenty-two other criminal charges of horse theft, larceny, burglary, assault, assault with intent to kill, maliciously exposing poison, breach of peace, abusive language, and unlawful taking of oysters from an oyster bed. Somehow, Frank wangled out of his charges.

[*Hartford Courant,* November 14, 1885]
The two criminal cases against Frank P. Smith, of Chester, charged with having the reputation of selling liquor without a license, and keeping liquor with intent to sell, have been nolled.

The only case against him which still remains on the docket is a civil case against his liquors which were seized a year ago, and that will not be tried during this term of the superior court.

## 1886 AND 1887

Chester continued to vote NO to serving alcohol in town. And Frank continued to serve it. In the exceptionally cold month of January 1887, three Hadlyme men stole two buffalo robes (buffalo hides, with the fur still on, were used as blankets in the nineteenth century) and a horse whip from horses tied to a hitching post in Chester. The men were brought before Justice Joseph E. Silliman. Joseph Silliman was another prominent Chester town father, politician, and close brother of Samuel Silliman, the county commissioner with the loud anti-immorality voice who once claimed that "the Silliman blood is pure." The Hadlyme men blamed their actions on getting drunk at the Chester House. It was their bad luck, and Frank's too, that one of the stolen robes belonged to Dr. Sylvester Turner, a good friend of the Silliman brothers.

I don't know what the punishment was for the Hadlyme men, but Frank received his punishment six weeks later when three saloons in Chester were raided by local deputy sheriffs. The raid was reported in the *Hartford Courant* on March 14, 1887. Here's a summary of the liquor seized:

| **Chester House, Frank P. Smith:** | **The place of Daniel LeVaugh:** | **The Park House, Edward O'Connor:** |
|---|---|---|
| 4 Kegs Beer | 100 Bottles Lager | 2 Kegs Beer |
| 3 Barrels Ale | 1 Jug Rum | 8 Gallons Whiskey |
| 76 Bottles Ale | 1 Bottle Gin | 1 Demijohn Whiskey |
| 7 Bottles Whiskey | | |
| 1 Gallon Whiskey | | |
| 1 Bottle Rum | | |
| ½ Gallon Rum | | |
| 1 Bottle Wine | | |
| 1 Quart Wine | | |
| 2 Gallons Gin | | |

The three saloon owners were arrested for "having the reputation of selling liquors contrary to law" and "keeping liquors with intent to sell." Frank was also charged with selling it. Who heard the case? Justice Joseph E. Silliman. The outcome of the case? No record. But Frank was likely fined again.

## 1888

Much to the chagrin of Joseph and Samuel Silliman and other anti-saloon men in Chester, the town's NO vote lasted only another year and a half. In October 1888, the town voted YES to liquor, with the NO votes suspiciously low. Frank could now legally serve liquor in Chester *if* — and it was a big *if* — the county commissioners would approve him for a license. They didn't.

Not everyone in Chester thought Frank was in the wrong. Of the town's voters, half were against prohibition of alcohol. Many people in the country and in Connecticut resisted townwide prohibition and spoke against the national temperance movement. Frank likely did not worry about his reputation as a lawbreaker. He probably viewed the arrests as a necessary part of his job, rather than a reflection on his character.

### A CHARMING MAN

Also in his favor, Frank was likable. He was a good-looking, clever gentleman with energy, enthusiasm, and a knack for salesmanship.

Proof certain that he had charm and friends: Frank was voted in as a member of a Chester club in which "good moral character" was required for membership. This club, the Chester Driving Park Association, had formed while Frank lived in Chester. According to *Kate Silliman's Chester Scrapbook,* "This association sponsored the improvement of the breed, and the development of horses; the prevention and the punishment of fraud in racing, and uniformity in the government of trotting and driving."[128]

Horse racing in Chester? Yes. The harness racing kind of racing, that is. Wildly popular in nineteenth-century America, harness racing,[129] sometimes called *trotting*, was a style of racing in which the driver sat on a vehicle called a *sulky* behind a horse attached by a harness, and in which the horse was required to race at a specific gait. It was the kind of horse racing that Professor Harold Hill in *The Music Man* called "wholesome" in his "Ya Got Trouble" song. In the song, the professor warns the mothers of River City that a pool hall could lead their sons to "horse race gamblin', not the wholesome trottin' race, no! but a race where they set down right on the horse!"

Races at the Chester Driving Park Association track were not for Chester trotters only. Participants came from Deep River, Ivoryton, Haddam, and East Haddam, as did spectators who would huddle and cheer from the grassed area around the association's half-mile, hard dirt circle track. Georgiana and Ulysses were likely on that grassy patch for more than a few races.

When the *New Era* (the newspaper whose editor was an anti-saloon advocate) wrote an article describing the horses that raced in Chester, he wrote this about Frank: "F. P. Smith has 'Grover' and has trotted him way inside the three minutes, but Grover is an 'ornery beast' and can't always be depended on to do his best." He added: "We must not forget Frank Smith's donkey, which, although not very speedy, is always on hand about breakfast time and can beat the best steam calliope ever made."[130] A calliope is a musical instrument that whistles and wheezes loudly, most often used in circuses or carousels. Was the editor mocking Frank? Yes, I think he was. Did Frank really own a donkey? Yes. You can see the donkey in the photo at the start of this chapter.

### A CHARMING FAMILY

And also in Frank's favor, he had a hardworking and supportive wife. Like nearly every couple in the nineteenth century, he and Sarah operated in different spheres: Frank in the masculine bread-winning sphere of finances, politics, saloons, tobacco, and horses; and Sarah in the feminine bread-baking sphere of housekeeping, cooking, clothing, soapsuds, and children. Sarah stayed out of Frank's court cases and the business end of the Chester House. She also stayed out of the smoke-choked saloon on the ground floor, where women were not welcome, not because of laws at that time, but according to social standards. She tended to the guests' comforts — making sure they had fresh rooms and good dining, which she apparently did exceptionally well. "Mrs. Smith has brought to the table service a first class reputation,"[131] reported *Beers 1903*. I envision Sarah as a slim Mrs. Patmore, the cook in *Downton Abbey*, flashing a forced smile when meeting guests, but working in a permanent frenzy behind the scenes to produce the "excellence of the cuisine" that *Beers 1903* also attributed to the Chester House.

Despite the run-ins with the town temperance groups, or maybe because of them, Frank and Sarah were a popular couple. *Beers 1903* reported: "The family is a charming one, and Mr. and Mrs. Smith are people of whom nothing but kind words can be said. Their hotel is made more like a home for their guests by their hospitality and genial manners, and they have made many friends, not only in the immediate vicinity, but throughout the country."

On April 1, 1888, when the snow from the mid-March Great Blizzard of '88 was still piled to record-breaking heights in Chester (where, according to *Kate Silliman's Chester Scrapbook*, the first stories of two-story houses were fully covered with snow), Sarah gave birth to their fourth child — a girl, Kittie Louise Smith. Frank and Sarah now had four young children from newborn to age eight, two girls and two boys. Perhaps it was Lucinda, Frank's mother, then in her early sixties, who was the linchpin in Frank and Sarah's success, helping with the childcare of her grandchildren. And possibly financially?

Lucinda may have inherited money from her father, Horace Arnold, when he died in 1884. I say this because she had enough money to make two real estate investments. Shortly after her father's death, Lucinda purchased a large (acreage not recorded) parcel of farmland in Chester for $750 [about $20,000 in 2020] near the railroad depot. The land included an income-producing, three-acre apple orchard with a hundred trees. Frank may have had something to do with this transaction. The property was convenient for railroad deliveries, and also included apples that were used for making cider.

Then, in 1888, Lucinda purchased a seventy-eight-acre parcel of land in East Haddam for $400 [about $11,000 in 2020]. This second real estate transaction raised my curiosity because of the several connections to her late husband, Abner C. Smith: First, the property was recorded as the "Moseley lot." The Moseleys were relatives of Electa Warner Smith, Abner C. Smith's biological mother who had died when he was an infant. Second, the property abutted the Smith homestead in Mount Parnassus. And third, Lucinda bought the property from a widow related to Smith families. Why Lucinda bought the property, I don't know. But four years later, in 1892, at age sixty-seven, she sold a tiny portion of it (less than an acre) to abutting neighbor, her half brother-in-law, Abner Comstock Smith (1846), for $5. These East Haddam transactions tempt me to conclude that Lucinda (and by extension, Georgiana) sustained a relationship with the Smiths on Smith Road in East Haddam after Abner C. Smith died in 1865.

Lucinda's story — her brave move as a teenage girl from her family farm in Haddam to the mills of Moodus, her disenchantment with farm life during the Civil War, and her later departure from rural Moodus to downtown Chester — is emblematic of America's shift from farm to town, a movement that spanned her lifetime. Lucinda was in her late fifties and a widow for more than fifteen years when she left Moodus for Chester. She left behind fruit trees, green pastures, placid cows, and familiar faces to enter a noisy world of fruit carts, dusty roads, clopping horses, and strangers. I think, though, that Lucinda was happy living in Frank's busy home in the center of the bustling Chester downtown. Lucinda would live with Frank and Sarah for the rest of her ninety-three years.

## 1889

In 1889, the end of the decade, Frank turned thirty-four and Sarah turned thirty. The oldest children, Georgia, Fred, and Donald were attending the Chester district schools. One-year-old Kittie Louise was learning to walk. It was a calm year at the Chester House. Frank did not get arrested, and the Chester House did not get raided. Chester had stayed a wet town, although Frank himself did not have a liquor license. Maybe he stopped serving alcohol, or maybe the town stopped serving papers.

## 1890–1892

Do you remember the opening credits of the 1980s television show *Cheers* with its sketches and vintage photos of people from the 1890s flashing on the screen? Did you notice the EST. 1895 on the iconic finger-pointing *Cheers* sign?? Do you remember the last line of the theme song, *You want to go where everybody knows your name?*[132] Those images and song lyrics can give you a flavor of tavern life in the 1890s, when Frank was providing the spot in Chester for men to go where everybody knew their name.

Frank spent the 1890 decade running the Chester House and its saloon, running guests to and from the railroad station, running his horses in races, and running into the law. Running a saloon in Chester in the 1890s was tricky. The livelihood of Frank and the other saloon owners revolved around those every-October votes that switched unpredictably between YES and NO. For the first ten months of 1890, liquor was legal in Chester. But in October 1890, Chester voted NO to liquor licensing. And within a couple months, Frank was in trouble. Again.

[*Hartford Courant,* March 18, 1891]
F. Smith of the Chester House was tried for violating the license law before Justice S. A. Wright [Samuel A. Wright, first selectman of Chester and a Chester town father] Tuesday. As it was his second offense, a fine of $75 [about $2,100

in 2020] was imposed and thirty days in jail. Appealing to the superior court, he was put under $250 [about $7,100 in 2020] bonds, which were furnished by Mrs. Lucinda Smith.

Did Frank's sixty-five-year-old mother, Lucinda Smith, put up the bond money?!? Yes. Perhaps she was only a messenger, delivering Frank's money from home. Perhaps Ulysses gave her the money. Or perhaps she used her own money.

Frank's appeal took over a year to be finalized. Before it was heard, Chester, in October 1891, voted NO to licensing again. A NO vote was not a good sign for Frank. A YES vote might have helped his defense, demonstrating that the people of Chester were in favor of licensing.

In April 1892, Frank's appeal was heard in the Middletown superior court. He lost. Although I can't find a record of his punishment, I can surmise that Frank paid the fine and served jail time, after which he would have collected the bond money, paid his mother back, and returned to work in May.

Later that year, in October 1892, Chester voted YES to licensing, winning by 12 votes of the 214 cast. Chester was on a seesaw over the liquor issue.

### 1893

Although Chester was now a wet town, Frank had to wait until April 1893, a year from his superior court conviction, to apply for a license. With the spotlight dimmed on Chester liquor issues because of the YES vote, it was now safer for Frank to serve liquor without a license, and he likely went back to doing so. (Did he ever stop?)

In October 1893, the town seesawed back to NO.

This was the same month that Frank's last child, Vernon Edgar Smith (1893–1967), was born. Frank and Sarah now had five children: two girls (thirteen and five) and three boys (nine, eight, and newborn).

The responsibilities of supporting his growing family and the bad news from the October vote did not seem to stifle Frank's zest for life. Vernon was born on October 9, and on October 14, Frank ferried his horse "Chester Boy" across the river and ran him in Frank C. Fowler's "Grand Trotting Event" at Fowler's Oak Grove Trotting Park in Moodus. Because the Oak Grove Trotting Park was virtually in Georgiana's backyard, Frank probably brought his two older sons, Fred and Donald, with him to Moodus for the race, where they could also enjoy some time with Aunt Georgiana and Uncle Ulysses. His daughter Georgia was away, attending her first year at a boarding school in Norwich, Connecticut. Kittie would have stayed home with her mother, grandmother, and week-old brother Vernon.

### 1894 AND 1895

In October 1894, Chester voted NO liquor licenses again. This time by only one vote.

I doubt Frank stopped selling liquor. He was making enough money to support his family, pay taxes, send his oldest daughter to private school, buy and race horses, buy himself a diamond shirt stud, and throw parties — big parties that made the news.

> [*Hartford Courant,* August 3, 1895]
> CHESTER
> A party of seventy-five people were entertained at the Chester House Thursday evening by the proprietor, Frank P. Smith.

What was the celebration? The newspaper's social news reported that Frank's daughter Georgia, who was fourteen and on a summer break from school, had a "Miss Dickinson from Waterbury" visiting her on this date. But I don't think the girls had anything to do with the party except to be dazzled by the scene or possibly to help Lucinda with the babysitting of the four younger Smith children so that Frank and Sarah could be gracious hosts.

I think the August party was timed so that Frank could show his hotel in a positive light, hoping to influence Chester voters to vote YES for licensing in the upcoming October 1895 election. If that was the reason, it almost worked.

In October 1895, the annual election had its largest turnout in fifteen years — 278 men voted on the liquor license question. It was in this election that Chester and all Connecticut towns were required to use the new secret ballot system aimed at curbing ballot box corruption. YES votes in previous elections had been thought to be inflated because of bribery and trickery at the ballot boxes. With the new corruption-free voting process, the NO votes were expected to slaughter the YES votes. The YES votes were not slaughtered, however. There were more YES votes than ever before. In the end, though, the NOS won — by a mere six votes.

By 1895, in Connecticut, in the nation, and in the world, temperance organizations had spread like wildfire. The World's Women's Christian Temperance Union had been formed under the leadership of Frances Willard and had built itself into the largest organization of women in the world. America's WCTU had powerful lobbyists in state and federal levels of government, as did America's Anti-Saloon League, which became a national organization in 1895 and would later overcome the WCTU as the most powerful temperance lobby in America.

Connecticut had its own fervid anti-alcohol bunch. In 1895, the state granted a charter to the newly-formed Law and Order League of Connecticut, whose motto was: "We demand obedience to the law." To the liquor law, that is. Under their charter, the league was authorized to investigate (read *raid*) establishments suspected of serving alcohol illegally. The Law and Order League investigators, called *detectives* by their supporters and *spotters* or *spies* by nonsupporters, made it their mission to drive liquor dealers and saloon owners out of business. They would conduct surprise raids, seize the liquor, then testify against the saloon operators in court. The courts would impose large fines and long jail sentences and order the liquor to be destroyed.

There were plenty of people critical of the Law and Order League's methods, sometimes considered sneaky. Letters of opposition to the league were printed in newspapers. In November 1895, the *Hartford Courant* carried a letter from the Rev. Dr. E. P.

Parker reading that "many law-abiding and order-loving citizens" have alleged that some of the league's agents or officers have used "means and instruments of doubtful propriety in the prosecution of the work."[133] And not all legislators were in favor of it. In April 1895, the General Assembly debated a bill for funding the league for three hours. Those legislators who opposed it argued, "the idea is to give a premium to informers, to give men a premium to seize upon other men ... this provision is the most infamous one imaginable."[134] The police, too, whom the league accused of incompetence and corruption, were not grateful for the criticism or the extra help. The police sometimes tipped off the saloons when the league was about to raid them. Ordinary citizens spoke up about the cost of paying for another law enforcement group in addition to the police. And, of course, the State Liquor Dealers Association wanted to muzzle the league and repeal their charter altogether.

In 1895 and most of 1896, the Law and Order League stayed away from the small town of Chester, who had voted to stay dry for the previous three years.

1896

In October 1896, Chester flipped back to voting YES to licensing, winning by a strong margin of thirty-four votes.

This YES vote reignited the Law and Order League's interest in the town. It took only a month for Chester to feel the heat. In early November, the league raided the town's saloons, with the Chester House their biggest target. League officials claimed they raided Chester at the request of leading citizens of the town; liquor dealers claimed the league came of its own free will. The confusion was likely stoked because one *leading citizen* of Chester was John B. Hardy, who was also a director of the state's Law and Order League. John B. Hardy became an unpopular man to many in Chester.

The court date for the Chester cases, which included Frank's case, was set for Saturday, November 14, 1896. Frank had some bad luck on Friday the 13th. Was that a bad omen?

[*Hartford Courant,* Monday, November 16, 1896]
**Lost His Diamond**
*He Was Making Sure He Wouldn't Lose $1,000.*
Frank P. Smith, proprietor of the Chester House at Chester, came to this city [Middletown] Friday afternoon [Friday, November 13] in search of James Slyne, whose hearing on the charge of perjury was assigned for Saturday [November 14] morning. Smith was desirous of insuring Slyne's attendance at the court as he was his surety for $1,000 [about $31,000 in 2020].

He found him and they started for the train. As they were about to board it three men collided with them. Nothing was thought of the accident until Smith arrived at his home, when his wife asked him what had become of the diamond stud which he had worn in his shirt from when he left home. The stud screwed in and was valued at $150 [about $4,600 in 2020]. The probabilities are that it was stolen by the men who ran into them at the depot. Smith telephoned his loss to the police in this city and they have found several who noticed the stud in Smith's shirt front as he was going to the train, and one or two who can describe the men who are supposed to be the thieves, although they have disappeared from town.

Things were getting messy: perjury charges, $1,000 bonds at risk, thefts.

Here are the results of the Chester court cases from November 14, 1896:

[*Hartford Courant,* Tuesday, November 17, 1896]
**Those Chester Cases**
*Convictions and Continuations.*
Judge W. U. Pearne has reserved his decision until Saturday [November 21] in the case of James Slyne of Chester, charged with perjury. The witnesses against Slyne were the two detectives of the State Law and Order League.

Frank P. Smith, proprietor of the hotel at Chester, was convicted Saturday on four counts and fined $25 [about $800 in 2020] and costs on each. He appealed to the December term of the superior court and gave bonds in the sum of $300 [about $9,300 in 2020]. A motion was made to destroy the liquors seized at his saloon and they were ordered destroyed. An appeal was taken from this order and bonds furnished in the sum of $300.

The case of Egbert Emmons was then called and ten witnesses examined, when the case was continued until Saturday [November 21].

It is thought that the Chester liquor cases will be finished in two weeks. [That did NOT happen.] Another license has been applied for by a third party for the Chester House and a remonstrance has been filed with the county commissioners. The hearing will not be held until after the cases now in the courts have been tried.

James Slyne, the man charged with perjury and for whom Frank paid a $1,000 bond, was Chester's Democratic registrar of voters. He was the thirty-seven-year-old son of a local land-owning farmer. A month before this November superior court appearance, Slyne had been accused of perjury in a lower court case when he gave testimony that contradicted the testimony of the Law and Order League. Slyne was likely suspected of corruption in the October 1896 liquor licensing vote, in which the YES votes won by thirty-four votes and the NO votes were particularly low. At his November superior court appearances, Slyne was ordered to appear in a trial in December. Slyne's case was not settled until ten months later. On September 30, 1897, he pleaded guilty, was sentenced to six months in the county jail, and was fined the costs of the case.

Egbert Emmons, another Chester saloon owner, had also applied for a license as soon as the October 1896 YES votes were known. On November 23, 1896, the week after Frank's November 14 court date, the county commissioners held a hearing in Chester to decide on Egbert Emmons's and Frank's applications. Presenting against them both was the top man of the state's Law and Order League, Secretary S. P. Thrasher, who, according to the newspaper account, presented a "large amount of testimony showing that neither was a proper person to be given a license."[135] Because both Frank and Egbert had December 2 trials scheduled with Judge Pearne, the county commissioners reserved both decisions until after their trials.

Trying to prepare alternatives lest he lose his case and his ability to (legally) serve liquor, Frank decided to find someone to lease the saloon portion of the Chester House, someone who could acquire a liquor license. He found a Mr. Barney Warner. Barney Warner officially leased the saloon and applied for a liquor license on December 1, the day before Frank's trial. No doubt, there was an undocumented financial arrangement between Barney and Frank. The commissioners tried to keep up with Frank's schemes:

> [*Hartford Courant,* December 2, 1896]
> **Liquor Question In Chester**
> MIDDLETOWN, DEC. 1
> The county commissioners today refused to grant a license to B. Warner at the Chester House until they can learn whether it is possible to impeach the reputation of the bar of the hotel under the new proprietor before he has obtained possession. Chester people oppose the license, claiming that Warner is the stool pigeon of F. P. Smith, the former owner, now under trial in the superior court.
>
> The commissioners decided to delay the decision for Barney Warner until the new year.

## DECEMBER 1896: FRANK LOSES BIG

On December 2, 1896, Frank's trial regarding the November raid by the Law and Order League was held. He lost.

[*Hartford Courant,* December 3, 1896]
**Heavy Penalty for Saloonkeeper Smith**
MIDDLETOWN, DEC. 2
The criminal term of the superior court was suddenly brought to a close today. Several witnesses testified as to the general reputation of the Chester House, as kept by Frank P. Smith during the past year, and two said they had bought liquor there. Both admitted that they had told Smith that they wanted liquor for medicinal purposes [alcohol for medicinal reasons was legal] as they had hard colds.

A laugh was caused by one witness, who said, "Smith said after his conviction in the lower court, 'I shall appeal in the superior court for there will surely be one drunkard on the jury.'"

The state showed that Smith had received over nineteen barrels of bottled liquors by freight within a few weeks, for which he had paid the freight. [Frank's trips to the railroad station evidently were not just to greet customers!] At the time of the raid there were seized 151 bottles of beer, one barrel of whisky, one and one half barrels of beer, one demijohn of whisky and several bottles of whisky and other liquors.

Smith pleaded guilty to three counts, general reputation, and actual sale and keeping with intent to sell. The two other counts charging actual sales were nolled.

Judge Elmer fined Smith $40 on the first count, $10 on the second and $30 on the third or in all $80 and costs. The costs are heavy, being $232.35 in the lower court and fully as much more in the upper court. Taking Smith's lawyers' fees into account, the case will cost him between $650 and $700 [about $20,000 and $22,000 in 2020].

The bartender at the time of the raid, John Mooney of Chester, was not part of this trial, but the Law and Order League went after him too. His case was heard a year later. He pleaded guilty and was fined $50 [about $1,500 in 2020] plus costs for violation of the liquor laws.

## 1897

Because of his convictions for liquor law violations, Frank could not apply for a liquor license for a year, not until November 1897, and only if Chester voted to stay a license town in the October 1897 vote. As might be expected, that did not stop Frank from finding ways to provide his customers alcohol.

Frank still had hope that county commissioners would approve Barney Warner for a license for his leased saloon space in the Chester House. Warner's case was to be heard February 3, 1897. The Law and Order League was planning to oppose Warner, but the league's headman, Mr. Thrasher, was a no-show. The judge directed the clerk to notify Thrasher that if he did not appear by the following Friday, the case would be stricken from the docket. Thrasher did indeed appear the next Tuesday, February 9, and brought forty witnesses with him. Barney Warner also had forty witnesses with him. The Law and Order League testified that Warner was really an agent of Frank P. Smith, who had been selling liquor illegally. The result: no license for Barney Warner.

Not to be taken down, Frank had another idea up his sleeve: he would sell the lot next door to the Chester House to someone who could build a saloon on it, and his hotel patrons could drink there. Within a month of the denial of Barney Warner's liquor license, in March 1897, Frank sold the parcel to Peter McIntyre of Hartford, who in turn, within a month, erected a building on it, then applied for a liquor license. And was approved!

[*Hartford Courant,* April 14, 1897]
**Hartford Man Gets a License in Chester**
MIDDLETOWN, APRIL 13
The county commissioners met here today and rendered

their decision to grant a license to Peter McIntyre of Hartford, who desired to run a saloon at Chester. McIntyre had erected a small building adjacent to the Chester House, but proved he had no connection with that house. It is expected that the Chester Law and Order League will appeal this decision to the superior court.

Frank's hotel customers could now buy a drink next door. There is no record of how Peter McIntyre and Frank conducted business together, but I doubt that all the income stayed with McIntyre.

Opposition to Frank calmed down in the summer of 1897, partially because of the Peter McIntyre deal, and partially because Chester had continued to vote YES to be a license town the October before. The Law and Order League officially conceded to Chester's results in 1896, but they insisted the voting process had been corrupted, an accusation they made in many towns. Liquor dealers and saloon owners around Connecticut were accused of influencing the outcome of the town license votes by bribery or by preventing people from reaching the ballot box. So as the October 5, 1897, voting day approached, the Chester temperance people went fishing. They caught a whopper: Frank was accused of trying to influence the voters.

[*Hartford Courant*, October 12, 1897]

**Alleged Election Bribery in Chester**

MIDDLETOWN, OCT. 11

Attorney Frank E. Haines was in Chester today as counsel for Grand Juror J. M. Watrous. Frank P. Smith, proprietor of the Chester House, was arrested this morning on the charge of bribery in connection with the last town election. The offense, it is charged, was committed on Sunday before election day [October 4], when Smith attempted to bribe one Meigs to stay away from the polls or else to vote [YES for] the license ticket. [John Rufus Meigs was a fifty-eight-year-old farmer in Chester.]

The complaint, drawn by Grand Juror Watrous, had three counts. Smith was arraigned before Justice F. W. Silliman and pleaded not guilty.

The case was continued until October 20 and Smith was released under $1,000 [about $31,000 in 2020] bail.

Maybe Frank did some other *lobbying* too, as the town voted YES in the election. The count of the YES and NO votes are missing from the town records for that year.

In December 1897, with Chester still a license town and the Chester House having stayed free of liquor violations for a year after the November 1896 raid, Frank applied for a license in his own name. His opposers were caught off guard.

> [*Hartford Courant,* December 14, 1897]
> A remonstrance was filed with the county commissioners yesterday against the granting of a license to Frank P. Smith of the Chester House at Chester. The remonstrance had only two signatures, but the accompanying letter said, "Do not be alarmed at the few signatures, there are plenty more and plenty of evidence." The grounds are as usual: unsuitable place and person. The house was condemned a year ago, but it has purged itself. The county commissioners will name a day for a hearing, which will be held in this city.

### DECEMBER 1897: FRANK IS GRANTED A LIQUOR LICENSE

Finally! On December 18, 1897, Frank was granted a liquor license. He had been trying to obtain one for sixteen years, since 1881, keeping his cool as the tempers of the temperance groups grew hotter and hotter.

> [*Daily Morning Journal and Courier,*
> (New Haven, Connecticut), December 29, 1897]
> MIDDLETOWN, CONN., DEC 28
> At a meeting of the county commissioners held here today, Frank P. Smith of Chester was granted a liquor license for

the Chester House. The town has voted [YES for] license for the past two years, but this is the first time a license has been granted owing to the opposition of the Law and Order League.

## 1898

A new year and a license for Frank! Was this the beginning of some easier years for Frank and the Chester House? No. It was too late. Frank had spent too much money on the legal cases, and likely (and as it turns out, rightly) foresaw more firestorms with the Law and Order League.

The temperance people were turning into a fiery bunch everywhere. Carrie Nation (1846–1911), a WCTU member, had escalated her protests from singing hymns outside of saloons in the mid-1890s to violent stunts by the end of the decade. By 1898, she was throwing rocks at the saloons. Within a few years, she would become famous for her *hatchetations*, when, armed with her trademark hatchet, she marched boldly into saloons, whacked the bottles off the shelves, and hacked the wooden bars to pieces.

Frank had been busy at the end of 1897 establishing himself at a new hotel in Middletown, where, in January 1898, he formally opened the former Germania Hotel on Main Street under a new name, the Middlesex Hotel. Not surprising, Middletown was a license town.

In March 1898, Frank needed income. He leased the Chester House to a Mr. Sylvester Looby of Centerbrook "for a term of years."[136] Frank still owned the building, and he and his family were able to live there as he launched his new hotel in Middletown.

In April 1898, the Chester House's barn burned down.

[*Hartford Courant*, April 18, 1898]

**Incendiary Fire in Chester**

CHESTER, APRIL 17

The large barn belonging to Frank P. Smith, proprietor of the Chester House, together with its contents, was burned early yesterday morning. The loss is about $1,500 [about $47,000 in 2020], partly insured. It is thought that the fire was set by someone through spite because of Mr. Smith's attitude in the many liquor cases here the past year.

The Chester selectmen (R. Clifford Tyler, Ezra G. Church, and Robert Saffrey) were getting fired up too — against the Law and Order League. On the same day of the barn burning, the selectmen refused to open town hall for the league officials, who had planned to hold a liquor trial there.

> [*Hartford Courant*, April 18, 1898]
> **Town Hall Closed**
> *Liquor Trial Was Not Held in Chester — A Meeting Called*
> The cases against Egbert Emmons and seven others, members of the Bicycle Club located at the Monterey House in Chester, which were to have been tried before Judge Pearne yesterday [April 17] were continued one week. The trial was to have been held in the town hall but the selectmen refused to open it pending action of the town meeting which has been called to act on the question of allowing the town hall to be used for liquor trials.
> 
> The action of the selectmen is due to the intense feeling in Chester against the Law and Order League, which has prevented any licenses being granted or saloons run during the past year and a half while the town has been a license town.

On the following day, April 19, 1898, a special town meeting was held, and a resolution was adopted — although not unanimously — that demanded the town hall be opened for *any* trial. From now on, the Chester selectmen would be required to open the town hall, free of charge, for the Law and Order League trials.

A day later, on April 20, the Law and Order League raided Egbert Emmons's house. Remember Egbert Emmons from two years ago in 1896? He had applied for a liquor license the same day that Frank had, but the Connecticut Law and Order League leader, Mr.

Thrasher, had appeared and presented a fire and brimstone case against the two of them.

May 26 was set as the day that the Law and Order League would present the results of their April 20 Egbert Emmons raid. The meeting was to be held at Chester's town hall. But when the league showed up on May 26, the town hall was locked again! Not to be outsmarted, the league found a way for the trial to be held in the nearby office of eighty-year-old Justice of the Peace Joseph E. Silliman.

Be careful what you wish for, Law and Order League, because the tables could turn on you. Which they did:

[*Hartford Courant*, May 27, 1898]

**More Trouble In Chester**
*Town Hall Locked — Law and Order League Men Arrested*
This morning [May 26] when officers arrived at the [town] hall, they found the doors locked. The janitor being found said he was ordered by the selectman not to open the doors unless ordered by him, necessitating an adjournment to the office of J. E. Silliman.

The case against E. G. Emmons, charged with perjury, three counts was finished. Decision was reserved. The case against him on charge of selling liquor illegally was partially heard. The case was continued until Tuesday.

John B. Hardy, a director of the State Law and Order League, was arrested at 3 o'clock this afternoon upon the charge of perjury. He was the principal witness for the state in the perjury case of Emmons. He was arrested upon complaint of Emmons's lawyer.

At the same time, Hardy and S. McClair, an agent of the Law and Order League, were arrested for breaking into the residence of Egbert Emmons on April 20, the day of the last raid by the league officials.

Hardy was placed under $1,500 [about $47,000 in 2020] bonds for perjury and Hardy and McClair were each placed under $100 [about $3,100 in 2020] bonds for breaking into Emmons's house. Bonds were furnished by E. C. Hungerford, treasurer of the Chester Savings Bank.

Secretary Thrasher of the Law and Order League claims that the arrests were malicious and threatens to prosecute everybody in Chester who had anything to do with the arrests.

I can guess how Frank reacted to the arrests of the Law and Order League agents, but it would have been a small satisfaction. The league had done their job of shutting down Frank Smith and the Chester House. In September 1898, Frank resorted to selling parcels of land around the Chester House and took a mortgage against the property. In mid-November, Frank moved his family to Middletown.

At this point, Frank was forty-four and Sarah was thirty-nine. Georgia had turned eighteen in October and was attending her final year at McLean Seminary in Simsbury. Frederick was fifteen and had been attending Middletown High School from Chester as a tuition student. Students from Middletown's surrounding towns who wanted to extend their education beyond the eighth grade could attend Middletown High School as tuition pupils starting in 1896.[137] Donald, Kittie, and five-year-old Vernon, who had been a member of Chester's first kindergarten class, switched to Middletown schools. Lucinda, now seventy-three, joined her son and family in Middletown.

The end of 1898 was a tough time for the Frank Smith family. Frank was sinking financially. They had to leave Chester, the only home his children knew. He had to turn an old hotel into a moneymaking enterprise to keep his family of seven afloat. And he still owned the Chester House where expenses exceeded income.

### 1899 – GEORGIANA BAILS FRANK OUT

Within two months of the Smiths moving to Middletown, Georgiana threw Frank a lifeline. On February 7, 1899, Ella Georgiana Cook

*Georgiana's nephew, Vernon E. Smith, age four, stands next to his teacher, Miss Dimock, in this 1897 photo of the first kindergarten class of Chester, Connecticut. Photo from Kate Silliman's Chester Scrapbook, page 72.*

## Vernon Smith In Chester's First Kindergarten Class

Frank and Sarah's youngest son, Vernon Edgar Smith, born in October 1893, is listed as a member of Chester's first kindergarten class in *Kate Silliman's Chester Scrapbook*, on page 78. The class was held in a room on the second floor of the Stone Store, a few buildings away from the Chester House. The building, now known as the Old Stone Store, was built in 1809, continues to be a landmark in Chester center.

bought the Chester House from Frank for $4,500 [about $141,000 in 2020], the same amount that Frank had paid Ulysses for the property in 1885. I assume this was with money from Ulysses, but ownership of the Chester House was in Georgiana's name alone.

Could Frank and his family now make plans to reopen the Chester House as a hotel and eventually move back home? No financial arrangement between Georgiana and Frank was ever recorded beyond this February 1899 real estate sale.

The blood of the Law and Order League must have boiled when they heard the news that the new owner of the Chester House, Georgiana Cook, was Frank Smith's sister. Would that mean Frank Smith would be coming back to Chester? The league and Chester were at odds. Chester had humiliated the league with the arrest of their agents in 1898. In October 1898, the town voted NO to licensing, giving a win to the league. But they won by only four votes. The league knew the town could have easily voted YES, had Frank Smith been in town. Now his sister owns the Chester House, which may mean he'll be back!

(I find it interesting that two weeks after Georgiana bought the Chester House in February 1899, her Westbrook cottage was burglarized. No, it can't be!)

Frank spent the next year running Hotel Middlesex in Middletown and making state-of-the-art renovations to the Chester House. He installed a new water heater so that each room had heat. And the town of Chester had invested in its first piped water system, so now the Chester House would have running water. He and Sarah redecorated the interior of the building for a refreshing look and to accommodate the new plumbing.

Then, they turned the peaked-roof top floor into a room for music, dancing, and gatherings. This room included a *spring dance floor*, a new type of flooring that allowed dancers to bounce gently as they waltzed and two-stepped. Was this new addition inspired by the Chester House's new owner, Georgiana, who loved to dance? The top floor, which had been used for town meetings in Chester's early days in the 1840s, would again be used for local events. According to the book *Old Homes of Chester, Connecticut*,[138] the Chester House's "attic room was known for its dance floor."

Yes, the top floor was a hall, and it was known for dancing, but I am resisting the term *dancehall* because of images that come to mind with that word. Especially in a story that involves a saloon, illegal liquor, traveling salesmen, and hotel rooms. That word has never been used in any publication to describe the Chester House's top floor, and I don't believe that Frank (and Sarah!) would have had *dancehall girls* floating around their home. I prefer the description of the top floor in the February 28, 1902, *Hartford Courant*: "A fine hall for accommodation of dancing parties, dinners provided by advance notice having been given."

Frank and his family continued to live Middletown until the Chester House reopened in April 1900, making their full stay in Middletown a year and a half. Georgiana continued to own the Chester House through the turn of the century. Chester continued to vote NO to liquor licensing. And the Chester House story, far from over, continues in the next chapters.

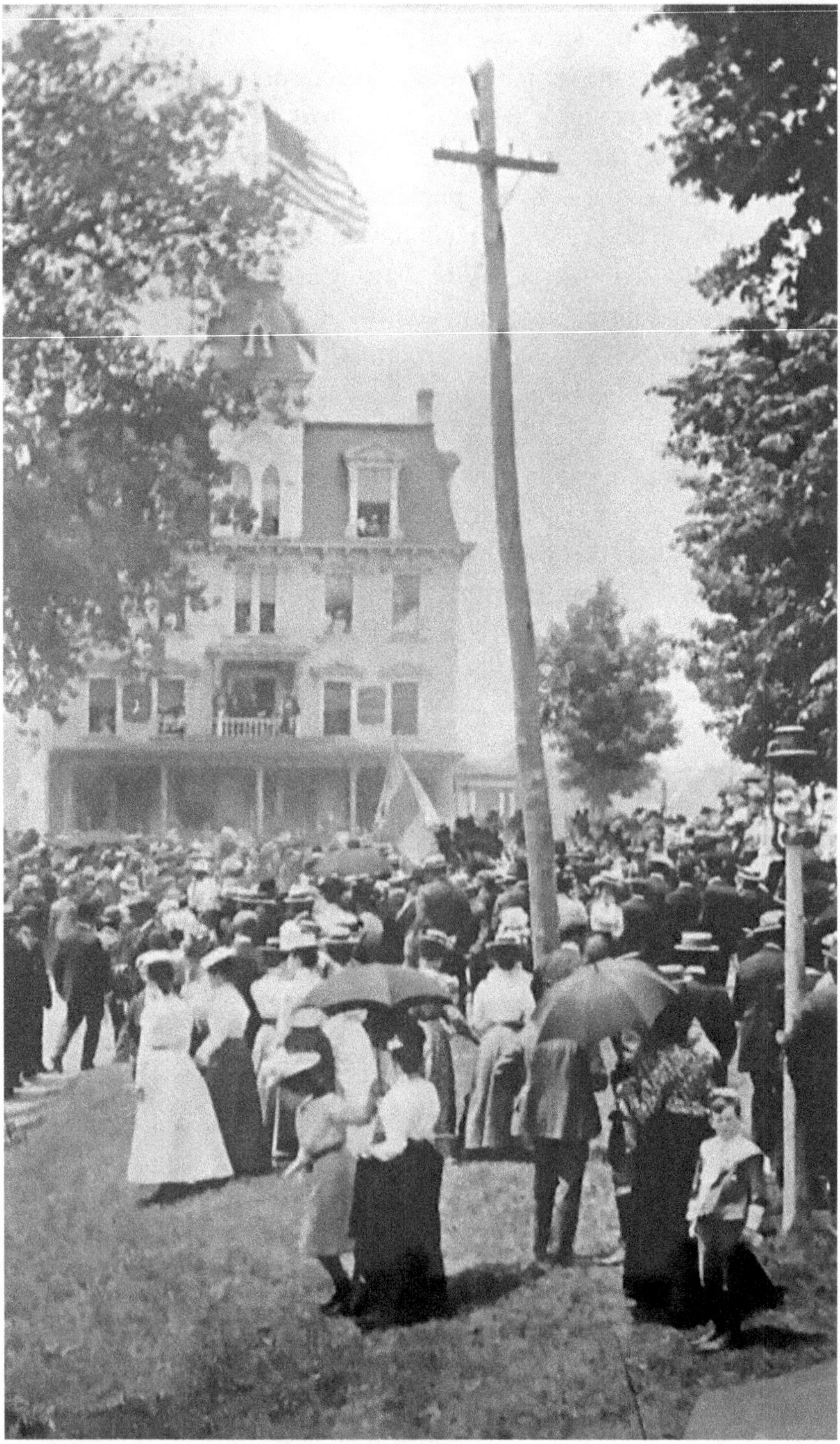

CHAPTER 10

# Turns

## Georgiana in Her Fifties
## 1900–1909

It seems that when the century turned, the world began turning faster. Americans were quick to adapt to the expanding worlds of communication and transportation. Telegraphs could send news from across the Atlantic to big city newspapers, who in turn sent the news to small town newspapers. Radios delivered news and entertainment even faster. Telephones were installed by the thousands, bringing business faster to businesses, doctors faster to sick people, gossip faster to homes, and fertilizer to the proverbial grapevines. Trains, trolleys, and bicycles improved. But in the new century, these modes of transportation would be left in the dust by the automobile, which had been invented in 1896. By 1900, there were eight thousand motor vehicles in the United States. By 1910, five hundred thousand. Humans were moving faster and further than ever before.

By the turn of the century, the circles of Georgiana's life had rippled out beyond its central swirl in Moodus. She could now count Westbrook and Chester as towns she knew well. And from November 1898 to April 1900, when Frank and his family, including Lucinda, lived in Middletown, Georgiana had come to know that town well too.

OPPOSITE: *The Goodspeed Opera House in East Haddam in 1900. The boy in the foreground is seven-year-old Vernon Smith, Georgiana's youngest nephew. This photograph was found in Georgiana's cottage and remains there today.*

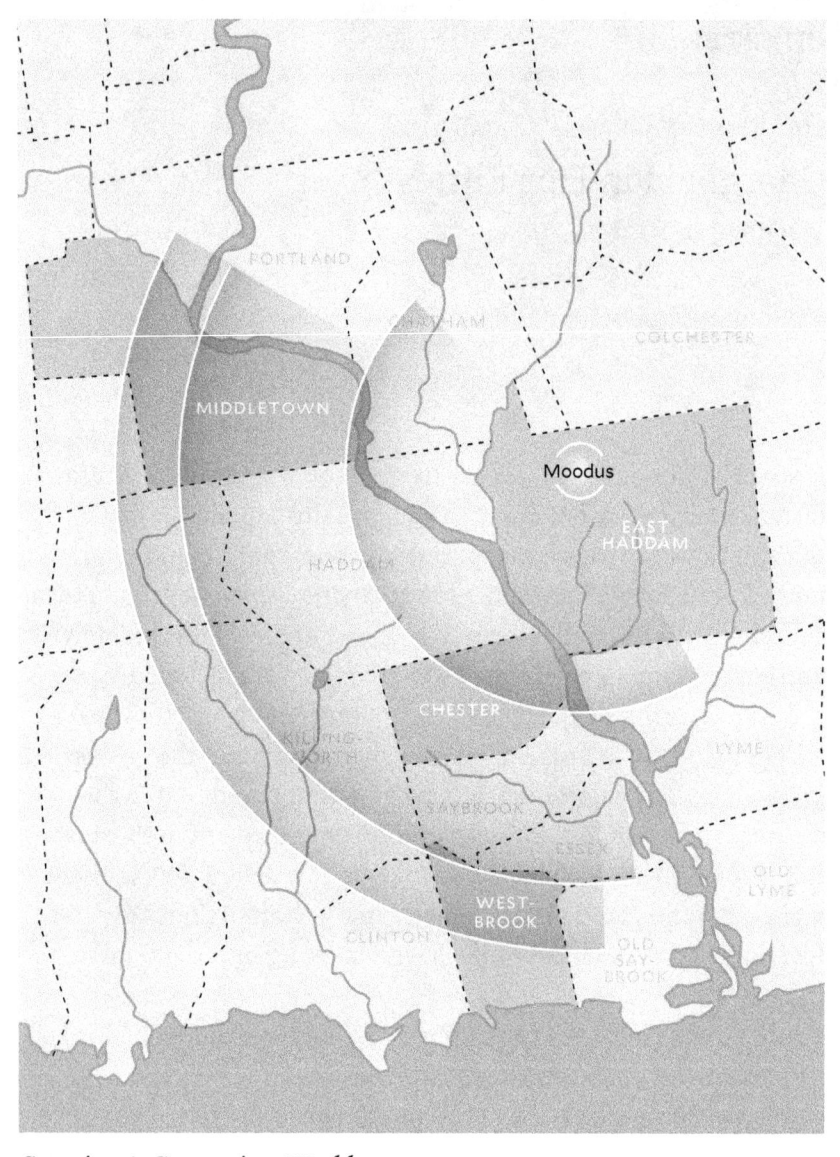

*Georgiana's Connecticut World*

## 1900 MIDDLETOWN

Middletown had turned into *the big city* for the people of Middlesex County, which included towns on both sides of the Connecticut River. Georgiana's East Haddam was one of the towns on the east side of the river. On the west side, the town of Middletown was the county seat in the days when Connecticut's county government was powerful. (In Connecticut, the county layer of government was removed in the 1960s.) Middletown had seventeen thousand residents, more by far than any other town in the county, and more than six times larger than East Haddam's twenty-five hundred.

Still growing in 1900, Middletown enjoyed (and tolerated) all the hubbub that goes with being the hub city with spokes that radiated out in all directions. From surrounding towns, workers came to the big city's busy manufacturing companies to make money, and shoppers came to the growing downtown to spend it. Lawyers with their documents, lawbreakers with their excuses, lawmakers with their proposals, businessmen with their plans, widows with their wills, newspaper reporters with their notebooks, and politicians with their glad hands flowed in a steady stream in and out of Middletown's courts and county government offices. Students from other towns and states walked the campuses of its schools, including the progressive coeducational[139] Wesleyan University. Many people arrived and departed by train; many used horse-drawn carriages; many more tried to negotiate the crowded, designed-for-horses streets with their new horseless carriages.

Georgiana needed to cross the Connecticut River to get to the town of Middletown. From Moodus, she could ride by carriage for thirteen miles to Portland, then pay a small toll to cross the river on the bridge between Portland and Middletown (built in 1896). In the good weather months, she could cross the river by ferry in East Haddam to either Tylerville or Chester and take the train straight into Middletown.

During the years Frank was in Middletown, Georgiana was a frequent weekend visitor to the town. Ulysses or Lillie or both may have joined her, or she may have traveled alone. In Middletown, Georgiana would have stayed at the Middlesex Hotel with Frank and Sarah, her mother, and her three nephews and niece Kittie. Her older niece, Georgia, during these years, was finishing up her school in Simsbury, Connecticut, then moving to New York to work as a governess.

And in Middletown, Georgiana would have shopped. I imagine Aunt Georgiana walking with eleven-year-old Kittie in downtown Middletown for a Saturday shopping spree, buying her pretty clothes and whatever the little girl's heart desired. I imagine Aunt Georgiana bringing home new purchases for the boys, too, and fresh baked goods from the local bakeries for the household. Then I imagine her staying for supper, doting more on Kittie, chatting about the new styles, the new foods, and the new gadgets, then spending the night so she could attend church in Middletown on Sunday.

Church? In Middletown? Yes. Georgiana joined a church there in 1900. She became an official member of Middletown's Christ Church, P. E. (Protestant Episcopal), also called the Church of the Holy Trinity. This is the beautiful stone church with double red front doors located at 381 Main Street. The church records show that on February 25, 1900, Georgiana, at age fifty, was baptized there. Also baptized were Frank's three oldest children: Georgia (nineteen), who came all the way from Brooklyn, New York; Fred (sixteen); and Donald (fourteen). A week later, on March 4, 1900, Frank's three children and Georgiana were confirmed.

What was behind her decision to join a church? One point to ponder is that she did this on her own, without husband or brother or sister-in-law or mother or any other adult. Was she exhibiting a little wave of independence? Did she have a religious epiphany at age fifty? Did she do it to influence her nieces and nephews? There had to be a reason why Georgiana chose to join an Episcopal church in Middletown. In Moodus, she had attended a Methodist Episcopal church. Methodist and Episcopal churches, both outgrowths of the Church of England, were once combined into one church, as in Moodus. If Georgiana had wanted to change to an Episcopal-only church for religious reasons, she could have joined St. Stephen's Episcopal Church in East Haddam, much closer to home.

I believe her reason for joining the Middletown church was linked to her nieces and nephews. I think she took all the children to church. The 1900 records don't name Kittie (eleven) and Vernon (six), as they were too young for official church membership, which required being fourteen, but Georgiana likely brought them to Sunday school. As far as I can tell, Frank and Sarah were not churchgoers[140] during these years, nor did they bring their children to church, a point that may have caused Georgiana some angst. It has occurred to me that there may have been a *quid pro quo* arrangement in 1899 between Frank and Georgiana, as in "I'll buy the Chester House for you, under one condition — your children must go to church."

Georgiana may have joined the church for Georgia's sake. In 1900, Georgia was at the *marrying age* of nineteen and may have wanted (or Georgiana may have wanted her to have) a church affiliation for a future wedding. At the time of her baptism and confirmation, Georgia was living in Brooklyn, New York, where she had secured a position as a full-time governess. Coming to Middletown for these ceremonies in the cold month of February would have involved an uncomfortable journey by train. Therefore, it must have been important, for whatever reason, to Georgia.

How often Georgiana attended church services in Middletown, and how devout a believer she was, it's hard to tell. In the years following 1900, she continued her connection with her Moodus Methodist Episcopal Church. No records show any involvement by Georgiana in the Middletown church after the baptisms and confirmations — not surprising, given that Frank and his family moved out of Middletown and back to Chester within two months of the February and March 1900 church ceremonies.

### 1900 — FRANK AND FAMILY RETURN TO CHESTER

By April 1900, Frank and his family, including Lucinda but without Georgia, who was working in New York, were back in the freshly renovated Chester House, now owned by Georgiana. The older boys, Fred and Donald, who were in their high school years, continued attending Middletown High School as tuition pupils, likely taking the train from Chester to Middletown. Kittie and Vernon returned to the Chester district school. The whole family, including seventy-four-year-old Lucinda, was probably thrilled to get back to the place they had called home for seventeen years.

Frank dove back into business with renewed confidence, advertising the Chester House's new modern luxuries of heat, indoor plumbing, and the new top floor hall designed for group dining and dancing. He also went back to soliciting traveling salesmen at Chester's railroad depot, a privilege the railroad granted him for a fee.

Georgiana and Ulysses visited Chester when their busy schedules allowed, and no doubt enjoyed some of the social events offered in the new top floor hall. There is no evidence that Georgiana or Ulysses became involved in the running of the day-to-day operations. There is also no evidence of family tension over Georgiana's ownership of the Chester House. Probably these two points are related.

### 1900 — A MONUMENTAL MOMENT
### FOR MOODUS AND FOR GEORGIANA

Moodus remained the axis of Georgiana's life. After living there fifty years, she knew every building, every tree, and every divot in every street. She knew three generations of families who in turn knew her. These families also knew about her father who had died in the unforgotten Civil War. So in early 1900, when Georgiana was asked to become a member of an executive committee to plan a monument to honor the soldiers who lost their lives in the Civil War, she accepted — most certainly with pride and eagerness. Her involvement with this monument was a major event in her life.

The funding for the monument came through the philanthropy of a local woman. Mrs. Eliza Wheeler Miller (1835–1898), who had died in September 1898, had bequeathed money for a monument to honor the thirty-two East Haddam soldiers who had died in the Civil War. Her young brother Alfred Wheeler had been one of them. He was the Wheeler boy across the street from the Smiths who was killed in September 1862, two weeks after his seventeenth birthday. At the time, Eliza was twenty-seven, unmarried, and still living with her Wheeler family on North Moodus Road. She would never forget her young brother, whom she probably cared for like a mother.

Eliza Wheeler Miller lived her entire life in Moodus. She was one of the nine children of the Wheeler family who lived across the street from Smiths. The families knew one another well. The oldest Wheeler son, Frank, born in 1833, never lost touch with the Smith family, even making a trip to visit Lucinda when she was ninety. Another son, Clarence, also paid visits to Lucinda. Eliza, the third child, born in 1835, was older than Georgiana by fourteen years. Her ill-fated brother Alfred, born in 1845, was born the same year as Ulysses. In 1862, when the just-turned-seventeen Alfred died in the Civil War, Georgiana was thirteen and the Wheeler children ranged in age from nine to twenty-nine, including twenty-seven-year-old Eliza.

In 1866, Eliza Wheeler married Charles Miller from Cromwell. They chose to live in Moodus near her family. Eliza and Charles never had children. When he died in 1882, Charles willed everything to Eliza. When she died in 1898, her will included this excerpt:

> I give and bequeath $2,000 [about $62,000 in 2020] to the town of East Haddam, on condition that it shall be used, and all it may increase, to purchase and erect a soldiers' monument ... to be placed in the park in the village of Moodus within five years after my decease.

Her will also detailed her wishes for the style of the monument and for a plaque acknowledging that the monument was "erected by Charles Miller and his wife Eliza Wheeler Miller."

The people of Moodus embraced the idea of a monument for the East Haddam men and boys lost in the Civil War. A number of Georgiana's women friends were on the monument executive committee with her, including Juliette Williams, the wife of the other Moodus physician, Dr. E. E. Williams. The executive committee met regularly starting in January, guiding the decisions that led to the September 1900 installation. The committee was also charged with organizing an October 1900 dedication ceremony, which was no small task and involved several subcommittees and daunting logistics. Two weeks before the event, the *Hartford Courant* announced the plans for the dedication. Here are some excerpts:

[*Hartford Courant,* October 10, 1900]
**Soldiers of Moodus**
*The Monument to be Dedicated in Their Memory October 24*
- The soldiers' monument recently erected on the park in this village by Stephen Maslen of Hartford, will be dedicated with appropriate ceremonies on Wednesday, October 24.
- The people of East Haddam are making great preparations for the event. Hatch's Band of Hartford and the famous Moodus Drum Corps will furnish music. [I bet Ulysses loved the word *famous*!]
- The procession will form at the Machimoodus House at 11 a.m., but the line of march has not yet been decided on. George Q. Emily, a Civil War veteran, will be chief marshal. It is expected to be the biggest parade in the history of the town.
- The visiting delegations and invited guests will be fed at the Continental, which will accommodate several hundred. The committee is endeavoring to secure one of the best speakers in the state to deliver the oration.

- At a recent meeting, a committee of over 100 of the leading citizens of the town was appointed to arrange the celebration. Albert E. Olmsted was elected chairman, George W. Hall secretary and Samuel P. Clark treasurer. The executive committee, which will have charge of the dedication, is composed of the following: A. E. Olmsted, the Rev. C. L. Eldredge [Moodus Baptist Church], C. H. Emily, W. C. Drown, the Rev. J. E. Duxbury [Moodus Methodist Episcopal Church], **Mrs. U. S. Cook**, Mrs. W. S. Purple, Mrs. E. E. Williams, Mrs. T. R. Spencer, Mrs. J. W. Chapman. The executive committee has appointed a large number of subcommittees.
- On three sides [of the monument] are inscribed the names of the soldiers of East Haddam, who died in the Civil War as follows: Twentieth Regiment — Corporal Abner C. Smith, Frederick A. Chapman, John Burns ...
- All business in Moodus will be suspended on the day of the dedication. The school children, who will take a prominent part in the exercises, are being drilled in singing by Professor R. R. Cone, who had charge of them at the Nathan Hale celebration.

When October 24 came, four thousand people turned out! The event was a huge success. The *Hartford Courant* detailed the program at great length in the next day's paper:

> [Excerpts from the *Hartford Courant,* October 25, 1900]
> **The Moodus Monument**
> *Dedication Of Memorial To Heroes Of The War*
> Result of the Bequest of Mrs. Eliza Miller — A Large Attendance at the Ceremonies — President [of Wesleyan University] Raymond the Orator.
>
> - The rain last night laid the dust in fine shape for the ceremonies today, connected with the dedication of the Soldiers' Monument. For weeks, the committee has been

preparing for this event, and today's exercises passed off without a break and were witnessed by some 4,000 people. Early this morning, they began to arrive in carriages and on their wheels, and the trains landed hundreds at Goodspeed's who were brought here in buses [horse-drawn omnibuses].
- The Civil War Veterans, Relief Council, O.U.A.M. [Order of United American Mechanics], and the reception committee, accompanied by the Moodus Drum and Fife Corps and Cornet Band, assembled at the monument to act as escort to the visiting organizations. Upon arrival they were escorted to Continental Hall where they were given a dinner. [According to another article, this banquet was served by the "ladies."] The parade was at 1 o'clock this afternoon and went through the principal streets of the village which presented a gala appearance.
- The committee in charge of the exercises were indefatigable in the care for their guests and everything was done that could be to make the day a memorable one.

"Indefatigable in the care for their guests." That's our Georgiana!

After the early morning preparations, after the welcome and escorting of the guests, after the dinner at the Continental, the one o'clock parade, the invocation by the Reverend Francis Parker, the four addresses by four important men, the children's singing, the bands' playing, the unveiling of the monument, the thirteen-gun salute, the benediction, the trotting away of the filled omnibuses, the closing down of the public library that had been "open for the ladies," the farewell hugs with family and friends, and after the final removal of her hatpin and hat at home, Georgiana must have flopped into her favorite corner of the parlor sofa to bask in the afterglow of her wonderful success.

The East Haddam's Soldiers' Monument still stands on Moodus's town green at the junction of Routes 149 and 151.

*Soldiers' Monument, located at the junction of Route 151 and Plains Road in Moodus, East Haddam, Connecticut. Photo taken 2022.*

### GEORGIANA'S FULL 1900 CALENDAR

Georgiana's calendar for the first year of the new century was filled with special events. The planning for the monument had begun in January. On February 5, she and Ulysses probably traveled to see John Philip Sousa in his annual concert at the Meriden Opera House. In late February and early March, Georgiana orchestrated the Middletown church ceremonies for her niece and nephews. In April, Frank and his family, including Lucinda, moved back to the newly refurbished Chester House, which Georgiana now owned and would have visited that spring. June was East Haddam's important Nathan Hale School House celebration. September was the monument installation. October was the dedication ceremony.

These special events were in addition to her already busy schedule which included the annual Moodus festivities of May's Decoration Day, June's Ladies Benevolent Society's Strawberry Festival, and July's Independence Day; which were on top of Ulysses's and Lillie's musical events and Ulysses's Continental Hall responsibilities that trickled into Georgiana's sphere; which were on top of her everyday household and hostessing duties in Moodus; and on top of her household and hostessing duties at her Westbrook cottage in the good old summertime.

### IN THE GOOD OLD SUMMERTIME

Westbrook did indeed have good old summertimes in the 1900s. The town had continued to grow in popularity as a summer beach resort through the 1890 decade and into the new century. The permanent residents of town (many of whom, as descendants of Westbrook's founding families, had roads and buildings bearing their names) could hardly recognize *their* Westbrook from Decoration Day to Labor Day. Some likely didn't appreciate it, but there were plenty who enjoyed the three months of business and busyness.

[*Hartford Courant,* July 30, 1901]

**Westbrook Notes**

*An Unprecedented Season at this Resort*

The present season of popularity here is almost unprecedented and, if Westbrook continues to be as lively and gay the rest of the summer, it will be a record-breaker. Almost every cottage along the crescent of the bay ... is occupied, and the hotel managers report an exceedingly prosperous season.

Perhaps one attraction is the good fishing ... Bluefishing and blackfishing are the most popular ... Several parties were out sailing by moonlight.

The hops [dances] at the Pochoug [Hotel] and the Seaview [Hotel, formerly Cooley's Hotel] Saturday night were well attended.

The peak month for Westbrook was August. That's when Georgiana and Ulysses vacationed there. For Westbrook and for Georgiana and Ulysses, even though the calendar had turned to a new decade, it was like the lively 1890s had never ended.

*Oompah-pah, oompah-pah, oompah-pah.* Set to the waltz rhythm that took off in the 1890s, the song "In the Good Old Summertime," written by Ron Shields and George Evans, was released in 1902. This is a classic example of a Tin Pan Alley hit song — a popular sing-along, dance-along, sway-along song of this era. The houseful in the Cook cottage would have sung this song as they swayed around the upright piano, sometimes with arms linked together, sometimes with arms lifting drinks, sometimes with someone adding harmony, and always with gusto. Lillie would have played it on the piano. Ulysses would have beaten the *oompah-pahs* on his drum. And Georgiana would have waltzed to it with friends and family and by herself.

For Georgiana and Ulysses, the song may have been an anthem to Westbrook.

## A RARE GLIMPSE OF GEORGIANA IN 1901

Of the many letters that Georgiana would have written and received in her adult years, the time when social letter writing peaked in popularity, only one letter survives. It is dated September 4, 1901. The letter was written to her and offers a wonderful glimpse at Georgiana's duties and cares.

The letter is from Mary (born Ackley) Cook (1825–1904). Mary was the third wife of Dr. Henry C. Cook (1824–1883), Ulysses's uncle, also a botanic physician. Both of Henry's previous wives, one of whom was Mary's sister, had passed away. Mary had married the twice-widowed Henry in 1878, when they were both fifty-three. At the time of their wedding, Georgiana was twenty-nine. When this letter was written, Mary was seventy-six and had been a widow for eighteen years. Georgiana was fifty-two. It came from Mary's home in Pittsfield, Massachusetts and is dated September 1901:

> *My dear Georgia* [Mary's nickname for Georgiana],
>
> *I received your long and interesting letter Aug. sixteenth, and hope you will not feel displeased because I have neglected to send the record you requested before.* [Georgiana had requested information to compile a family record.] *I might have done that, but I was thinking all the time that I wanted to write and so put it off. My excuse is, I have not felt very well some of the time, and we have had company, so I feel sorry for the long delay.*
>
> *Edward* [Edward Cook Perkins (1886–1904), fourteen at the time of this letter, was Mary's grandson.] *came to visit us during his short vacation from Aug. 17 to the 30eth and as I didn't expect to see him again before the holidays I spent considerable time with him. He entered the Mount Hermon School* [a boarding school in Gill, Massachusetts, near the Vermont line] *last May. The term commences May first but he went*

*the day before so as to be ready the first day of school — the Principal requested him to do so. He likes it there better than he did at Amherst and I feel as if it is a better place. The religious influence there is very good. He has grown quite tall in nearly eight months since I saw him and looks like his mother.* [His mother was Mary (born Cook) Perkins who had died three years before this letter was written. She was Ulysses's cousin, daughter of his uncle Henry C. and Margaret Cook.] *He seems ambitious to learn and I noticed he used good language to express his thoughts. Last term his studies comprised Arithmetic, Grammar, U.S. History. This term he is advanced to Ancient History, Algebra, and continues Grammar. Besides they have a bible lesson every week, drawing and singing, also composition.*

*I was very glad you wrote about your nieces — I like to see you have such a care over them and a love for them and also for all your brother's children.*

*I think of your mother — she is about my age — only a little younger, and I hope she is well. The last time I saw her was at your house and we talked over our ages.* [Mary and Lucinda were both born in 1825 and were seventy-six at the time of this letter ] *I think it was at Christmas when we all had gifts — the smaller children, each a bright silver dollar* [probably the Morgan dollar, minted from 1878 to 1904] *from our host.*

*I send you the record as Father Cook wrote it in his family bible. His last entry was the death of his son John S. Cook. Only the birth and death of his children are recorded, except his own marriage. The maiden name, surname I mean, of his wife is not given but I know it was Clark — Sally Clark. I have not the date of Seth's death but have that of Elizabeth. Neither have I the date of Henry's marriage to Abbie's mother* [Henry

C. Cook's first wife]. *Margaret Pamela Ackley* [Henry C. Cook's second wife and Mary's sister] *was married Feb. 22, 1854, and died Nov. 17, 1877. I was married Sept. 11, 1878.*

[Henry C. Cook's family tree is one of the most complicated and one of the saddest I've read in writing this book. At the time of this letter, Mary lived with her stepdaughter, Abbie (born Cook) Button and her husband, Edward Button, who were about the same age as Georgiana. Abbie was the daughter of Henry C. Cook and his first wife, also named Abbie, who lived only three months after her daughter's birth. Abbie was raised by Henry's second wife, Margaret Pamela (born Ackley) Cook. When Abbie was twenty-four, Margaret died and Henry married his third wife, Mary, who penned this letter.]

*I thank you for your newsy long letter, also your pleasant invitation to visit you. Write again when you can get time from your duties and cares. And I can't say when we'll go to East Haddam, but will consider it a standing invitation.*

*Myron* [Myron W. Perkins (1853–1911) was Edward Perkins's father. He had been married to Mary Cook, Henry's daughter who had died in 1898. Myron lived in Springfield, Massachusetts, and was in the newspaper business] *sent me last week's Advertiser and I noticed an account of the flood which did so much damage. Also the death of Mrs. Pierce and some others.*

*Edward* [Edward L. Button (1849–1919)] *continues his business* [as an optician] *but his health is poor and he has very little ambition about going away from home. Abbie also is not strong and cannot endure as she could once. They both wish to be remembered to you all, as I also do, with love and thanks for your kindness.*

*Mary.*

Mary died three years after she wrote this letter, at age seventy-nine in February 1904. Her grandson Edward Perkins died of appendicitis four months later at age seventeen in June 1904. Abbie Button died in 1917. There are no descendants of Henry C. Cook.

This letter reveals a warm relationship and mutual respect between Mary and Georgiana. It confirms that Ulysses had a familial bond, not only a professional one, with his uncle Dr. Henry C. Cook, and that the Cook family was part of Georgiana's family celebrations. It also fully convinced me that Georgiana gave special attention to Frank's daughters (Kitty was thirteen, and Georgia was twenty when this letter was written), a point I had only deduced, contemplated, mused over, and admittedly hoped for, as I tried to get inside her head and heart while examining her life.

And this letter made me think that Georgiana would laugh out loud in agreement with me that genealogy is messy.

### GEORGIA: TURN-OF-THE-CENTURY GIRL

Georgiana's namesake niece, Georgia, had entered the new century as a well-educated young lady. She had graduated from McLean Seminary for Young Ladies in Simsbury, Connecticut, at age eighteen in 1899. She then stayed in Simsbury to work for the summer. According to the *Hartford Courant* on July 20, 1899, she and a Miss Annie A. Phelps of Simsbury took charge of a group of children for a Mrs. Norman Dodge. Mrs. Dodge had arranged for ten children from New York City to be entertained and stay at her "cottage" on the grounds of her Simsbury home during the summer of 1899.[141] Georgia then moved to Brooklyn, New York, where she worked as a governess (for an unknown family) for two years. It was during early 1900 that Georgia made a brief trip back to Middletown, Connecticut, to be baptized and confirmed with Georgiana in the Middletown church.

*McLean Seminary, Simsbury, Connecticut, which Georgiana's niece Georgia attended in the late 1890s and 1900. (Postcard)*

## What Was a Seminary?

In the nineteenth and early-twentieth centuries, the words *seminary* and *college* were used to describe private schools at a variety of educational levels. A seminary could be a preparatory school (high school level), a school at the post-high school or the graduate levels, as well as an institution that offered professional training. A college might give instruction to those of high school age and even younger, or to university students.

The idea of a college for women was horrifying to many people in the 1830s when Mount Holyoke Seminary, the first of the seven women-only colleges in the United States which became known as the Seven Sisters, was founded. The founder, Mary Lyon, chose to use the term *seminary* to avoid controversy with and loss of financial backers who were uncomfortable with colleges for women. The institution was later called Mount Holyoke Seminary and College, and in 1893, simply and finally Mount Holyoke College.

The word *seminary* has evolved to mean an institution for training priests, ministers, and rabbis.

Like most twenty-one-year-old women in the early 1900s, Georgia did not have a career goal. Her main mission was to get married, a goal she soon achieved. In January 1902, invitations to her wedding were sent out, an event reported in the social news section of the *Hartford Courant*.

[*Hartford Courant,* January 27, 1902]

CHESTER

Invitations cards are out for the marriage of Miss Georgiana Smith, daughter of Mr. and Mrs. F.P. Smith of the Chester House, and J.F. Strong, manager of the South Norwalk telephone exchange, February 11, at the home of the bride's parents.

How and where Georgia met Jack (John Frederick) Strong (1873–1922), I don't know. He came from Pittsfield, Massachusetts, the son of Charles Worthington Strong and Sarah Burghardt Strong. Jack was seven years older than Georgia. Perhaps they met through Georgiana's Pittsfield connections of Mary Cook, Edward Button, and Abbie Button.

For her maid of honor, Georgia chose Miss Bessie Gridley (1878–1964) from South Hadley, Massachusetts. My guess is that Georgia and Bessie had become friends at McLean Seminary. It was customary in the early 1900s for a bride to pick a close friend as maid of honor. Georgia's wedding is the only connection I found between Bessie and Georgia, but somehow Bessie was important enough to Georgia to serve in that special role. In 1902, at the time of Georgia's wedding, Bessie was about to graduate from Mount Holyoke College in South Hadley. Jack's mother had attended Miss Wells Seminary in Pittsfield, Massachusetts, and was probably quite pleased that her son was marrying a seminary-educated woman whose friend attended the prestigious Mount Holyoke College.

The wedding took place at one o'clock on Tuesday, February 11, 1902, at the Chester House. Did Georgiana help plan the wedding? I think so. Aunt Georgiana would have been Georgia's idol — the aunt she was named after, the aunt with the seashore cottage, the aunt who doted on her and showered her with gifts, the aunt who (probably) paid for her to go to private school, the aunt who loved to dance, the aunt who was married to her jolly, musical uncle, and the aunt who took her to church. The minister of Middletown's Christ Church, the same minister who had baptized and confirmed Georgia in 1900, Reverend Edward Campion Acheson, officiated the ceremony.

A *Hartford Courant* article published the day after the wedding provided the details of the event:

> [*Hartford Courant,* February 12, 1902]
> The rooms [of the Chester House] were handsomely decorated with laurel and cut and potted flowers. The bride wore a gown of tucked white crepe de chine and duchesse lace over white taffeta [White had become the standard color for wedding gowns after 1840 when Queen Victoria wore a white dress for her wedding with Prince Albert.] and carried a shower [cascade] bouquet. The maid of honor wore yellow crepe de chine over yellow taffeta and carried a bouquet of roses. The gifts were numerous and included much solid silver and beautiful cut glass.

Miss Gertrude E. Gladding played the wedding march on the piano. Gertrude was a thirty-one-year-old music teacher and musician in Chester. Gertrude and her parents were friends of Frank and Sarah's in Chester, close enough to have Kittie as a houseguest in Chester when Kittie was older, and close enough to vacation with Sarah in the Westbrook cottage. (Musicians had a leg up on getting invitations to the beach.)

A reception was held immediately after the ceremony, no doubt using the Chester House's new top floor hall. I don't know if the father of the bride served alcohol at his daughter's wedding reception. The owner may not have approved!

Wedding guests came from Connecticut, Massachusetts, and New York City. Georgiana, Ulysses, and Lillie would have had prime seats at the wedding ceremony, sitting with Lucinda, Sarah, the three boys, and Kittie, as Frank walked Georgia down the aisle. Imagine the thrill for thirteen-year-old Kittie watching her glamorous big sister amid the pomp and circumstance.

After the wedding and the honeymoon, Georgia and Jack made their home in South Norwalk, Connecticut, near Jack's work. As soon as she married, Georgia became *Mrs. John F. Strong*, following the naming custom of the day in which the husband's first name followed *Mrs*. When Georgia and Jack visited Frank and Sarah a month after the wedding, the newspaper reported their visit with the socially accepted formality.

[*Hartford Courant,* March 25, 1902]
Mr. and Mrs. John F. Strong of South Norwalk are guests of Mrs. Strong's parents, Mr. and Mrs. Frank P. Smith, at the Chester House.

After she married, Georgia continued her visits to Westbrook, which was about a two-hour train ride from South Norwalk. Six months after their wedding, Georgia and Jack were probably in Westbrook when this article appeared.

[*Hartford Courant,* August 22, 1902]
James Balen[142] of Moodus is the guest of Dr. Ulysses Cook. Dr. Cook and family will return to Moodus tomorrow. The nightly orchestral concerts given at the cottage will be greatly missed by the beach people.

The "and family" in this article were certainly Georgiana and Lillie, but it could have also meant his extended family of Lucinda, Sarah, Fred, Donald, Kittie, Vernon, and the newlyweds, Georgia and Jack. The cottage often made room for Frank's family. Frank did not always go to Westbrook when his family did. He had his hands full tending to the Chester House business.

## 1903 — I WONDER, I WONDER

The spillover from the bubbly 1890s into the new century was bound to dry up, as it did for the Chester House during 1903.

Like many Connecticut small towns in the early 1900s, Chester continued to vote NO to serving alcohol in the town. When Frank reopened the Chester House in 1900, did he abide by this law and give up serving alcohol? There were no raids or arrests or incidents involving liquor at the Chester House after Frank made his return. Perhaps he behaved himself because of a promise to new owner Georgiana. Or perhaps he had simply mastered the art of dodging the enforcers.

The members of Connecticut's Law and Order League still had a short fuse when it came to Frank Smith and the Chester House. The hotel that had been their nemesis for so many years was back in business, and bolder than ever with the added pizzazz of new conveniences and a new décor. The league's concerns: This attractive makeover might make drinking alcohol more appealing. It might create more pro-alcohol voters. It might tip the scales in Chester from dry/NO to wet/YES in the October vote.

In 1903, Connecticut's Law and Order League, which had been trying to control the serving of liquor in the state for over eight years with the futility of rubbing two sticks together, was still trying. They would have watched Frank Smith closely. I wonder, I wonder — did they have anything to do with what happened on February 9, 1903?

> [*Daily Morning Journal and Courier*,
> New Haven, Connecticut, February 10, 1903]

**Fire in Chester**
*Hotel Burned*
CHESTER, FEBRUARY 9
The Chester House caught fire shortly before 2 o'clock this afternoon and was practically destroyed. A gale of wind was blowing and it was feared for a time that the whole business section of the town would be burned. The local hose

companies were called and quickly laid three lines of hose and the company from Deep River was summoned to give assistance.

The Chester House was three stories and a half high and was built in 1840. It has been a well-known hostelry. Frank P. Smith is proprietor. The post office, a livery stable and five stores are within a stone's throw of the house. The fire started in the space between the attic and the roof of the hotel and is supposed to have been caused by a defective flue. By 2:30 the fire companies had the fire under control. The building was owned by Mrs. Ulysses S. Cook of Moodus. It was insured for $4,000 [about $117,000 in 2020]. Mr. Smith had an insurance of $1,000 [about $29,000 in 2020] on the contents. Little was saved.

Mr. Smith attempted to go upstairs after the fire started but was driven back by the smoke. The firemen did excellent work in saving the adjoining buildings.

The *Hartford Courant* reported more details:

[*Hartford Courant*, February 10, 1903]

**Fire in Chester**

*Hotel Building Practically Ruined — Once a Famous Hostelry*
CHESTER, FEBRUARY 9
About 1:30 this afternoon, Frank Watrous noticed smoke coming through the roof and from the upper windows of the Chester House. He gave the alarm to the proprietor, Frank P. Smith. Word was telephoned to the factories nearby and the employees hurried to the spot. Two lines of hose were attached to hydrants and the streams turned on the roof, through which the flames had burned. When the Deep River Hose Company arrived two more streams were turned on and after an hour and a half the flames were subdued.

The house was erected in the thirties of the last century. During the years before the opening of the Valley

Railroad it was a noted hostelry. In 1881, Frank P. Smith of Moodus took possession and had continued since with the exception of a year when he conducted the Hotel Middlesex at Middletown. During the last year he had had the house thoroughly renovated. The building, which was about 40 × 50 feet and three and a half stories in height, was owned by Mrs. U.S. Cook, wife of Dr. Cook of Moodus, and was insured for $4,000. Mr. Smith had an insurance of $1,000 on the furniture.

It is supposed that the fire caught from the chimney in the attic on the east side. The building is practically ruined by the fire and water.

Also up in smoke were Frank and Georgiana's hopes for the Chester House. Georgiana collected the insurance money, but she did not reinvest in the Chester House. Frank and his family may have stayed with her in Moodus while they sought a new place to live. Within three months, Frank and his family, including Lucinda, moved out of Connecticut. And Georgiana continued as owner of the "practically ruined" Chester House.

---

**OBITUARY: The Law and Order League of Connecticut (Born 1895; Died 1903)**

In 1895, Connecticut took a statewide approach toward controlling illegal liquor sales. Local authorities seemed to be ignoring the liquor and vice laws, so the General Assembly approved a charter for a new group of enforcers for the state, calling it the Law and Order League of Connecticut.[143] The charter allowed the governor to appoint four agents. Their headquarters would be on Church Street in New Haven. A prestigious board of directors was selected. The league's motto: We demand obedience to law. Mr. Samuel Powers Thrasher (1858–1925) was the secretary and general manager of the league from start to finish. In 1903, the league was abolished.

During its short life, the league had many supporters from the clergy and from the growing number of pro-temperance advocates. In 1898, the league published a pamphlet which reported on "Six Months' Work of the Law and Order League of Connecticut." Their list of achievements included investigating 225 places, conducting 25 raids, seizing and destroying nearly 900 gallons of liquor, and generating $5,515 [about $173,000 in 2020] in fines and forfeited bonds. They covered the whole state. Greenwich, New Haven, and Hartford received a lot of attention. As did Chester.

Several groups, and not only the self-serving saloon owners and liquor dealers, were against the league and tried to destroy it. Some groups were openly critical of their methods of enforcement, an accusation that was virtually admitted to when a pro-league Baptist minister, in a long, published sermon, said "as officers of the league are human, no doubt some of this prejudice [criticism] was deserved." The minister also blamed the press for misrepresenting the facts.[144] The league was also unpopular with the local police, whom the league accused of corruption and incompetence, which may or may not have been true. The police couldn't enforce the liquor laws because saloons had posted men who, as soon as they saw their well-known local policeman approaching, would alert the owners to clear away evidence.

Over the years, public sentiment about the Law and Order League swung both ways. In 1899, a formal proposal to abolish the league titled the "Resolution Repealing the Charter of the Law and Order League of Connecticut," was presented to the General Assembly. Who submitted it? There was lots of finger-pointing in this Keystone Kop-like whodunit, but the answer led back to someone in Chester, where, according to the Baptist minister's sermon "nineteen places have been cleaned up by the Law and Order League, and in which, therefore, a certain element is bitter against the league."[145]

In May 1903, three months after the burning of the Chester House in February, the Law and Order League was abolished by the state. (I'm not saying the two events are related.)

> The Law and Order League of Connecticut lasted eight years, from 1895 to 1903. National Prohibition lasted thirteen years from 1920 to 1933. Lesson learned? Prohibition in America doesn't work.

## The Chester House's Get-rid-of-the-liquor System?

In the early 1900s, if a town voted NO to liquor licensing, some saloonkeepers in the town tried to serve liquor illegally. To elude the authorities, saloonkeepers came up with all sorts of ideas: befriending and bribing officials to alert them about scheduled raids; paying lookout men to send warning signals when enforcers were approaching; engineering hiding places for the liquor; and installing gadgets and processes to swiftly get rid of the liquor if enforcers made it into the bar.

The newspaper account below is from 1905, when Chester was a no-license town, which it had been since 1898. Georgiana owned the Chester House at this point but had little to do with it. Her brother Frank Smith had been proprietor of the Chester House until 1903, when he moved out of Connecticut.

Had Frank installed this get-rid-of-the-liquor system when he ran the Chester House from 1900 to 1903?

[*Hartford Courant,* September 25, 1905]

### Sheriff Finds Beer In Bottom Of Well

Friday evening, Deputy Tyler went to the [Chester] hotel, accompanied by Russell Stannard. They suddenly entered the hotel, and went direct to the room which, in license years, had contained the bar. Proprietor Frank Bottomly was behind the counter, and reaching under, he pulled a string and in a second the officer heard the sound of glass breaking in an adjoining room. Deputy Tyler rushed into this room just in time to see liquid of some sort disappearing through the cracks in the floor while lying about were the frag-

> ments of a jug upon which a heavy stone had just descended. The deputy managed to save a little of the liquid and has it for evidence.
>
> Then Tyler went direct to the opening of a well in the cellar, pulled off his clothes and clambered down the stone sides. The water was some three feet deep, but the officer jumped in and feeling about with his feet succeeded in securing a bottle, which inspection proved to contain lager. Over the mouth of the well hung an overturned basket from which a cord led to the bar room.
>
> Bottomly was immediately taken before Justice Lewis ...

### 1903 — FRANK TURNS TO MASSACHUSETTS

Frank moved his family to Ashley Falls, the first patch of Massachusetts touching the Connecticut line in Connecticut's northwest corner. Ashley Falls, a tiny village in the town of Sheffield, Massachusetts, is the little foyer in the majestic mansion of Berkshire County, home of the famous Berkshire Mountains. In 1903, Ashley Falls had the same permanent population (about eight hundred) as Westbrook. Like Westbrook, during the summer it attracted vacationers for relief from the heat, not with a sea breeze but with the shade of trees.

The railroad that ran between New York City and Pittsfield, Massachusetts, made stops at the Ashley Falls depot, only a few steps from the beautiful Ashley Falls Hotel. In 1903, the hotel was for sale. How Frank learned of the Ashley Falls opportunity, I don't know. Perhaps Georgia's in-laws from nearby Pittsfield had heard about it.

Or perhaps the train-traveling dealers of liquor told him. The village of Ashley Falls was part of Sheffield, a *license town*. Massachusetts, like Connecticut, conducted a vote on liquor licensing each year, and on March 31, 1903, the town of Sheffield had voted YES, beating the NO votes by four votes and reversing the NO vote of the year before. (I can feel Frank smiling.)

CHAPTER TEN

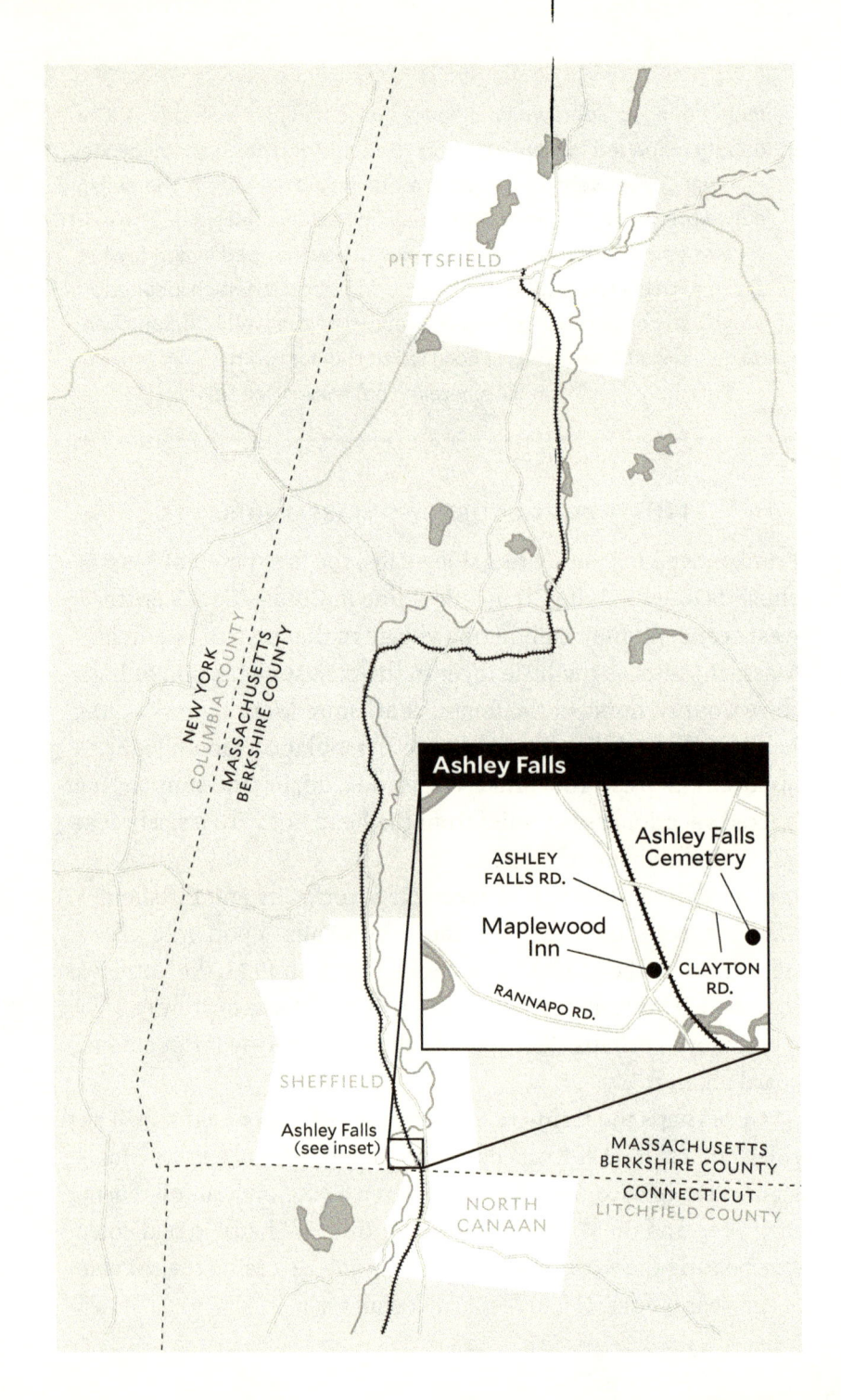

## Was Ashley Falls Wet or Dry?

In Massachusetts, as in Connecticut, individual towns had the right to prohibit the sale of alcohol within their town before Prohibition in 1920. During Frank Smith's proprietorship of the Maplewood Inn in the town of Sheffield, in which Ashley Falls is a village, had the question on their ballot every year. A YES vote meant the town would officially be a license town or *wet town*. A NO vote meant the town would be a no-license town or *dry town*.

## Town Of Sheffield, Massachusetts (Includes Village of Ashley Falls) Results of Liquor Licensing Votes, 1902–1919

*"Shall licenses be granted for the sale of intoxicating liquors in this town?"* \*

| Year | YES | NO | TOTAL | MARGIN |
| --- | --- | --- | --- | --- |
| 1902 | 137 | **148** | 285 | 11 |
| 1903\*\* | **139** | 135 | 274 | 4 |
| 1904 | **156** | 146 | 302 | 10 |
| 1905 | **144** | 140 | 284 | 4 |
| 1906 | **170** | 122 | 292 | 48 |
| 1907 | 140 | **151** | 291 | 11 |
| 1908 | 142 | **155** | 297 | 13 |
| 1909 | **171** | 124 | 295 | 47 |
| 1910 | **153** | 117 | 270 | 36 |
| 1911 | **155** | 110 | 265 | 45 |
| 1912 | **178** | 102 | 280 | 76 |
| 1913 | **180** | 107 | 287 | 73 |
| 1914 | **145** | 103 | 248 | 42 |
| 1915 | **140** | 107 | 247 | 33 |
| 1916 | **153** | 127 | 280 | 26 |

| | | | | |
|---|---|---|---|---|
| 1917† | 110 | **159** | 269 | 49 |
| 1918 | 70 | **146** | 216 | 76 |
| 1919 | 87 | **107** | 194 | 20 |

\*   This was the question on the ballot every year.

\*\*  In 1903, Frank became proprietor of Maplewood Inn. He remained there until his death in 1938.

†   On April 6, 1917, America entered the Great War/World War I; an armistice was declared November 11, 1918.

The Eighteenth Amendment, which prohibited the manufacture, sale or transportation of "intoxicating liquors" nationwide, was ratified in January 1919 and went into effect in January 1920, lasting until 1933.

Frank didn't take long to get back to business. In early May, the Sheffield newspapers announced that Frank P. Smith was the new landlord of the Ashley Falls Hotel. Frank soon renamed it Maplewood Inn. But Frank wasn't the new owner. The new owner, who had purchased it on May 8, 1903, was Dr. Ulysses S. Cook of Moodus, Connecticut.

On May 13, proprietor Frank P. Smith was issued a *License to Sell Intoxicating Liquors* by the selectman of the town of Sheffield in the Commonwealth of Massachusetts. The permit stated that he was licensed to sell liquor "at his place of business being all the rooms in the Ashley Falls Hotel called the Maplewood Inn in the village of Ashley Falls." The license, good for one year, cost $300 [about $8900 in 2020].

Like the hotels in Chester and Middletown, the Maplewood Inn also served as home to Frank's family, Lucinda included, beginning in the spring of 1903. All of Frank and Sarah's children (except the married Georgia) would come to know Ashley Falls as home. Fred (nineteen), moved with his parents. He had graduated from high school and had been working at the Pratt, Read and Company in Deep River, Connecticut, the manufacturing firm that first processed ivory from imported elephant tusks for piano keys, then manufactured pianos during the can't-make-pianos-fast-enough days. At this time, Pratt, Read and Company and Comstock, Cheney & Company in nearby Ivoryton processed 90 percent of the ivory imported to the United States. Donald (seventeen) was in his final year at Middletown High School and likely stayed with friends in Chester or Middletown until he graduated in June. Vernon (nine) switched to the Sheffield, Massachusetts, school system.

Kittie had turned fifteen in April 1903, the month before her father took over the Maplewood Inn. She was a freshman in Middletown High School at the time and continued there. In June 1904, sixteen-year-old Kittie is listed in the school yearbook as K. Louise Smith, a sophomore with an address of Ashley Falls, Massachusetts. But a daily commute from Ashley Falls to Middletown would have been impossible. Kittie may have lived with a Smith family friend during this time. Another possibility is that during the school terms Kittie lived with Aunt Georgiana in Moodus. East Haddam was one of the towns that used the Middletown High School's tuition program for high school education.

By July 1904, Frank was promoting the Maplewood Inn for summer business. His July 1904 newspaper advertisement read:

> Maplewood Inn
> ASHLEY FALLS, MASS.
> The Southern Gate of the Berkshires
> Summer board for adults. Livery and care. Attractive surroundings.
> FRANK P. SMITH, Prop.

Frank was running his favorite business once again. And once again, Ulysses or Georgiana owned it.

## 1903 TO 1905 — WESTBROOK SUMMERS CONTINUE

Like the unwavering rhythm of the tides, Georgiana and Ulysses continued their annual summertime fun at West Beach. Even with the rough start to 1903, the year that had begun with the Chester fire, Georgiana and Ulysses went to Westbrook with their usual open arms, welcoming a houseful of family, friends, and music. In late July, musician James Balen, who had been in Westbrook the year before, was again their guest and again provided musical entertainment with Ulysses for the cottagers. In early August, John and Frank Cone of Moodus stayed with them. It's possible that the Cones were also part of the musical entertainment.

The end of August 1903 was an especially festive time for Georgiana and Ulysses. It was the month that West Beach, after a five-year hiatus, brought back the Annual Illumination.

[*Hartford Courant,* August 24, 1903]

**Display at Westbrook**

*Old-Time Illumination — Many Cottages Elaborately Decorated*

West Beach had an old-time illumination last night, the first in five years, and the cottagers entered into the spirit of the occasion. The rain and wind of the early evening destroyed many of the Chinese lanterns [Chinese and Japanese were interchangeable terms for the lanterns] which had been put in place and somewhat injured some of the larger displays, but as the weather became pleasant later, a crowd gathered. The Citizens' Band of Ivoryton, stationed on the piazza of F. W. Heins's residence, began to play and the fireworks were set off. Viewed from the west end toward the east, the scene was one of beauty and red fire burning at every cottage adding greatly to the general effect. The crowd was large and orderly.

    John H. Parker of Meriden, besides having his cottage well decorated with lanterns, had a row of lanterns reaching across the street. Mrs. A. D. Cook [no relation to Ulysses] of Hartford had both verandas of Arcadia Lodge [two houses from Georgiana and Ulysses] handsomely lighted.

This news article goes on to list some of the cottage owners by name (Georgiana and Ulysses were not mentioned in this article) with descriptions of house decorations, lanterns on balconies, and clever lighting patterns on sidewalks. The article concluded by reporting that the band gave a concert until ten o'clock, after which the crowd went to one of the hotels for a couple of hours of dancing.

In the following year, 1904, Georgiana and Ulysses came to Westbrook for the first two weeks of August. It was a particularly hot couple of weeks that year, with the hotels and cottages filled by people trying to escape the inland heat. Yet it wasn't too hot, according to the newspaper accounts, for dancing, sailing parties, fishing parties, whist parties, card parties, or for a bazaar and concert at the Westbrook Town Hall. People could always cool off with a swim, day or night, which they did.

The rhythm, the music, and the fun of Westbrook repeated for Georgiana and Ulysses during the summer of 1905. But one of Georgiana's favorite guests missed that year. Her niece Georgia had given birth to a baby in June and did not come to Westbrook with her two-month-old.

In June 1905, three-and-a-half years after they were married, which was a little longer than what was expected for newlyweds in the early 1900s, Georgia and Jack had their first child. It was a boy. He was the first of the next Smith generation, Georgiana's grandnephew.

They named him Frederick Worthington Strong (1905–1974), whom the family called "Worth." Frederick was a family name on both sides. It was Jack's middle name and the name of Georgia's brother Frederick Abner Smith, who had been named after his uncle, Little Freddy, the never-forgotten five-year-old who died during the Civil War. The name Worthington came from Jack's father, Charles Worthington Strong. Worth would be an

# Georgiana's World

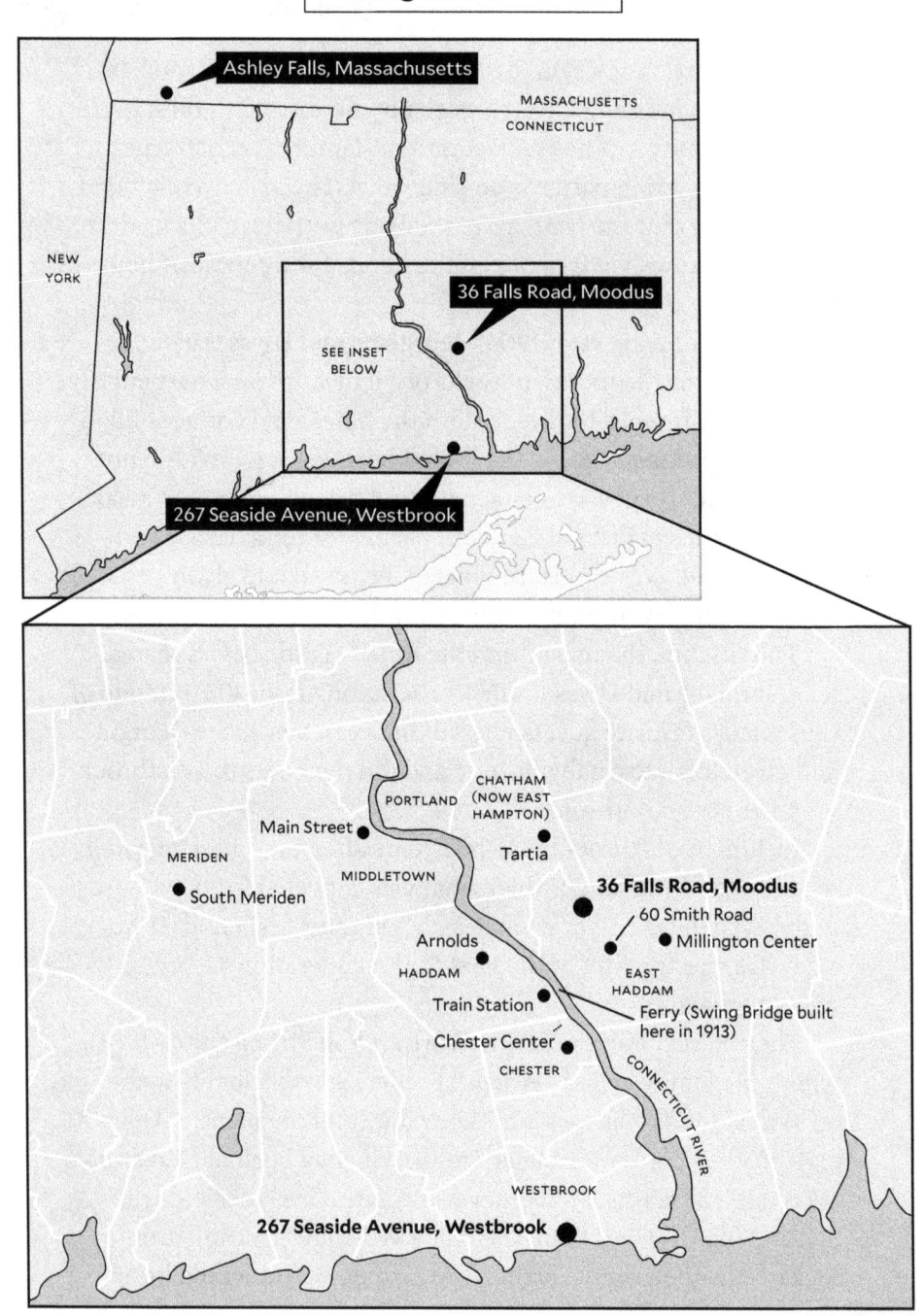

CHAPTER TEN

only child. He was an adored Smith relative. His Worthington name was passed down in the Smith family to my husband, Peter Worthington Smith, and to our grandson born in 2017, William (Billy) Worthington Demiris. Worth was a great joy in Georgiana's life. He and his mother often spent time with her in Westbrook, Moodus and in Ashley Falls.

At the end of 1905, everyone in Georgiana's life seemed happy as a clam at high tide.

## 1906 — TURNING POINT

In 1906, the tide would turn. Before the year had barely begun, on January 18, 1906, the Great Moodus Center Fire ripped through Main Street in Moodus, taking with it a part of Georgiana's everyday life that would never be replaced. Destroyed were the village stores she had patronized for years, including T. R. Spencer's, Purple & Silliman's, which also housed the probate and business office of Judge Albert E. Purple, and Henry Labensky's store, which was located in the Music Hall building. Yes, the old Music Hall Building was burnt to the ground. I can't help but think that the loss of the Music Hall was the symbolic prelude to the decline in Georgiana and Ulysses's musical lives.

As a musician, Ulysses had started off the 1900 decade with as much vigor as ever, still leading the Moodus Drum and Fife Corps, playing in the Moodus Cornet Band, and performing in his own orchestra. The year 1900 was particularly active for the Moodus Drum and Fife Corps with out-of-town travel, East Haddam's Nathan Hale School House ceremony in June, and the Soldiers' Monument ceremony in October. But as the years moved on, the Moodus Cornet Band and the Moodus Drum and Fife Corps performed at fewer and fewer events.

In 1905, the cornet band disbanded altogether and 1906 witnessed the final performance of the Moodus Drum and Fife Corps at Moodus's Decoration Day ceremonies. The celebration of Decoration Day would continue in Moodus with school children decorating the soldiers' graves in the cemetery, and townspeople gathering at Soldiers' Monument for a reading of the Gettysburg Address, songs, and prayers. But after 1906, there was no longer the celebrated drum corps adding their traditional color and drama to the event — only drumbeats by a few individual drummers, of which Ulysses was one. *Parker's*, when recording the history of the drum corps, says that "since 1906, members of the corps as individuals, assisted in some instances by young men who have been under their instruction, have annually provided music for Decoration Day. Dr. Ulysses S. Cook, long the leader of the corps, never failed to appear with the other members as long as his health and strength permitted."[146]

Ulysses had given up marching but not drumming. For the rest of the decade and beyond, he continued to give drumming lessons. He would teach new members of the drum corps the unique continental style of drumming that would be passed down the generations to many more Moodus drummers. The Moodus Drum and Fife Corps is still admired today for playing the unique style of drumming that Dr. Ulysses Cook devoutly preserved.

## The Unique Drumming Style of the Moodus Drum and Fife Corps

*"'Twas the works of a great musician
Named Dr. U. S. Cook."*

These are lines from a poem written in 1950 by successful Connecticut drummer Peter Mietzner (1895–1978). In the poem he gives credit to Ulysses for first preserving the authentic Revolutionary War style of drumming, the style Nathan Hale and George Washington had marched to and the unique style still preserved by the Moodus Drum and Fife Corps today.

James Clark, in *Connecticut's Fife & Drum Tradition*,[147] writes in depth about the preservation of the unique Moodus style drumming and includes the full Mietzner's poem "How and Where I Learned to Drum." Here are a few lines:

> *They had a system too, quite unique,*
> *Not found in any book,*
> *'Twas the works of a great musician*
> *Named Dr. U. S. Cook.*
> *Yes, the style was quite unique indeed*
> *But for all they did not boast,*
> *And eighty years ago and more*
> *'Twas the talk from coast to coast.*
>
> Mietzner had learned his drumming fundamentals from Ulysses, starting as a young boy in 1900 on a pine needle drum pad. He joined the drum corps as teen, and remained a lead snare drummer in the corps for over seventy years. In 1914, at age eighteen, Mietzner and a fifer formed an ensemble. He later formed the "Spirit of '76" group, which successfully played up and down the East Coast, using the style of drumming taught by Ulysses.

I'm not sure which came first — the downturn of Ulysses, the downturn of the drum corps, or the downturn of Moodus with its declining mill industry and devastation from the downtown fire. The three — Ulysses, the drum corps, and the village of Moodus — all seemed to slow down together.

Ulysses had been slowing down as a physician too. As with his musical life, Ulysses had started off the 1900s as active a doctor as ever, treating patients for cancer in his Moodus infirmary. Here are two newspaper excerpts from early in the decade:

> [*Hartford Courant,* November 2, 1901]
> FUNERAL OF MRS. NORTON. Deceased had been a victim of cancer, and was treated last spring by Dr. U. S. Cook of Moodus. Returning home apparently cured, she recently suffered a relapse, passing away as above stated. Mrs. Norton was sixty-one years of age and had passed most of her life in Guilford.

[*Hartford Courant*, August 8, 1902]
Mrs. Mary E. Leete, who has been receiving treatment for a cancerous growth at the sanitarium of Dr. U. S. Cook, of Moodus, for several months, is at her home in Guilford for a few days. Mrs. Leete has nearly recovered, the cancer having been removed. More time will be required, however, for the abscess to heal, and she will return to the sanitarium in a few days.

Ulysses turned sixty-one in August 1906. By that time, newspaper references to the medical practice of Dr. Ulysses S. Cook had stopped, a clue that he had slowed down. He officially stopped practicing in 1909.

### BRIGHT SPOTS IN 1906

Not everything was discouraging for Georgiana and Ulysses in 1906. There were a couple of bright spots during the year.

One occurred in June, when Lillie got married. She became Mrs. Merton Henry Lee. Lillie's marriage took place on Thursday, June 21, 1906, at East Haddam's St. Stephen's Episcopal Church Rectory, with the Reverend Reginald R. Parker presiding. It looks like the wedding was not a lavish affair as Georgia's had been in 1902. There was no *Hartford Courant* article to tell us about the wedding dress, flowers, gifts or attendees. Records of her marriage were hard to find; the marriage license certificate, signed the day before the ceremony by East Haddam Registrar M. H. Watrous, had both the bride's and groom's name misspelled as Lelly White and Martin Lee. But I was able to find a short paragraph about her wedding in the "Moodus Items of 25 Years Ago" section of the 1931 *Connecticut Valley Advertiser* scrapbooks at East Haddam's Rathbun Free Memorial Library.[148]

[*Connecticut Valley Advertiser*, June 26, 1931]
**Moodus News Items of 25 Years Ago** [1906]
*Items of Interest as Recorded by The Advertiser a Quarter of a Century Back*
The marriage of Miss Lillian B. White of Moodus and Merton H. Lee, son of Mr. and Mrs. Joseph H. Lee of Mount Parnassus, took place in the Episcopal rectory at East Haddam Thursday evening, June 21. Rev. R. R. Parker, rector of St. Stephen's church, performed the ceremony. They will live in the Fred Mack place, near Boardman's upper shop.

Perhaps Lillie and Merton wanted a private ceremony and no hoopla. However, it's difficult for me to imagine that Georgiana and Ulysses would not have had some type of celebration for Lillie; I'd like to think that there was a nice wedding and a nice reception, and I was unable to locate an article about it.

I can't think of Lillie without a bit of sympathy. She was six years older than Georgia, and fourteen years older than Kittie. Except for Georgiana, Lillie had little in common with her two cousins. Lillie had been educated in the Moodus district schools only; Georgia and Kittie had furthered their educations in seminaries. Lillie had stayed in Moodus her entire life; Georgia and Kittie had lived part of their lives at schools away from home. Lillie had musical talent and spent time performing; I didn't find any musical accomplishments for Georgia or Kittie. Lillie's friends were from local working families; Georgia's close friend attended the prestigious Mount Holyoke College.

At Georgia's fancy 1902 wedding, Lillie was an unmarried twenty-seven-year-old, still living with Georgiana and Ulysses. Lillie would have watched Georgiana smile with pride at her niece who was wearing her fashionable wedding dress, and was surrounded by flowers and gifts and a loving family. Lillie probably dreamed of her own wedding someday. And when Georgia delivered her prized son into the family in 1905, the still unmarried Lillie probably took a worried glance at her biological watch.

Lillie married a good guy. Merton Henry Lee was raised by his parents, Joseph and Fannie (Martin) Lee, on their family farm in Moodus. In 1900, at age nineteen (he was six years younger than Lillie), Merton was working on his father's farm. The Lee farm shared a property line with the farm of Abner C. Smith (1846). (Remember him? He was one of the three Abner C. Smiths. He was the half brother of Georgiana's father, Abner C. Smith.) Perhaps Georgiana and Lillie visited the Smith farm occasionally, and that is how Lillie met Merton. Or perhaps Lillie met Merton when he delivered the mail to Falls Road. At some point after 1900, Merton had escaped farm life, a trend of his age group. After their 1905 marriage, Merton and Lillie lived in East Haddam Village, where Merton earned a living as a mail carrier.[149]

Another bright spot for Georgiana and Ulysses in 1906 was Frank's success at the Maplewood Inn in Ashley Falls. Despite the eighty miles between Moodus and Ashley Falls, they made the trip back and forth several times a year — in their newly purchased automobile. By 1906, Americans were turning their attention, their wallets, and their lives over to automobiles. Ulysses, given his fiscal health and his personality, would have been one of the first to buy one. Driving the early cars on horse-friendly unpaved roads made the trip between Moodus and Ashley Falls an all-day trip, taking up to eight hours. Today it can be driven in less than two hours.

I found this 1906 picture postcard of the Ashley Falls Maplewood Inn. It was postmarked July 23, 1906, and was sent by a guest of the inn to a woman in Bridgeport, Connecticut. Neither the sender nor the receiver was connected to the Smith family. The black and white photo on the card shows the white inn, set behind white fences that were connected by a white arched gateway, standing stately below several tall, dark shade trees. The handwritten message reads, "Things are not as dark as they appear on this card. Everything shines. Even nails."

*Maplewood Inn, Ashley Falls, Mass.*

*July 23 — Over the gateway you may read — Things are not as dark as they appear on this Card. Everything smiles — even nails. — G. H.*

Everything in Frank and Sarah's life seemed to shine at this time. They were running a successful inn. Their family, including Lucinda, were in great health and had made many new friends. Their daughter Georgia was happily married with a one-year-old son. Their two older sons, in their early twenties, were attending college at Norwich University in Vermont. Twelve-year-old Vernon was attending the Ashley Falls grammar school, where he was one of three students who was never tardy or absent for the school year ending in June 1906. And eighteen-year-old Kittie was a student at a seminary in South Norwalk, the town in Fairfield County, Connecticut, where Georgia had lived.

 Kittie had followed the same path that Georgia had, attending a private seminary. I think Georgiana may have been responsible for the privileged education her nieces received, not just financially — she likely paid (really, Ulysses paid) for her nieces to attend the seminaries — but also by influencing them to get a good education. I'm remembering the letters from Georgiana's father when she was a teen — how he repeated and repeated and repeated how important education was, how he tried to guide Edgar and Frank to be better students, how proud he was of Georgiana's success at school, and how he encouraged her to be a teacher. I'm also remembering the 1901 letter from Mary Cook to Georgiana in which Mary complimented Georgiana for paying special attention to her nieces. Georgiana, I believe, was the source for much of the shine in Frank and Sarah's family.

### 1906 TRAGEDY

But all would abruptly turn dark for Georgiana's Ashley Falls family. Kittie became ill with typhoid fever. In 1906, the largest ever American typhoid epidemic hit New York and surrounding areas. This was the epidemic in which "Typhoid Mary" became infamous as the young New York City cook who unknowingly (she was an asymptomatic carrier) spread the disease to many people. How did Kittie catch this terrible disease? She was on a summer break from her seminary at the time. The newspaper reported that "it is thought that she contracted the disease while on an automobile trip."

Kittie made it back to her home in Ashley Falls at the end of July. She suffered for four weeks under a doctor's care and died on Friday, August 24. She was eighteen years old.

Her funeral was August 27 at the Maplewood Inn. The Reverend James S. Ellis of Christ Episcopal Church in Sheffield officiated. She was buried in the Ashley Falls Cemetery which was a short walk from the Maplewood Inn. Frank (or maybe Ulysses) bought a large cemetery plot that could accommodate several more graves in the future. Kittie's was the first. She lay there alone for twelve years, until her grandmother Lucinda joined her in 1918.

> ### How Health Has Changed Since Georgiana Was Born
>
> Georgiana was born into a world of infectious diseases that took the lives of many. During her lifetime, advances in preventive medicine — sanitation, education, inoculations — reduced or eradicated most.

In the chart below, you can compare the top ten causes of death in 1850 during Georgiana's first year of life to the top causes in 1900 when she was fifty, and to 2019.

## Top Leading Causes of Death in the United States

*The causes are ranked in descending order based on percentage of all deaths.*

| 1850 | 1900 | 2019 |
|---|---|---|
| Tuberculosis | Pneumonia or Influenza | Heart Disease |
| Dysentery or Diarrhea | Tuberculosis | Cancer |
| Cholera | Gastrointestinal Infection | Accidents |
| Malaria | Heart Disease | Chronic Lower Respiratory Diseases |
| Typhoid Fever | Stroke | Stroke |
| Pneumonia | Nephropathies | Alzheimer's Disease |
| Diphtheria | Accidents | Diabetes |
| Scarlet Fever | Cancer | Nephropathies |
| Meningitis | Senility | Pneumonia and Influenza |
| Whooping Cough | Diphtheria | Intentional Self-harm |

1850 source: "1850 Census: Mortality Statistics of the Seventh Census of the United States." census.gov. 1900 source: "Mortality and Top 10 Causes of Death, USA, 1900 vs. 2010," UNC Carolina Demography, June 16, 2014. ncdemography.org. 2019 source: Kenneth D. Kochanek, M. A., Jiaquan Xu, M. D., and Elizabeth Arias, Ph.D. "Mortality in the United States, 2019," Center for Disease Control and Prevention, NCHS Data Brief No. 395, December. 2020.cdc.gov.

> Typhoid is a bacterial infection caused by salmonella and spread by contact with an infected person or by contaminated food and water. A vaccine was developed in 1911, five years after Georgiana's eighteen-year-old niece, Kittie, died from the disease in 1906.
>
> Cancer, Ulysses's medical specialty, was not a leading cause of death in 1850. It was detected in his days of medical practice (he stopped practicing around 1909) through visible or felt tumors. At that time, cancer was thought to be caused by trauma. Although Ulysses did not perform surgery for treatment of cancer, some doctors did attempt removal, but tumors would grow back. In 1896, the X-ray was introduced and used to detect breast cancer. In 1899, radiation was used to treat cancer. In 1915, it was discovered that cancer was caused by carcinogens. In the 1960s, screenings to detect early cancers began.[150] And as you can see from the chart, as other diseases were eradicated through vaccinations and better sanitation and education, cancer moved into a top cause of death.

Kittie's unexpected death at such a young age would have dealt Georgiana a keen-edged blow. She had not experienced a tragic death in the family for over forty years, not since she was a young teenager and her little brother and father had died. She had not yet experienced the death of her mother, who was eighty-one when Kittie died.

There was no Westbrook for Georgiana and Ulysses in 1906. Georgiana likely spent time in Ashley Falls, consoling and helping Frank and Sarah.

Perhaps connected in some way to the tragedy of Kittie's death, in October 1906, Georgiana quitclaimed the ownership of the Chester House to Frank. Georgiana had owned the Chester House for seven years, since 1899. (Since 1877, a married woman was allowed by law to own property in her own name.) An interesting conundrum: at the time of the quitclaim, Ulysses's name accompanied Georgiana's on the Chester House's deed. Yet I cannot find a record of when his name was added. I'm guessing there was some purely practical reason for this documentation change. I am not suggesting there was any controversy between Ulysses and Georgiana; in writing about their lives, I can only conclude that they were like many couples of their era — those who worked as a team, each content with their position on the team.

As for Thanksgiving and Christmas that year, there is no guest record for the Maplewood Inn. I hope Georgiana and Ulysses spent their holidays there with her family, as was their usual pattern. The press did not report on the guests or on anything about the Maplewood Inn for months after Kittie's death.

## 1907

At the start of 1907, Georgiana and Ulysses stayed close to home in Moodus, near Lillie, their large circle of Moodus friends, Ulysses's orchestra, and Continental Hall. Their Chester House ownership was now a thing of the past, as were Frank's liquor licensing schemes and violations.

The Maplewood Inn, which Ulysses had owned since 1903, was in the capable hands of Frank and Sarah. They had made Ulysses's investment popular, profitable, and free of entanglements with anti-saloon groups — three accomplishments made possible because alcohol could be legally served. Which Frank did, having been issued licenses each year by the town of Sheffield.

But. But. But. In March 1907, the town of Sheffield voted NO to liquor licensing for the first time during Frank's proprietorship. Would Frank comply with the new law and stop serving alcohol? There were no incidences reported in the newspapers after March that year to suggest he didn't (or that he did).

Yet. Yet. Yet. It's hard to believe that the Maplewood Inn packed the liquor away with the level of entertainment they offered guests in the summer of 1907, the year after Kittie's death. According to an August 1907 newspaper article, "The third of a delightful series of musicals given at the Maplewood Inn by the host and hostess, Mr. and Mrs. F. P. Smith, took place last Saturday evening. After the entertainments, dainty refreshments were served by Mrs. F. P. Smith."[151]

It looks like Georgiana and Ulysses — with his fiddle — were at this August 1907 musical, as it was after this weekend that the press reported that they headed to Westbrook for a month at the shore, bringing Lucinda with them! They also brought twenty-six-year-old Miss Florence Hall from Ashley Falls who had attended the musical and who I can guess served as a companion for the eighty-two-year-old Lucinda. From weekend parties in Ashley Falls to Westbrook Illuminations, Lucinda's life was not short on pleasures.

In October 1907, prime leaf-peeping season in the Berkshires, the Ashley Falls Smiths enjoyed weekend convivialities. On Friday, October 11, Frank and Sarah threw a surprise birthday party at the inn for their daughter Georgia, who turned twenty-seven that day.

[*Berkshire County Eagle* (Pittsfield, Massachusetts), October 16, 1907]

On Friday evening [October 11], a surprise party was given to Mrs. John P. Strong of New Haven, Conn., who has been spending several weeks at the Maplewood Inn. Mrs. Strong received during the day over a hundred postals [postcards] from friends. A delightful supper was served in the evening to about thirty guests. The evening was spent in music and games.

The next day, October 12, Frank and Sarah's friends threw them an anniversary party.

[*Berkshire County Eagle* (Pittsfield, Massachusetts), October 16, 1907]

**Sheffield**

*Observed Wedding Anniversary*

On Saturday evening [October 12], a reception was given to Mr. and Mrs. F. P. Smith at the Maplewood Inn by their many friends, it being the 29th anniversary of their marriage. [Frank and Sarah's wedding was October 6, 1878.] The marriage ceremony was again read, though not by a minister, but by John Hall, who was elected by the guests assembled to again perform the marriage ceremony. About fifty guests assembled to congratulate Mr. and Mrs. Smith upon this delightful occasion.

    The toastmaster was George Hall, who had prepared a list of toasts which were duly given, many of which were of local interest. Mr. and Mrs. Smith received their friends in the parlors which were very tastefully decorated with autumn leaves and ferns. After supper, games and music were indulged in. Among the out-of-town guests attending were Mr. and Mrs. John Strong of New Haven, Conn. [Georgia and Jack], Harold Glendenning of Hartford, Conn., Mr. and Mrs. John Moody [Sarah's brother and his wife] of Haddam, Conn., Mrs. L. K. Broeck of Ocean Grove, N. J., John Hall of Palmer, Mass., and Miss Bertha Powell of New Britain, Conn.

Did Georgiana and Ulysses attend the parties? On one hand, they made frequent trips to Ashley Falls and were exceptionally close to Frank and his family, so it's hard to think they would have missed these events. On the other hand, their names are not included in the newspaper report. My guess? They did not.

    They probably saved their trip to Ashley Falls for Thanksgiving, which turned out to be quite an entertaining day — and night!

> [*Berkshire County Eagle* (Pittsfield, Massachusetts), December 4, 1907]

Mr. and Mrs. F. P. Smith, host and hostess of the Maplewood Inn, gave a large Thanksgiving dinner on Thursday [November 28] in honor of their two sons Donald and Frederick, who are attending Norwich University at Northfield, Vt., this being a reunion of relatives which consisted of four generations.

> The out-of-town guests united with them were Dr. and Mrs. U. S. Cook, of Moodus, Ct.; Mr. and Mrs. Edgar C. Smith of Saybrook, Ct.; Mr. and Mrs. C. C. Wheeler [Clarence Wheeler was a son of the Wheeler family from North Moodus Road] of Fresno, Cal., and Mr. and Mrs. J. F. Strong and son Worthington of New Haven, Ct.
>
> In the evening, some thirty immediate friends of the village were delightfully entertained by the host and hostess. Dancing commenced at 9 o'clock with Prof. Rolf as prompter, which continued until 12 o'clock. It was partially a masquerade party, and some very pretty costumes were shown. Mr. Smith, the host, acted the part of Queen Elizabeth, in a costume of the centuries past, while George Hall delighted the guests in a costume of the Scotch Highland, dancing the double shuffle and the highland fling.
>
> The music was furnished by Cook's orchestra. At 11, delightful refreshments were served. It was one of the pleasantest affairs that has enlivened the village this season.

I'm wondering about Georgiana and what costume she wore. (I'm also wondering how you throw a Thanksgiving dinner for a large family, then throw a masquerade party for thirty more people at night.)

Lillie was not the pianist in Ulysses's orchestra for this Thanksgiving performance. She was busy in East Haddam — giving birth to a baby girl! On December 1, the Sunday after Thanksgiving, Doris H. Lee was born. Doris would be Lillie and Merton's only child. The little family of three lived in a house in East Haddam Village. They did not live within walking distance of Moodus, but Lillie and Doris were frequent visitors at Falls Road, no doubt bringing joy and music into Georgiana and Ulysses's home.

## 1908

In April 1908, Georgiana and Ulysses made the trip to Ashley Falls for a short visit at the Maplewood Inn. Staying at the inn during their visit were all of Frank and Sarah's children and their grandson Worth.

And, oh yes, this time the inn was filled with twenty-somethings — Georgia, Fred, and Don, plus several friends of theirs. Was it Spring Break? Hmm. There was still a ban on liquor in Sheffield in 1908. The town had voted NO again to liquor licensing in March.

Frank and Sarah's children were learning the art of Smith hospitality and party-giving. In June 1908, the Smiths hosted a "delightful house party" with "dancing and games and refreshments" in honor of Donald's graduation from Norwich University.[152] Many of their friends attended and remained through the Fourth of July, staying in partying mode. They celebrated the Fourth with fireworks, picnics, a musical performance, baseball games, and, in the days that followed, an *auto party* through the Berkshires.

Can you feel the shift into a new generation of merry-making that was beginning at the inn? Frank and Sarah's children had become the main hosts, and, I assume, pulled their weight to help Frank and Sarah. As you'll read below, Lucinda, eighty-three in 1908, was still pulling her weight!

> [*Berkshire County Eagle* (Pittsfield, Massachusetts), July 15, 1908]
>
> A fire started in the icehouse of the Maplewood Inn on Sunday morning and burned about three feet before it was discovered. Mrs. Lucinda Smith saw the smoke coming out of the door. Although advanced in years, she managed to put it out. A singular coincidence is that it caught fire last summer about the same time and in about the same place. The damage this time was only slight.

The popularity of the Maplewood Inn continued through 1908. Frank continued to invest in the business with improvements to the property. He installed gas lines and gas lamps along the short sidewalk between the inn and the train depot, where the train hissed to a stop and spewed out many customers looking for good lodgings and good food. (And good drink?)

## 1908 WESTBROOK

For Georgiana and Ulysses, Westbrook in August continued to be their look-forward-to-all-year vacation, with Ulysses bringing his fishing pole, fiddle, and drumsticks, and Georgiana bringing her fan, a sun hat, and a trunk full of clothes. And both bringing their good natures.

In July 1908, some were predicting a less busy season in Westbrook. The *Hartford Courant* began their summer reporting with some man-on-the-street opinions of what the summer would bring.

[*Hartford Courant,* July 8, 1908]

**Summer Days at Westbrook**
A native of this vicinity who hasn't missed an incoming or outgoing train since he could walk and is considered an authority on the prognostication of summer colonies here [said that] it didn't look very chipper to him, because "the traffic aren't so heavy as 'twas and there's a whole lotta cottages for rent at the beach, and also that 'money trouble' a little while ago!"

The article went on to report that a popular hotel was not opening for the season because of decreased demand. Yet in the next breath, the article reported:

The crowd at Quotonsett Beach [next to West Beach] has been active as ever since the season began ... with several big contests which furnished no end of sport ... a [boat] race of Barnegat sneakboxes [small boats] over a triangular course .... golf ... and entertainment.

Not since the last appearance of James Richmond Glenroy ... and his clever vaudeville troupers, has Westbrook been so stirred up over affairs theatrical. For are not "Keith's Moving Pictures" [silent films accompanied by live music, often piano only] on their way? July 10 is the date, and not only will the pictures be moved, but in addition there will be illustrated songs galore. Mr. Somebody-or-Other will feature the beautiful "ballad" entitled "She Was Weeping as She Leaned against the River." [Was this title real? Or was the reporter poking fun at the sentimental ballads of the era? It may simply have been lazy titling by the reporter for the 1889 W. B. Yeats Irish poem-turned-song, "Salley Gardens," which had become a popular ballad at this time.] The beachers will turn out in numbers. It's the event of the week!

And three weeks later, the *Courant* was reporting on the August influx.

[*Hartford Courant,* July 25, 1908]
Westbrook has gained materially in population this week. The hotels, there are only two of them, now report good bookings for August ... even at that, though, the 1908 season will fall short of expectations, because it has taken so long for the people to be up and doing [due to a heat wave].

Over at West Beach [Georgiana's beach], the Improvement Society has started action again. Now that they have good sidewalks [Georgiana's cottage did get sidewalks], and plenty of lights [oil streetlights] to find the sidewalks, the West Beachers have got the athletic hunch. They want a tennis court; and they'll probably get one very soon, because they are untiring hustlers over that way, and best of all, work in close harmony.

It was an exceptionally hot August. The August 15 *Hartford Courant* reported: "These warm days have taken somewhat of the social energy of the Westbrook cottagers and they say that their most enjoyable moments are spent in the water."

Georgiana and Ulysses were part of the August 1908 influx. As were Georgia and Jack and three-year-old Worthington. There is nothing like a three-year-old boy at a summer cottage to stop the complaining about a heat wave — with his simple delight in filling and carting heavy pails of water to you over and over again, his fascination with examining and saving tiny hermit crabs, and his high-pitched scream as he high-steps away from the incoming water and then goes back for more.

Lucinda did not go to Westbrook in August 1908. At eighty-three, she was probably more comfortable in the shade of the Maplewood Inn. But in November, Georgiana had Lucinda stay with her for the full month in Moodus. Including Thanksgiving. That year in Ashley Falls, Frank and Sarah had a small Thanksgiving. Perhaps because they were sick with worry about their son Don, who was severely ill with typhoid fever in West Virginia, where he was working. Unlike Kittie, Don would survive the disease.

During this Thanksgiving week, Ulysses was preparing to sell the Maplewood Inn to Frank. Perhaps the July fires at the inn two years in a row reminded Ulysses of the Chester troubles. Perhaps Ulysses, who was intimately familiar with Frank's pattern of breaking of the liquor laws and had enjoyed many happy hours himself at the inn during the past two "NO" years, saw the tide of public opinion moving in favor of temperance in Ashley Falls and wanted out of the business. Perhaps Ulysses wanted to wind down his responsibilities or turn more of his assets into cash. Or perhaps Frank had accumulated enough money to buy the Maplewood Inn. Whatever the reason or reasons, Ulysses sold the Maplewood Inn to Frank in late November 1908 for an amount unknown.

And it looks like it was a good decision by Ulysses.

### 1909 ASHLEY FALLS — OH, BROTHER (AGAIN)

Within three months of Ulysses selling the Inn to Frank, in February 1909, Frank was caught illegally serving liquor. He was slapped with a relatively small fine and given a relatively strong tongue-lashing from a judge who told him he was "old enough not to need a second warning!" (Frank was fifty-five.)

[*Berkshire County Eagle* (Pittsfield, Massachusetts), February 11, 1909]

**Ashley Falls Hotel Proprietor Pays Heavy Fine**

Imposing sentence upon Frank P. Smith of Ashley Falls for the illegal sale of liquor, Judge Walter B. Sanford said: "This court passes a fine of $75 [about $2,000 in 2020] on you and I want to state to you in public that I have had several letters from your town complaining that you were conducting a liquor nuisance and parents have written me that their sons were being ruined because of it. I will add that if you come before this court again for a similar offense, the case will not stop at a fine. You are old enough not to need a second warning."

Frank P. Smith was quick to pay the fine for he had been caught right in the act, having made a sale to Deputy Sheriff Truesdell. The arrest of the Ashley Falls proprietor attracted interest, for Ashley Falls had been popular for some time and it had been rumored that the "beverages" could be secured there without difficulty. The fact that the deputy sheriff was able to get the drink served out to him shows that the business was conducted quite openly.

Six weeks after the fine, Sheffield voted YES to liquor licenses by an overwhelming number of votes and stayed voting YES until 1917. (I can feel Frank smiling again.) Temperance was a fickle issue.

### 1909 MOODUS

Back in Moodus, Georgiana and Ulysses were enjoying life with social events, often involving Ulysses's orchestra. In April, they attended — and Ulysses's orchestra played for — a farewell event to honor the popular Reverend and Mrs. Francis Parker. Reverend Parker had been the pastor of the First Congregational Church of East Haddam since 1892. Georgiana and Ulysses had been married in the parsonage of this church in 1868.

[*Hartford Courant*, April 3, 1909]

MOODUS

A farewell reception was given Rev. and Mrs. Francis Parker by members and friends of the Congregational Church in the chapel adjoining the church building Thursday evening. The chapel was tastefully decorated with potted plants and evergreens. Music was an important feature of the reception. An orchestra composed of Miss Jennie Williams,[153] pianist; Harold Chapman, clarinet; and Dr. U. S. Cook, violin, rendered several delightful selections. Piano solos were rendered by Mrs. Merton Lee and Miss Olive Crocker, which were heartily enjoyed. Miss Minnie Labensky and Carrie L. Bowers played a duet. A purse of money was given to Mr. Parker by the parishioners and Mrs. Parker's Sunday school class gave her a brooch.

Note that Lillie — Mrs. Merton Lee — played a piano solo at the event. My heart warms when I realize that Lillie continued enjoying the piano and the music that Georgiana and Ulysses had brought into her life, even after becoming Mrs. Merton Lee and a mother.

It also warms my heart to see that Ulysses, at age sixty-four, led his orchestra and played his violin at this event. Even with Moodus Music Hall, the cornet band, the drum corps, and their youth in their past, Georgiana and Ulysses still had some music in their lives.

### 1909 WESTBROOK

Westbrook in 1909 turned out to be extra special for Georgiana and Ulysses. They arrived in Westbrook in July, and Ulysses, ever the leader, along with two friends, took the baton to lead West Beach's most important event, the Annual Illumination.

[*Hartford Courant*, August 3, 1909]
This year, "Illumination Night" will take place Saturday [August 7, 1909]. Formerly this distinctive feature of West

Beach life took place during the second week of September when the cottagers were about to leave for home, but this had its disadvantages since many were preparing to depart and could not give it their undivided attention. [This is the only record I found that reported the Illumination happening in September.] This year extra arrangements have been made to make it a banner celebration.

The Illumination committee is composed of Dr. Cook, Sim Brooks, and Dr. Roberts. They have already engaged the Chester Band to lead the evening parade and have seen that thousands of Japanese lanterns are in the hands of the cottagers who dwell along the beach. There will be a dress parade in the evening for which the young men and ladies are already preparing elaborate costumes, grotesque and of many colors.

Sim Brooks was Simeon S. Brooks (1865–1916), a successful businessman and amateur musician in Chester. He had lived in Chester his whole life and was active in the town during Frank Smith's Chester House years. He had attended Wilbraham Academy, the same school as Ulysses, but twenty years later than Ulysses. He and Mrs. Brooks (born Mary B. Wright) had a cottage near the Cooks in West Beach. Staying with the Brookses at the time of the Illumination was Miss Jennie Williams, one of the pianists who often played in Ulysses's orchestra. I imagine the Brookses and the Cooks were summer friends.

Georgiana and Ulysses stayed in Westbrook until September that year. Lucinda joined them for the month of August. Other family and friends came too.

### A HAPPY END TO THE DECADE

During the month of November 1909, Frank sold the remaining portion (he had sold some sections to others before this) of the Chester House property to a Mr. Tobias of Hartford, Connecticut for $7,000 [about $197,000 in 2020].

With pockets full, Frank and Sarah held a large gathering on Thanksgiving for friends and family, including Georgiana and Ulysses. In the 1909 guest book for Thanksgiving on November 25, they are second on the list identified as *Dead Heads*, a term used for nonpaying guests by the hotel industry. Based on the wording of the guests' names, the entries were written by one of Frank and Sarah's children, likely Georgia, who was first on the list. The Dead Heads, in the order in which there were written, were:

- John F. Strong and wife [Georgia]   New Haven
- Dr. and Mrs. U. S. Cook   Moodus
- Edith K. Weston   Fenville, Mich. and Brooklyn
- F. Worthington Strong [Worth]   New Haven
- Pop Smith [Frank]   Ashley Falls
- Mom Smith [Sarah]   Ashley Falls
- Fred A. Smith   Northfield, Vt
- Vernon Smith   Ashley Falls
- George Spencer   Guilford, Ct
- Lucy Bishop   Guilford, Ct
- Gram Smith [Lucinda]   Turkey Hill
- Chas Ferrer   New York

Edith K. Weston and Charles Ferrer (friends of Georgia) may have become engaged over this weekend. Their engagement was announced in December 1909; they were married on May 28, 1910. George Spencer (1849–1935) was the uncle of Lucy Bishop (1893–1944). George lived with the family of his sister, Lucy's mother, in Guilford. In censuses, he is listed as a *music maker* or a *piano tuner*. George was likely a musical performer with Ulysses. George and Lucy also frequently visited Westbrook.

The Berkshire County newspaper reported on the crowd at the Maplewood Inn as "the largest gathering for Thanksgiving" in Ashley Falls.[154]

## WOMEN'S TURN

By the end of this decade, the spheres of women and men had started to overlap. In 1909, the nation had seven thousand women doctors, three thousand women ministers, and one thousand women lawyers. Women were earning college degrees and entering professions. One clear indicator that women were making headway toward equality: Beers's *History of Middlesex County* had changed the extended title of their book from *With Biographical Sketches Of Its Prominent **Men*** in 1884 to *Containing Biographical Sketches Of Prominent And Representative **Citizens*** in 1903.

> ### The Title Says It All
>
> One of the most authoritative sources for the history of Middlesex County is a book published in 1884 by J.B. Beers & Co., New York. The title: **History of Middlesex County, Connecticut, with Biographical Sketches of Its Prominent Men.** (No, there is not a companion book with biographical sketches of prominent women.)
>
> Nineteen years later, in 1903, a second Middlesex County reference book was published by J.H. Beers & Co., Chicago. This time the title read: ***Commemorative Biographical Record of Middlesex County, Connecticut, Containing Biographical Sketches of Prominent And Representative Citizens.*** The Godfrey Memorial Library,[155] a library of genealogy, history, and biography in Middletown, Connecticut, describes this 1903 book as featuring "biographies of more than a thousand men — and a few women — that were prominent at the turn of the twentieth century."
>
> The Beers publishing houses were experts at producing histories, biographies, and maps for numerous American counties at the turn of the twentieth century. By 1903, their titles had changed from men to citizens. It was a significant word change that represented a sweeping change in America. Between the publications of 1884 and 1903, women had leapt forward in education, earning power, property rights, speaking up, and speaking out.

> Georgiana was a mature woman when the Beers books were published. She was thirty-five for the first book and fifty-four for the second. She likely saw and read parts of both books — her ancestral Arnold family is included in the 1884 book; her brother and husband are two of the more than one thousand men included in the 1903 book.
>
> I wonder if Georgiana and the other women of Middlesex County noticed the word change in the two books' titles.

Around the nation, state by state, women's rights activists were increasing in numbers and in decibels. In 1908, California staged the first women's suffrage march, greasing the wheels of the women's suffrage movement. In Connecticut in this decade, however, the wheels were as stubborn as ever. The Connecticut Women Suffrage Association, which had been formed in 1869 with 138 members, had dwindled to fifty members during this decade. Isabella Beecher Hooker, the organization's founder and leader, had died in 1907 at age eighty-five, and new leadership was needed.

In East Haddam, most women — and Georgiana was one of them — stayed in the women's sphere. Most women — and Georgiana was one of them — were married and were homemakers. Most women — and Georgiana was one of them — quietly watched as a few other women spoke out for the women's suffrage cause. And my guess is that, like so many American women of her era, Georgiana was thinking, thinking, thinking about changes for women.

### TURN, TURN, TURN

During this first decade of the new century, the world was turning in new directions at a new speed.

Americans, including Georgiana and Ulysses, had turned with unbridled enthusiasm to the automobile for their preferred mode of transportation. The new automobile assembly lines were unable to turn out cars as fast as Americans wanted them; dirt roads were unable to turn into paved roads as fast as the cars turned out; and lawmakers could not turn out the safety laws and regulations fast enough. Speed limits were set for the first time. In May 1901, Connecticut was the first state to set speed limits — 12 mph on city streets and 15 mph on country roads.

> ## With Automobiles Came Accidents
>
> On the Saturday before Thanksgiving in 1909, Georgiana's sixteen-year-old nephew Vernon was in a car accident. Well, a half-car/half-carriage accident.
>
> *[Berkshire County Eagle* (Pittsfield, Massachusetts), November 25, 1909]
>
> **Auto Crashed into Carriage**
>
> While Vernon Smith of Ashley Falls was driving from Great Barrington Saturday afternoon an automobile ran into his carriage about midway been Sheffield and Great Barrington. The wheels were broken, but Mr. Smith escaped injury. The automobilists, as is said to be frequently the case now, hurried off without inquiring how much damage was done. Mr. Smith was forced to walk to his home in Ashley Falls.
>
> With automobiles, came a new type of accident and the need for new laws. The making of laws could not match the speed of the making of automobiles. In 1909, there were no hit-and-run laws. Even if there were, the getaway scenes were in favor of perpetrators, with the dust from the dirt roads, the hard-to-read early license plates, and goggles that masked the drivers' faces making identity nearly impossible.

Marconi turned the communication world on its ear when he developed a way to send messages with airwaves instead of wires. At record speeds, families turned to radios for news. And also to phonographs for at-home entertainment, to Eastman Kodak's new Brownie cameras for photographs, to telephones for business and conversation, and to movie theaters to see the new moving pictures. President Teddy Roosevelt, who led the country during this progressive decade, turned the nation's attention to conservation and preservation. He turned acres of the nation's national resources into national parks and turned many historic and scientific structures into national monuments.

New York City, trying to move millions of people quickly from place to place, turned to the underground for a solution and opened what would become the largest American subway line. And to the amazement of the human race, transportation was turned on its head when the Wright Brothers successfully flew their airship in North Carolina, and air travel became a real possibility.

Parts of America were turned upside down and inside out: San Francisco by an earthquake; Monongah, West Virginia, by a coal mine explosion, the worst mining disaster in American history[156]; New York City (and the hopes of nine million new immigrants) by overcrowded urban housing conditions; Chicago's gruesome meatpacking industry by Upton Sinclair's book *The Jungle*; and taverns in many towns by Carrie Nation and the temperance advocates.

During these ten years, the village of Moodus negotiated some tough turns — a hairpin curve with the devastating downtown fire in 1906, and a long slow downhill bend as the mill business declined. To recover, the village cleverly turned its energies to tourism for new business opportunities. Moodus began to develop resorts around its beautiful lakes, a brilliant move that would contribute mightily to its economy over the next fifty years and to the memories of vacationers for a long time after that.

The first ten years of the new century brought Georgiana her own set of twists and turns. She was caught in the downward spirals of the fire at the Chester House, the move to Massachusetts of her mother and Frank's family, and the death of eighteen-year-old Kittie. But she also watched Lillie and Georgia turn into wives and mothers, her older nephews turn into college boys, her youngest nephew turn into a teenager, and the memory of her father turn into a tangible, permanent landmark in Moodus. During these years, Georgiana stood steadily by Ulysses as he turned over ownership of properties to Frank, turned off his medical practice and turned down his musical activities.

Together, as the worlds around them changed at dizzying speed, Georgiana and Ulysses could count on the unchanging anchors of friendships, family, music, the tides and joys of Westbrook, the routines and the comforts of Moodus, and each other.

In 1909, Georgiana turned sixty. One more thing that had not changed for Georgiana — her hair! By the end of the decade, Ulysses's hair had turned white, but Georgiana's had not.

*The Westbrook Cottage during the August 1913 Illumination. From left to right: Frederick Abner Smith (29), Lucinda (born Arnold) Smith (88), Dr. Ulysses S. Cook (67), Ella Georgiana (born Smith) Cook (64), two unknown men, possibly Sarah Jane (born Moody) Smith (54), Georgia Cook (born Smith) Strong (32), rest of adults unknown. Children on fence are unknown, except that third boy (left to right) is "Worth," Frederick Worthington Strong (8). Photo taken in 1913 by Wm. J. Neidlinger, Westbrook, Conn. Photo restored in 2019 by Joe Pecoraro, Joseph's Photography, Inc., Chester, Conn.*

CHAPTER 11

# Before the Parade Passes By
## Georgiana in Her Sixties
## 1910–1919

*I'm gonna carry on*
*Give me an old trombone*
*Give me an old baton*
*Before the parade passes by!*

THE LAST LINES OF "BEFORE THE PARADE PASSES BY"
FROM THE BROADWAY MUSICAL *HELLO DOLLY!*
MUSIC AND LYRICS BY JERRY HERMAN, 1964

Do you remember Dolly from the hit Broadway musical *Hello Dolly!*? The *Hello Dolly!* story takes place in the early years of the twentieth century when both Georgiana and the fictional Dolly were entering their later years. Georgiana and Dolly were the same age — both were in their sixties during the 1910 decade, although, true to the social construct of the times, Dolly's age is never revealed. In the show, Dolly is a dazzling, charming, working-as-a-matchmaker widow who realizes that her youth is behind her. The plot centers around her decision to embrace life before it's too late, or, as she famously belts out in one of the most memorable Broadway songs of all time, "Before the Parade Passes By."

Georgiana, who had spent a parade-filled lifetime among her own renditions of whistles, cymbals, sparklers, trombones, and batons, had Dolly's same spirit when it came to aging. Dolly's life is a work of fiction. She watches the famous parades in New York City, mixes among city slickers, wears feathers and glitter, and flashes a Carol Channing smile with Hollywood-style perfect, bright white teeth. Georgiana's life, however, is nonfiction. She watched the homegrown parades of Connecticut, mixed among small town folks, wore practical clothing, and smiled more inside than out, avoiding a display of her imperfect teeth in the days of poor dental care. Just like Dolly, Georgiana made it her business to carry on enjoying life.

When Georgiana entered the 1910s at age sixty, and Ulysses at sixty-four, they had a comfortable home base. They lived in comfortable Moodus in a comfortable house, within comfortable walking distance of many lifelong friends, and surrounded by comfortable familiarity. But they were not quite ready to just be comfortable. They had an automobile, and they used it to travel in these last of their go-go years before entering their slow-go and no-go years.

Americans had begun to use automobiles for pleasure by this decade. A long car ride was a novelty, even a thrill, for the owners of the first automobiles. My guess is that Ulysses replaced his drum corps time with *automobiling*—a term commonly used in the early twentieth century.

I don't know what model of car Ulysses and Georgiana had in the early 1910s, but no car had an integrated storage area for luggage until the 1930s. If they took an overnight trip with a traveling trunk, Ulysses would have had to fasten it to the back of the car. (This was why the American term *trunk* came to mean the luggage compartment of a car.) I envision Georgiana sitting corset-straight in the front passenger seat, wearing a hair-protecting hat and body-protecting clothing (there were no heaters in cars or sunscreen products until the 1930s), as they headed for the mountains, to the shore, or to nowhere in particular on a Sunday afternoon.

Riding in an automobile in the 1910s wasn't all that comfortable. I wonder if Georgiana found the rides bumpier and dustier and muddier than rides in a horse-drawn carriage. I wonder if she found the smell of gasoline exhaust worse than the smell of horses. She and Ulysses evidently liked *automobiling* well enough.

The roads between the three ports of her life — Ashley Falls in the Berkshire mountains, Westbrook at the shore, and Moodus in the inland center — became the well-worn routes that marked the perimeter of their world.

### TRIPS TO ASHLEY FALLS

In this decade, Georgiana and Ulysses made many trips to Frank's Maplewood Inn in picturesque Ashley Falls. Did they go there for the peace and quiet of a country inn? To gaze at the splendor of the foliage in the fall? To visit Georgiana's in-her-late-eighties mother under the peaceful coverlet of the Berkshire trees? They surely went to visit Lucinda, but amid peace and quiet? Ah, no. Their visits were filled with loud holiday festivities, family celebrations, and visits with friends in the Maplewood Inn. The inn was filled with guests checking in and out, going up and down stairs, eating in the dining room, chattering with one another, playing games, singing around the piano in the parlor, and in the basement, bellying up to the bar.

It is my good luck that the Maplewood Inn kept guest registers, and even better luck that the Sheffield Historical Society[157] preserved many of these pages dating back to 1909. What a thrill for me to see the handwritten entries for Georgiana and Ulysses over the years. Take 1912 for example:

- On April 2, a Tuesday, among guests checking in from Springfield and Boston, Massachusetts; Hartford, Connecticut; Newburgh, Poughkeepsie, and New York City, New York; Louisville, Kentucky; and New Orleans, Louisiana, there is the entry for "Dr. U. S. Cook & wife, Moodus, Ct." Georgiana and Ulysses likely stayed for a week or more, at least through Easter on April 7. Perhaps through their wedding anniversary on April 9. Or perhaps longer. Were they there on April 15 when the shocking news about the sinking of the Titanic broke, and the world could talk of little else? I don't know. Checkout dates for guests were not recorded.

- On June 10, Georgiana and Ulysses signed in again, this time to prepare for her mother's birthday on June 12. Lucinda, the Maplewood Inn's resident mother, grandmother, and great-grandmother, was in good health. She lived in a separate section of the inn with a private entrance and with her own big rocking chair on her own little veranda.

- On June 12, "Birthday Gathering in Honor of Grandma Smith's 87th Birthday" has its own page in the guestbook. First on the list? "Dr. U. S. Cook and wife." Second is "Edgar C. Smith and wife [Hattie]." It's interesting to note that there is not a mention that June 12 was also Sarah's birthday, her 53rd. I presume that Georgiana and Hattie helped Sarah with this party. The names of fourteen residents of Ashley Falls whom the Smith family had befriended in their nine years in the village were also entered in the guest book for Lucinda's party. They were:

    1. Mrs. Sarah E. Manville
    2. James Heaton
    3. Henry Ferry
    4. Henry Joiner
    5. Myron Decker
    6. Arthur Parsons
    7. Charlotte C. Wilcox
    8. William Sackett
    9. William White
    10. Ira Manville
    11. — Dunbar
    12. Levi Van Duesen
    13. Dougal McGregor
    14. Jane Snyder

- Thanksgiving fell on November 28 in 1912, and Georgiana and Ulysses returned to the Maplewood Inn for the family gathering. I learned this from a newspaper article,[158] not from the guest register, which, for some reason, was not filled in for the last two weeks in November. Perhaps the inn was closed to the public to accommodate Frank and Sarah's family feast. Twenty people attended the Thanksgiving party.

1. Frank, Sarah, and Lucinda
2. Georgiana and Ulysses
3. Edgar and Hattie
4. Georgia, Jack, and Worthington Strong (age seven) of West Haven, Connecticut
5. Fred Smith and his new-as-of-September wife, the former Mary (Mae) Bertha Welch (1885–1937) of Ashley Falls. Fred was thirty-years old and had been coproprietor of the inn for six years.[159]
6. Donald Smith, who was "employed as one of the engineers on the Ohio River at Parkersburg, Va."[160]
7. Mrs. Helen M. Heald (1883–1965) (Donald's future wife) and her son, Robert (age six), of Newark, New Jersey
8. Mr. and Mrs. Charles E. Ferrer of New York
9. Mr. Albert Baker of New Haven, Connecticut
10. Mr. and Mrs. Harold F. Glendenning of Danielson, Connecticut

- On Christmas Eve, Georgiana and Ulysses again checked into the Maplewood Inn. They had probably stuffed a trunk full of presents for everyone. Georgia, Jack, and Worth also checked in on Christmas Eve. I imagine seven-year-old Worth had one great Christmas that year. Santa, or perhaps Aunt Georgiana and Uncle Ulysses, may have given him a toy train, one of the top presents requested in Dear Santa letters at the time. The top ten gifts requested in Dear Santa letters in 1913 were candy, nuts, rocking horses, dolls, mittens/gloves, oranges, books, handkerchiefs, toy trains, and skates.[161]

Surprisingly, the guest registers of and newspaper articles about the Maplewood Inn, eighty miles away from Moodus, helped me get closer to Georgiana. They offered some unexpected glances into what must have filled her mind, her heart, and her dinnertime conversations with Ulysses. Take these six months of register entries and news clips from 1915:

- On May 29, for the first time, there is an entry of "Mr. and Mrs. D. U. Smith of Newark, New Jersey." Georgiana's thirty-year-old nephew Donald Ulysses had just married his sweetheart of many years, Helen. Helen would end up sharing good times — and sad times — with Georgiana in Westbrook and in Ashley Falls as the years went on. Helen was likely a favorite of Ulysses — Helen could sing!

- On June 4, four couples and two children checked in. A note written next to their entry reads: "Some party from Prattsville, N.Y., on a tare." The Maplewood Inn, advertised in the South Berkshire Directory[162] as an "American Motor League Official Hotel," was a popular destination for the motoring public from New England, New York, and New Jersey. Prattsville is seventy miles west of Ashley Falls. (Wordsmiths, take note: the word tare should be spelled tear, rhyming with bear. "On a tear" means "on a spree," but in 1915, almost certainly meant "on a drinking spree."[163]) Frank's business was booming — legally.

- On June 12, printed in large, bold, and formal calligraphy across the top of the page, is "90th Birthday Party. Mrs. Lucinda A. Smith, June 12, 1915. Ashley Falls, Mass." Two pages of names, which include forty local friends, are entered. Georgiana is the first name on the page. Ulysses's name is missing. This is the only entry in all the available Maplewood Inn registers that records Georgiana as being there without Ulysses. It was for this June 12, 1915, event that Georgiana's grandnephew, ten-year-old Worth, penned his own name, Worthington Strong, in perfect script into the guestbook. He listed his "residence" as Ashley Falls, so he may have been staying at the inn for the summer. Worth's mother and father, Georgia and Jack Strong, did not attend the party. But they weren't far away. The family of three had moved to Jack's hometown, Pittsfield, Massachusetts, near Jack's siblings, and where Jack's widowed mother had died in 1911. Ashley Falls was a short train ride (thirty miles) from Pittsfield, a ride Worthington and Georgia took quite often.

- Three weeks later, on July 3, close friends of Georgiana and Ulysses from Moodus, "S. P. Clark and wife" and "Chas. H. Rogers and wife," checked into the inn. Georgiana and Ulysses may have been there, although their names are not in the guest book. Georgiana may have been staying at the inn since the June birthday event.

- Every month from July to December in 1915, "Mr. and Mrs. Donald Smith" came to the Maplewood Inn for a few days. In 1912, Frank had purchased the nearby Ashley Falls marble quarry as a business opportunity for his sons. The quarry was located within walking distance of the Maplewood Inn, but the business was registered in New Jersey where Don and Helen took up residence. Don managed the business in New Jersey, and Fred managed the business in Ashley Falls. The successful "D. U. Smith and Brother" quarry business took off. The quarry would operate and thrive and, as the years went one, impact the lives of many Smiths. The income from the quarry allowed the Smiths to use the entire Maplewood Inn as their home.

- In mid-November, the local Berkshire County newspaper reported that "Frank Wheeler of Meriden, Ct., an old friend and neighbor of Mrs. Lucinda Smith, has been spending a week at the Maplewood Inn."[164] Frank Wheeler was seventy-eight, the oldest son of the Wheelers who had lived across the street from Abner and Lucinda on North Moodus Road. He was also the brother of Eliza Miller, who had bequeathed the Moodus Soldiers' Monument, and the brother of young Alfred who had died in the Civil War. He was one of few remaining people who had known Georgiana's father. I'm guessing Georgiana was the energy that kept the Moodus-rooted Wheeler/Smith communication alive over the years, even though both families spread out to new states and towns within Connecticut.

- November 25, 1915, was Thanksgiving Day, and the guest book was filled. Georgiana and Ulysses were at the Maplewood Inn with Lucinda and nearly the entire Frank Smith family. Georgia, Fred, and Don came with their spouses and with one son each: Fred and Mae's almost-two-year-old Frederick Abner, Jr. (who would always be called Ab); Georgia's ten-year-old Worth; and Don and Helen's nine-year-old Robert, whom Don had immediately adopted and made a Smith when he married Helen. Only Edgar and Vernon were missing. Edgar and Hattie likely spent Thanksgiving with Hattie's family in Old Saybrook. Vernon, who had started a new job in Providence, Rhode Island, in October, was not there. But Miss Helen Hanlon (1894–1942), the young lady Vernon would marry, was. She would become Vernon's wife two weeks before Thanksgiving the following year. Ninety-year-old Lucinda might have wondered if this was her last Thanksgiving. (It wasn't.)

Georgiana and Ulysses developed a pattern of visiting Ashley Falls two or three times a year — in April and November, and often in June. As the next generation of the Smith family grew, which it rapidly did in the 1910 decade, the Maplewood Inn became Smith Family Central.

In summers, though, the Westbrook cottage was the place to be. And Georgiana and Ulysses packed as many Smiths and as much fun as they could into it, for as long as they could.

*By the sea, by the sea, by the beautiful sea!*
*You and I, you and I, oh how happy we'll be!*
*When each wave comes a-rolling in*
*We will duck or swim,*
*And we'll float and fool around the water.*
*Over and under, and then up for air.*
*Pa is rich, Ma is rich, so now what do we care?*
*I love to be beside your side, beside the sea,*
*Beside the seaside, by the beautiful sea!*[165]

MUSIC BY HARRY CARROLL;
LYRICS BY HAROLD ATTERIDGE
1914

### TRIPS TO WESTBROOK

I don't think Georgiana ever had an empty room in her Westbrook cottage in summer. She was constantly welcoming and accommodating overnight visitors. It's quite likely — and I hope — she had some help with the cooking and also with the towel-washing, bed-changing, sand-sweeping, and outhouse-cleaning.

Family members packed themselves into the rooms and porches of the cottage. Sleeping space was at a premium. Abiding by the unspoken cottage rule of "the older the person, the more privileged the sleeping space," single men of the younger generations would sleep in the loft of the horse barn. Women and girls slept in the cottage, some in hammocks on the verandas. As the 1910 decade moved on, Georgiana's nephews brought girlfriends, then wives, then children to Westbrook. Sarah, Lucinda, Georgia, and Worth were frequent visitors. Frank, busy running his own summer resort, did not come as often as his family did. But he came often enough to build some memories. When he was in his eighties, visiting the cottage in the 1930s, Frank would ask his grandsons to row him in the family rowboat over to Menunketesuck Island "for old times' sake." This rowboat memory was told to Peter Worthington Smith by his father, Hal Smith, Frank's grandson.

Vernon spent many of his teenage summers (he became a teenager in 1906, the year Kittie died) at the cottage, presumably to help Georgiana and Ulysses. Newspapers frequently reported Vernon staying at the Cook Cottage. He would have enjoyed the summer beach days (and nights) in the way teens have been enjoying West Beach for over a century. Teens in the 2020s still walk the sidewalks in separate groups of girls or boys — except those in summer romances who walk hand in hand, oblivious to everyone else. During the day, teens still jump back and forth between beach blankets, run in for a swim, play ball on the sandbars at low tide, balance themselves on and push each other off the jetties, whisper, mumble, and act cool. The girls flock together like birds, females lined up on the seawall preening themselves, and every now and then, a male struts around to attract the females. At night, they bunch together in groups, staying in the dark on the beach, where the pairing off begins. Sometimes you can see a sparkling tip of cigarette that has been snuck away from an adult for all to try.

Speaking of cigarettes, every flat surface of the cottage — the windowsills, the pantry shelves, the Hoosier cabinet's pullout workspace, the bookshelves, the tops of end tables, the tops of bedside tables, the arms of chairs, the fireplace mantle, and the piano — held an ashtray that was often a large quahog shell. This was true for almost every seaside cottage in the early twentieth century. In most cases, women did not smoke. They did, however, have the morning duty before others arose to clean out the ashtrays and sweep up the spilled tobacco.

Women might have been as delighted as men when, in 1913, R.J. Reynolds came out with the first packaged cigarettes — Camels — that replaced the messy roll-your-owns. Camel cigarettes took off in America, as did a surge in cigarette smoking that did not peak until the 1960s. In the 1910s, smoking was not officially linked to lung cancer, although people must have connected smoking with the ghastly coughing and choking heard in the cottages (as well as in any building, on any sidewalk, or anywhere and everywhere) in those days. Ulysses, a cancer specialist, certainly must have seen the connection. Did he smoke? Maybe after-dinner cigars. He is not smoking in any of his photographs, a point I can't make for the other men in the family.

Friends of Georgiana and Ulysses from Moodus often visited them in Westbrook. Georgiana's lady friends from her church would pop down to the cottage for day-trips. Most overnight visitors came as couples. Many were associated with Ulysses's musical groups. He and his buddies would give musical performances in front of the cottage for the beachers. The wives would visit with Georgiana, take dips in the water, and prepare food. Sometimes Carrie Bowers, the pianist in Ulysses's orchestra in Moodus, stayed overnight. I imagine the crowd singing and swaying around the cottage piano in the evenings when Carrie was there.

Westbrook's 1910 Annual Illumination, held August 13, was one of the most spectacular. West Beach was celebrating construction of its new pier[166] — a 767-foot monster of a pier that served as a boardwalk, a fishing spot, and a dock for boaters. It was the longest pier between New Haven and New London, the "Granddaddy of them all," according to *Westbrook History Happenings and Hearsay*.[167]

*West Beach Pier, the largest on the Westbrook shore, was constructed in 1910 within easy view of Georgiana and Ulysses's summer cottage. Photo by Wm. J. Neidlinger, Westbrook, Connecticut. Postcard on display at Westbrook Historical Society, Connecticut.*

For the celebration that year, the beachers decorated their new pier and their homes with thousands of Japanese lanterns. Set up on the pier[168] and providing lively music was the Chester Band, led by Sim S. Brooks, Ulysses's coleader for the Annual Illumination the year before. Also playing was the brand new Westbrook Drum Corps,[169] which had debuted only three months earlier in the town's Decoration Day parade. Ulysses would have been eager to see the new group perform during his August visit, eager to encourage them, and eager to give them advice. Westbrook's drum corps would have certainly known of the famous Moodus Drum and Fife corps, and likely of Ulysses's leadership too.

For this 1910 celebration, Georgiana and Ulysses entertained a cottageful of friends and family. They would have enjoyed the music, the fireworks, the cake and food sales, the sidewalk promenading, the dancing, and the latest attraction — strolls on the new pier.

The Cook cottage had a front row seat to watch the goings-on at the new pier. It was only a hundred yards to the east of their cottage, within easy eyeshot of porch-sitters. I'm sure the pier activities provided great entertainment for Georgiana and Ulysses and their guests, who could rock on the porch and tune into new episodes of "The Pier" every day. Starting in 1913, they could tune in every night, too, because the street and the new pier were awash with light from the new electric lights, which pleased everyone except the teens.

[*Hartford Courant*, August 9, 1913]
A noticeable improvement on the beach is the changing of the oil street lamps to electric lights, which make the beach road much brighter at night. Preparations are now being made for putting electric lights on the West Beach pier; a plan to which the young people are objecting strenuously.

Good fishing was another draw to Westbrook. People could cast lines from their boats, from the beach, from the new pier, or from the several smaller piers. Blackfish were a favorite catch; they still were in 2020. Ulysses loved fishing, and it appears he was good at it — or good at telling fish stories, based on the newspaper accounts of his catches.

*Ulysses enjoyed fishing for blackfish in Long Island Sound in front of his and Georgiana's cottage. This photo is undated. Note the West Beach Pier (built in 1910) in the background.*

This photo of an older Ulysses in his fishing clothes on the beach in front of his cottage shows he never lost his love for the sport. I surmise, too, that Georgiana became an expert at cooking blackfish, which they would have eaten within a few hours of catching it. Whether she loved cooking fish as much as he loved catching them, I'll never know.

After a crammed cottage and a crammed August schedule, home in Moodus must have been a welcome change in September. Not that Georgiana plopped down in the house for long.

### HOME IN MOODUS

To get a feel for what Moodus was like in the beginning of the 1910 decade, think of the musical *The Music Man* with its 1912 small town setting. Georgiana could easily have been one of the sixtyish "Pick-a-Little, Talk-a-Little, Pick-a-Little, Talk-a-Little" townswomen who gathered in gossiping broods and worked together on the town's charitable events.

It looks like Georgiana stayed connected to her Moodus Methodist Episcopal Church, at least to the social parts. She had become the leader of the church's Dorcas Society. Dorcas societies gave clothing to the poor. Named after a woman in the Bible who made clothing, they were established by churches in America in the early 1800s. There are still Dorcas societies in some American towns at this writing. Many of Georgiana's Moodus lady friends were members as well. In 1912, the Moodus Dorcas Society voted Georgiana in as president. Also elected at the meeting were Georgiana's friends: Mrs. E.E. (Juliette) Williams as associate president; Mrs. Elizabeth Brainerd, Mrs. Nellie E. Clark, Mrs. W.W. Gates, and Mrs. M. Gates as vice presidents; and Mrs. O. Percival (Helen) Fowler as secretary and treasurer.[170]

In August 1912, newly elected Dorcas Society president Georgiana, accompanied by Ulysses, entertained the members of the society at their Westbrook cottage. The new minister of the church, Rev. Jesse Martin, who had also spearheaded an active

Dorcas Society in his previous church in Bolton, Connecticut, joined them, along with his wife and daughter. I'm sure Georgiana was proud to give the minister, his family, and her women friends a day at her beach house. It's just a guess, but probably a good guess, that Ulysses added music to the day.

By this decade, Georgiana and Ulysses were masters at "friend-shipping." They had accumulated sixty years' worth of friends in Moodus. From his music connections, Ulysses had a circle of men friends; from her church and social activities, Georgiana had a circle of women friends; and overlapping, in Venn diagram style, were couples with whom they socialized.

One couple, Charles and Phoebe Rogers, were in the center of Georgiana and Ulysses's intersecting friendships. Charles Rogers (1863–1947) was a longtime drum corps fifer, one of the first stockholders of the drum corps with Ulysses in 1892.[171] He also played in the Moodus Cornet Band with Ulysses. Professionally, he served as editor of the *Connecticut Valley Advertiser*, a newspaper in downtown Moodus that covered many Connecticut River towns.[172] Phoebe (born Emmons) Rogers (1867–1952) was in Georgiana's circle of church friends. When Georgiana was elected president of the Dorcas Society in 1912, the meeting had been held at Phoebe's home.

The Cooks and the Rogerses lived within walking distance of each other. I can only assume that Georgiana and Phoebe enjoyed some cups of coffee or tea together. Ulysses and Georgiana were almost twenty years older than Charles and Phoebe, yet the couples were great friends. The Rogerses were frequent visitors at the Westbrook cottage and at the Maplewood Inn in Ashley Falls.

In June 1913, Georgiana and Ulysses did not take their usual trip to Ashley Falls. They remained in Moodus to attend one of the proudest events in East Haddam's history — the opening ceremonies of the East Haddam Swing Bridge — on June 14, Flag Day in Connecticut. Flag Day had been a statewide holiday since 1906, when Connecticut's Governor Henry Roberts issued the first known Flag Day proclamation for a state. Later in the decade, in 1916, President Woodrow Wilson proclaimed June 14 as the nationwide Flag Day.

The Swing Bridge, designed with unique mechanisms to swing open for tall boats, connected East Haddam and Haddam over the Connecticut River. No longer did horses, carriages, bicycles, automobiles, and feet need the ferry to cross the river. On the west side of the river, the train tracks and a road for vehicles ran as double stripes parallel with the river, carrying people from Haddam in two directions — one way to Chester, Essex, and Saybrook, and the other way to Middletown and Hartford. The bridge, of course, also allowed the west-siders to travel easily to East Haddam, where the grand bridge led directly to its grand companion, the Goodspeed building. At the time of the bridge opening, the building housed W. C. Reynolds grocers.

Georgiana and Ulysses would have driven their car to the bridge-opening event with friends, maybe the Rogerses, in the back seat. Thousands dressed in their best finery attended. Automobiles filled the streets for the festivities. Photographers, reporters, and dignitaries did as well. Governor Simeon Baldwin delivered a speech. And there was music, of course, including the Moodus Drum and Fife Corps. For Ulysses, the event may have been acutely emotional. According to *Parker's,* this celebration was "the last time drums were beaten by any of the original members of the [Moodus Drum and Fife] corps in a public parade."[173] Ulysses was one of those "original members." He was no longer the drum major, but I bet he put on his uniform and played his snare drum with the corps for this important event.

The East Haddam Swing Bridge was and still is a photographer's dream. It remains an iconic image of East Haddam in the newest books about the town. In 2019, two books about East Haddam were published and each highlighted the bridge. It is the first photo in *Essence of Architecture in East Haddam*[174] in which a full section of the book is dedicated to the bridge's "many faces." *Images of America: East Haddam"*[175] includes several photos of the

*The East Haddam Swing Bridge opened in June 1913, connecting Haddam to East Haddam across the Connecticut River. The bridge is shown here in February 1913 as construction wound down.*

bridge, including the photo on its cover, taken at the bridge when it was under construction in February 1913.

A bit further down the river, near the Hadlyme–Chester ferry crossing, another East Haddam iconic structure was about to be built. Within a year of the bridge opening, William Gillette, a well-known actor who famously portrayed Sherlock Holmes, broke ground for his unique, unconventional, and amusing castle. He finished construction in 1919, then lived and entertained there (with great panache) for almost twenty years. Today it is part of Gillette Castle State Park, a popular Connecticut tourist attraction.

Three East Haddam iconic structures were built right before the eyes of Georgiana and Ulysses — the Goodspeed, the East Haddam Swing Bridge, and Gillette's Castle. Imagine what they'd think if they could see that the three are still defining East Haddam today.

A few weeks after the Swing Bridge opening ceremony in 1913, on July 1, another meaningful event was celebrated. This one touched the heart of Georgiana, as well as the hearts of the entire nation. It was the fiftieth anniversary of the Battle of Gettysburg, considered by many to be the most significant battle of the Civil War. In so many ways, this anniversary connected to pieces of Georgiana's life: her young days on North Moodus Road when she received her father's letters and read them aloud to her mother and brothers; the attention she received over the years from Horatio Chapman and other local Civil War veterans who never forgot her father; the fifty-year passion to honor the Civil War soldiers of her husband's drum corps; Moodus Decoration Days; the Continental Hall in which she and Ulysses hosted so many Civil War commemorations and post-parade ceremonies for more than twenty years; and the Moodus Soldiers' Monument, on which her father's name was etched.

I wonder if, for this fiftieth anniversary, she dug out and reread her father's letter from the Battle of Gettysburg, which had begun on July 1, 1863, her fourteenth birthday.

### STILL ROLLING, HALFWAY THROUGH THE DECADE

As the decade reached the halfway point, Georgiana at age sixty-five and Ulysses almost seventy kept rolling along on their Moodus/Ashley Falls/Westbrook circuit. Cars were improving at a fast clip. Ford Motor Company had emerged as the top car manufacturer, outpacing the competition, which was plenty and ever-changing. Buick, the predecessor of General Motors, was also pulling away from the pack. Buick wasn't Cadillac, the top of the line, but it was only a step below. In 1915, Ulysses bought a new Buick Touring car, designed for luxurious long-distance traveling.

While all sorts of automobile ads appeared in the inside pages of Connecticut's *Hartford Courant* in 1915, and while, that summer, the paper carried articles such as "Few Changes Are Seen at Westbrook" and "Standing Room Only at Cottages," as well as baseball scores, baseball stars, baseball schedules, and baseball stats, the front pages featured maps of Europe with headlines shouting words such as GERMANY, FRANCE FORCES, FIGHTER BOMBS, and WAR. Europe was in the Great War, which was getting more intense each month. Americans read about it but were not involved.

Georgiana and Ulysses began 1916 with a significant financial and emotional transaction. Ulysses gave up his guardianship of Continental Hall, the building he had fathered and raised for more than twenty years.[176] In February 1916, he sold the Continental and its property to Mr. David Zavodnick.[177] After that, Georgiana and Ulysses resumed their usual rhythm of traveling to Ashley Falls in April, Westbrook in August, and Ashley Falls again for Thanksgiving.

Thanksgiving fell on November 30 in 1916. November had been a game-changing month for the Maplewood Inn and Frank. Only three weeks before, the inn had been raided in what was reported as "one of the biggest liquor raids ever pulled off in southern Berkshire County."[178] Yet every member of the four-generation Smith family still gathered for Thanksgiving. There would have been room at the inn. It was empty of guests.

Sixty-seven-year-old Georgiana and seventy-one-year-old Ulysses strolled into 1917 in good health. In February 1917, the newspapers reported that Ulysses provided emergency medical help to a seventy-year-old man who had been struck by a train in Haddam.[179] In this same month, Ulysses filled out the required *State of Connecticut Military Census* form and claimed no "serious physical disability." He was mandated to fill out the form because of the Great War in Europe.

Georgiana, Ulysses, and Americans across the country were still marching forward, not affected by the Great War across the ocean. Until April 6, 1917.

# 1916–1919 at the Maplewood Inn: The Four Years before Prohibition

With the national temperance movement gaining strength and on the path to nationwide Prohibition, each year, towns in Massachusetts asked their citizens to vote on whether to allow liquor licenses to be issued or not. Since March 1909, Sheffield, Massachusetts, and its village of Ashley Falls, had voted YES. And each April, Frank P. Smith and Frederick A. Smith of the Maplewood Inn had applied for and were granted a one-year "License to Sell Intoxicating Liquors" at the inn.

In March 1916, the citizens of Sheffield voted YES once again to allow liquor licensing in Sheffield. However, despite the YES vote of the citizens, the selectmen had always had the power to approve or disapprove applications for a license. And this year, with rising attention toward temperance among their constituents, they chose to grant only one liquor license in Ashley Falls, and it wasn't to the Maplewood Inn. Starting May 1916, Frank was no longer allowed to serve liquor.

The Maplewood Inn had made a lot of money serving a lot of alcohol. The 1916 Maplewood Inn account books record Frank as doing a substantial business with his suppliers—distilleries, breweries, and beer suppliers. The account book also gives the financial situation of the inn: for the month of May 1916, the inn took in $696 [about $16,600 in 2020] after expenses.[180] That's about $200,000 net income a year in 2020 dollars. And it may have been higher, because 1916 was only the third year of federal income tax, and who knows if Frank recorded all the income.

But not having a license did not stop Frank from selling liquor in the basement barroom of the Maplewood Inn, and in November, the law caught up with him.

[*Berkshire County Eagle* (Pittsfield, Massachusetts), Tuesday, November 7, 1916]

### Big Liquor Raid on Hotel in Southern Berkshire

*"Wet Goods" Secured Filled Two Motor Trucks—*
*Maplewood Inn, the Victim*

One of the biggest liquor raids ever pulled off in southern Berkshire, from the standpoint of the quantity of "wet goods" secured, was made at the Maplewood Inn at Ashley Falls last evening at 8:30 o'clock. The liquor secured, which was in barrels, bottles, cases, etc., completely filled two large motor trucks and when carried to Great Barrington and stored in the town lockup it completely filled one of the largest cells.

The Maplewood Inn is conducted by Frank P. Smith and his son, Frederick Smith. But one license to sell intoxicating liquor was granted by the Ashley Falls selectmen this year and this license was given to the town tavern, which is located about half a mile from the Maplewood Inn. Canaan, Conn., a dry town, is situated two miles south of the inn.

The Maplewood Inn has done a good business all summer with motoring parties, etc. It has been well advertised and is generally well-known throughout southern Berkshire and northern Connecticut.

The officers who made the raid on the inn last night were Deputy Sheriff Frank A. Minkler of Great Barrington, Deputy

> Sheriff Clarence Kinne of Monterey, Chief of Police William J. Oschmann of Great Barrington, who is also a deputy sheriff in criminal cases, and Deputy Sheriff Benjamin Frank Clark of Sheffield. The trip to Ashley Falls was made in Sheriff Minkler's automobile.
>
> There were cases upon cases of bottled goods found, a quantity of beer in casks and bottles, a barrel of whiskey which was on tap and about two-thirds empty, and a dress suitcase full of bottled goods on a counter that had either been left there full or was about to have been taken away by some person. The value of the goods was placed at several hundred dollars. [$100 in 1916 is equivalent to $2,400 in 2020.]
>
> Mr. Smith and his son were summoned to appear in the Great Barrington court on Friday morning at 9 o'clock. Mr. Smith, senior, was in the Great Barrington court once before on a charge of the illegal sale of liquor and he was fined $50.00 [about $1,200 in 2020].
>
> The liquor business continued to be wrung dry.
>
> #1 Squeeze: In March 1917, the town voted NO to liquor licensing for the first time since 1909.
>
> #2 Squeeze: In March 1918, the town voted NO again.
>
> #3 Squeeze: In January 1919, the Eighteenth Amendment, prohibiting alcohol nationwide was ratified.
>
> #4 Squeeze: In March 1919, the town voted NO again.
>
> #5 The final squeeze: On January 16, 1920, national Prohibition began. It lasted until December 5, 1933.

### HALT

On April 6, 1917, every household in the country halted life as usual. America had joined the Great War over in Europe.

*On this 1918 sheet music cover, note the illustrator is Norman Rockwell (1894–1978). He was twenty-four years old at the time and would become the star illustrator for The Saturday Evening Post magazine for the next fifty years.*

*Over there, over there
Send the word, send the word over there
That the Yanks are coming
The Yanks are coming
The drums rum-tumming
Everywhere.*

*So prepare, say a prayer
Send the word, send the word to beware
We'll be over, we're coming over
And we won't be back till it's over
Over there.*[181]

CHORUS OF "OVER THERE"
LYRICS AND MUSIC BY GEORGE M. COHAN
1917

Georgiana and Ulysses were in Ashley Falls on their annual April trip when they heard the news. They knew what this might mean for the young men in the Smith family, especially for twenty-four-year-old Vernon. All men twenty-one to thirty-one were called to register for the draft.[182] On June 5, 1917, Vernon, who had married Helen in 1915, registered in Hartford, Connecticut.

Immediately after the April 6, 1917, announcement, East Haddam Company H of the Sixth Regiment, Connecticut Home Guards was formed. One hundred thirty-four men stopped their usual lives and prepared for battle through strenuous drills. On August 30, a military ball was held at Continental Hall to raise money for Company H. On September 17, the Moodus Drum and Fife Corps led the company in a parade from Soldier's Monument to Continental Hall, where a fund-raising banquet was held as a farewell for the first squad of East Haddam soldiers about to leave for battle.[183] I think it's a safe assumption that Georgiana and Ulysses attended both the ball and the banquet to support the hometown boys. They likely knew the families of each soldier.

The rest of 1917 in America was consumed with the wartime activities of sending men and supplies overseas. Herbert C. Hoover, America's Food Administrator, called for "continued rigid economy in consumption so that America may meet the increased demands from Europe."[184] Households rose to the call with patriotic duty. Small American villages, Moodus included, did their part.

Food, especially, was a focus for housewives like Georgiana, who were asked to find ways to waste less and grow more. To maximize food resources, including the resources needed to transport food, people were asked to grow their own vegetables, fruits, and herbs. These *victory gardens* blossomed. My guess is that Georgiana and Ulysses had a victory garden.

I guess, too, that Georgiana knitted socks and rolled bandages to be sent to soldiers, as her mother had during the Civil War. Ulysses would have bought Liberty Bonds to support the war effort. Together, Georgiana and Ulysses would cut back on using gasoline for pleasure, including abiding by the *gasolineless Sunday* rules.

They would use the train to make trips to Westbrook, where, that summer, the cottages were still filled with families and Long Island Sound was still filled with blackfish, but where the sky was no longer filled with firecrackers, as the Annual Illumination had been called off.

Georgiana and Ulysses made it to Ashley Falls for a small Thanksgiving gathering in 1917. A group of only nine family members were present, one of whom was the physically frail Lucinda. One newspaper had reported earlier in the year that "Mrs. Lucinda Smith received a bad fall going into her bedroom, sustaining bad bruises about the limbs and shoulders." They qualified this bad news by adding: "Mrs. Smith has reached the advanced age of ninety-two, but her mind has not lost any of its keen wit."[185]

After the family Thanksgiving, the Maplewood Inn had one more set of outside guests in early December. Then, with war filling the minds and the time of Americans while draining their wallets and their gas tanks, the Maplewood Inn closed for guests.

## 1918

In February, Frank and Sarah, free of hotel responsibilities, visited Georgiana and Ulysses in Moodus. They came to attend the golden wedding anniversary celebration of Sarah's sister Maggie (born Moody) Murkett and her husband Nehemiah Murkett at their home on Barton Hill in East Hampton. (Chatham had changed its name in 1915 to East Hampton.) In April, Georgiana and Ulysses skipped their usual trip to Ashley Falls. They stayed put in Moodus, where a victory rally (a fund-raiser celebrating a hoped-for victory) was held in Continental Hall, at which Ulysses's buddies provided the music. Ulysses and Georgiana would have walked next door for this event.

In Europe in 1918, the war was at its peak, creating what became known as the *lost generation*. This term, coined by American-turned-Parisian Gertrude Stein, is used to identify the men and women born between 1883 and 1900 whose lives or spirits were lost forever because of the Great War. Between fifteen and twenty-two million individuals died; up to twenty-three million more were wounded. Most of the casualties were young men from Europe.

America's casualties were small in comparison, but only in comparison. Of the 4.7 million American soldiers sent to Europe during the war, twenty-two thousand died and twenty-three thousand became sick or were wounded. The American home front took action to inspire young men to enlist and to raise funds to support war expenses. American patriotism was high, measured by the large sums of money collected during the Liberty Loan campaign. In Connecticut, every town received a quota of bonds to sell, and a few towns — East Haddam was one — reached their quota in one day. Patriotism was also evident in the ten thousand flags that were waved on Main Street in Hartford for a Liberty Parade in May. The Moodus Drum and Fife Corps, with only seven members, was one of the many marching bands that day.

### LUCINDA DIES IN JUNE 1918

Amidst these peak war days, in June 1918, Georgiana's mother died. Lucinda died on June 7, five days before her ninety-third birthday. She had "fallen and hurt her limbs," according to the death record.[186] Georgiana had not seen her mother since Thanksgiving of 1917. There is no record of a funeral. Her obituary, printed in the Moodus news section of the *Hartford Courant,* does not mention a service. Lucinda was buried near Kittie in the Smith plot in the Ashley Falls Cemetery.

In Lucinda's final days, the Great War was raging. With unforgettable memories of the Civil War over fifty years before, Lucinda would have agonized over the possibility of her youngest grandson, Vernon, going to war. Vernon and Helen had become parents of Lucinda's only great-granddaughter, Margaret Louise Smith (1917–2003). Lucinda's death in June would spare her the additional agony of hearing that in September, the age criteria for registering for the draft expanded to include ages eighteen to forty-five, which would include her older grandsons. On September

12, 1918, Fred Smith (34), Don Smith (33), and Georgia's husband, Jack Strong (45), registered in Lee, Massachusetts. Lucinda would never know the joy that her sons and grandsons were not called to go to war. Or that their wives would never become war widows as she had. Or that her seven great-grandchildren[187] would never lose their father at young ages, as her four children had.

The Maplewood Inn reopened for guests for a short time in the middle of 1918, had a filled-to-capacity Fourth of July weekend, but then closed again. Frank and Sarah joined Georgiana and Ulysses in Westbrook for the rest of the July. Georgiana and Ulysses continued their summer in Westbrook, welcoming friends from Moodus and East Hampton for another no-Illumination year.

### THE SPANISH FLU ARRIVES IN CONNECTICUT IN SEPTEMBER 1918

At the end of summer 1918, the Spanish Flu hit America with ferocity. The first outbreak in Connecticut occurred in September 1918 among servicemen in New London County, when vessels from foreign ports discharged patients into the Groton Navy Yard hospital, and a large number of men from the Boston Navy Yard transferred there. The virus quickly spread among the naval community, its civilian employees, and the families in the area who housed the nearly seven thousand naval men in private homes. The virus then whipped through the state from east to west. Some estimate 25 percent of Connecticut's residents contracted it. Monthly deaths in Connecticut from the flu and the pneumonia it caused peaked in October 1918 at 5,000. Penicillin, the treatment for pneumonia, would not be available for another ten years. There were not enough caskets.

The virus reached East Haddam by mid-October.[188] Small rural towns in Connecticut (with the exception of towns in Tolland County which were severely hit) suffered much less than large cities. And small towns *untouched by a railroad* (a phrase used to categorize towns in the Connecticut's final influenza report), such as East Haddam, suffered the least.

Ashley Falls and Sheffield were touched by the railroad. The Maplewood Inn, which tried to reopen for guests to enjoy autumn in the Berkshires, had almost no guests for the rest of 1918. In October, six residents of Sheffield died from the flu.

### NOVEMBER 1918 ARMISTICE

November 11, a date Americans now know as Veterans Day, has its roots in 1918. It was November 11, 1918, when the armistice that ended the Great War was announced. The United States, along with Great Britain and France, proclaimed November 11 Armistice Day, a day to annually honor veterans of the Great War, later called World War I. After World War II, the United States adopted a new name for the holiday — Veterans Day — as an honor to all veterans of all wars. Georgiana and Ulysses witnessed firsthand the jubilation that rippled through America on the day of the Great War's armistice. According to *Parker's*:

> When the news of the armistice reached Moodus on the morning of November 11, 1918, Walter W. Beckwith with his bass drum and accompanied by his wife, appeared upon the streets and led an impromptu parade. He was soon joined by Charles H. Rogers and members of the [Moodus Drum and Fife] corps, which thus contributed its full share to the noisy jubilations of that long-to-be-remembered day.[189]

I can picture Georgiana and Ulysses cheering and waving flags from the sidelines, maybe even from their front porch, as the parade passed by. Ulysses would have yearned to grab an old baton and lead the parade as he had in the good old days.

In the United States, the war ended in November 1918, but the flu carried on, taking lives until February 1919. In the end, more Americans died from the flu than from the war nationwide. That was true for Connecticut, too, where approximately 1 percent — 8,500 — of the state's residents died from the virus[190] and 1,100 from the war. East Haddam, a microcosm of Connecticut and the nation, followed the same pattern. Three residents died from the virus; and of the ninety residents of East Haddam who served in the war (sixty-seven Army, twenty-two Navy, one support), one died.[191]

Thanksgiving was November 28 in 1918, but there was not a Thanksgiving gathering in Ashley Falls that year, the first year without Lucinda and in the middle of a flu pandemic.

For the country, for the state, and for Georgiana, the cadence was off.

The war had ended in November 1918, but it took until April 1919 for the Connecticut soldiers to come home. Connecticut towns held parade after parade after parade after parade for the returning soldiers who stepped off the ships they had boarded in Europe and onto American soil in Boston. On April 7, the *Hartford Courant*'s front page headlines exploded:

> BOYS FROM CONNECTICUT! WITH HEARTS FULL OF GRATITUDE AND THANKFULNESS, YOUR OWN PEOPLE WELCOME YOU HOME. BOSTON FILLED WITH DELEGATIONS FROM CONN. EAGER TO GREET TROOPS ON AGAMEMNON [battleship] TODAY.

Tucked inside the multi-page news story about the Connecticut attendees at this welcome was this sentence: "The Waterbury delegation is accompanied by the Mattatuck and Moodus Drum Corps, whose quaint costumes are exciting considerable interest in Boston."

Wouldn't Ulysses have loved to drum for this event in his quaint uniform!

Wouldn't Georgiana and Ulysses have loved to be back in the good old days!

But their world had changed. In Westbrook, roof-raising Illuminations had been replaced with fund-raising fairs for the Red Cross and the Blue Cross (an organization which cared for wounded horses and dogs). In Ashley Falls, automobile parties no longer stopped at the Maplewood Inn for refreshment. In Moodus, German helmets were offered as prizes:

[*Hartford Courant,* April 28, 1919]
German helmets, offered as prizes in connection with the Victory Loan, are on exhibition at the Moodus Savings Bank, the store Purple & Silliman in Moodus, the National Bank of New England, and Allison's drug store in East Haddam.

### TWO LONG PARADES END IN GRAND FINALES IN 1919

In 1919, two groups of Americans, who had been beating their drums for more than seventy years and had willingly marched in place during the war, could finally advance to the finish line. One group was the temperance movement, the other the women's suffrage movement. Both groups were briskly stepping toward their grand finales — the approval of amendments to the United States Constitution. And the drum majors of both parades, who were getting ready to throw their drumsticks high in the air in victory, were straight-faced, iron-jawed, chins-held-high, eyes-boring-in-to-the-future women.

Their efforts culminated in the Eighteenth and Nineteenth Amendments:

- **The Eighteenth Amendment prohibited alcohol nationwide:** "The manufacture, sale or transportation of intoxicating liquors ... for beverage purposes is hereby prohibited." The temperance movement had been brewing since the mid-1800s when prohibitionists advocated a ban on alcohol for health and social reasons. After Americans joined the war in April 1917, there was one more reason to ban alcohol — the nation needed to preserve grain for the war effort. In December 1917, the United States Senate proposed the Eighteenth Amendment, which required thirty-six states to ratify it before it could be in effect. But war issues took over, including pushes for and against a temporary Wartime Prohibition Act of Congress. The Eighteenth Amendment was eventually ratified two months after the November 1918 armistice, on January 16, 1919. Prohibition did not become effective until a year later, giving proprietors of saloons — and inns — a full year to stock up and find hiding places.

- **The Nineteenth Amendment gave women the right to vote**: "The right of citizens of the United States to vote shall not be denied or abridged by the United States or by any State on account of sex." Twenty-eight words, seventy-two years in the making. The women's suffrage movement, which had also been brewing since 1848, had drawn new support from citizens and politicians after women's vital contributions to the Great War. In June 1919, Congress approved the proposed Nineteenth Amendment. The final step was for thirty-six states to ratify it. By the end of 1919, the suffragists needed fourteen more states. And they kept going, state by state, with the 1920 presidential election in view. (They made it!)

For women, the temperance and the women's suffrage movements were bound together. Most women were dependent on men for food, clothing, and shelter; they wanted to — and needed to — vote for laws, especially laws that prohibited alcohol.

East Haddam was officially in favor of women's right to vote. In May 1919, the citizens of East Haddam sent a petition through their United States Senator to Washington, D.C., in support of the women's suffrage amendment. Behind this petition were local women who had formed a suffrage group, called the Equality League of East Haddam and Moodus.[192] As for the Prohibition amendment, several local women became active in the Woman's Christian Temperance Union (WCTU). Many of the women in the Equality League and the WCTU were also leaders of the Nathan Hale Chapter of the Daughters of the American Revolution (DAR), the Red Cross drives and the Liberty Loan campaigns for the war. More and more, women were joining together in groups to support causes they believed in.

Some of Georgiana's friends, all at least ten years younger than she was — Phoebe Rogers, Juliette Williams, and Helen Fowler — were active leaders of these groups. Through these friends, and through her many Methodist church friends and acquaintances, I expect Georgiana stayed up to speed on the women's point of view for both temperance and suffrage issues. (Methodists were especially anti-alcohol!)

I believe Georgiana had a well-informed perspective on issues that affected women in 1919. She would have heard the modern point of view from the younger generation of women in her life — Lillie, Georgia, and her three Smith nieces-in-law, Helen, Helen, and Mae. And past experiences would have informed her. She had watched the voting and alcohol issues develop from birth to maturity, then marry into a united cause. She had seen men spend too much of their household money on alcohol at her brother's bars — men who were married to women powerless to change their circumstances and desperately wanting the right to vote, if only for the right to ban alcohol. But Georgiana, like most women of her era, did not publicly take a stand.

Did Georgiana support both causes privately? I would love to know the answer. My guess? YES.

### FORWARD, MARCH

In 1919, recovering from the war years, Moodus and East Haddam took steps to create a new normal as they approached a new decade.

- The Moodus mills had prospered during the war years from government contracts, but the locally owned (by the Chaffee family) New York Net and Twine Company, which ran two mills (Red Mill and Falls Mill) and a dozen tenement houses, had fallen victim to a swindler and had been forced to close their large Falls Mill for almost two years.[193] In 1919, the Chaffee family sold New York Net and Twine, one of the oldest manufacturing concerns in Moodus with roots of the first cotton twine factories in the country, to an Illinois company. The company promised to reopen the Falls Mill and hire 150 workers — a high-impact boost to the local economy — which they did in September.[194]
- Outsiders also came to the rescue of East Haddam's historic and grand Champion House, a large summer riverfront hotel,

which had attracted the top society of New York and Connecticut for years but had been closed for two years. The new owners announced plans to spare no expense to restore it to its "former high estate"[195] for year-round use, giving the Moodus resort industry a nice high tide. (A rising tide lifts all boats!) Many resorts and camps on the lakes of East Haddam began their rise to popularity and profitability at this time.
- In the Millington area near the old Smith homestead, the thousand acres known as Devil's Hopyard since the early 1800s, became a state park in 1919.
- The construction of a new Moodus library, donated by Judge Albert E. Purple, began.

The landscape of Moodus was changing — even in Georgiana and Ulysses's own front yard, where a prominent aging tree with deep sentimental roots had to be cut down.

*Left to right: Three unknown people, Georgiana, and Ulysses, circa 1919.*

On the back of the photo is a message written by Georgiana to her niece Georgia, reading "Taken in front of the spruce pine tree cut down March first. 65 ft. tall, set out [planted] by Uncle Ulysses' Father in his Mother's flower bed when he was a little boy. Over front chamber. Do you remember it? Wish you could have seen it fall. Beautiful tree. I know Worthington would have been interested."

As Georgiana and Ulysses left this decade, they knew their future would be quite different than their past. Georgiana no longer had a mother to talk with. Lillie, Merton, and Doris had moved to New Haven. Georgiana's childhood North Moodus Road home had been sold.[196] Ulysses no longer carried the drum major's mace. Georgiana and Ulysses, at ages seventy-four and seventy-nine, were not the parade leaders anymore.

### GEORGIANA'S PARADE

As I write about Georgiana's life, I feel like a spectator at a parade in which Georgiana's life is a marching band. At first, she was far away, and I could only hear the low, sad drumbeats of the Civil War. Then, from a distance, I heard music, which grew louder and louder, until her life marched directly in front of me with seventy-six trombones, bright red uniforms, and a proud, decorated drum major in the lead position.

Then I heard the whistle that halted the parade — when the cymbals stopped crashing and the sparklers stopped lighting the sky.

Now, as I write about Georgiana in her seventies, she and her drum major have marched past me, carrying on with an old trombone and an old baton. I watch their backs moving away from me into the distance. Their uniforms have lost their vivid color. Their drumbeat has slowed. Their music has faded to almost out-of-hearing range.

But when they turn to look back at me, they are still smiling.

*Ulysses (76) and Georgiana (72) on their West Beach cottage porch, 1921.*

CHAPTER 12
# Coda
## Georgiana in Her Final Years 1920–1930

Georgiana and America had been in perfect step with each other since the day Georgiana had been born. As a child during the Civil War, she had huddled with America in fear of bad news and wept with her when the bad news came. Then they recovered together, each with the help and love of someone named Ulysses.

Side by side, like close friends, Georgiana and America learned how to enjoy life again. America taught Georgiana how to ride an iron horse and a bicycle. Together they discovered summer fun at the seashore and danced their way through the turn of the century to new music. When clever America produced electricity, indoor plumbing, the telephone, the radio, and her masterpiece, the automobile, Georgiana was an "early adopter" before the term was invented.[197] When innovative America created the zipper, crayons, the teddy bear, the fountain pen, shredded wheat cereal, the mousetrap, the tea bag, the toaster, the ice cream scoop, cotton candy, and so many more delights, Georgiana was right there trying them all. And when America halted life as usual to enter the Great War, Georgiana halted her life as well.

She had walked and skipped and paraded alongside America her whole life. But when the 1920s arrived and America roared on, Georgiana couldn't keep up.

Georgiana was seventy when 1920 began. Let me tell you about seventy: you ache, your feet hurt, you can't hear, your eyes give you trouble, your knees and hips wear out, you can't get out of a chair like you used to. I could go on. I'm sure Georgiana experienced her seventies as most of us do (or will), but she did it without the help of AARP (American Association of Retired Persons, founded in 1958 to promote healthy aging), ibuprofen (introduced in the 1960s as an alternative to aspirin which had been introduced in the early 1900s), or Medicare (enacted in 1965 to provide people sixty-five and over with access to health care). She was not able to join America on the dancefloors, in the speakeasies, at the automobile races, or at the new cinemas in the Roaring Twenties. Nor could Ulysses.

Ulysses entered 1920 at age seventy-four. In July, a month before his seventy-fifth birthday, three visitors came to his home to "pay their respects."

> [The *Norwich Bulletin*, July 19, 1920]
> Dr. A. S. Wheeler, leader of the Worcester [Massachusetts] Continental Drum Corps, Manager Odell M. Chapman and Leader William H. Small of the Thread City [Willimantic, Connecticut] Continental Drum Corps are in Moodus today, paying respects to Dr. U. S. Cook, of that place, formerly leader of the famous Moodus Drum Corps.

The men were not paying *last* respects, but this little clip hints that Ulysses was a respected elder whose active days were behind him.

Georgiana and Ulysses were spending more and more time at home, or I should say homes.

### WESTBROOK ROARS AGAIN IN THE TWENTIES

After skipping Illumination parties during the Great War, Westbrook held its first Illumination Night in four years in August, 1920. Georgiana and Ulysses did not miss this "event of the season" at their beloved West Beach, even if they could only sit in rocking chairs on the porch.

[*Hartford Courant*, August 14, 1920]
**West Beach Will Have Celebration**
*Event of Week Will Be Fete for Benefit of Big Pier*

The event of the season at West Beach will be the celebration of "Illumination Night," Saturday, August 21. Extensive plans are being made by the various committees in charge of the affair, which will be given for the benefit of the West Beach Pier. For a number of years, "Illumination Night" was an annual event of the social season at Westbrook, but the affair of the coming weekend will be the first observance of the custom in four years.

Summer residents from shore resorts along the Connecticut beaches will attend the event in large numbers, and no efforts are spared by the committees to make the enterprise a success financially or socially.

The West Beach Pier, for the benefit of which the "Night" will be observed, was constructed about ten years ago by property owners at the resort, and has the reputation of being the longest pier between New Haven and New London. It is a decided attraction to the popular Westbrook Beach and is especially advantageous for diving and other water sports, as well as for a boulevard. The storms and rough weather of the past ten seasons have badly undermined the foundations of the pier, as well as the boardwalk, and consequently its structure is in need of immediate repair.

Throughout the season, various entertainments and enterprises have been undertaken by the summer residents to raise money for the pier's benefit: the Sunday afternoon sales of homemade root beer, candy and cream, and tag day [a day on which solicitations were made for a charity — in this case, the pier — for which small tags were given in exchange] being particularly successful. But the event of "Illumination Night" will be the most extensive undertaking of the season.

Throughout Saturday afternoon, at the gayly decorated booths to be constructed for the occasion, all the requisites of a lawn fete will be sold. Cake, candy, ice cream, root beer, grab bag, "knick knacks," etc. will be disposed of by the various committees in charge of their respective booths. Games and sports will also be features of the afternoon, as well as the fortune teller, who will tell the secrets past and future of the residents and their guests. The climax of the event will be the dance in the Fowler House in the evening, which is expected to attract 160 couples. The lawns and the dance hall of the Fowler House will be lighted with Japanese lanterns and the effect is to be both picturesque and unusual. The announcement that "Illumination Night" is to be revived has created widespread interest along the shore. The following committees have been appointed: Publicity, Candy, Cashier, Music, Cake, Grab bags, Printing, Cigars, Barrel Game, and Hot Dogs.

The party-loving Smith family joined Georgiana and Ulysses in Westbrook. Frank and Sarah and the next generations of Smiths filled the cottage. Georgia and Jack, Fred and Mae, Don and Helen, and Vernon and Helen all brought their children. In 1920, the seven cousins ranged from age two to fifteen. As their parents had before them, the cousins would grow up summering on West Beach at Aunt Georgiana's cottage, where they would make lifelong friends. Mae's obituary in 1937 (she was fifty-two) from the Moodus News section of the *Connecticut Valley Advertiser*, begins with the headline, "Mrs. Frederick A. Smith, Death of Massachusetts Woman — Summer Resident of Westbrook." It ends: "Mrs. Smith was known to many people here and also at West Beach, Westbrook, where she passed the summers at the Smith cottage."[198]

## WOMEN ROAR IN THE 1920S

I wonder if Georgiana and the other Smith women set off a sparkler or two at the August 1920 Westbrook Illumination to celebrate the ratification of the Nineteenth Amendment. Three days prior to the event, the thirty-sixth state had voted in favor of giving women the right to vote. Thirty-six was the magic number! The United States could not amend the Constitution unless 75 percent of the forty-eight states were in support. When Tennessee voted favorably (by only one vote!) on August 18, 1920, word flew through the country's newspapers. For the first time in American history, women would be able to cast votes for president of the United States. The election was only two-and-a-half months away, on November 2.

As soon as cities and towns could arrange voter registration days, women around the nation registered to vote. In East Haddam, townspeople had the choice of three days in October to register — two days at the East Haddam Town Hall and one at the Probate Office in Moodus. Altogether, 237 people registered, of which 207 were women![199] That means about 39% of East Haddam women twenty-one years and over registered to vote as soon as they were able to.[200]

On Election Day, November 2, the polls were open from 5:30 a.m. to 6:00 p.m. at East Haddam Town Hall. How many women voted? Did all the women who registered vote? Voting records in the United States, except in the state of Illinois, did not distinguish between the sexes. So to answer this question for any polling place in America (except in Illinois), mathematics are used to estimate. For East Haddam, the math looks like this: Four years prior, in the 1916 presidential election, 365 men had voted in East Haddam. In 1920, the number of voters jumped to 516 — a 41 percent increase over 1916,[201] which, by the way, is very close to the nation's increase in the number of voters of 44 percent.[202] If women made up all of the increase in voters, then 151 women voted (516 less 365). Of course, it could be higher, as high as the number of women who registered to vote. While the records can't prove it, in any report I've read about this jump in number of voters in November 1920, the Nineteenth Amendment gets the credit.

Newspapers estimated that in many towns in Connecticut, more than 90 percent of registered women cast their votes. This excerpt about women's first day of voting in nearby Norwich, Connecticut, which had a population ten times the size of East Haddam, captures the enthusiasm of women who participated in this watershed moment in American history.

> [The *Norwich Bulletin,* November 3, 1920]
> **Women Vote for the First Time**
> Equal suffrage for men and women brought the women into the election for the first time, and there were few who did not exercise their privilege. In some of the polling districts they were among the earliest voters when the polls opened at 5:30 in the morning, but in the First or Central district they heeded the advice to vote between the hours of 9 and 11:30, with the result that by noon 1,200 women had voted in the district ... the line of men and women who gathered to vote had to be folded back and forth in the hallway of the town hall and down the stairs and out into the street on Union Square.

Yet the majority of women did not vote. Only 36% of eligible women in the nation voted in 1920. Compared to 68% of men. In fact, women did not vote at the same level until the 1980s. From then on, women voted at equal or higher levels than men.[203]

Georgiana was one of the majority of women in East Haddam and in the nation who did not register to vote in 1920. Her name does not appear in the *Record of Voters, East Haddam*.[204] Listed in this record are the names of voters, their ages, and their occupations on the date they registered. The September[205] and October 1920 entries are almost all women, including several in Georgiana's circle: Carrie Bowers, 37, nurse; Helen Fowler, 51, housewife; Phoebe Rogers, 53, no occupation listed; and Juliette Williams,

57, housewife. Most women were listed as housewives or housekeepers. An occasional entry of another occupation — such as nurse, schoolteacher, milliner, bookkeeper, artist, post office clerk — shows up.

Why didn't Georgiana and other women register to vote? In a study done in the 1920s, these were the top reasons collected for not voting or registering: 34% General indifference; 13% Disbelief in women's voting; 10% Ignorance or timidity; 13% Illness. Various other reasons were given in small percentages, including a half of one percent of non-voting women citing "fear of disclosing their age" as the reason.[206]

I am not suggesting that Georgiana was one of those whose vanity prevented her from registering. But perhaps aging had something to do with her not making the effort. She was seventy-one. Only a small number of women over seventy registered to vote. (Elizabeth Brainerd registered at age 82.) Perhaps the visit to the Probate Office in Moodus to register in October and the trip to Town Hall in November were physically too much for her. Within a few weeks, she and Ulysses went to Ashley Falls for Thanksgiving, where there is a hint that Georgiana wasn't in tip-top shape.

### A SMITH FAMILY THANKSGIVING 1920

Yes, at ages seventy-one and seventy-five, Georgiana and Ulysses made it to Ashley Falls for Thanksgiving in 1920. *Dr. and Mrs. U.S. Cook of Moodus, Connecticut* tops the list of names neatly written in the Maplewood Inn guestbook on a page entitled *Thanksgiving, Nov. 25, 1920*. Second in the guestbook was Edgar, alone. He had lost his wife Hattie earlier in the year. Frank and Sarah, their four children and spouses were next. Then came six of the seven grandchildren (Robert was missing). Nineteen family members in all. With Lucinda gone, Georgiana had become the matriarch of the family.

This Thanksgiving may have been the last time Georgiana and Ulysses traveled together to Ashley Falls. The hint that aging may have been impacting their activities came after their visit, when Sarah sent a postcard dated December 8, 1920. It read: **"We called you by phone last night but did not have a good wire. Assume you arrived home safe. Hope you keep well. Don't try to do too much. So glad you could be with us. Hope Dr and you keep well."** Georgiana and Ulysses's names do not appear in the Maplewood Inn guest book again.

*Georgiana and Ulysses in front of their cottage at West Beach, Westbrook, Connecticut, 1921. Note the West Beach pier.*

### THE LAST TRIPS TO WESTBROOK

It looks like they made it to Westbrook for two more summers. The old handwritten records of owners of Westbrook post office boxes, which can be viewed firsthand in the now century-old giant record books at the Westbrook Historical Society,[207] show that Dr. U. S. Cook rented a box from July 1 to September 30 in 1921 and for the same dates in 1922. But not in 1923.

As the 1920s roared on around them, Georgiana and Ulysses more and more stayed in the comfort of their home in Moodus.

Changes in radio technology provided some new at-home entertainment for them. Radio had taken a broad jump in the early twenties and landed right in the middle of home parlors. Georgiana and Ulysses probably spent hours sitting near the radio listening to news, music, drama, comedy, and baseball. They likely huddled around the radio in October 1923, tuning in to the broadcast of the World Series on the future WNBC, in which the New York Yankees won the series in their new stadium with the phenomenal Babe Ruth, who had left the Boston Red Sox with a curse that began in 1918. Their phonograph, almost assuredly a Victrola, would have received a workout too. I bet Ulysses wore out many needles playing the 78 RPM record of John Philip Sousa's "Stars and Stripes Forever." And maybe, a big maybe, they played some of the new music called jazz.

However, for a couple as gregarious as Georgiana and Ulysses, technology could not substitute for company and conversation.

THE BEST TONIC

Perhaps recognizing how much Georgiana and Ulysses missed socializing, Frank and Sarah threw a party for them in 1924. The gathering was held on Georgiana and Ulysses's fifty-sixth wedding anniversary — Wednesday, April 9. The local newspaper covered the event in detail.

[The *Connecticut Valley Advertiser*, April 1924]
**Dr. And Mrs. U.S. Cook Celebrate Their Anniversary**
Seventy-five or more relatives, friends and neighbors gathered at the residence of Dr. and Mrs. Ulysses S. Cook Wednesday afternoon and evening to extend their congratulations and participate with the esteemed couple in celebrating the fifty-sixth anniversary of their wedding. There were no printed or special invitations issued, only a general desire expressed to receive as many of their friends as would favor them with their presence, it being the spirit

*Photos from the April 1924 Connecticut Valley Advertiser article about Georgiana and Ulysses's 56th wedding anniversary.*

now, as ever with them, "the more the merrier" and the happier. The spacious rooms were tastily decorated with flowers in profusion, many of which were kind remembrances of friends. The couple also received numerous nice gifts and many letters and cards of congratulation. A fine and generous lunch — the Cook kind — was served, and, of course, the customary anniversary cake was in evidence.

Music, vocal and instrumental, added to the pleasure of the occasion.

The couple were assisted in receiving their guests by her brother and sister [sister-in-law], Mr. and Mrs. Frank P. Smith, of Ashley Falls, Mass., at whose suggestion the anniversary was celebrated.

Dr. and Mrs. Cook were married at the parsonage of the First Congregational Church of East Haddam, April 9th, 1868, by the pastor, Rev. Silas W. Robbins, and have always resided here [Moodus].

He was born in Portland August 25th, 1845, a son of Dr. H. Evelyn and Elizabeth B. (Strickland) Cook, and has been a resident of Moodus since he was nine years[208] old. After a common school and Wilbraham Academy education, he studied medicine under his father, making a specialty of treating cancer and carried on the treatment successfully for many years, retiring from practice fifteen years since.

Mrs. Cook before her marriage was Miss Georgiana Smith, a daughter of Abner and Lucinda (Arnold) Smith, and was born in Tartia, Chatham, (now East Hampton), July 1st, 1849, the family moving to Moodus when she was quite young. She has been an ideal companion and homemaker, contributing her full share to the mutual happiness that has made married life worth living.

Dr. Cook is a musician of considerable talent, and is best known in that line as leader of the once famous Moodus Drum and Fife Corps, of which he is one of the few original members now living. He was considered one of the best snare drummers in this state.

Dr. and Mrs. Cook are enjoying good health, and admit the gathering and hearty greetings of the friends on their anniversary is the best "tonic" they have had in a long time. Their many friends wish for them many happy returns of their wedding anniversary.

The Cook home has always been a delightful place to go to, either on special occasion or to make a friendly call, and all were pleased this week to show their esteem and express congratulations.

Out of town relatives and friends present included Mr. and Mrs. Frank P. Smith; Mr. and Mrs. Fred Smith and two sons; Mr. and Mrs. Donald Smith and two sons of Ashley Falls, Mass.; Edgar C. Smith, of Saybrook; Mr. and Mrs. W. A. Brown and son of Middletown; Mr. and Mrs. E. B. Baker; Mr. and Mrs. Merton H. Lee and daughter, Doris;

Harold Lewis and Miss Emily Lewis of New Haven; Mrs. Harriet Phelps, Mrs. Paul Dugan and Miss Emma Maesing of Chester; Edward C. Mitchell and Mrs. Allie Clark of East Hampton.

Perhaps this mention is not germane to the subject, but Dr. Cook has been a subscriber to the *Hartford Times* and the *Advertiser* for over fifty years, and it is a question whether he would prefer to "lose" a ten pound blackfish or miss a copy of either publication.

The admiration, respect and love for Georgiana and Ulysses can't be missed. The article even tops all the accolades off with a bit of affectionate teasing for a couple who possessed a good sense of humor. The author was their good friend Charles H. Rogers, the editor of the paper. If I could meet Mr. Rogers today, I would thank him for the insight he gave me into Georgiana, when he word-sculpted her as "ideal companion and homemaker, contributing her full share to the mutual happiness that has made married life worth living." Yes, it's a tad sexist for the twenty-first century, but I wonder if there is any better achievement in life than contributing your full share to happiness.

### LILLIE

At the party was Mrs. Merton H. Lee — Lillie — with her husband and her sixteen-year-old daughter. Lillie may have played the piano, contributing to the pride and pleasure of Georgiana and Ulysses at this special event.

I wish I could say that Lillie was a part of all the Smith family celebrations, but she wasn't. Lillie, however, did stay close to Georgiana and Ulysses her whole life. After she and her family moved to New Haven in the 1910s, they often returned to East Haddam for visits with Merton's family and with Georgiana and Ulysses. Sometimes Lillie and Doris came alone, as Merton had to work. He earned a living as a private chauffeur. Lillie and Doris often stayed at the Lee farm in the Mount Parnassus section of

East Haddam, where Doris could drink in the fresh air at her grandparents' country farm.

Lillie also had friends in East Haddam. One friend was Carrie Bowers, who was eight years younger than Lillie. Carrie looks as if she'd be a fun-loving friend. There is a picture of Carrie from the early 1900s in *Images of America: East Haddam*[209] in which she is one of four women, possibly boosters for the Moodus baseball team, who are hamming it up for the photo. Several ties bound Carrie and Lillie together. They had both been brought up in musical homes. Both had become accomplished pianists. And both had grown up under the influence of the Moodus Drum and Fife Corps — Carrie's father was George Bowers, one of original members of the drum corps and a great friend of Ulysses. Possibly because of Carrie's friendship with Lillie, Carrie became close to the Cooks. She took Lillie's place in Ulysses's orchestra when Lillie moved to New Haven with her family. And Carrie visited the Westbrook cottage more than once.

Did Lillie go to Westbrook for the summer fun? She and Doris could have easily taken the train from New Haven. They must have gone, but I can find only one newspaper article that lists Lillie staying in Westbrook. The article is from July 1926 when Lillie, Merton, and Doris, then nineteen years old, spent a weekend in a cottage around the corner from Georgiana's, but when Georgiana had stopped going to Westbrook.[210] The year before, in 1925, Merton had been stricken with polio, leaving his stomach and back paralyzed.[211] Perhaps Georgiana had something to do with this Westbrook arrangement in order to help Lillie and her family.

Based on finding no record of Lillie visiting Georgiana in Westbrook or Lillie visiting Ashley Falls, and because no one in the current Smith family has any recollection of Lillie or her daughter, Doris (who lived in East Hampton until her death in 1990), I don't think Lillie was viewed by the Smiths as a close family member. But I do think that Lillie and Georgiana maintained a strong, healthy, and loving relationship over the years.

### GEORGIA

Missing from the April 1924 party was Georgia. I assume it was purely practical reasons, likely a job or Worth's school schedule, that kept Georgia from attending the party. Georgia had been a widow for two years. In February 1922, her husband, Jack Strong, had died at their home in Pittsfield, Massachusetts. He was forty-nine; Georgia was forty-two; Worth was sixteen. After Jack's death, Georgia and Worth had moved in with her parents and brothers at the Maplewood Inn, which took in its last guest in June 1924 and closed to remain a private residence for the Smith family. Georgia and Worth lived there until Worth moved to Seattle to attend the University of Washington in the fall of 1924, and Georgia moved to Rhode Island to work as a private governess for a wealthy family. Georgia never remarried.

### THANKSGIVING 1924

For Thanksgiving 1924, seventy-five-year-old Georgiana and seventy-nine-year-old Ulysses stayed in Moodus. I don't know everyone who visited them that holiday (my guess is that they had many callers), but because of a tiny newspaper clip, I know that Lillie was there. She, Merton, and Doris paid Georgiana and Ulysses a visit the weekend before Thanksgiving.[212] Surely their visit was combined with one to Merton's mother who had recently been widowed.

Unlike Georgiana and Ulysses, America's Thanksgivings did not slow down. They went the other way. (It was the Roaring Twenties, after all.) In New York City, the new Macy's department store held its first Thanksgiving Day Parade. That first year, 250,000 people watched as professional marching bands, giant floats, and zoo animals made their way down the streets of the city. Parade-lover Ulysses would have consumed every word in the papers about this parade-of-parades, reading the descriptions out loud to Georgiana with a touch of awe and perhaps envy for the youthful marchers.

## CODA

[coda, noun. co·da | \ kō-də \ A concluding musical section]

Ulysses would not live to see Thanksgiving 1925. He died on November 18, eight days before the holiday. He was eighty.

[*Hartford Courant*, November 18, 1925]
**Dr. Ulysses S. Cook, 80, Dies in Moodus**

Dr. Ulysses S. Cook, for years a practicing physician in this town and a specialist in the treatment of cancer, died at his home late today. He was 80 years old. Dr. Cook was born in Portland, August 15, 1845, the son of the late Dr. H. Evelyn Cook and Elizabeth Strickland Cook.

He had lived in Moodus since he was nine years[213] old and studied medicine under his father. Dr. Cook is survived by his wife. They had no children. Dr. and Mrs. Cook celebrated their 56th wedding anniversary April 9, 1924.

Dr. Cook was a musician of unusual ability on the violin. He was one of the original members of the Moodus fife and drum corps, which was famous throughout the state, and played the snare drum.

Some would say Ulysses was also "survived by" the Moodus Drum and Fife Corps. *Parker's* eloquently phrased the relationship this way: "Dr. Cook's attachment to the Moodus Drum and Fife Corps was akin to that of a **parent to a favorite child** and for many years, the continuance and success of the Moodus Drum and Fife Corps was largely dependent upon his enthusiastic support and never-failing devotion to its welfare."[214]

Ulysses had a wonderful life. If he'd been George Bailey in *It's a Wonderful Life,* the angel Clarence would have shown him what Moodus would have been like without him. He would have shown him a less-famous drum corps in less-snappy uniforms; no Continental Hall; no one remembering *Moodus-style* drumming; young men holding pool sticks instead of drumsticks hanging around a Falls Road building owned by Frank Fowler; and people suffering in their homes from untreated cancer. Then Clarence would have brought him to Chester and shown him Lillie working in a tobacco field pretending to play a piano in the air; Frank working as a clerk in the Chester House with his hands shoved into his empty pockets and dreaming of owning a hotel of his own; and Sarah explaining to her children why they couldn't go to seminaries and universities. Then he would have brought him to an empty cottage in Westbrook with no music playing and no blackfish on ice. And then back to Moodus, where he would show him Georgiana, still Georgiana Smith.

Ulysses was buried next to his father, mother, and sister in the Cook family lot in the Moodus Cemetery. A place next to him was reserved for Georgiana.

### AFTER THE BALL

*After the ball is over*
*after the break of dawn —*
*After the dancers' leaving;*
*after the stars are gone;*
*Many a heart is aching*
*If you could read them all*
*Many the hopes that have vanished,*
*After the ball.*[215]

WRITTEN BY CHARLES K. HARRIS
1892

(This waltz song was the biggest hit
in Tin Pan Alley history.)

The ball was over for Georgiana when Ulysses died. She was never the same. Frank and his family helped her immediately. Six days after his death in 1925, she signed an East Haddam Probate Court document acknowledging that she had been selected as sole executrix of Ulysses's estate, as spelled out in his 1906 will. But she "refused to accept executrixship" and granted the power to administer the will to her forty-five-year-old nephew Donald Ulysses Smith, Sr. Her handwriting was shaky.

Three months later, in January 1926, her handwriting was even shakier when she applied for monthly payments of $150 [about $2,200 in 2020] from Ulysses's estate while it was being settled, for which she was the sole beneficiary. She was also likely shaken because of a January 7 traumatic event in her house: Giles P. LeCrenier, serving as an appraiser of her house, suffered a stroke while taking inventory for Ulysses's estate. Frank and son Donald were with Georgiana when it happened. Mr. LeCrenier "did not lose consciousness immediately, but soon after lapsed into a state of coma, in which condition he remained until his death about nine hours later. He was placed in bed by Charles H. Emily, Frank P. Smith and Donald Smith."[216]

In April, she wrote her will. The first clause bequeathed Lillie the sum of $500 [about $7,400 in 2020]. The second clause directed the executors of the will, who were named as her nephews Donald Ulysses Smith and Frederick Abner Smith, to invest her estate and pay the income from it, annually and in equal shares, to Frank, Edgar, and — this is nice! — Sarah.

She then moved to Ashley Falls to live with Frank and Sarah and family.

### TENDERLY CARED FOR

Georgiana lived with Frank and Sarah for the rest of her life, about five more years. When she arrived at the Ashley Falls house, which was no longer the Maplewood Inn, it was home to three generations of Smiths: Frank and Sarah; Frederick and Mae with their two sons, Frederick Abner ("Ab") Smith, Jr. (1914–1994), and Harold ("Hal") Franklin Smith (1916–1999); and Donald and Helen with their two youngest sons, David ("Dave")Arnold Smith (1917–2002), and Donald ("Don") Ulysses Smith, Jr. (1918–1984). Robert, age twenty, was away at college or at work most of the time. In 1926, the four young Smith boys — Don, Dave, Hal, and Ab — were ages eight, nine, nine, and twelve. They grew into teenagers during Georgiana's final years in Ashley Falls.

"Aunt Georgiana" lived in the lovely and spacious two-floor section — the original section of the house, and the same quarters Lucinda had used — next to the noisy household filled with the boys being boys, fathers running the quarry business from sun to sun, and mothers tending to the women's work which was never done. An aging Frank and Sarah did their best to serve as caregivers for an ailing Georgiana, who by then was an invalid. According to Georgiana's obituary: "In all her afflictions, she was most tenderly cared for by Mr. and Mrs. Smith and other members of the family."[217]

As if in synchronicity with America, which fell into the Great Depression in 1929, Georgiana failed to the point of near helplessness. A live-in private nurse was hired to care for her.

### GEORGIANA'S LIFE ENDS

On October 3, 1930, at age eighty-one, Georgiana died from nephritis, a kidney disease, and (this is painful for me to write) from extreme emaciation.

[*Connecticut Valley Advertiser,* October 7, 1930]
**Mrs. Cook Dies after Long Illness**
*Moodus Woman Passes at the Age of Eighty-One Years*

The funeral of Mrs. Ella Georgiana (Smith) Cook, widow of Dr. Ulysses S. Cook, formerly of Moodus, who died last Friday night [October 3, 1930] at the home of her brother, Frank P. Smith, in Ashley Falls, Mass., was largely attended at the [Moodus] Methodist church Monday afternoon [October 6, 1930] at 2:30. Rev. E.R. Thurlow, rector of the

Episcopal church in Sheffield, Mass., officiated. The burial was in the Cook family lot in Moodus Cemetery. [Her name is engraved as Georgiana S. Cook.] The bearers were Henry B. and George O. Fielding, Edgar P. Simpson,[218] and Charles C. Richmond.[219] There were many beautiful flowers.

Mrs. Cook was born in Moodus, July 1, 1849, daughter of Abner C. and Lucinda (Arnold) Smith. Until the death of her husband about five years ago, she had always resided in Moodus. Since that time, owing to failing health, most of the time she had lived with her brother. She had gradually failed and for some time previous to her death had been practically helpless. In all her afflictions she was most tenderly cared for by Mr. and Mrs. Smith and other members of the family.

Besides her brother, Frank P. Smith, she leaves three nephews and one niece, besides several grandnieces and grandnephews. [Her brother Edgar had passed away in 1928.] Mrs. Cook's father was killed in the Civil War and his body lies in an unknown grave in the South.

Mrs. Cook was a woman of many many friends, both in Moodus and elsewhere. The Cook home, with the doctor and his wife, was noted for its hospitality and many social gatherings held there and at their cottage with great pleasure by a host of friends.

### HER LIFE RECORDED

How satisfying that Georgiana's death did not go unnoticed in Moodus, and that her life was recorded in Moodus's main newspaper, *the Connecticut Valley Advertiser*. How wonderful to read that her life was filled with bringing happiness to others. How telling that the word *many* is repeated three times in the final paragraph. How charming that *cottage* is one of the final words used to memorialize her. And how perfect that the last bell to ring out her life is *friends*.

The Westbrook "Cottage" in 2019. From left to right: David Sermersheim, Sarah Lucinda (born Smith) Sermersheim, Peter Worthington Smith, Claire Smith, Dayle Smith, Jay Bradford Smith, Henry Lopez Andrade (holding Theo), Caitlin Smith, William Worthington Demiris (held by) Anne (born Smith) Demiris, Phillip Demiris, Hayley Smith, Chris Hildebrandt, Sarah Smith, Megan (born Smith) Lavoie, Jonah Lavoie, Chris Lavoie. Photo taken by Joe Pecoraro, Joseph's Photography, Inc., Chester, CT.

# Epilogue

A family tree with a hundred leaves can shed a satisfying light on history. But spending a hundred hours on one leaf is a hundred times more powerful. By turning it over and over, you learn the pattern of its veins by heart. By observing every moment in its lifespan, you see how it opens in sunshine and droops in drought, how it dances in breezes and hunkers down in storms, how it changes color as it ages, and how it falls to earth at the end of its life. And how it becomes part of the soil that forever nourishes future leaves.

Georgiana was my one leaf. I didn't unearth much about her in the history books. But from her father's letters, I witnessed a headstrong adolescent as she uncurled into a determined young lady. From the guestbook of her brother's inn, I felt her strong family veins. And from her event-filled, music-filled, fun-filled, cottage-filled, and friend-filled experiences, I found the essence of a woman who lived a full life with the love of her life.

I have portrayed Georgiana in this book as a fulfilled woman, one who opened in the sunshine and danced in the breezes. But I am not naïve. Her life was surely not as rosy as I have painted it. I will never know how her father's death affected her. Nor will I know her most intimate thoughts about her mother, Lillie, or Frank. Nor her true relationship with Ulysses. I will never know who among her "many many friends" were closest to her, or whether she was tired or energized from all the hostessing, or the look on her face when she listened to one more story about drums, or whether she stayed silent in subservience or spoke up in confidence with her husband, or if she sensed the permanent sweeping changes ahead for women that her generation began. And I will never know if she tried to imagine what life would be like for a woman living in her cottage a century later.

> **Like So Many Women of her Era**
>
> "In the early 20th century, most women in the United States did not work outside the home, and those who did were primarily young and unmarried. In that era, just 20 percent of all women were 'gainful workers,' as the Census Bureau then categorized labor force participation outside the home. And only 5 percent of married women were categorized as such … Most women lacked significant education. Fewer than 2 percent of all 18- to 24-year-olds were enrolled in an institution of higher education and just one-third of those were women … [There existed] widespread sentiment against women, particularly married women, working outside the home." [220]
>
> Janet L. Yellen (1946–) in May 2020.<br>She became 78th United States<br>secretary of the treasury in January 2021.

Georgiana was like so many women of her era. She was not a *new woman* — at least not in her actions. But was she thinking, thinking, thinking as so many women were? Did the emergence of the *new woman* put questions in her head? Did she view the transformed woman as too radical? Or was she privately cheering for the women who blazed the trail? Did some unfulfilled dreams surface? Did she ever yearn to work outside the home, or get more education? Or was she content in her role as "an ideal companion and homemaker, contributing her full share to the mutual happiness that made married life worth living?" I don't know.

What I *do* know is that Georgiana continued to give happiness to others after she died. First, by bequeathing the cottage to her family. And second, through her spirit which she left in the cottage, believed by some to be embedded in the walls.

### HER COTTAGE

Georgiana's Westbrook cottage stayed in her name, under the "Estate of Ella G. Cook," for forty-two years after she died—through the Great Depression of the early thirties, through the repeal of Prohibition in 1933, through the hurricane of 1938 (which the cottage survived), through the big band swing era of the forties, through World War II when the cottage used dark shades to prevent any enemy ships on Long Island Sound from seeing shoreline lights, through the postwar baby boom, through the first rock 'n' roll songs of the fifties, through the second women's liberation movement in the sixties, and through the debut of the Rolling Stones.

Over those forty-two years, three more generations of Smiths filled the cottage in summers. Among them: Frank's son, Fred, married to Mae; their son, Hal, married to Connie; their son, Peter, who would later marry me. Peter, great-grandnephew of Georgiana, bought the cottage from Georgiana's estate in 1972, when he was twenty. The transaction was complicated: there were seven legal heirs in different parts of the country, but each agreed to Peter's purchase.

### HER SPIRIT

Our three daughters are the fifth generation to absorb the spirit of Georgiana in the cottage. Sarah, our firstborn, swears that when she was nine, she saw the ghost of Georgiana dressed in a long white dress. She remembers not being afraid as Georgiana seemed friendly. Sarah is not the first to say that the house has a happy spirit in it. A summertime West Beacher born in 1937[221] told me, "Every time I have walked by the Smith house, even as a child in the 1940s, there was music playing and laughter from a crowd of people inside."

This fifth generation enjoys the cottage in the same way Georgiana did: music blaring, singing and dancing in the street, rocking in the porch rocking chairs, with aunts, uncles, cousins, neighbors, overnight guests, friends, friends, and more friends on the porch, coming in and out of the front door, ladling chowder into mugs from the giant chowder pot in the kitchen, awaiting ice cream (now from the legendary Daisy in her ice cream truck), and gathering together to watch fireworks on the Fourth of July.

The youngest generation, the sixth, has begun to hear the echoes of Georgiana's heartbeat. One September day, after the summer crowds had left and our porch was empty and quiet with no music playing, our first grandchild, Billy,[222] at two years old, stood under the GEORGIANA sign on the porch. Glancing from right to left and peering into the other rooms, he asked, with a look of confusion on his face, "Where are all the people?"

I think Georgiana smiled down.

# Chapter Notes

1 ***autumn:*** "People who find it necessary to leave the shore in September are missing the most beautiful month of the year by the water. The still days are flooded with yellow sunlight. The water looks bluer and the sky clearer then than at any time during the year." *Hartford Courant,* August 27, 1908, 14. The special look of the water at West Beach in autumn has been a topic of conversation in Westbrook for generations.

2 ***1884:*** J. B. Beers & Co., *History of Middlesex County, Connecticut, with Biographical Sketches of its Prominent Men* (New York: J. B. Beers & Co., 1884).

3 ***1903:*** J. H. Beers & Co., *Commemorative Biographical Record of Middlesex County, Connecticut: Containing Biographical Sketches of Prominent and Representative Citizens, and of Many of the Early Settled Families* (Chicago: Beers, J. H. & Co., 1903).

4 ***Haddam:*** Horace Tyler Arnold inherited the land from his father, David Arnold, who died in April 1812. David Arnold's probate documents (dated May 25, 1812, four days before Horace's seventeenth birthday) are on file at the Connecticut State Library in a packet entitled "Estate of Arnold, David, Town of Haddam, 1812, No. 65, Middletown Probate District." The will contains bequests of his land in Haddam. He designated acres to each of his nine children, one bequest reading: "To Horace Arnold, son of the deceased, a piece of land containing about three acres & half ..." Connecticut, Will and Probate Records, 1609–1999, Middletown District, Private Packets A–Austin, Joseph, 1752–1880. Probate date: 1812. Ancestry.com.

5     **"death.":** *Beers 1903*, 750.

6     **related:** Thankful Arnold's information is from the Haddam (Connecticut) Historical Society website, haddamhistory.org. Lucinda Arnold's information is from the family tree of "Joseph Arnold (1625–1691)" compiled on Ancestry.com.

7     **factory:** Letter from Abner C. Smith to Lucinda Smith, November 13, 1862. Full letter can be found in *The Civil War Letters of Abner C. Smith*, companion to this book.

8     **81 cents for each dollar men made:** "Women in the U. S. earn 81 cents for every dollar men make in 2020. That's the raw gender pay gap, which looks at the median salary for all men and women regardless of job type or worker seniority." Kathleen Elkins, "Here's How Much Men and Women Earn at Every Age," July 18, 2020, cnbc.com.

9     **Mills along the River:** Bruce R. Sievers, *Mills along the River, the History of the Cotton Industry in Moodus, Connecticut* (East Haddam: East Haddam Historical Society, 1985), 49–52.

10     **Paree:** Lyrics.com, STANDS4 LLC, 2021. "How Ya Gonna Keep 'Em Down on the Farm? Lyrics." Accessed November 4, 2021.

11     **By 1900, 40 percent:** Michael S. Katz, "A History of Compulsory Education Laws," Fastback Series, No. 75. Bicentennial Series. Education Resources Information Center (ERIC), an online library sponsored by the Institute of Education Sciences (IES) of the U. S. Department of Education, 1975, Eric.ed.gov.

12     **"nineteen.":** *Beers 1903*, 750.

13     **"farming.":** *Beers 1903*, 749.

14     **records:** Connecticut, Church Record Abstracts, 1630–1920, Haddam, First Congregational Church 1739–1908, digital image, s.v. "Lucinda Arnold," 6. Ancestry.com.

15     **reads:** Original 1718 deed to Matthew Smith for property. Courtesy of Smith Farm Gardens, Smith Road, East Haddam, Connecticut.

16     **"plain.":** Hosford B. Niles, *The Old Chimney Stacks of East Haddam, Middlesex County, Connecticut*. (New York: Lowe & Co, 1887), 113.

17     **"homestead.":** Ibid, 115.

18     **reported:** Mason, Karen Oppenheim, and Lisa G. Cope. "Sources of Age and Date-of-Birth Misreporting in the 1900 U. S. Census." *Demography* 24, no. 4 (1987): 563–73. doi.org/10.2307/2061392.

19 *"grammar.":* Letter from Abner C. Smith to Edgar Smith, August 24, 1863. Full letter can be found in *The Civil War Letters of Abner C. Smith*, a companion to this book.

20 **information:** Du Pont De Nemours, *National Education of the United States,* Translated from the Second French Edition of 1812 and with an Introduction by B. G. Du Pont (Newark, Delaware: University of Delaware Press, 1923), 4.

21 **shoemaker:** *Beers 1903,* 750.

22 **Sarah Josepha Hale (1788–1879):** Wikipedia's "Sarah Josepha Hale" entry, accessed May 10, 2021.

23 **holiday:** "Thanksgiving in North America: From Local Harvests to National Holiday," Smithsonian Institution, Revised March, 1998, Si.edu/spotlight/thanksgiving/history.

24 **The Haddam Town Marriage Record:** The Barbour Collection of Connecticut Town Vital Records, Connecticut Town Marriage Records, pre-1870, Haddam, digital image, s. v. "Lucinda Arnold," 74. Ancestry.com.

25 **Shailer:** Rev. Simon Shailer (1776–1864) became the minister of the Baptist Church of Christ in Haddam in 1822. He performed the marriages of many Arnolds, Tylers, and Dickinsons in Turkey Hill, Haddam over the years. The Shailers (spelled in various ways, including Shailor, Shayler, Shaler) were a prominent family in the Haddam area. (1) "Old Baptist Church," Historical Society, accessed July 1, 2020, haddamhistory.org; (2) "The Simon Shailor House (1827)," Historic Buildings of Connecticut, accessed July 1, 2020, historicbuildingsct.com.

26 **births:** In 2018, the infant mortality rate in the United States was 5.7 deaths per 1,000 live births. "Infant Mortality," Center for Disease Control and Prevention, September 10, 2020, cdc.gov.

27 **twenty-four:** Dana Smith, "Postpartum Health in Crisis," Spring 2022, harvardpublichealth.org.

28 **deaths in the United States:** Cancer was fatal to 1,704 persons in 1850, about 61 in 10,000 of all deaths. In 1860 it caused the death of 1,230 males and 2,062 females, 3,292 in all—nearly twice as many as in the former year. The number and proportion to total mortality were much larger among women than among men. US Census Bureau, "Statistics of the United States (including mor-

tality property, etc.) in 1860," (Washington, D.C: Government Printing Office, 1866, 241), census.gov.

29   **lives:** "Penicillin: An Accidental Discovery Changed the Course of Medicine," August 10, 2008, Healio.com.

30   **"holes in our stockings?":** Anonymous author, "Bolting Among the Ladies," *Oneida Whig* (Oneida, New York), August 1, 1848. Accessed at Newspaper Coverage of Seneca Falls Convention, senecafallscoverage.tumblr.com.

31   **time:** "Ella" and "Georgiana," Baby Names Finder, BabyCenter, babycenter.com. The name Ella is the 130th most popular name of the 714 different female names recorded on the nationwide 1850 census, taken a year after Georgiana was born. This statistic is not for babies born in 1850; it is for all females living in 1850 in the United States. New baby names were not recorded and ranked as they are today, or as they were in 1885, when Ella had risen to the seventeenth most popular name for females. The name Ella, after dropping to a virtually unchosen name at the end of the twentieth century, bounced back in popularity in the twenty-first century. In 2011, Ella was the twelfth most popular name for newborn girls and has since continued to rank in the top twenty. The name Georgiana ranked 237th in 1850 in the census. After a brief spurt in popularity at the end of the nineteenth century, the name Georgiana went downhill and has yet to make a comeback.

32   **hick'ry stick:** Lyrics.com, STANDS4 LLC, 2021. Accessed November 4, 2021.

33   **life:** Joanne M. Marshall, "Common School Movement," Education Publications. Iowa State University Digital Repository, 2012, 67. lib.dr.iastate.edu.

34   **schoolhouse:** Dr. Karl P. Stofko and Rachel I. Gibbs, *East Haddam Connecticut: A History* (East Haddam: East Haddam Historic Commission, 1977), 10.

35   **Mount Holyoke Female Seminary:** "The Founding of Mount Holyoke Female Seminary," accessed July 1, 2020, mtholyoke.edu.

36   **laws:** Patrick J. Mahoney, "Child Labor in Connecticut," April 18, 2021, Connecticuthistory.org.

37   **Little Women:** Louisa May Alcott, *Little Women* (Boston: Roberts Brothers, 1868/1869).

38   ***Wheeler:*** Alfred Wheeler (1845–1862) died September 22, 1862, in Fortress Monroe, Virginia. Connecticut, Hale Collection of Cemetery Inscriptions and Newspaper Notices, 1629–1934, Charles R. Hale Collection, Image 345 of 583, digital image, s.v. "Alfred Wheeler," Ancestry.com.

39   ***scarlet fever:*** Karl P. Stofko, East Haddam Municipal Historian. Paper: "Abner C. Smith 2nd of East Haddam," updated April 29, 2010, 4.

40   ***deadliest battle of the Civil War:*** The Battle of Gettysburg was a three-day battle and had the greatest number of casualties of any battle in the Civil War. The top three costliest battles, in terms of killed, wounded, missing, and captured were: (1) Battle of Gettysburg, Pennsylvania: 51,112; (2) Battle of Chickamauga, Georgia: 34,624; (3) Battle of Chancellorsville, Virginia: 30,099. Abner C. Smith fought in #1 and #3. "The Ten Costliest Battles of the Civil War," accessed August 24, 2017, civilwarhome.com.

41   ***Mr. Semes:*** I was unable to determine who this was, even after considering different spellings of this phonetic sound.

42   ***Mother-Daughter Conflict:*** Michelle Silver and Roni Cohen-Sandler, *I'm Not Mad, I Just Hate You! A New Understanding of Mother-Daughter Conflict* (New York: Penguin Publishing Group, 2000).

43   ***aunt and uncle:*** In a letter from Elizabeth to Lucinda two years earlier, in December 1862, Elizabeth added a note to 13-year-old Georgiana, "Well, Georgy, I will say a word to you. I want you to be a good girl. Do all you can. Learn all you can. For like enough [in all probability], I will want you next summer." Georgiana did not go to her aunt and uncle's Meriden home the "next summer" in 1863. She went in April 1864.

44   ***guardianship:*** The Probate Court, District of East Haddam, document dated August 9, 1866, reads: "Present, J. Attwood, Esquire, Judge, Ella G. Smith, Edgar C. Smith and Frank P. Smith, residing in East Haddam in said District, minors aged respectively 17 – 14 – 12 years, having no father, guardian or master. Therefore, this Court doth accept of the choice of Lucinda Smith, Guardian of said minors, who appeared in Court, accepted said trust, and gave bonds with surety, in the sum of One Hundred Dollars for a faithful discharge of her trust according to law, which bond is accepted by the Court."

45   **Kandie Carle Victorian Lady:** kandiecarle.com

46   **Goodspeed:** William Goodspeed (1816–1882) was sometimes called "The Vanderbilt of Connecticut." He owned prosperous enterprises in shipbuilding, banking, railroads, and retail. And he loved the theater. He was the mastermind behind the Goodspeed Opera House building and became the theater's producer. T. M. Jacobs, *Goodspeed's Folly*, (United States of America, 1996).

47   ***"cancer curer.":*** *Beers 1884*, 179.

48   **Hooker:** Susan Campbell, *Tempest Tossed, the Spirit of Isabella Beecher Hooker* (Middletown, Connecticut, Wesleyan University Press, 2013).

49   ***vote:*** Jessie Kratz, "Harriet Beecher Stowe: A Fighter for Social Justice." Posted in Woman Suffrage, Women's History Month. March 8, 2019. Accessed at prologue.blogs.archives.gov, a blog of the US National Archives.

50   ***"established.":*** *Parker's*, 142a.

51   ***"you.":*** "Till There Was You" was written by Meredith Willson and performed in his musical play *The Music Man* (1957). Lyrics from Lyrics.com, Accessed November 6, 2021.

52   **(GAR):** The Grand Army of the Republic (GAR) was an organization for Northern Civil War veterans. Inspired by local observances held in many towns after the war, in May 1868, Major General John A. Logan, head of the GAR, proclaimed, "The 30th of May, 1868, is designated for the purpose of strewing with flowers, or otherwise decorating the graves of comrades who died in defense of their country during the late rebellion." The towns and cities in the Northern/Union states began planning annual May 30 Decoration Day commemorations. Southern/Confederate states continued honoring their soldiers on different days until after World War I, when Decoration Day evolved to include those who lost their lives from all wars. In 1971, Congress designated the last Monday in May as a federal holiday, Memorial Day. "Memorial Day History," VA, US Department of Veterans Affairs, va.gov., and "Civil War Dead Honored on Decoration Day," History.com. Last updated May 26, 2021.

53   **Montgomery Ward catalog:** (1) Judy Hevrdejs, "Montgomery Ward's First Catalog," December 18, 2007, chicagotribune.com. (2) Anna Kathryn Lanier, "Montgomery Ward Catalog." August 19, 2011, seducedbyhistory. Blogspot.com.

54  **Haddam:** Tom Nelligan, *The Valley Railroad Story* (New York, New York: Quadrant Press, Inc., 1983). At this writing, the building is still standing and in use as Goodspeed's Station Country Store, 22 Bridge Street, Haddam, Connecticut.

55  **residents:** "Connecticut Population by Town 1830–1890," portal.ct.gov/SOTS/Register-Manual/Section-VII/Population-1830–1890.

56  **Botanic Family Physician:** J. W. Comfort, J.D. *The Practice of Medicine on Thomsonian Principles*, 7th ed., (Philadelphia: Lindsay and Blakiston, 1867).

57  **health craze of the 1820s:** David Mikkelson, "The Origin of Graham Crackers," August, 2002, snopes.com.

58  **fuel of the fashionable:** Robert Khederian, "Beyond Fireplaces: Historic Heating Methods of the 19th Century," November 30, 2017, curbed.com.

59  **Victorian style, the fashion of the Gilded Age:** The Victorian Age, 1837–1901, overlapped with the Gilded Age, 1870–1900.

60  **1900:** *Parker's,* 142b.

61  **"Music Hall.":** *Parker's,* 142b.

62  **Connecticut's Fife & Drum Tradition:** James Clark, *Connecticut's Fife & Drum Tradition* (Middletown, Connecticut: Wesleyan University Press, 2011), 114.

63  **"purposive.":** Ibid, 113.

64  **spectators:** Diane Longley and Buck Zaidel, *Heroes for All Time* (Middletown, Connecticut: Wesleyan University Press, 2015), 290–291.

65  **"rip-roaring melodrama with thrills and laughter":** These are words from the poster promoting the 1938 production of the play by the Federal Theatre Project. Wikipedia"s "The Drunkard" entry, accessed May 13, 2021.

66  **The Drunkard:** *The Drunkard* continued to be performed through Prohibition (1920–1933), and through the 21st century. Except for a pause during the COVID-19 pandemic, the play has been performed every Saturday night at the Tulsa Spotlight Theater in Tulsa, Oklahoma. Wikipedia's "The Drunkard" entry, accessed May 13, 2021.

67  **Irish immigrants:** Sievers, *Mills,* 45.

68 **home:** "Moodus News Items of Fifty Years Ago," *Connecticut Valley Advertiser,* November 28, 1930. Mary S. Bigelow Scrapbook, 1924–1938, 2. Local History Archives, Rathbun Free Memorial Library, East Haddam, Connecticut.

69 **"the Cook kind.":** "Married Fifty-Six Years. Dr. and Mrs. U. S. Cook Celebrate Their Anniversary." *Connecticut Valley Advertiser,* April 1924. Bigelow, *Scrapbook.*

70 **"home.":** Beers 1903, 846.

71 **location:** *Parker's,* 180c. *Parker's* also reported that Henry E. Cook's son performed this 1883 transaction and mistakenly reported the son's name as Henry, instead of Ulysses.

72 **wealthiest man in town:** Sievers, *Mills,* 54. Albert E. Purple was owner of two mills in 1880: Card's Lower Mill and the East Mill. He went on to become the largest mill owner in Moodus. He was also partner in the Moodus downtown Purple and Silliman dry goods store, the judge of probate, the president of the local bank, an elected representative in the Connecticut State Legislature, and leader of many community activities.

73 **still stand today:** The Johnsonville property was purchased in 2017 by Iglesia ni Cristo (Church of Christ), a Filipino Christian organization.

74 **"benevolence.":** Beers 1884, 328–329

75 **"reading room.":** Beers 1903, 293

76 **surviving mill owner:** Sievers, *Mills,* 2.

77 **Simon:** Ken Simon is the producer/director of the "Saving Land, Saving History" documentary series (2021) as part of the "Saving Land, Saving History" project in collaboration with the East Haddam Historical Society and East Haddam Land Trust. The series can be accessed at easthaddamhistory.org.

78 **"family.":** "Ulysses S. Cook. M.D." *Beers 1903,* 426.

79 **"[missing word]":** "Moodus News Items of Fifty Years Ago," *Connecticut Valley Advertiser,* July 1937. Bigelow, *Scrapbook.*

80 **published in 2012:** Eric D. Lehman and Amy Nawrocki, *The History of Connecticut Food* (Charleston, S.C.: American Palate, 2012), 42.

81 **food:** "According to the 1975 *Better Homes and Gardens Heritage Cookbook* [Des Moines: Meredith Corporation, 1975], canned pork

and beans was the first convenience food." Wikipedia's "Pork and Beans "entry, accessed July 14, 2021.

82 **Christian Endeavor Societies and the Home Circle:** Amos R. Wells, *Social Evenings: A Collection of Pleasant Entertainments for Christian Endeavor Societies and the Home Circle* (Boston and Chicago: United Society of Christian Endeavor, 1899).

83 *"performers"*: *Daily Morning Journal and Courier* (New Haven, Connecticut), June 24, 1881.

84 *receiving line:* Parker's, 142b, c.

85 **East Room:** Clark, *Tradition*, 124.

86 *1963:* Jacobs, *Goodspeed's Folly*.

87 *there:* refers to "... the Music Hall building (where the great showman P. T. Barnum had once made an appearance)." Sievers, *Mills*, 55. P. T. Barnum (1810–1891) started his "Grand Traveling Museum, Menagerie, Caravan, and Hippodrome" in 1871, promoting it as "The Greatest Show on Earth." His show later became the Barnum and Bailey Circus.

88 *attended*: *Connecticut Valley Advertiser*, January 15, 1887. Sievers, *Mills*, 52.

89 *"abroad.":* *Beers 1884*, 562. The word "abroad" in this context means "away from one's home."

90 *"William E. Odber and Mattie C. Odber (wife).":* *Beers 1884*, 310 and *Beers 1903*, 815–816. Captain William Odber (1842–1921) of Haddam, Connecticut, listed as a "prominent and representative citizen" in *Beers 1903*, was educated in Haddam's Brainerd Academy. He registered for the Civil War in 1863 at age 21 and became one of the few survivors of an ill-fated ship that burnt off the coast Cape Hatteras, North Carolina, in 1865. (Strangely, his records reveal that during the war, he went under the alias, George W. Murphy. This fact is found in his widow's 1921 application for a Civil War pension.) From 1877 to 1901, William Odber was the jailer for the principal jail of Middlesex County, located in Haddam, under the administration of Sheriff Thomas Brown. When Odber managed the Haddam jail, it was so decent (as jails go) that it was nicknamed "Hotel d'Haddam" by the locals and later called "The Country Club." **Mrs. Mattie Odber** (1848–1930), his wife, was born Martha Clarissa Burr, in Haddam. She also was educated at Brainerd Academy. The couple and their family lived in the

large built-in-1878 granite addition to the original built-in-1845 stone cellblock jail, located at the intersection of Jail Hill Road and Saybrook Road, Haddam, which remains a significant historical landmark in Haddam.

91   **"Dr. Ulysses S. Cook.":** *Parker's,* 148b. This excerpt goes on to say: "New lights were a long time coming into general favor for business and household uses. By 1917, village streets of Moodus and 80 percent of dwelling houses in East Haddam were electrically lighted."

92   **"Full Line of Millinery, Dry and Fancy Goods.":** *Directory of Essex, Deep River, Chester, East Haddam, Moodus, and Haddam* (New Haven: The Price and Lee Company, 1896), 161.

93   **bicycle built for two!:** Lyrics.com, STANDS4 LLC, 2021. Accessed November 6, 2021.

94   **extinction:** Gary Allan Tobin, "The Bicycle Boom of the 1890s: The Development of Private Transportation and the Birth of the Modern Tourist." *The Journal of Popular Culture VII(4),* March 2004, 838–849.

95   **"untrammeled womanhood.":** "Pedaling the Path to Freedom," National Women's History Museum. June 27, 2017, womenshistory.org.

96   **entry:** Both sources were accessed July 1, 2020.

97   **towns:** *Parker's,* 158d.

98   **Miss Carrie Bowers (1882–?):** In 1910, Carrie Bowers was 27, single, and working as a companion for and living in the home of George and Rebekah Buell in Moodus. George Buell was an original member of the Moodus Drum and Fife Corps. Carrie Bowers is listed in the 1920 East Haddam census as a thirty-seven-year-old nurse and living with her mother in Moodus in the home of Elizabeth Hurd. The last record I can find for Carrie Bowers is a 1921 newspaper item that reads: "Miss Carrie Bowers who has been nursing in the family of Judge R. U. Tyler of Tylerville, has returned to her home in Moodus." *Norwich Bulletin* (Norwich, Connecticut), January 28, 1921, 7. I cannot find a death record for Carrie. She may have married and taken a new last name.

99   **"great manhood.":** "How the Connecticut Knights March," *Daily Morning Journal Courier* (New Haven, Connecticut), August 29, 1895.

100 ***"United States."***: *Parker's*, 142d.

101 **Sound Money**: McKinley's Sound Money monetary policy was a response to the country's economic depression, a key issue in the presidential election of 1896. McKinley won the election. A silent documentary about the Sound Money Parade can be viewed at imdb.com. Sound Money Parade (1896), documentary, short, November 1896 (USA). New York City, USA. William K. L. Dickson, director.

102 **corps:** *Parker's*, 143b.

103 **begun:** "Fashionable Dances of the Day," *Harper's Bazar*, December 22, 1896. Found on vintagevictorian.com/dance_1890.html.

104 **[2020]:** On July 26, 1893, Ulysses paid Mary Brainard $375. Three months prior, in April 1893, Ulysses had paid $325 to the Trustees of Brainerd Academy of Haddam for a quitclaim deed to the same property. The trustees included J. H. Odber, brother of William E. Odber, the Haddam jailer who had sold Ulysses the western half of the cottage in 1882.

105 **Cooley House:** In 1896, the Cooley House/Hotel was located on the corner where Bay Shore Road (now Seaside Avenue) met Long Island Sound. In 1893, the hotel had been caught serving alcohol, which was illegal in Westbrook at the time. It was caught again in 1899, reducing its popularity and its profit. In 1900, it then changed its name to the Seaview Hotel and soon disappeared from its original location. Gail Colby, in her 2019 book, *People and Places of West Beach*, 27–28, wrote: "I continue to wonder if the old Cooley Hotel, renamed the Seaview, was indeed moved to the western end of the beach," and offers insights into the unsolved mystery.

106 **Maplewood Music Seminary:** Hosford B. Niles, *The Old Chimney Stacks of East Haddam, Middlesex County, Connecticut* (New York: Lowe & Co., 1887), 145.

107 **record:** *Builders of Our Nation, Men of 1914*, (Chicago, Illinois: Men of Nineteen-Fourteen 1915).

108 **Life: How to Enjoy and How to Prolong It:** Prof. F. C. Fowler, *Life: How to Enjoy and How to Prolong it, 21st Edition*. (Philadelphia: Blake Publishing Company, 1896).

109 **brothel:** "The ferryboat *F. C. Fowler* was brought upriver to Hartford in 1895 when the wooden bridge between Hartford and East

Hartford burned. It notoriously provided services to the customers of the River House, Hartford's premium upscale brothel at the time." Wick Griswold and Stephen Jones, *Connecticut River Ferries* (Charleston, S.C.: The History Press), 2018, 123.

110   **race horses:** "Moodus Horse Races in Gay 90s," *Connecticut Valley Advertiser,* December 16, 1938.

111   **Main Street:** Fowler opened his business in the Meckensturm hat and boot shop building, owned by Charles Meckensturm. In 1887, Fowler moved to the Music Hall building, which he expanded several times. He left the Music Hall building in 1904, selling it to Henry Labensky. "Moodus News Items of Fifty Years Ago ," *Connecticut Valley Advertiser,* November 1937. Bigelow, *Scrapbook.*

112   **"liberated.":** "Superior Court—Divorces Granted," *Hartford Courant,* April 18. 1896. The word "liberated" was used to describe women who secured a divorce. It is defined as "freed from or opposed to traditional social and sexual attitudes or roles," and was first used in 1887. *Merriam-Webster.com,* accessed August 8, 2020, merriam-webster.com.

113   **after-game showers:** Fred Post, *Hartford Courant,* February 18, 1998, 76.

114   **operation:** Wick Griswold and Stephen Jones, *Connecticut River Ferries* (Charleston, S.C.: The History Press, 2018), back cover and 13–14.

115   **freeze:** Curtis S. Johnson, Compiler, *Three Quarters of a Century, The Life and Times in The Lower Connecticut Valley As Chronicled for Seventy-Five Years by* The New Era. (Privately Printed, 1949). 19. The *New Era* was first a monthly, then a weekly, newspaper founded in Chester in 1874, covering the lower Connecticut River Valley towns.

116   **"chloral.":** The full newspaper article read: "CHESTER. Landlord Weaver of the Chester House, formerly of North Manchester, was found dead in bed at ten o'clock Thursday. The cause is supposed to be an overdose of chloral." *Hartford Courant,* January 22, 1881.

117   **death:** H. H. Kane, M.D., *Drugs that Enslave, The Opium, Morphine, Chloral and Hashisch Habits* (Philadelphia, 1881).

118   **issues:** According to the US Census for Chester, Connecticut, June 1880, Erastus Weaver's 22-year-old son, Clinton, lived with his parents in Chester. Clinton's occupation is listed as "physi-

cian." Clinton was 23 when his father died the following January. Had he been treating his father? Had he prescribed the chloral for his father? Clinton later became a minister and moved to Iowa, then Maryland. He died at age 58 in 1915 and was buried in Manchester, Connecticut, with a gravestone reading: "Reverend Clinton Hosmer Weaver (M.D.–D.D.)," acknowledging that he was both a Medical Doctor and a Doctor of Divinity.

119 *Kate Silliman's Chester Scrapbook:* Thelma Clark, ed., *Kate Silliman's Chester Scrapbook, Edited and revised by Thelma Clark* (Chester, Connecticut: The Chester Historical Society, Inc., 1986). Thelma Clark (1908–1999) lived in Chester for forty years. She assembled the 1953 Scrapbook and edited and revised the 1986 edition.

120 *"of the town itself.":* Beers 1903. 749–750.

121 *7 cents:* Annual Report of the Bureau of Statistics of Labor, July 1884. Part IV, Comparative Prices, 1860–1883, Table I, Prices in Massachusetts, 1883, p 440. Version 11/23/20. Accessed through Babel.hathitrust.org.

122 *day's salary ($1.34):* "If you worked in manufacturing, as many did during this period of mechanization, you could have expected to make approximately $1.34 a day in 1880." Michelle Leach, "Salaries in the 1880s," updated August 23, 2019. careertrend.com.

123 *"The Silliman Blood is Pure.":* Clark, *Chester Scrapbook*, 111–112.

124 *"agin' its enforcement!":* Johnson, *Three Quarters of a Century*, 19.

125 *"Come Home, Father,":* Margaret Bradford Boni, ed., *Songs of the Gilded Age* (New York: Gold Press, 1960), 131.

126 *anthem:* Jon W. Finson, *The Voices That Are Gone: Themes in Nineteenth Century American Popular Son* (New York: Oxford University Press, 1994), 56–57.

127 *Willard:* Miss Frances E. Willard (1839–1898) was a national temperance reformer and women's suffragist who served as the national president of the Woman's Christian Temperance Union from 1879 to her death in 1898.

128 *"driving":* Clark, *Chester Scrapbook*, 188.

129 *harness racing:* Andrea Rapacz, "And They're Off!: Harness Racing at Charter Oak Park," August 28, 2020. Connecticuthistory.org.

130  *"made.":* Clark, *Chester Scrapbook,* 189.

131  *"reputation,":* Beers 1903, 751.

132  **name:** Theme from *Cheers* by Gary Portnoy and Judy Hart-Angelo, 1982. Source for lyrics: lyricsondemand.com.

133  *"work.":* "Law and Order League. Two Open Letters that Speak for Themselves," the *Hartford Courant,* November 23, 1895, 4.

134  *"imaginable.":* "General Assembly" *Hartford Courant,* April 18, 1895, 10.

135  *"license.":* "News of the State. Middletown." *Hartford Courant,* November 24, 1896, 10.

136  *"years.":* *Hartford Courant,* March 17, 1898, 10.

137  **1896:** "About 1896 a new law had passed [in Connecticut] whereby pupils desiring a high school education could obtain it in an out-of-town school, and have their tuition paid by their own town." Clark, *Chester Scrapbook,* 79.

138  **Old Homes of Chester, Connecticut:** Theodore Foster (author), Gertrude C. Lowe, ed., *Old Homes of Chester, Connecticut* (West Haven: Church Pr., O. K. Walker, publisher, 1936). From unnumbered page within "Historic Sketch" section written by Gertrude Lowe, ed.

139  **coeducational:** Wesleyan University, founded in 1831 for men, admitted women from 1872 to 1909. The university began admitting women again in 1970.

140  **churchgoers:** There is no mention of religious affiliation in Frank's biographical entry in *Beers 1903,* in which most biographical entries include one. In this book, Sarah is described as "of staunch Presbyterian stock" (*Beers 1903,* 751), yet the only connection I can find to a church in Connecticut is their 1878 marriage listed under the East Haddam Congregational Church (*Connecticut, U.S. Church Record Abstracts, 1630–1920, Volume 025 East Haddam,* 212.) At some point after Frank and Sarah moved to Massachusetts in 1903, they joined the Christ Episcopal Church in Sheffield, Massachusetts, where they and their children attended. A June 28, 1906, article in the *Pittsfield Sun* (Pittsfield, Massachusetts) reads: "The ladies of Christ Church will meet with Mrs. Frank P. Smith at Ashley Falls today."

141  **1899:** "Simsbury," *Hartford Courant,* July 20, 1899.

142 **Balen:** James D. Balen (1834–1916) was a Moodus resident, a Civil War veteran, and a member of Ulysses's orchestra. In 1902, he was 68.

143 **Law and Order League of Connecticut:** "A Brief History of the Connecticut State Police," Connecticut State Police Museum History, accessed March 31, 2019, cspmuseum.org.

144 **misrepresenting the facts:** Rev. Harold Pattison, "Who Want [sic] to Have Its Charter Repealed?" *Hartford Courant,* March 20, 1899.

145 **"bitter against the league.":** Ibid.

146 **"permitted.":** *Parker's,* 157c.

147 **Connecticut's Fife & Drum Tradition:** Clark, *Tradition,* 118–119.

148 **Rathbun Free Memorial Library**: *Connecticut Valley Advertiser,* June 26, 1931. Bigelow, *Scrapbook.*

149 **mail carrier**: Merton is listed as a mail carrier in the US Census for East Haddam, Connecticut, May 1910.

150 **cancers began:** Nigel Hawkes, "A Comprehensive History of Cancer Treatments," June 4, 2015, Raconteur.net.

151 **"Smith.":** *Berkshire County Eagle* (Pittsfield, Massachusetts), August 7, 1907, 15.

152 **Norwich University:** "Ashley Falls," *Berkshire County Eagle* (Pittsfield, Massachusetts), July 1, 1908, 16.

153 **Williams:** Jennie Williams (1888–1974) was 21 at the time of this article in 1909. She was a teacher living with her mid-80-year-old grandparents, her parents, and her siblings near Comstock Bridge on Moodus Road in East Hampton, where she grew up. Jennie's name continues to appear in articles about Ulysses's musical events for several years. She was a frequent Westbrook visitor, and she likely performed as a pianist with Ulysses for the cottagers in Westbrook. Jennie never married. At times during her life, she lived with her brother Edgar D. Williams, who became a prominent East Haddam figure, founding Williams Chevrolet in East Haddam Village near Goodspeed Opera House, of which he was also a founder. The Williams family later purchased a cottage in West Beach next door to the Cook/Smith cottage.

154 **Ashley Falls:** "Ashley Falls," *Berkshire County Eagle* (Pittsfield, Massachusetts), November 24, 1909, 13.

155   **Godfrey Memorial Library:** "Historic Middlesex County Book Project," Godfrey Memorial Library Online, the internet branch of Godfrey Memorial Library. Godfrey.org.

156   **worst mining disaster in American history:** In December 1907, a coal mine explosion took the lives of 362 workmen. Wikipedia's "Timeline of the United States (1900–1929)" entry, accessed July 14, 2021.

157   **Sheffield Historical Society:** The Sheffield Historical Society and the Mark Dewey Research Center are located at 159–161 Main Street in Sheffield, Massachusetts. Documents, sincere interest, and patience were provided by James (Jim) R. Miller, Archivist at the Mark Dewey Research Center.

158   **newspaper article:** *Berkshire County Eagle* (Pittsfield, Massachusetts), November 27, 1913, 13.

159   **years:** On April 10, 1906, a Bond for License was issued and signed by Frank and Fred as principals. It reads: "We, Frank P. Smith and Frederick A. Smith as 'Maplewood Inn' at Ashley Falls, Mass. in the Town of Sheffield and County of Berkshire as Principal and the National Surety Company … as Surety, are held and firmly bound unto the Treasurer of the Town of Sheffield, in the sum of One Thousand Dollars [about $28,800 in 2020], to which payment, well and truly to be made, we bind ourselves and our legal representatives. The condition of this obligation is that, if the above-bounden Principal, this day licensed by the Board of Selectmen for the Town of Sheffield in the County of Berkshire to sell intoxicating liquors in the said Town shall well and truly comply with all the provisions of law under which he has been so licensed, and shall also pay all costs, damages and fines which may be incurred by a violation of the provisions of Chapter 100 of the Revised Laws, then this bond shall be void, otherwise shall be in force."

160   **"Parkersburg, Va.":** *Berkshire County Eagle* (Pittsfield, Massachusetts), November 27, 1912.

161   **skates:** Joanna Prisco, "Most Popular Gifts in 1913 and 2013," December 9, 2013, abcnews.go.com.

162   **South Berkshire Directory:** "The Maplewood billed itself as 'American Motor League Official Hotel' in the 1907/1908 South Berkshire Directory." Bernard A Drew, *Spend a Summer in Shef-*

*field & Environs. The Tourism Trade in the Railroad Era* (Sheffield, Massachusetts: Sheffield Historical Society, 2003), 34.

163 **"on a drinking spree.":** The *Merriam-Webster Dictionary* definition of the word *tear* in this context is "spree." The *Oxford English Dictionary* shows *tear* was used in 1896 to mean alcohol was involved. The OED, which includes examples of words in published sentences, uses an example of *tear* from *Harper's Magazine*, April 1896, which reads "Got me off a tear somehow, and by the time I was sober again the money was 'most gone."

164 **"Maplewood Inn.":** "Ashley Falls," *Berkshire County Eagle* (Pittsfield, Massachusetts), November 10, 1915, 14.

165 **sea:** Lyrics from ragpiano.com. Accessed November 6, 2021.

166 **pier:** For a good history of the West Beach pier, see *People and Places of West Beach* by Gail Colby (Westbrook, Connecticut, 2019), available at the Westbrook Library and the Westbrook Historical Society.

167 **Westbrook History Happenings and Hearsay:** Louise Chapman Dibble and Lynda Stannard Norton, editors, *Westbrook History Happenings and Hearsay.* (Westbrook, Connecticut: Westbrook Bicentennial Committee, 1976), 174.

168 **Set up on the pier**: "Westbrook Plans Big Celebration ... Plans are progressing rapidly for the great celebration in honor of the completion of the new pier on Saturday. Thousands of lanterns will decorate the pier, and the Chester Band and Westbrook Drum Corps will furnish the music from the pier. Ice cream, cake and candy will be plentiful, and preparations have been made to take care of the crowds which will doubtless throng the beach." *Hartford Courant*, August 10, 1910, 16.

169 **Westbrook Drum Corps**: Louise Chapman Dibble and Lynda Stannard Norton, editors, *Westbrook History Happenings and Hearsay.* (Westbrook, Connecticut: Westbrook Bicentennial Committee, 1976), 153.

170 **treasurer:** "Moodus News Items of Twenty-Five Years Ago," *Connecticut Valley Advertiser,* May 1937, 30. Bigelow, *Scrapbook.*

171 **1892:** Parker's, 143b.

172 **towns:** James Swift Rogers, *James Rogers of New London* (Boston: The Compiler, 1902), Section 592, and Johnson, *Three Quarters of a Century,* 70. Charles Rogers was editor of the *Connecticut Valley*

173     *Advertiser* in 1902. When the *New Era* newspaper bought the *Advertiser* in 1929, Charles became the Moodus correspondent.

173     **"parade.":** *Parker's,* 143a.

174     **Essence of Architecture in East Haddam:** George Fellner, *Essence of Architecture in East Haddam* (East Haddam, Connecticut: Stone Insights Books. 2019).

175     **Images of America: East Haddam:** Russell Shaddox, *Images of America East Haddam* (Charleston, S.C.: Arcadia Publishing, 2019).

176     **twenty years:** *Parker's,* 143b. Ulysses had gifted the land for Continental Hall to the Moodus Drum and Fife Corps in 1892, when it was built. In 1897, the corps deeded the land and the building to Ulysses, who took over the financial burdens.

177     **Zavodnick:** (1879–?) *Parker's,* 123, 143b; Fred Post,"Levine, Sam Pear and Moodus," *Hartford Courant,* February 18, 1998, 76; James M. Owens, "Meet Mr. Moodus," *Hartford Courant Magazine,* August 19, 1951, 4, 9. David Zavodnick kept the hall open for public entertainment after he purchased it in 1916. In 1921, he sold it to his brother, Max Zavodnick (1873–1952), who also kept the hall open. In the 1920s and 1930s, among other uses, the Moodus Meteors and the Moodus Noises basketball teams used the facility. But renovation was needed. In 1942, the 50-year-old building was condemned.

178     **"Berkshire County.":** "BIG LIQUOR RAID ON HOTEL IN SOUTHERN BERKSHIRE. 'Wet Goods' Secured Filled Two Motor Trucks — Maplewood Inn, the Victim," *Berkshire Eagle* (Pittsfield, Massachusetts), November 7, 1916, 2.

179     **Haddam:** "Saybrook Train Hits Haddam Man," *Hartford Courant,* Feb 21, 1917, 11.

180     **after expenses:** Bernard A Drew, *Spend a Summer in Sheffield & Environs. The Tourism Trade in the Railroad Era* (Sheffield, Massachusetts: Sheffield Historical Society, 2003), 5.

181     **Over there:** Lyrics.com, STANDS4 LLC, 2021. Accessed November 6, 2021.

182     **draft:** The Selective Service Act of 1917 initially authorized a selective draft of men between 21 and 31. The ages were soon changed to include those 18 to 45. Ulysses (71 in 1917) did not register for the draft, but in February 1917, he filled out a Military Census form.

183 ***battle:*** *Parker's,* 143a,d.

184 ***Europe:*** *Hartford Courant,* August 18, 1918, 1.

185 ***"wit.":*** *Berkshire County Eagle* (Pittsfield, Massachusetts), March 14, 1917, 15.

186 ***record:*** Massachusetts, Town and Vital Records, 1620–1988. Provo. UT.

187 ***great-grandchildren:*** F. Worthington Strong (1905–1974), Robert Smith (1906–1963), F. Abner Smith (1914–1994), Harold Franklin Smith (1916–1999), David Arnold Smith (1917–2002), Margaret Louise Smith (1917–2003), and Donald Ulysses Smith, Jr. (1918–1984).

188 ***mid-October:*** David Drury, "The Spanish Influenza Pandemic of 1918," September 20, 2020, Connecticuthistory.org.

189 ***"day.":*** *Parker's,* 143a.

190 ***virus:*** Tasha Caswell, "Eighty-Five Hundred Souls: the 1918–1919 Flu Epidemic in Connecticut." December 12, 2015. Connecticuthistory.org.

191 ***died:*** *Hartford Courant,* May 19, 1919, 15. The first East Haddam boy to die in service was Louis Yindar. He was killed in France on October 23, 1918. His brother was severely wounded and spent 6 months in the hospital.

192 ***Moodus:*** Mrs. Arthur W. (Emma) Chaffee (1856–1938) of Moodus was a prominent leader in the local and state WCTU, DAR, and Equality League. Her husband was on the state board favoring prohibition. Apart from living fairly near one another, and Mr. Chaffee managing the New York Net and Twine Company across the street from Georgiana, I find no connections between the two women. The *Hartford Courant* reported on May 15, 1919: "Equality Leagues will meet with Mrs. A.W. Chaffee," and on November 19, 1919: "Mrs. Arthur Chaffewwe to speak on Social Purity in Essex."

193 ***years:*** Sievers, *Mills,* 55–56.

194 ***September:*** "Big Industrial Deal in Moodus," *Hartford Courant,* March 14, 1919, 16; and "Moodus Mill to Run Again after Two Year's Idleness," *Hartford Courant,* September 17, 1919, 5.

195 ***"former high estate":*** *Hartford Courant,* June 15, 1919, 36.

196 ***sold:*** On June 10, 1910, the North Moodus Road house and lot was

sold to Joe Attkess of New York City. He paid $1,000 to "Lucinda Smith and Frank P. Smith (of Ashley Falls, Massachusetts), Edgar C. Smith (of Old Saybrook, Connecticut), E. Georgiana Cook and Ulysses S. Cook (of East Haddam, Connecticut)." East Haddam Land Records, Volume 45, 222.

197   **invented:** The term *early adopter*, which means being one of the first customers of a new product, was coined in 1962 by Everett M. Rogers in his book, *Diffusion of Innovations (NY, NY; The Free Press, 1962)*.

198   **"cottage.":** Note that this article, written in 1937, now refers to the cottage as the Smith Cottage, not the Cook Cottage. Georgiana had died in 1930, leaving the cottage to Smiths.

199   **women:** "Making Voters. The Selectmen and Town Clerk of the Town of East Haddam will be session at the Town Clerk's office on Saturday October 9th, 1920, from 10 A.M. until 5 P.M. for the purpose of admitting as Electors those persons who shall be found qualified and whose names appear on the lists of the registrar's under title 'To be made.' They will also be in session at the Probate Office in Moodus on Saturday Oct 16 from 9 o clock A.M. until 5 o clock P.M. for the same purpose. They will also be in session at the Town Clerk's office on Tuesday Oct 19 from 10 A.M. until 8 o clock P.M. as the last day of Making Voters for the November 2nd Election of 1920. [signed] Wm W. Gates, Charles C. Sanford, Eugene B. Peck, Selectman. M. H. Watrous, Town Clerk. East Haddam, October 1, 1920." [Then this entry] "Pursuant to above notice the 3 meetings were held and Electors were found qualifying and duly recorded in the Electors book as follows: Total number 237 of which 29 were men and 207 were women. [I realize the math is off by 1]. Attest M. H. Watrous. October 20, 1920." *Admission of Electors, Vol. 1858–1961 Part II*. October 20, 1920. Records are housed at the East Haddam (Connecticut) Town Hall.

200   **were able to:** The 39 percent was estimated as follows: 207 women registered of the estimated 531 women who were 21 and over in the 1920 East Haddam census. The 531 was estimated assuming that 50 percent of the 2,312 East Haddam residents in the census were women and 46 percent of the residents in the census were 21 or over. The 50 percent and 46 percent estimates were derived

from census counts for the State of Connecticut and US Census Bureau, "General Characteristics Connecticut. Table 14 — Race by Sex, for the State, Urban and Rural, 1950, and for the State, 1880 to 1940," and "General Characteristics Connecticut, Table 16 — Age by Color, and Sex for the State: 1880 to 1950," www2.census.gov/library/publications/decennial/1950/population, accessed July 14, 2021.

201 **1916:** *Admission of Electors, Vol 1858–1961 Part II*, November 7, 1916 [results announced by the Moderator, Everett E. Swan], and November 2, 1920 [results announced by Moderator, Charles H. Rogers.] Records are housed at the East Haddam (Connecticut) Town Hall.

202 **44 percent:** The 44-percent increase is based on the 1916 total number of votes of 18,537,000, compared to the 1920 total number of votes of 26,750,000, representing an increase of 8,213,000 votes. Vote totals taken from Wikipedia's entries of "1916 United States Presidential Election," and "1920 United States Presidential Election," accessed July 14, 2021.

203 **men:** Anna Csar, "How many women voted in 1920 presidential Election?" (in response to Darren Cole) Historyhub.history.gov/thread/3568, March 11, 2019. This source cites three Wikipedia entries "Women Suffrage in the United States," "1920 United States Presidential Election," and "Nineteenth Amendment to the United States Constitution."

204 **Record of Voters, East Haddam:** *Record of Voters, East Haddam 1899–1926*. Housed at the East Haddam (Connecticut) Town Hall.

205 **September:** A few women, presumably the leaders in the women's suffrage activities in East Haddam, registered to vote on September 18, 1920, before the three October sessions were announced. Among them were Elizabeth Brainerd, Emma Chaffee, Helen Fowler, Phoebe Rogers, and Juliette Williams, and other names that have appeared in Georgiana's story.

206 **reason:** "The Woman's Vote in National Elections." In *Editorial Research Reports 1927*, vol. II, 413. Washington, DC: CQ Press, 1927. http://library.cqpress.com/cqresearcher/csresrre1927053100

207 **Westbrook Historical Society:** Westbrook Historical Society, 1196 Boston Post Road, Westbrook, Connecticut.

208 **nine years**: This is a typo made by the newspaper. Ulysses was

nine **weeks** old. *Beers 1903,* 846.

209 **East Haddam:** Russell Shaddox, *Images of America: East Haddam* (Charleston, S.C.: Arcadia Publishing, 2019), 99.

210 **Westbrook:** *Hartford Courant,* July 25, 1926, 19. Lillie, Merton, and Doris stayed at the Hersie cottage on Post Avenue, Westbrook.

211 *paralyzed:* "Merton H. Lee, 72, who lost one leg through an infection and was stricken with polio 30 years ago [1925]—leaving stomach and back paralyzed—learned how to operate a car equipped with amputee's driving apparatus and has built up a paying sales route. Housewives help out by doing business with him through the car door." *The Boston Globe,* August 16, 1955, 36.

212 **Thanksgiving:** "Mr. and Mrs. Merton H. Lee of New Haven were guests of Dr. and Mrs. U. S. Cook over the weekend." *Hartford Courant,* November 25, 1924, 9.

213 **nine years:** This is typo of newspaper. Ulysses was nine **weeks** old. *Beers 1903,* 846.

214 *"welfare.":* *Parker's,* 143b.

215 *ball:* Lyrics.com. STANDS4 LLC, 2021. Accessed November 6, 2021.

216 *"Smith.":* *Connecticut Valley Advertiser,* January 8, 1926. Bigelow, *Scrapbook.*

217 *"family.":* "Mrs. Cook Dies after Long Illness." *Connecticut Valley Advertiser,* October 7, 1930. Bigelow, *Scrapbook.*

218 **Simpson:** Henry B. Fielding (1871–1958), George O. Fielding (1873–1952), and Edgar P. Simpson (1868–1937) were members of the Fielding family who had been Falls Road neighbors of Georgiana for many years. Henry and George were sons, and Edgar was a son-in-law (married to Effie Fielding), of Henry and Mary Fielding who, as their children were growing up, had lived one house away from Georgiana and Ulysses on Falls Road in Moodus. The Fielding parents had both passed away. The Fielding children were likely friends of Lillie, who was approximately their age. Lillie may have arranged the service in Moodus and called on her Fielding family friends to be pallbearers. Henry and George had played in the Moodus Drum and Fife Corps when Ulysses was leader. Henry, George, Effie, and two other Fielding siblings

likely knew the Cook house and Georgiana well.

219 **Richmond:** Charles Richmond (1867–1940) was 63 when he served as Georgiana's pallbearer. He had known her all his life. He was 18 years younger than her and lived a couple houses away from her on North Moodus Road. As an adult, Charles worked in one of the general stores in Moodus Center, where he would have seen Georgiana frequently. He also belonged to Moodus Methodist Episcopal Church, which Georgiana attended. Charles's wife Abbie (born Stevens) (1879–1914) died in her mid-thirties, and Charles never remarried. He lived near Georgiana and Ulysses' good friends, Charles and Phoebe Rogers.

220 **"outside the home.":** Janet L. Yellen (1946–), United States Secretary of the Treasury, 2021. "The history of women's work and wages and how it has created success for us all." brookings.edu, May 2020.

221 **1937:** Sandra (born Fournier) Galloni (1937–2017).

222 **Billy:** William Worthington Demiris, born November 25, 2017, of Westbrook, Connecticut, is Georgiana's great-great-great-grandnephew.

# Selected Bibliography

*Sources selected for this bibliography are sources used multiple times. Sources used one time are included only in Chapter Notes.*

### BOOKS

Alcott, Louisa May. *Little Women.* Boston: Roberts Brothers, 1868/1869.

Beers, J.B. & Co., *History of Middlesex County, Connecticut, with Biographical Sketches of its Prominent Men.* New York: J.B. Beers & Co., 1884.

Beers, J.H. & Co., *Commemorative Biographical Record of Middlesex County, Connecticut: Containing Biographical Sketches of Prominent and Representative Citizens, and of Many of the Early Settled Families.* Chicago: Beers, J.H. & Co., 1903.

Bigelow, Mary S., *Scrapbook of Connecticut Valley Advertiser clippings 1924-1938, 2.* Local History Archives, Rathbun Free Memorial Library, East Haddam, Connecticut.

Boni, Margaret Bradford, ed., *Songs of the Gilded Age.* New York: Gold Press, 1960.

Borst, Ruth Wilson, *A Turn-of-the-Century Child.* Framingham, Massachusetts: Wendover Press, 1979.

Campbell, Susan. *Tempest Tossed, the Spirit of Isabella Beecher Hooker.* Middletown, Connecticut: Wesleyan University Press, 2013.

Chapman, Horatio Dana. *Civil War Diary of a Forty Niner.* Hartford, Connecticut: Allis, 1929. The Connecticut State Library lists this diary in their collection as follows: *Civil War diary. Diary of a forty-niner.* Chapman, Horatio Dana, 1826-1910; Price, Carl F. Hartford, Conn. Allis 1929. Available at Connecticut State Library Stacks E601.C35.1929. (cscu-sdi-primo.hosted.exlibrisgroup.com).

Clark, James. *Connecticut's Fife & Drum Tradition.* Middletown, Connecticut: Wesleyan University Press, 2011.

Clark, Thelma, ed. *Kate Silliman's Chester Scrapbook.* Chester, Connecticut: The Chester Historical Society, Inc., Assembled in 1953 and edited and revised in 1986.

Colby, Gail. *People and Places of West Beach.* Westbrook, Connecticut, 2019.

Dibble, Louise Chapman and Lynda Stannard Norton, editors, *Westbrook History Happenings and Hearsay.* Westbrook, Connecticut: Westbrook Bicentennial Committee. 1976.

Fellner, George. *Essence of Architecture in East Haddam.* East Haddam, Connecticut: Stone Insights Books. 2019.

Finson, Jon W. *The Voices That Are Gone: Themes in Nineteenth Century American Popular Song.* New York: Oxford University Press, 1994.

Fowler, Prof. F. C. *Life: How to Enjoy and Prolong It.* Philadelphia: Blake Publishing Company. 1896.

Griswold, Wick and Stephen Jones. *Connecticut River Ferries.* Charleston, S.C.: The History Press. 2018.

Jacobs, T. M. *Goodspeed's Folly.* United States of America. 1996.

Johnson, Curtis S., Compiler. *Three Quarters of a Century. The Life and Times in The Lower Connecticut Valley As Chronicled for Seventy-Five Years by The New Era.* Privately Printed. 1949.

Lehman, Eric D. and Amy Nawrocki. *The History of Connecticut Food.* Charleston, S.C.: American Palate, 2012.

Longley, Diane and Buck Zaidel. *Heroes for All Time.* Middletown, Connecticut: Wesleyan University Press, 2015.

Nelligan, Tom. *The Valley Railroad Story.* New York: Quadrant Press, Inc., 1983.

Niles, Hosford B. *The Old Chimney Stacks of East Haddam, Middlesex County, Connecticut.* New York: Lowe & Co. 1887.

Parker, Francis Hubert. *Contributions to the History of the Town of East Haddam, Connecticut, a compilation of newspaper articles written 1914–1927, originally published in Connecticut Valley Advertiser, Moodus, Connecticut.* Compiled in 1938.

*Record of Service of Connecticut Men in the Army and Navy of the United States During the War of the Rebellion.* Hartford: Case, Lockwood and Brainard, 1889. Accessed through Connecticut State Library, cslib.contentdm.oclc.org. Company C begins on page 697.

*Records of the Moodus Drum and Fife Corps, December 31, 1887, to October 3, 1892.* Reproduced in 1974 from the original records of the Moodus Drum and Fife Corps dating back to 1887. Courtesy of the East Haddam Historical Society.

Shaddox, Russell C. *Images of America: East Haddam.* Charleston, S.C.: Arcadia Publishing. 2019.

Sievers, Bruce R. *Mills along the River: The History of the Cotton Industry in Moodus, Connecticut.* East Haddam: East Haddam Historical Society, 1985.

Stofko, Dr. Karl P., and Rachel I. Gibbs. *East Haddam Connecticut: A History.* East Haddam: East Haddam Historic Commission, 1977.

OTHER SOURCES

Ancestry.com
Civil War Pensions Index
fold3.com
Church Records
   Connecticut, Church Record Abstracts, 1630-1920
   Moodus Methodist Episcopal Church Records
   Middletown's Christ Church, P. E. (Protestant Episcopal), also called the Church of the Holy Trinity

Connecticut Historical Society
Dictionary
   Merriam-Webster.com
Documentary Film
   Simon, Ken. Producer/Director of "Saving Land, Saving History" documentary series (2021) in collaboration with the East Haddam Historical Society and East Haddam Land Trust. Accessed at easthaddamhistory.org
Findagrave.com
Interviews
   Carle, Kandie (East Haddam. Conn.)
   Clark, James (East Hampton, Conn.)
   Colby, Gail (Westbrook, Conn.)
   Denette, Debra (East Haddam, Conn.)
   Doane, Catherine (Westbrook, Conn.)
   Fuller, Marcy (Westbrook, Conn.)
   Halpin, Marianne (East Haddam, Conn.)
   Miller, James (Sheffield, Mass.)
   Reuter, Priscilla Hall (Ashley Falls, Mass.)
   Shaddox, Russell (East Haddam, Conn.)
   Sievers, Bruce (East Haddam. Conn.)
   Smith, Fred (Ashley Falls, Mass.)
   Parker, Mia (Ashley Falls, Mass.)
   Winkley, Peggy and Travis (East Haddam, Conn.)
Lyrics
   Lyrics.com, STANDS4 LLC, 2021
Newspapers, accessed through Newspapers.com
   *Berkshire County Eagle* (Pittsfield, Mass.)
   *Boston Globe* (Mass.)
   *Daily Morning Journal and Courier* (New Haven, Conn.)
   *Hartford Courant* (Conn.)
   *Meriden Record* (Conn.)
   *New Haven Journal* (Conn.)
   *Norwich Bulletin* (Conn.)

Newspapers
  *Connecticut Valley Advertiser,* accessed at Rathbun Library, East Haddam, Conn.
  *East Haddam Advertiser,* accessed at Rathbun Library, East Haddam, Conn.
  *The New Era,* accessed at Deep River Historical Society, Conn.
Research Document
  Stofko, Dr. Karl P., East Haddam Municipal Historian, "Abner C. Smith 2nd of East Haddam," April 29, 2010
Speech
  Stofko, Dr. Karl P., East Haddam Municipal Historian, "Who's Buried in the Graveyard behind the Dr. Cook Place in Moodus?" to East Haddam Historical Society, November 10, 1999 (accessed at Rathbun Library, East Haddam, Conn.)
Town Records (Probate, Property, Tax, Voting), Town Historical Societies and Libraries
  Connecticut: Chatham/East Hampton; Chester; East Haddam; Rathbun Free Memorial Library; Essex; Haddam; Middlesex County Historical Society; Middletown; Old Saybrook; Portland; Westbrook
  Massachusetts: Massachusetts, Town and Vital Records, 1620-1988; Sheffield Historical Society and Mark Dewey Research Center
United States Census Bureau (census.gov)
Wikipedia.org

# Index

Acheson, Rev. Edward Campion, 312
Ackley and Smith (The Smackleys), 35–39
Ackley family in Tartia, 31, 112
Ackley, Delos, 33
Ackley, Elizabeth (born Spencer) (widow of Capt. Nathaniel Ackley), 6, 32
Ackley, George Buckley, 6, 32
Ackley, Isaac (adoptive father of Isaac Ackley Smith who was renamed Isaac Ackley, Jr.), 37–39
Ackley, Isaac, Jr. (adopted son of Isaac Ackley), 37–39
Ackley, John S., 124
Ackley, Nathaniel (Capt.), 6, 32
Ackley, Rebekah (born Cone), 37
Ackley, Rhoda A., 1, 6, 31–36, 58. *See also* Brainerd, Mother.
Ackley, Warren, 6, 32–33
Ackley, Washington S., 6, 162
*Age of Innocence* (Wharton), 196
Alcott, Louisa May, 76, 418
Allison's Drug Store, 384
Allopathy, 237
American Hotel, 162
American Ladies' Magazine, 42
*Anne of Green Gables* (Montgomery), 65
Anthony, Susan B., 160, 217

Anti-Saloon League, 276
Anti-suffrage, *see* Women's Roles and Rights, Anti-suffrage
Armistice Day, 382
Arnold, Benedict, 20, 189
Arnold, Davis Tyler (son of Horace and Sylvia Arnold), 1, 19, 56, 112, 178
Arnold, Elizabeth (born Wakeman), 18
Arnold, Elizabeth (firstborn daughter of Horace and Sylvia Arnold), 1
Arnold, Elizabeth (Georgiana's aunt) *See* Ventres, Elizabeth
Arnold, Horace (firstborn son of this name of Horace and Sylvia Arnold), 19, 46, 178
Arnold, Horace Edgar or Edgar Horace, (Georgiana's uncle), 1, 19, 41, 55, 79, 112, 178
Arnold, Horace Tyler (Georgiana's grandfather), 1, 3, 4, 18–19, 26, 55–56, 69, 112, 164, 178, 253–254, 271
Arnold, Joseph, 17–18, 20, 416
Arnold, Lucinda, *see* Smith, Lucinda (born Arnold)
Arnold, Susan, 55
Arnold, Sylvia (born White) (Georgiana's grandmother), 1, 3, 4, 18–19, 164, 178, 180, 253
Arnold, Thankful (born Clarke), 19–20, 416
Arthur, Chester A., 189
Ashley Falls (Sheffield), Mass., 319, 320–323, 326–327, 332–334, 336, 338–340, 344–345, 348, 351, 357–362, 369, 372–373, 374–376, 377–381, 383, 397, 400–401, 403, 407–408, 428–431
Attwood, Julius, 120, 419
Austen, Jane, 14, 247
*Awakening, The* (Chopin), 218
Baker, Albert, 359
Baker, Mr. and Mrs. E. B., 401
Baldwin, Simeon, 370
Balen, James, 313, 324, 429
Ballek, Anita (born Ackley), 36
Ballek's Garden Center (East Haddam, Conn.), 36

Barker (House) Hotel, 162, 250
Barker, Charles, 162
Barker, Mrs. Charles, 162
Barry, Michael, 226
Battle Flag Day, 156–157
Beckwith, Walter W., 191, 230, 382
Beecher, Catharine, 63–65, 134
Bicycle, 142, 210, 215–218, 220, 235, 286, 293, 370, 391, 424
Bishop, Lucy, 201, 348
Bissell, Nancy M., 161
Blackwell, Elizabeth, 46
Blizzard of 1888 (Great Blizzard of '88), 206, 271
Blue Back Square (Conn.), 63
Blue Cross, 383
Blue-backed Speller, 63
Boardman, Luther and family, 130, 148, 157, 196, 331
Bottomly, Frank, 318–319
Bowers, Carrie, 227, 230, 346, 365, 396, 403, 424
Bowers, George, 191, 230, 403
Brainard, Francis W. (Frank), 123–124
Brainard, Mary, 236, 423
Brainerd Academy, 423, 425
Brainerd, Aaron (Capt.), 46
Brainerd, Charles Edgar, 46
Brainerd, Charles Smith, 46
Brainerd, Elizabeth, 368, 397, 435
Brainerd, Juliette, 46, 68
Brainerd, Julius, 6, 32
Brainerd, Louisa F., 46, 68
Brainerd, Mother, 111. *See also* Ackley, Rhoda A.
Brainerd, Rhoda (born Ackley), *see* Ackley, Rhoda A.
Brainerd, Sylvia (born Arnold) (also Mrs. Warren Pardee), 46, 68–69
Broeck, Mrs. L. K., 339
Brooks, Mary B. (born Wright), 347

Brooks, Simeon S., 347, 366
Brooks's Orchestra (Chester, Conn.), 234
Brown, Elizabeth (born Chapman), 233
Brown, Mr. and Mrs. W. A., 401
Brown, Thomas S., 233–234, 423
Brown, William, 124
Brownell, Crary, 177
Buell, George Rinaldo, 124, 190, 424
Bulkeley, Morgan Gardner, 219–220
Burns, John, 301
Burr, Frances Ellen, 134
Button, Abbie (born Cook), 308–309, 311
Button, Edward, 308, 311
Cancer, 47, 130, 146–148, 151, 170–172, 237, 329–330, 335–336, 365, 401, 405–406, 417, 420, 429
Card, Stanton, 175
Carle, Kandie, 129, 420
Carnegie Hall, 220
Carroll, Harry, 363
Carroll, Thomas H., 226
Cemetery in Cooks's yard, mystery of, 169–172
Chaffee family, 110–111, 386
Chaffee, Edward (manager of New York Net & Twine), 433
Chaffee, Emma (Mrs. Arthur W.), 433, 435
Champion House, 386
Chapman, David O., 124
Chapman, Fred or Frederick A., 99, 301
Chapman, Harold, 226–227, 346
Chapman, Horatio Dana, 106, 128, 148–149, 156, 191, 233–234, 372
Chapman, J. Wilbert, 226
Chapman, Mrs. J. W., 301
Chapman, Nathaniel, 60
Chapman, Odell M., 392
*Cheers* theme song, 273, 428
Chester Band, 347, 366, 431

Chester Driving Park Association, 269–270
Chester Hotel, 249–250, 252–253, 261, 265, 279. *See also* Chester House.
Chester House, 180, 253–254, 256–261, 265–268, 271, 273, 275, 277–286, 288–291, 297–298, 304, 312–318, 336–337, 347, 352, 406. *See also* Chester Hotel.
Chloral, 252, 426–427
Chopin, Kate, 218
Christmas, 22, 70, 91, 103, 307, 337, 359
Christmas hymns, 70
Church socials, 185–188, 205
Church, Ezra G., 286
Churches
    Moodus Methodist Episcopal Church, 69, 92, 112, 137, 176, 185–187, 232, 297, 301, 368, 437
    St. Stephen's Episcopal, 297, 330–331
    Christ Episcopal Church in Sheffield, 334, 428
    Chatham Congregational Church, 131
    First Church of Christ Congregational Church in East Haddam, 127, 185–186, 345–346, 400
    First Congregational Church of Haddam, 41, 178
    Middletown Christ Church, P.E. (Church of the Holy Trinity), 296, 441
Citizens' Band of Ivoryton, 324
Civil War, Chapter 3 *passim*
    Atlanta, battle of, 104
    Bentonville, battle of, 105
    Chancellorsville, Va., battle of, 104, 419
    Fort Sumter, battle of, 73
    Gettysburg, battle of, 86–87, 104, 372, 419
    Gettysburg, battle of, Fiftieth Anniversary, 372
    Goldsboro, N.C., 105–107
    The Rebellion, beginning of, 73, 420
    Savannah, battle of, 104
    Sherman's March to the Sea, 102, 104

Civil War, *continued*
   20th Connecticut Volunteer Regiment, 74-75, 103, 106, 108, 156
   Veterans, Relief Council, Order of United American Mechanics, 302
Civil War Widow's Pension, 113, 119-120, 122, 423
Clark, Allie, 402
Clark, Benjamin Frank, 376
Clark, Mr. and Mrs. Samuel P., 361
Clark, Nellie E., 368
Clark, Samuel P., 301
Clarke, Henry, 113
Clarke, Louisa Fidelia (born Brainerd), 179
Cleveland, Grover, 228
Clevonshire, James Edward, 226
Cohan, George M., 225, 377
Comstock, W. J., 230
Comstock, Wilbur S., 124, 190
Cone, Frank, 324
Cone, J. Herbert, 226
Cone, John, 324
Cone, Joseph A., 226
Cone, R. R., 301
Cone, William, 190
Connecticut Ancient Fife and Drum Corps, 153
Connecticut River, 16, 17, 21, 90, 96, 117, 143-144, 183, 192-193, 198, 229, 249-252. 295, 369, 370, 371, 426
   Swing Bridge, *see* Swing Bridge (East Haddam Swing Bridge)
Connecticut River ferries, *see* Ferries
Connecticut schools, 59-66
Connecticut Spirit of '76 ensemble, 329
Connecticut State Capitol Hall of Flags, 156
Connecticut State Library, 60, 186, 415, 440-441
Connecticut Valley Railroad, *see* Railroads, Connecticut Valley Railroad (Valley Railroad)

Continental Hall (Moodus, Conn.), 230–232, 245–246, 300, 302, 304, 337, 372–373, 378–379, 406, 432
Cook, Elizabeth B. (born Strickland), 129, 131, 163, 171, 180, 401, 405
Cook, Ella Georgiana. *See* Cook, Georgiana (born Smith)
Cook, Georgiana (born Smith), *passim*
    Birth of, 1, 45
    Chester House, 289, 316
    Civil War, Chapter 3 *passim*
    Dancing school, 83–84, 100
    Death of, 408–409
    Estate of, 407, 413
Cook, Georgiana (Smith) and Ulysses S., 119 and onward *passim*
    Adoption of Lillie, 179–181
    Building of Moodus home, 167–169
    Social events, 157–158, 185–188, 190, 192–195, 213, 226, 229, 345
    Wealth of, 196–197
    Wedding, 127
    Wedding anniversary (56th), 399–402
Cook, Henry C., 306–309
Cook, Henry Evelyn, 117, 124, 129–132, 163, 169–172, 400–401, 402, 405
Cook, John S., 307
Cook, Margaret Pamela (born Ackley), 307
Cook, Mary (born Ackley) (third wife of Dr. Henry C. Cook), 306
Cook, Mrs. A.D., 324
Cook, Sarah, 129, 171
Cook, Sarah/Sally (born Clarke), 132, 307
Cook, Selden, 132, 168–169
Cook, Silas, 117, 119–122. *See also* Cook, Ulysses S.
Cook, Ulysses S., 2, 119 and onward *passim*
    Blackfishing in Westbrook, 235–236
    Continental Hall, 246
    Death of, 405

Cook, Ulysses S., *continued*
   Moodus Cornet Band, 226
   Moodus Drum and Fife Corps musical director, 122–124, 228, 328–329, 405
   Name change, 122, 124
   Orchestra, 227
   Physician, Dr. Cooks Infirmary, 146–148, 172, 237, 329–330
Cooley House (Hotel) (Westbrook, Conn.), 203, 234, 305, 425
Cowdery, Sarah (born Ackley), 6
Crocker, Olive, 346
CWSA, *see* Women's Roles and Rights, Connecticut Woman Suffrage Association (CWSA)
D. U. Smith and Brother (Ashley Falls marble quarry), 361
Dacre, Harry, 215
Daisy (ice cream truck), 414
Daughters of the American Revolution (DAR), 238, 385
Davison factory (mill), 21
Davison, Roswell, 21
Death and Disease Near Baby Georgiana, 47–49
Death during childbirth, 33, 45, 102
Death of children, 47–49
Death, causes of in the U.S., 47–49, 334–336
Decker, Myron, 358
Decoration Day, 137, 191–192, 228, 232, 304, 327–328, 366, 372, 420
Deep River Drum Corps, 234
Deep River Hose Company, 315
Demiris, Annie (Smith) (Daughter of Peter and Claire Smith), 8, 410
Demiris, William (Billy) Worthington, 327, 410, 437
Devil's Hopyard (Conn.), 387
Dibble, Harriett (Hattie), see Smith, Harriett (Hattie) (born Dibble)
Dickinson family, 68, 121, 178, 417
Dickinson, Edwin A., 46
Dickinson, Emily, 121

Dickinson, Jerusha Abigail (born Arnold) (Georgiana's Aunt), 41, 46
Doane, Elizabeth (born White), 3, 56
Dodge, Mrs. Norman, 309
Donaldson, Walter, 24–25
Donation Suppers, 92–93
Dorcas Society of the Moodus Methodist Episcopal Church, 368–369
*Downton Abbey* (television program), 271
Dr. Rudolphe's Specific Remedy, 239–241, 244
Drown, W.C., 301
*Drunkard, The,* a.k.a. *Vice and Virtue,* play, 158, 421
Dugan, Mrs. Paul, 401
Dunbar (Ashley Falls), 358
Duxbury, Rev. J. E., 301
East Haddam (Conn.) schools, 59–66, 116, 176, 331
East Haddam Advertiser (Advertizer), 157, 443
East Haddam Company H, Sixth Regiment, Connecticut Home Guards, 378
East Haddam Historical Society, 34, 68, 152, 169, 173, 190, 229, 416–419, 422
East Haddam Swing Bridge, *see* Swing Bridge (East Haddam Swing Bridge)
East Haddam, Conn., settling of, 17, 117
Eighteenth Amendment (Prohibition), 255, 322, 376, 384. *See also* Prohibition
Eldredge, Rev. C.L., 301
Ella, name, 57–58
Elliott J. Rogers, 214
Ellis, Rev. James S., 334
Elmer (judge), 281
Emily, C. H., 301, 407
Emily, George Q., 300
Emmons, Egbert, 279–280, 286–288
Emmons, Frank, 54

Evans, George, 225, 305
Falkner's Island (Conn.), 236
Falls Mill, 173–174, 386
Ferrer, Charles (Chas.), 348–349
Ferrer, Mr. and Mrs. Charles, 359
Ferries
    Chester–Hadlyme ferry, 143, 250–251, 295, 371
    Goodspeed's ferry (from Goodspeed's Landing to Tylerville), 68, 111, 143, 251, 295, 370
    Warner's Ferry, 250
Ferris Wheel, 210
Ferry, Henry, 358
Fielding, George O., 409, 436
Fielding, Henry B., 409, 436
Flag Day, 369–370
Fleming, Sir Alexander, 50
Fort Sumter, 73
Fourth of July (Independence Day), 8, 22, 42, 124, 304, 341, 381, 414
Fowler, Frank Chester, 198, 220, 226, 230, 239–245, 275, 406, 423, 426
Fowler, Frank Mrs. (first), 244
Fowler, Frank Mrs. (second), 244
Fowler, Helen (Mrs. Oscar Percival), 368, 385, 396, 435
Fowler, Oscar P., 244
Framingham Normal School (Mass.), 65
Fuller, Lucy, 65
G. Fox (Hartford), 214
Gates, Mrs. M., 368
Gates, Mrs. W. W., 368
Gay Nineties, 206, 209–210
Georgiana, name, 57–58
Georgiana, *see* Cook, Georgiana (Smith)
Georgiana Boat Sign, 8, 10–12
Germania Hotel, (Hotel Middlesex), Middletown, 285

Gilded Age, 141–144, 150, 161, 196, 242, 420, 436, 439
*Gilded Age, a Tale of Today* (Twain), 144
Gillette Castle, 371
Gillette, William, 371
Gilman, Charlotte Perkins, 218
Gladding, Gertrude E., 312
Glendenning, Harold, 339
Glendenning, Mr. and Mrs. Harold, 359
Glenroy, James Richmond, 342
*Godey's Lady's Book* (Hale), vii, 41, 127
Goldsboro, N.C., cemetery, *see* Civil War: Goldsboro, N.C.
Goodspeed Opera House, 21, 136, 143–144, 192–194, 197, 206, 228, 293, 370–371, 420, 427, 429
Goodspeed, William H., 130, 143, 148, 194, 197–198, 242, 420
Grand Trotting Event, 275
Grant, Ulysses S., 108, 121–122, 135, 160
Graveyard, Dr. Cook's Moodus, 169–172
Great Depression, 408, 413
Great War, 322, 373, 376–380, 382–383, 385, 391–392
Gridley, Bessie, 311
Griswold, Florence, 134
Grundshaw, Edward J., 191, 226
Haddam Historical Society, 20, 416
Haddam, Conn., settling of, 17–18
Haines, Frank E., 283
Hale, Sarah Josepha, 41–42, 417
Hall, Florence, 338
Hall, George, 301, 339–340
Hall, John (Ashley Falls), 339
Hanlon, Helen, *see* Smith, Helen (born Hanlon) (wife of Vernon Smith)
*Happy Days* (television program), 210
Hardy, John B., 277, 287
Harness racing, 242, 244, 269–270, 427
*Harper's Bazar*, 214, 232, 425

Harpers Ferry, Va., 79
*Harper's New Monthly Magazine,* 121
Harris, Charles K., 224, 406, 445
Harris, Henry C., 119–121
Harris, Nathanial Otis, 238–239
Harrison, Benjamin, 219, 228
Hartford Female Seminary (CT), 64
*Hartford Times,* 161, 402
Hatch's Band, 300
Hawley, Joseph R., 189
Heald, Helen M., *see* Smith, Helen (born Smith) (wife of Donald U. Smith, Sr.)
Heald, Robert, 359
Health care, improvements, 47, 49–50, 392
Heaton, James, 358
Hefflon, Fred, 230
Heins, F.W., 324
*Hello Dolly!* musical (Herman), 355–356
Hepburn, Katharine Martha Houghton, 134. *See also* Women's Roles and Rights, Connecticut Woman Suffrage Association
Hildebrandt, Hayley (Smith) (Daughter of Peter and Claire Smith), 410
Hills Academy (Essex, Conn.), 117
Hooker, Isabella (born Beecher), 65, 134, 160–161, 196, 350, 420
Hooker, Thomas, 160
Hoover, Herbert C., 378
"How and Where I Learned to Drum," poem (Mietzner), 328–329
Howe, Julia Ward, 137
Hungerford, E.C., 288
Hurricane of 1938, 204, 413
Hyde's shoe last factory, 40–41
*It's a Wonderful Life* (Capra), 176, 405–406
Illuminations, annual event in Westbrook, 202–204, 234, 324–325, 338, 346–347, 355, 365, 381, 383, 392–395

Independence Day (Fourth of July), *see* Fourth of July
 (Independence Day)
Jagger, Mick, 223
Jenkins Up, 276
Johnson family (Moodus), 148, 176, 186
Johnson, E. Emory (younger), 176, 197
Johnson, Mrs. E. Emory, 186
Johnson, Emory (elder), 175–176
Johnsonville (Conn.), 174–177, 197, 422
Joiner, Henry, 358
Jollification, 220, 228, 233
*Kate Silliman's Chester Scrapbook* (Clark, ed.), 254, 261–262, 269,
 271, 289, 427
Keith's Moving Pictures, 342
Kellogg, Martin David, 162
Kidd, Captain, 235
Kinne, Clarence, 376
Knights of Labor, 24, 195
Labensky, Henry, 327, 426
Labensky, Minnie, 346
Ladies Benevolent Society (Moodus Methodist Episcopal
 Church), 186–187, 205, 232, 304
*Ladies' Home Journal,* 183
Law and Order League of Connecticut, 276–290, 314, 316–318,
 428–429
LeCrenier, Giles P., 226, 242, 407
Lee, Doris H., 340, 301, 402
Lee, Fanny (born Martin) (Mrs. Joseph Lee), 331–332
Lee, Joseph, 331–332
Lee, Lillie Belle (born White), 178–181, 183, 186–187, 189, 197, 205,
 206, 211, 214, 218, 227, 232–233, 236, 260, 296, 304–305,
 312–313, 330–332, 337, 340, 346, 352, 386, 389, 401–404,
 406–407, 436
Lee, Merton Henry, 330–332, 340, 389, 401–404, 436

Lee, Robert E., 108
Leete, Mary E., 330
Lewis, Emily, 401
Lewis, Emory, 124
Lewis, Harold, 401
Lewis, Justice, 319
Liberty Loan, 380, 385
Lincoln, Abraham, 42, 70, 73, 108
    Thanksgiving, 42
Liquor Licensing Voting Record
    Ashley Falls, 321–322
    Chester, 257–259
Little Haddam Cemetery, 137
*Little Women* (Alcott), 76–77, 418
Long Island Sound, 12, 184, 198, 367, 379, 413, 425
Looby, Sylvester, 285
Lord, Daniel Chapman, 163
Lord, Elizabeth, 163
Lowell, Francis Cabot, 22
Lyman, Charles N., 106–107
Lyon, Mary, 310
Machimoodus House (Moodus, Conn.), 300
Maesing, Emma, 401
Manville, Ira, 358
Manville, Sarah E., 358
Maplewood Inn (Ashley Falls Hotel), 320–323, 332–334, 337–341, 357–362, 369, 373–375, 379, 381, 383, 397–398, 404, 407, 430–432
Maplewood Music Seminary (East Haddam), 239, 425
Martin, Rev. Jesse, 368
Mattatuck Drum Corps, 155, 383
McClair, S., 287
McGregor, Dougal, 358
McIntyre, Peter, 282–283
McLean Seminary (Simsbury), 288, 309–311

Meckensturm's Boot & Shoemaker, 423
Meigs, John Rufus, 283
Menunketesuck Island (Point) (Westbrook), 12, 208, 235, 364
Meriden Opera House, 304
Meriden (Conn.), 95–101, 114, 119, 221, 324, 361, 419
Middletown (Conn.), 64, 116, 143, 161, 199–201, 252, 259–260, 265, 274, 278–285, 288, 290–291, 293–298, 304, 309, 312, 316, 322–323, 349, 370, 401, 415, 419–420, 428, 432, bibliography
   High School, 298, 323
Mietzner, Peter, 328–329
Miller, Charles, 299–300
Miller, Eliza (born Wheeler), 299–301, 361
Millington (village in East Haddam), 25–26, 28–29, 54, 326, 387
Millington Historic District (East Haddam), 29
Mills
   Moodus, Twine Capital of America, 21, 144
   Neptune Twine and Cord Mill, 173–176
   New England mills, 24
   New York Net and Twine, 211, 386, 430
   Triton Mill, 175–176
   Unions, 24
   Mill girls, 21–23, 132
   Moodus mills, 173–177
   Lowell (Mass.) mills, 22–24
   Moodus mills, bells, 174, 176
   Moodus mills, child labor, 67–68, 418
   Moodus mills, Knights of Labor, *see* Knights of Labor
   Moodus mills, Moodus Reservoir, 173
Minkler, Frank A., 375–376
Miss Wells Seminary (Mass.), 311
Mitchell family, 148
Mitchell, Edward C., 402
Mitchell, Louis G., 226
Montgomery Ward catalog, 142, 420
Montgomery, Lucy Maud, 65

Moodus Celebration (July 4, 1871), 140–141, 157–159
Moodus Cemetery, 137, 171, 176, 192, 242, 406, 409
Moodus Center Fire (1906), 174, 327, 329, 352
Moodus Cornet Band, 192, 205, 225–227, 244, 327, 369
Moodus Dramatic Association, 157, 176
Moodus Drum and Fife Corps, 70, 122–124, 135–137, 151–155, 188–192, 228–230, 380, 405, 424, 436. *See also* Continental Hall.
    Dedication of the Washington Monument, 189
    Centennial celebration of 1775 Battle of Bunker Hill, 151–153
    Final performance at Decoration Day, 327
    Final performance of original members, 370
    Revolutionary War-era drumming, 328–329
    Uniforms, 152–155
    Westbrook visit, 1888, 201–202
Moodus Gun Club, 244
Moodus Library, 387
Moodus Music Hall, 195, 205, 346
Moodus Savings Bank, 384
Moodus, Catskills of Connecticut, 144
Moody, Mr. and Mrs. John, 339
Moody, Sarah Jane, *see* Smith, Sarah Jane (born Moody) (wife of Frank)
Mooney, John, 282
Moseley lot, 272
Moshier, Charles H., 226
Mott, Lucretia, *see* Women's Roles and Rights, Mott, Lucretia
Mount Hermon School (Mass.), 306
Mount Holyoke Female Seminary (College) (Mass.), 64, 310–311, 418
Mount Parnassus Burying Ground, 28–29
Murkett, Maggie (born Moody), 379
Murkett, Nehemiah, 379
*Music Man* (Willson), 136, 241, 270, 368, 420
Nathan Hale School House Celebration, 304, 327
Nation, Carrie, 285, 352

*Naugatuck Daily News,* 221
Nephritis, 408
*New Era* newspaper, 252, 262, 270, 426, 432
*New Guide to Health, or, Botanic Family Physician* (Thomson), 146, 421
New York Net and Twine, 211, 386, 433
Nightingale, Florence, 49–50
Niles, Hosford B., 176, 416, 425
Nineteenth Amendment (Women's Right to Vote), 160, 218, 385, 396, 435
Norton, Mrs., 329
Norwich University (Vt.), 333, 339, 341, 429
Oak Grove Stock Farm (Moodus, Conn.), 242, 244
Oak Grove Trotting Park, 275
Oberlin College (Ohio), 64
O'Connell, Jeremiah, 226
Odber, Mattie (born Burr), 201, 421–422
Odber, William E., 190, 201, 229, 421–423
Oldorf, J., 227
Olmstead or Olmsted, Albert E., 301
Oschmann, William J., 375
Pardee family, 68
Pardee, Harriett Ellen, 69
Pardee, Mrs. Warren, *see* Brainerd, Sylvia (born Arnold)
Pardee, Warren Washington, 46
Parker, Francis Hubert., 123, 170
Parker, John H., 324
Parker, Rev. and Mrs. Francis (East Haddam), 302, 345–346
*Parker's,* 123, 135, 151–152, 189, 211, 226–227, 231, 328, 336, 370, 382, 405, 420–425, 431–433
Parsons, Arthur C., 358
Patent drug, 239–242, 244–245
Pear, Bertha, 169–172
Pearne, W. U., 278, 280, 286
Percival, Helen (born Fowler), 368

Percival, Hezekiah W., 70, 118, 123–124, 154, 243
Percival, Mary, 243
Percival, Orville, 118, 123–124
Perkins, Edward Cook, 306–309
Perkins, Myron, 308
Phelps, Annie A., 309
Phelps, Harriet, 401
Pianos, 136, 138, 142, 181, 197–200, 206, 210, 223–224, 305, 312, 323, 342, 346, 348, 357, 365, 402, 406
Pochoug House (Hotel) (Westbrook), 235, 305
Pope Manufacturing Company, 215
Pope, Albert A., 215
Portland (Conn.), 117, 127, 129, 131–132, 170, 295, 400, 405
Post, Oliver R., 74
Powell, Bertha, 339
Pratt, Read and Company (Deep River, Conn.), 323
Prohibition, 158, 255, 257, 262, 265, 269, 318, 321–322, 374–376, 384, 385, 413, 420. *See also* Eighteenth Amendment (Prohibition)
Puerperal fever, 68
Purple and Silliman Dry Goods, 195, 231, 327, 384, 422
Purple family, 111, 148, 168, 195
Purple, Albert E., 168, 195–197, 198, 231, 327, 387, 422
Purple, Mr. and Mrs. David, 195
Purple, Mrs. W. S., 301
Purple, William S., 124
Purple's (grocery), 183, 195
Putnam Phalanx, 153
Queen Victoria, wedding of, 127, 312
Quotonsett Beach (Westbrook), 342
Railroad, 141, 144, 183, 233, 381
    Ashley Falls, 319
    Chester Station, 254, 271–273, 281, 298
    Connecticut Valley Railroad (Valley Railroad), 142–143, 156, 161, 198, 249, 315, 420
Raleigh, N. C., National Cemetery, 107

Rappahannock River, 89
Red Cross, 383, 385
Rich, George W., 226
Richmond, Charles C., 409, 437
Robbins, Rev. Silas W., 127, 400
Roberts, Henry, 369
Roberts, Dr., 347
Robinson, Silas Arnold, 260–261
Rogers, Charles H., 226, 230, 382, 402, 431, 435
Rogers, Mr. and Mrs. Charles H., 361, 369, 370, 437
Rogers, Phoebe (born Emmons), 369, 385, 396, 435
Rolf, Professor, 340
Rolling Stones, 413
Roosevelt, Teddy, 352
Rosenfeld, Monroe, 224
Sackett, William, 358
Saffrey, Robert, 286
Salt Island (Westbrook), 12, 235
Sanford, Walter B., 345
Schmitt, Raymond, 175
Seaview Hotel (Westbrook), 305, 425
Semes, Mr., 88–89, 419
*Sense and Sensibility* (Austen), 247
Sexton, Lyman R., 227
Shailer, Reverend Simon, 43, 417
Sheffield Historical Society, 357, 430–432
Sheppard, Abby, 67
Sheppard, Chester (born Sheperd), 67
Sheppard, Eunice, 68
Shields, Ron, 225, 305
Sievers, Bruce R., 24, 177, 415, 420–421, 430
Silliman, Alfred, 124
Silliman, Arthur, 195, 231
Silliman, F. W., 284
Silliman, Joseph E., 268–269, 287

Silliman, Kate, *see Kate Silliman's Chester Scrapbook* (Clark, ed.)
Silliman, Samuel C., 261–262, 268–269
Silliman, Thomas, 124
Silliman, William, 124
Simpson, Edgar P., 409, 436
Skinner, Nellie B., 149, 182
Skinnerville, Conn., 149
Slyne, James, 278–279
Small, William H., 392
Smallpox, 49, 95
Smith Farm Gardens (East Haddam), 7, 27, 29, 416
Smith, Abner C., 1, 3–6, Chapter 1–3 *passim*, 111–115, 118–121, 162, 185, 191, 254, 272, 332, 361, 401, 409
   Civil War: Chapter 3 *passim*
   Question of parentage, 31–36
   School tax collector, 62–63
   Soldiers' Monument, *see* Soldiers' Monument (Moodus Civil War Monument)
   Wounding and death of, 105–108
Smith, Abner Comstock (1796), 1, 5, Chapter 1 *passim*, 57, 66–68
Smith, Abner Comstock (1846), 5, 25–31, 66–67, 272
Smith, Asa, 36
Smith, Azariah (1786), 5, 35, 39
Smith, Calvin, 30
Smith, Candace, 5, 66
Smith, Charles, 5
Smith, Connie (born Dawe) (Mrs. Hal Smith), 413
Smith, David Arnold, 2, 408
Smith, Donald U. III, 75
Smith, Donald U., Jr., 2, 408
Smith, Donald U., Sr. (Georgiana's nephew), 2, 305, 248, 273, 296, 323, 339, 359, 361, 401, 407, 408, 433
Smith, Edgar C. (Charles Edgar) (Georgiana's brother), 1, 2, 56, 62, 66, 74, 103, 104, 113, 114, 116, 120, 128, 161, 243, 333, 340, 358, 359, 362, 401, 409, 417, 419, 434

Smith, Electa Brainerd (born Warner), 1, 5, 31, 33-34, 57-58, 272
Smith, Ella Georgiana, *See* Cook, Georgiana (born Smith)
Smith, Fluvia (born Ackley), 35
Smith, Franklin Pierce (Frank) (Georgiana's brother), 1,5,57, 66, 73,
    81, 101-105, 113-114, 116, 120, 128, 161-164, 180, 205, 243, 247,
    Chapter 9-10 *passim,* 357-362, 364, 373-376, 379, 381, 394,
    397, 399-401, 406-409, 411, 413, 419, 428, 430, 434
Smith, Frederick Abner, Sr. (Georgiana's nephew), 2, 206, 248,
    254, 260, 273, 275, 288, 296, 298, 313, 322-323, 325, 339, 341,
    348, 354, 359, 361-362, 374-375, 380, 394, 401, 407, 413, 430
Smith, Frederick Abner, Jr. (Ab), 2, 408
Smith, Frederick C. (Little Freddy) (Georgiana's brother), 1, 2, 55,
    57, 74, 80-81, 83, 112, 118-119, 243, 325
    Death of, 80-81
Smith, Georgia Cook (Georgiana's niece), *see* Strong, Georgia
    Cook (born Smith)
Smith, Harold Franklin (Hal), 2, 364, 408
Smith, Harriett (Hattie) (born Dibble), 2, 161, 358-359, 362, 397
Smith, Helen (born Hanlon) (wife of Vernon Smith), 2, 362, 378,
    380, 386, 394
Smith, Helen (born Smith) (wife of Donald U. Smith, Sr.), 2,
    359-362, 386, 394, 408
Smith, Henry C., 74
Smith, Hope (born Marshall), 5, 27, 31
Smith, Isaac Ackley (three with same name), 37, 39
Smith, Jeremiah, 5, 29-30
Smith, Jeremiah, Jr., 5
Smith, Julia, 5, 66
Smith, Kittie Louise (Georgiana's niece), 2, 205, 218-219, 271, 273, 275,
    288, 296-298, 312-313, 323, 331, 333-337, 344, 352, 364, 380
    Death of, 334-337
Smith, Lucinda (born Arnold), 1, 3-5, Chapter 1-4 *passim,* 132,
    163-164, 178, 180, 185, 205, 243, 248, 250-254, 260, 271-272,
    274-275, 288, Chapter 10 *passim,* 354, 357-362, 364, 379-380,
    383, 397, 401, 408-409, 416-417, 419, 420, 433

Smith, Lucinda (born Arnold), *continued*
   Civil War letters from Abner, Chapter 3 *passim*
   Death of, 380
   East Haddam Land Purchase, 271–272
   Moodus Mill Employee 21–23
   Thankful Arnold, relation to 19–20
   Widow's Pension 113, 119–120, 122
Smith, Margaret Louise, 2, 380, 433
Smith, Mary (Mae) Bertha (born Welch), 2, 359, 362, 386, 394, 407, 413
Smith, Matthew (1685–1751), 5, 28–30, 416
Smith, Matthew, Jr. (1722–1804), 5, 28–30
Smith, Peter Worthington, 12, 28, 327, 364, 410, 413
Smith, Robbins T., 5, 66–67
Smith, Robert, 2, 359, 362, 408, 433
Smith, Ruth or Ruthy (born Ackley), 5, 35, 39
Smith, Sarah (daughter of Peter and Claire Smith), 410, 413
Smith, Sarah (born Mack), 5, 28–30
Smith, Sarah Hill (born Rogers), 37, 39
Smith, Sarah Jane (born Moody) (wife of Frank), 2, 162–164, 180, 205, Chapter 9–10 *passim,* 354, 358–359, 364, 379, 381, 394, 397–401, 406–408, 428.
Smith, Temperance (b.1837), 5
Smith, Temperance Comstock (1764–1843), 5, 30
Smith, Temperance Comstock (1790–1812), 5, 35
Smith, Vernon Edgar (Georgiana's nephew), 2, 248, 274–275, 288–289, 293, 297–298, 313, 323, 333, 348, 351, 362, 364, 377, 380, 394
Smith, Watrous B., Jr., 36
Smith, Watrous Beckwith, 36–39
Snyder, Jane, 358
Soja, Louis and Helen, 170–172
Soldiers' Monument (Moodus Civil War Monument), 298–304, 327–328, 361, 372, 378

Songs
- "After the Ball" (Harris), 224, 406
- "Battle Hymn of the Republic" (Howe), 137
- "Before the Parade Passes By" (Herman), 355
- "By the Beautiful Sea" (Carroll, Atteridge), 363
- "Come Home, Father" (Work), 263–265
- "Daisy Bell (Bicycle Built for Two)" (Dacre), 215
- "How Ya Gonna Keep'em Down on the Farm?" (Donaldson), 24–25
- "In the Good Old Summertime" (Evans, Shields), 225, 304–305
- "Over There" (Cohan), 377
- "School Days" (Cobb and Edwards), 58
- "She Was Weeping as She Leaned against the River," 343
- "The Stars and Stripes Forever" (Sousa), 222–223, 399
- "When You Were Sweet Sixteen" (Thornton), 211
- "Ya Got Trouble" (Willson), 270

Sousa, John Philip, 136–137, 220–223, 227, 304, 399
Sousamania, 221–223
Spanish flu (1918), 381–383, 433
Spencer, Charles T., 227
Spencer, George, 348
Spencer, Mrs. T. R., 301
Spencer, Thaddeus R. (T. R.), 124, 226
Stannard, Russell, 318
Stanton, Elizabeth Cady, *see* Women's Roles and Rights, Stanton, Elizabeth Cady
State Liquor Dealers Association, 277
Stephens (Stevens), William Newell or Newel, 93
Stephens, Jonathan D., 93
Stephens, Rosetta (born Banning), 93
Stoddard (judge), 259
Stofko, Karl, 54, 169, 418–419
Stowe, Harriet Beecher, 64, 134, 419
Strawberry Festival (Moodus), 186, 205, 232, 304

Strickland family (Silas Cook's mother's family), 117, 131–132
Strickland, Elizabeth, *see* Cook, Elizabeth B. (born Strickland)
Strickland, Noah, 131
Strickland, Phebe (born Bement), 131
Strong, Charles Worthington, 311, 325
Strong, Frederick Worthington (Worth), 2, 325, 327, 340, 343, 348, 354, 359–362, 364, 388, 433
Strong, Georgia Cook (born Smith) (Georgiana's niece), 2, 164, 180, 248, 310-311, 313, 354, 361, 394, 404
Strong, John (Jack) Frederick, 2, 311, 360, 380, 404
Strong, Mr. and Mrs. J. F., 313, 338–340, 348, 360
Strong, Sarah (born Burghardt), 311
Swing Bridge (East Haddam Swing Bridge), 369–371
T. R. Spencer's store, 327
Talbot, Bernice William, 227
Tartia (Conn.), 16, 31–34, 41, 54, 58, 102, 110–112, 162, 326, 401
Teacherage, Moodus, 169–171
Temperance Movement, 158, 238, 256–260, 263–265, 269, 271, 276, 283–285, 316–318, 344–345, 352, 373–376, 384–385, 427.
    *See also* Prohibition
Temperance Plays, 158
Thankful Arnold House (Haddam), 19–20
Thanksgiving, 22, 41–42, 103, 260, 337, 339–340, 344, 348, 351, 358–359, 362, 373, 379–380, 383, 397, 404–405, 417, 436
Thanksgiving Day Parade, Macy's, 404
Thomas, Eugene B., 227
Thomas, William J., 226
Thomsonian System of Medical Practice (Thomsonian medicine), 130, 146, 149, 172, 237, 421
Thornton, James, 211
Thrasher, Samuel Powers, 280, 282, 287–288, 316
Thread City Continental Drum Corps, 392
Thurlow, Rev. E. R., 408
Tin Pan Alley songs, 142, 223–225, 305, 406
Tobias, Mr., 347

Treat, D. J., 191, 230
Trinity College (Conn.), 63
Truesdell (deputy sheriff), 345
Tucker, Sophie, 25
Turkey Hill boys, 74
Turkey Hill Cemetery (Haddam), 18, 178
Turkey Hill School (Haddam), 21
Turner, Sylvester, 268
Twain, Mark, 144
Tyler (deputy), 318–319
Tyler family, 68
Tyler, R. Clifford, 286
Typhoid fever, 48, 334–336, 344
Typhoid Mary, 334
Ulysses's orchestra, 227, 232, 327, 337, 340, 345–347, 365, 403, 429
*Uncle Tom's Cabin* (Stowe), 134
Uncle Washington, *see* Ackley, Washington S.,
Van Duesen, Levi, 358
Ventres, Daniel W., 96, 124
Ventres, Elizabeth (Lib, Elib) (born Arnold), 95–96, 419
Ventres, Fisk Brainard, 95
Veterans Day, 382
Victory Gardens, 378
Voting records of women in 1920, 395–397
    East Haddam, 395–397, 435
*Vice and Virtue* aka *The Drunkard* (Willson), play, see *Drunkard, The,* a.k.a. *Vice and Virtue,* play
*Vogue,* 214
W. C. Reynolds grocers, 370
Ward, Aaron Montgomery, 142. *See also* Montgomery Ward catalogue.
Warner Cemetery (East Haddam), 34
Warner, Barney, 280, 282
Warner, Electa Brainerd, *see* Smith, Electa Brainerd (born Warner)

Warner, Frederick, 57
Warner, Oliver, 57–58
Warner, Phoebe E. (born Moseley), 57
Washington Monument Dedication, *see* Moodus Drum and Fife Corps, Dedication of the Washington Monument
Washington, George, 153, 154, 328
    Continental Army uniforms, 153
Washington's Birthday, 41
Watrous, Frank (Chester), 315
Watrous, J. M. (Chester/grand juror), 283, 284
Watrous, M. H. (East Haddam Town Clerk, 330, 434
WCTU. *see* Women's Christian Temperance Union (WCTU)
Weaver, Carile (born Hosmer), 249
Weaver, Clinton, 249–250, 427
Weaver, Erastus, 249–250, 252, 256, 426
Webster, Noah, 63
Welch, Mae Bertha, *see* Smith, Mary (Mae) Bertha (born Welch)
Wesleyan Academy (Wilbraham Academy) (Mass.), 118–119, 176, 347, 401
Wesleyan University (Conn.), 63, 295, 301, 420–421, 428
West Beach (Westbrook Beach), Conn., 199, 200–205, 233–236, 324, 342–343, 346–347, 364–367, 390–394, 398, 413, 415, 425, 429, 431
    Cottage photos, 201, 354, 398. 410
    Fishing photo, 367
    West Beach Pier, 431, photo 366
Westbrook Drum Corps, 366, 431
Westbrook Historical Society, 366, 398, 431, 435
Westbrook Improvement Society, 343
Westbrook, Conn., 12, 161, 198–206, 208, 211, 229, 233–237, 245, 290, 293, 304–305, 312–313, 319, 324–327, 336, 338, 342–344, 346–348, 353, Chapter 11 *passim,* Chapter 12 *passim,* 410, 413, 415, 425, 429, 431, 436–437
    Westbrook Illumination, *see* Illuminations, annual event in Westbrook

Weston, Edith K., 348
Wharton, Edith Jones, 196
Wheeler family, 65, 111, 299, 340, 361
Wheeler, A. S., 392
Wheeler, Alfred, 80, 299, 419
Wheeler, Clarence, 299, 340
Wheeler, Frank, 299, 361
Wheeler, Mr. and Mrs. Clarence C., 340
White family, 68, 178
White, Jennie L., 179
White, Lillie Belle, *see* Lee, Lillie Belle (born White)
White, Louisa, 3, 179
White, Sylvia (later Sylvia Arnold), *see* Arnold, Sylvia (born White)
White, William (Sylvia White Arnold's brother and Lillie White's grandfather), 3, 178, 358
Whitman, Walt, 121
Wilbraham Academy (Mass.), *see* Wesleyan Academy
Wilcox, Charlotte C., 358
Wilcox, Samuel B., 154
Willard, Frances E., 265, 276, 427
Williams, Daniel Lamond, 124, 190
Williams, DeWitt Clinton, 124
Williams, Dr. Eugene E., 226, 237-239, 300
Williams, Jennie, 346-347, 429
Williams, Juliet or Juliette (Harris) (Mrs. E. E. Williams), 238, 300-301, 368, 385, 396, 435
Willson, Meredith, 136, 420
Wilson, Woodrow, 370
Womanity, 52, 54
Women's Christian Temperance Union (WCTU), 158, 264-265, 276, 285, 385, 425
Women's Rights National Historical Park (Seneca Falls, N.Y.), *see* Women's Roles and Rights, Women's Rights National Historical Park (Seneca Falls, N.Y.)

Women's Roles and Rights,
  Amendment, Fourteenth, 133
  Amendment, Fifteenth, 133
  Amendment, Nineteenth (Women's Right to Vote), 218, 384, 396, 432
  Anthony, Susan B.
    Votes for president, 160
    Bicycles, 217
  Anti-suffrage, 42, 65, 134
  Connecticut Woman Suffrage Association (CWSA), 51, 134, 160–161
  Connecticut Women Opposed to Women's Suffrage, 134
  Connecticut's Married Women's Property Act, 18, 37, 160–161
  Declaration of Independence, 51–52, 157
  Declaration of Sentiments, 51–53
  Dower rights as a widow, 114
  Electricity, impact on women, 148–150, 211
  Equal Pay Act, 22
  Equality League (Conn.), 385, 433
  First women's suffrage march, 350
  *Keep house* on census, 132
  Leisure time for women, 211–212
  Mott, Lucretia, 50–51
  "New Woman," 158, 160, 218, 412
  Oneida Whig (Oneida County, N.Y.), 54, 435
  Stanton, Elizabeth Cady, 51–54, 133, 135
  Subjects taught, girls vs. boys, 63, 65
  "The Destructive Male" speech, 133
  *The Revolution,* 133
  Wesleyan Methodist Chapel (Seneca Falls, N.Y.), 51
  Women's chores/women's work, 69, 82, 182–183, 408, 437
  Women's right to vote, *see* Nineteenth Amendment (Women's Right to Vote) *and* Voting records of women in 1920
  Women's Rights/Suffrage Convention, 1868 (Seneca Falls, N.Y.), 50–54

Women's Roles and Rights, *continued*
    Women's Rights National Historical Park (Seneca Falls, N.Y.), 51
    Women's suffrage movement, 50–53, 132–135, 158, 160, 196, 218, 238, 350, 384–386, 396, 419, 434–435
    World Anti-Slavery Convention, 51
    Yellen, Janet, 412, 437
Wood, Olin, 250, 253
Wood, Roselle (born Weaver), 249–250
Worcester Continental Drum Corps, 392
Work, Henry Clay, 263–265
World War I, *see* Great War
Worthington, Edward, 115
Wright Brothers, 352
Wright, Samuel A., 273
Yale University (Conn.), 63
"Yellow Wallpaper, The" (Gilman), 218
Zavodnick, David, 373, 432

# About the Author

Claire Smith is a lifelong Connecticut resident who spent too many years commuting to work in other states. She now blissfully spends her time researching and writing in her Connecticut home.

Having experienced firsthand the significant changes in the role of women during her own lifetime (She was born in 1949), Claire takes deep dives into the lives of the women in her family's past, seeking information and insight on how the changes for women that occurred during their lives impacted them.

Claire lives on the beach in Westbrook, Connecticut, with her husband, Peter. Their three adult daughters and their growing families live nearby and visit often (especially in the summer).

Claire is the author of *The Life and Unsolved Mystery of Jane Anthony* and the companion books, *Georgiana, Like So Many* and *The Civil War Letters of Abner C. Smith*.

clairesmith@snet.net

COLOPHON

The text of this book is set in MERCURY TEXT, a serif font designed in 1999 by Jonathan Hoefler and Tobias Frere-Jones. Maps, charts and boxes are set in MALLORY, designed by Frere-Jones in 2015. Book and map design by Russell C. Shaddox.

CPSIA information can be obtained
at www.ICGtesting.com
Printed in the USA
LVHW041501261122
733857LV00003B/39

9 780981 606011